D1348677

Race, Science and Medicine, 1700–1960

Studies in the Social History of Medicine
Series Editor: Bernard Harris

Life, Death and the Elderly
Edited by Margaret Pelling and Richard M. Smith

Medicine and Charity Before the Welfare State
Edited by Jonathan Barry and Colin Jones

In the Name of the Child
Edited by Roger Cooter

Reassessing Foucault
Power, Medicine and the Body
Edited by Colin Jones and Roy Porter

From Idiocy to Mental Deficiency
Edited by David Wright and Anne Digby

Nutrition in Britain
Edited by David F. Smith

Health Care and Poor Relief in Protestant Europe 1500–1700
Edited by Ole Peter Grell and Andrew Cunningham

Migrants, Minorities and Health
Historical and Contemporary Studies
Edited by Lara Marks and Michael Worboys

Midwives, Society and Childbirth
Edited by Hilary Marland and Anne Marie Rafferty

The Locus of Care
Edited by Peregrine Hordern and Richard Smith

Insanity, Institutions and Society
Edited by Joseph Melling and Bill Forsythe

Illness and Healing Alternatives in Western Europe
Edited by Marijke Gijswit-Hofstra, Hilary Marland and Hans de Waardt

Race, Science and Medicine, 1700–1960

Edited by Waltraud Ernst
and Bernard Harris

London and New York

First published 1999
by Routledge
11 New Fetter Lane, London EC4P 4EE

Simultaneously published in the USA and Canada
by Routledge
29 West 35th Street, New York, NY 10001

Routledge is an imprint of the Taylor & Francis Group

Typeset in Garamond by Routledge
Printed and bound in Great Britain by Biddles Ltd,
Guildford and King's Lynn

British Library Cataloguing in Publication Data
A catalogue record for this book is available from the British Library

Library of Congress Cataloguing in Publication Data
Race, science and medicine, 1700–1960 / edited by Waltraud Ernst and Bernard Harris.
Includes bibliographical references and index.
1. Medicine–Social aspects–History. 2. Colonization–Health aspects–History. 3. Imperialism–Health aspects–History. 4. Science–Social aspects–History. 5. Social medicine–History. I. Ernst, Waltraud, 1955– . II. Harris, Bernard, 1961– .
R133.R33 1999 98–55200
610'.9–dc21 CIP

ISBN 0–415–18152–6

Contents

Contributors

David Arnold is Professor of South Asian History at the School of Oriental and African Studies. His publications include *Colonizing the Body: State Medicine and Epidemic Disease in Nineteenth-Century India* (Berkeley: University of California Press, 1993) and *The Problem of Nature: Environment, Culture and European Expansion* (Oxford: Blackwell, 1996). He has recently completed a volume for the *New Cambridge History of India* on *Science, Technology and Medicine in India, 1760–1947*, and is currently conducting research into the issue of 'tropicality'.

Hanna Franziska Augstein studied history at Berlin, Bielefeld, and the University of Sussex. In 1996 she completed her Ph.D. dissertation at the Wellcome Institute for the History of Medicine, London, on the Bristol doctor and anthropologist James Cowles Prichard (1786–1848) which was subsequently turned into a book focusing on Prichard's unique concept of mental illness and the development of ethnological and racial theories from the late eighteenth century to the middle of the nineteenth. Currently she is an editor at the Feuilleton of the *Frankfurter Allgemeine Zeitung*.

Harriet Deacon is a historian currently employed at the University of Cape Town, South Africa, writing computer-based history courseware for university students. She did her Ph.D. in History at Cambridge University (1994, on the history of the Robben Island hospitals in the nineteenth century) and subsequently completed a three-year Junior Research Fellowship at Queen's College, Oxford, where she researched the medical history of the nineteenth-century Cape Colony.

Waltraud Ernst is a Lecturer at the Department of History, University of Southampton. She is the author of *Mad Tales from the Raj* (London: Routledge, 1991), and has published widely on the history of psychiatry in British India. She is currently working on a comparative study of colonial psychiatry in British India and New Zealand.

Bernard Harris is a Senior Lecturer in the Department of Sociology and Social Policy at the University of Southampton. He is the author of *The Health of the Schoolchild: A History of the School Medical Service in England and Wales* (Buckingham: Open University Press, 1995), and has published widely in the areas of anthropometric history and the history of British social policy. He is currently writing a general history of social welfare provision in England and Wales from 1800 to the present day.

Mark Jackson trained in medicine before completing his doctoral work on the history of infanticide. His publications include *New-Born Child Murder*, a monograph published in 1996, and a range of articles on the histories of infanticide and mental deficiency. A further monograph, *The Borderland of Insanity*, is to be published in 2000. Currently a Senior Lecturer at the University of Exeter, he is developing a new research project on the history of allergy and asthma.

Norris Saakwa-Mante is researching a Harvard University Ph.D. thesis, 'Medicine and the construction of race in Britain, *c.* 1660–1800'. He is an Honorary Research Associate at the Wellcome Institute for the History of Medicine, London. His interests include the History of Tropical Medicine and the Social History of Medicine.

Jonathan Sawday is a Senior Lecturer in the Department of English at the University of Southampton. He is the author of *The Body Emblazoned: Dissection and the Human Body in Renaissance Culture* (London: Routledge, 1995), and co-editor of *Literature and the English Civil War* (Cambridge University Press, 1990). He is currently working on a study of attitudes towards race at the time of the Piltdown 'discoveries' in the early part of the twentieth century.

Mathew Thomson lectures in the Department of History at the University of Warwick. He is the author of *The Problem of Mental Deficiency: Eugenics, Democracy and Social Policy in Britain, 1870–*

1959 (Oxford, 1998). He is currently researching the impact of psychology within British society during the first half of the twentieth century.

Paul Weindling is Wellcome Trust Research Professor in the History of Medicine at Oxford Brookes University. His research interests cover international health organisations, eugenics and Social Darwinism, and medical refugees in Britain from the 1930s. His publications include *Health, Race and German Politics Between National Unification and Nazism* (1989), and *Epidemics and Genocide in Eastern Europe* (1999).

Michael Worboys is Head of Research in the School of Cultural Studies at Sheffield Hallam University. He has worked on the history of tropical medicine and colonial science. Recently he has been working on the history of bacteriology and his book on germ theories of disease in British medicine will be published by Cambridge University Press in 2000.

Chapter 1

Introduction

Historical and contemporary perspectives on race, science and medicine

Waltraud Ernst[*]

During the last two decades the study of race and ethnicity as an important independent academic specialism has become well established within a range of social science disciplines such as sociology, political sciences, anthropology, cultural studies and geography.[1] This 'explosion of academic interest in the subject of race'[2] does, however, not suggest an agreement on the conceptualisations most adequate to explain the category of race. On the contrary, among academics the concept of race remains a controversial and contested one.[3]

Traditionally most historians have been careful to distance themselves from the moral and political implications of biological definitions of race; they have referred to it as a given (albeit characteristic and problematic) preoccupation of certain periods during the last two centuries. The interactions of particular colonial and migrant communities were conceived of as mere manifestations of the frictions of cultural contact. Racial attitudes and behaviours came to be viewed as but constitutive elements of particular groups' traditions and folklore, of the same order as ethnic idiosyncrasies, national costumes, food preferences and other cultural practices. Such historical accounts tended to remain almost at the anecdotal level and tended to ignore the wider power structures within which these episodes were embedded.

As recent authors of the postcolonial and subaltern[4] schools of thought have shown, the writing of colonial histories has had an enduring effect on representations of race, in the popular media as well as the scientific community. Notwithstanding honourable

* I would like to express my thanks to the Wellcome Trust for financial support and to B. Harris and M. Williams for helpful comments and proof-reading.

exceptions, such as V.G. Kiernan and Eric Hobsbawm, the tendency to relegate the analysis of race to a realm beyond historical research, and to provide instead collections of variably amusing or sinister historical vignettes, has in itself contributed to the reification of race.[5] Whether historians see their role as unavoidably political or not, writing about race in history cannot merely involve a dispassionate assessment of historical evidence: it provides the basis for the construction of historical – and thus necessarily also for present-day – political discourse.[6] As the historian D.A. Lorimer put it: 'the subject of race is at root a question of power and is, therefore, whether we like it or not, profoundly political'.[7]

Historians write history (and get their work refereed and published) within the constraints and preoccupations of present-day political and academic contexts. Any historical account of race – as much as any present-day study of racism – therefore needs to be created in awareness of its own specific political and academic context. The political positions and strategies that may be encoded in it need to be made explicit. Long before the advent of postcolonial, postmodern and subaltern studies, Gunnar Myrdal expressed this point succinctly in the (German) introduction to his *Asian Drama*, appropriately subtitled 'the mote in one's own eye':[8]

> The issue of objectivity in research cannot simply be sidestepped by striving to exclude value judgments. On the contrary; the investigation of any social problem is, and has to be, affected by value judgments. There never was such a thing as 'disinterested social science' and there never will be. The attempt to run away from value judgments is futile and even harmful. Value judgments are in us – however much we try to repress them – and they direct our work.[9]

Contributors to this book share an ambition to break away from and to expose some of the 'dangerous and destructive patterns that were established when the absurdity of "race" was elevated into a central political, cultural and economic concept and endowed with a power to both determine and explain the unfolding of history'.[10] That these 'dangerous patterns' have been persistent and enduring is evidenced by the current academic revival and general popularity of writing based either on socio-biological theories[11] or on ideas that encode and legitimate racial discrimination in terms of 'culture'.[12]

Opinions diverge as to the extent to which post-Enlightenment thinking and the various responses to and extensions of it (such as Romanticism) were inherently flawed.[13] Some believe that the categories themselves, although laying claim to universal truth, were part of but one particular philosophical mind-set that came to prominence already inherently implicated with racial ideology. Others hold that Enlightenment traditions projected the possibility of human emancipation, yet were limited in the expression of their emancipatory potential by social and political circumstance, and economically based class interest during the emergence of capitalism.

According to the former view, the elevation of scientific discourse to a major component in the project of modernity and the Eurocentrism inherent in the Western scientific enterprise has aided both the development of racial hierarchies and the creation of the long-enduring myth of science as an impartial, pure and value-free endeavour, superior to other peoples' modes of thinking. Alternatively it could be argued that it is one thing to 'discover', identify, categorise and classify plants, beetles as well as peoples, but quite another to transform such categories and classifications into hierarchies that suggest stratification in terms of social and moral inferiority. The process of categorisation would then not in itself be normative, but rather evaluative attributions would be based upon moral and social preferences, subjective value judgements and the striving for political power. The unfounded transformation of a statement about perceived difference into one about social or moral desirability and thence political dominance is starkly illustrated by Disraeli's well-known proclamation that 'race implies difference, difference implies superiority, and superiority leads to predominance'.[14]

The conundrum of the conceptual status and the socio-political consequences of the Enlightenment has not been resolved satisfactorily. Yet there now exists agreement on some parameters. The consensus is that scientific racism, racial medicine and colonial rule were for a time closely linked, variously reinforced and justified each other. Claims to racial superiority and Western scientific and medical hegemony are seen to have emerged alongside each other in the wake of the Enlightenment, culminating eventually not only in scientifically based racism in the nineteenth and racial medicine in the twentieth century, but also in the perceived enhancement and legitimisation of colonial expansion by reference to medical and scientific progress. Lyautey's dictum that 'medicine is the only excuse of colonialism'[15] vividly encapsulates this. The interrelatedness of race, science and medicine, and its extension to the colonial realm during the nineteenth century, in particular, therefore constitutes one major focus for this book.

Taking issue with the Enlightenment roots of hierarchical racial thinking and with Western scientific and medical hegemony is, however, vital not only for colonial history. Debates on the ontological status and political implications of ideas such as freedom, equality and individual rights on the one hand, and of claims to difference and particular group rights on the other, are also central to Western theories of decolonisation and multiculturalism in the twentieth century. The tendency to transform questions of politics, rights and morals into questions about nature, biology and culture has persisted. Immigrants and minority groups in Britain and elsewhere in Europe have been caught up in the tension between claims to equal rights and citizenship on the one hand, and to difference and the rights to cultural and political self-expression on the other.

Historically, the conflation of ideas of racial difference with moral values and political rights was facilitated during the nineteenth century by newly emerging biological and anatomical frameworks that constructed the qualities of particular peoples as fixed and transhistorical, thus quasi-naturalising social and political formations in terms of a racial logic of belonging. As a critical historian of 'scientific racism' put it: 'In effect, a theory of politics and rights was transformed into an argument about nature; equality ... was taken to be a matter not of ethics, but of anatomy'.[16] In the early twentieth century, in contrast, important changes occurred as race was increasingly encoded not only as biologically determined but also as culturally based. Since then equality has become more a matter of culture than of biology alone.[17] It is this shift in conceptual emphasis that is at the centre of the essays on aspects of early twentieth-century racial theories and medical practices in Britain itself.

Research on the crucial role of the Enlightenment in the creation of a racialised science and in the scientific and cultural justification of racism has also alerted us to the dangers of overgeneralisation and homogenisation of historical perspectives. Despite the value of critical analyses of the all-pervasive and powerful Enlightenment and post-Enlightenment gazes and discourses, not least in the eminent tradition of Foucault, many authors have pointed out that we also need to see the great variety and plurality, not to say ambiguities, of these discourses. These argue that the attribution of any singular train of thought and intention to Enlightenment or post-Enlightenment thinkers is misleading – in regard to racial theories as well as medical practices.[18]

Much recent literature on the link between science and race suggests that Western science and its representatives assumed a pre-eminent role in the invention, justification and dissemination of ideas of racial hierarchies as part of the project of the civilising mission and the universal spread of Western scientific knowledge. This led, first, to the formation of nineteenth-century 'scientific racism' and, subsequently, to the 'retreat of scientific racism' between the World Wars, when the definition of race as a biological concept was complemented by cultural notions of race. Arguably, we then witnessed the unravelling of the post-war scientific consensus on race, signalled by the 'return of racial science'.[19] These whole-scale characterisations of particular historical periods in terms of the varying ways in which science and race are thought to be intertwined constitute an important challenge to positivist thinking and are useful for the purposes of conveniently clear-cut classification and accentuation of long-term historical trends. At the same time they are problematic precisely on account of the generalisation on which they are based. They might therefore more appropriately be taken as the starting point for, rather than the conclusion of, further debate and in-depth probing of the historical evidence.

The concept of 'scientific racism', for example, rightly highlights the point that from the early nineteenth century to the present day the various branches of science and their representatives have not simply been involved in the pursuit of a socially and politically disinterested and objective enterprise, but have, to various extents, been implicated in the justification and construction of racist categories. In the main, 'scientific racism' has become synonymous with 'biologistic' racism as it emerged alongside evolutionary and Social-Darwinist ideas. Yet in-depth studies of particular strands of late nineteenth- and early twentieth-century medical and psychological theories of racial difference (see Harris, Sawday, Thomson and Worboys in this volume) suggest that such an equation may be too simplistic. 'Scientific racism' was variously and diversely refashioned during this period in biologistic as well as cultural terms. As Harris shows, medical observers in the late nineteenth and early twentieth centuries interpreted differences in the health status of Jews and Gentiles in cultural rather than biological terms. Worboys suggests that, contrary to general trends, commentators on tuberculosis favoured biological explanations from 1914 onwards. Thomson discerns a move away from biology to culture within the discipline of psychology in the period between the World Wars and suggests that different scientific disciplines produce or favour different sorts of scientific racism, as in the case of psychology which seems to have shifted away from biology-based conceptualisations to a cultural emphasis under the influence of anthropological ways of thinking.[20]

These findings indicate first of all that, once we look at the historical evidence of racism in science and medicine in more detail, we may be confronted with diverse strands and complex configurations of 'scientific racism' within particular scientific disciplines and in relation to different medical syndromes and socio-political settings. 'Scientific racism' presents itself in cultural as well as biologistic guise. Further, even when expressed in the language of 'culture' , a biologically based perspective may, in the last instance, still be at work, as when 'culture' is evoked as if intrinsically linked to the biological inheritance of a race. Unlike earlier debates on the role of the environment (in contrast to a people's constitution and character) that predate the advent of scientific racism (see essays by Saakwa-Mante and Augstein in this book), the cultural coding of race rose to prominence once it was realised, from around the late nineteenth century onwards, that biological differences between 'races' were *in themselves* not very significant. Cultural differences were referred to as quasi-inherited – as if culture was 'in the genes'. The move between, and conflation of, biological and cultural definitions of race still haunts present-day debates and popular conceptions. The long-standing debates on the status of 'biology' and 'culture' (progressing from previous ones about the role of 'constitution' and 'environment') raise the further important question as to whether binary distinctions, such as those of notions of racial difference based on biology and those based on culture, can legitimately be sustained.

As has been shown in earlier post-World War II methodological debates, researchers have indeed a tendency to iron out evidence of inconsistency and to smooth over ambiguities that might distract from the perceived desirability of arriving at unequivocal statements and clear-cut dichotomies. In addition, historians make allowance for what are seen as the exuberant style and lack of logical consistency in much Victorian writing, for example, and dismiss these as idiosyncratic contingencies, not relevant to the core arguments. By so doing, an important point in regard to the way in which racialised discourses strengthen their hegemony may be overlooked. In fact, the ambiguities, contradictions and discrepancies manifest within particular racial theories and racialised medicine are more likely to strengthen than weaken racial discourses. Racial discourses work well not despite their logical inconsistencies, ambiguities and mixing up of premises but *because* of them. They are destructively all-pervasive precisely because they are overdetermined and multivariant, creating the possibility for different arguments or perspectives (moral, biological, cultural, etc.) to be accentuated within different contexts and depending on the aims pursued.

It is not least this chameleon-like versatility of racialised discourses, their facility in shifting from ethical norms to biological arguments or to those of cultural identity, that has proved so painfully overpowering to those victimised by it.[21] The insistence that the presumption of 'a single monolithic racism' needs to be replaced by context-specific analyses of the multifarious historical formulations of particular 'racisms' has rightly led to an increased awareness of the multidimensionality of racial discourses, encouraging a focus on the variable spatial and temporal contexts within which particular discourses are articulated.

A number of chapters in this collection look at how the heterogeneity of racial discourses manifests itself. They deal with aspects such as the diversity of thinkers in any particular period (e.g. Augstein); the variety of perspectives employed in any one particular thinker's writings (e.g. Saakwa-Mante, Thomson); differences of outlook and opinion present in scientific and philosophical, in contrast to public, discourses and practices (e.g. Jackson, Sawday, Worboys); differences in the tenor of scientific debates in the colonial and metropolitan intellectual environments (e.g. Deacon on psychiatry in Africa, and Thomson on psychology in Britain), and, finally, the different social and political forces that influence particular strands of thought (e.g. Arnold, Ernst, Harris, Weindling).

The move away from overly generalising accounts that *only* stress the all-pervasiveness of racial domination has to some extent been due to the recognition that they contributed to the reification of the very structures they intended to expose. An exclusive emphasis on specific contexts rather than universal forces might on the other hand merely constitute another ploy in the politics of difference that not only produces new kinds of thinking about race, ethnic strife, body and mind, but promotes with it also new kinds of intolerance.[22] While it is vital to contextualise racialised medical theories and practices, we should not lose sight of the wider structures of political and economic power within which these are situated. Furthermore, the current proliferation of histories that focus *exclusively* on cultural and literary representations invites us to ask whether we really could write a social history of the interrelationship of race, science and medicine from contextualised, self-contained case-studies, travellers' diaries and cultural forms alone. In order to avoid the Scylla of conceptual fragmentation and the Charybdis of essentialist homogenisation, work on race and medicine will have both to situate itself within specific contexts and to proceed to relocate itself within the wider structures of political discourse and global power relationships.[23]

Current writing insists that race needs to be looked at in combination with the other categories that feed into it. As Solomos and Back have argued, 'racist discourse needs to be placed in the conditions surrounding the moment of its enunciation. This means irrevocably crossing the analysis of racism with other social relations.'[24] The aim is to do justice to complex realities by 'complicating the categories'.[25] Gender and class messages as well as discourses of nationhood and citizenship have been focused on as vitally informing and intersecting with racial discourses.

Even before the heyday of postmodern and feminist writing, historians highlighted the conflation of race with class in the West's construction and categorisation of colonial peoples. Take, for example, Kiernan's important observation in his classic *The Lords of Human Kind*: 'Discontented native in the colonies, labour agitator in the mills, were the same serpent in alternate disguises. Much of the talk about the barbarism or darkness of the outer world … was a transmuted fear of the masses at home.'[26] Arguments such as these evolved, of course, during a period when the concepts of race and gender still coexisted in uneasy relationship with social class, as questions of explanatory primacy were for a time the dominant theme in academic discourse.[27] More recently, in contrast, a pronounced shift has occurred, not only away from simplistic, determinist models that attribute conceptual precedence to one particular factor, but also from more sophisticated dialectical thinking. However, there exists as yet no agreement on the precise relationship between these various analytical categories in social and historical analysis, and the relative weight to be attributed to each of them. The common ground currently appears to be that the major categories need to be assessed in their interconnectedness. As Brah expressed it, emphasis is on the 'gendered racialisation of class' as constitutive in the rise of Europe.[28]

While issues of social class have been somewhat neglected by many academics during the last two postmodernist decades, work on the intersection of race and gender in particular has made considerable progress. Both race and gender have come to be seen as based on a number of similar principles: the locking of particular groups of people into fixed and quasi-transhistorical identities, for example, which enable some to lay claim to positions of power and to the right to self-determination, while excluding others. As pointed out by O'Hanlon in connection with Asian communities, the principles of their representation within Western Orientalist writing from the late eighteenth century were based on the 'persistent reference to the effeminate sensuality of Asiatic subjects, their inertia, their irrationality, their submissiveness to despotic authority, the hidden wiles and petty cunning of their political projects'.[29] Lewis therefore further expanded Said's pathbreaking work on 'Orientalism' by not only exposing the flawed construction by the West of peoples in the East in racialised terms, but also by 'gendering Orientalism'.[30] In a similar vein, Sinha exposed the case of the 'effeminate Bengali' – the crude stereotypical image of one particularly important group of Britain's colonial peoples in India, in which gender and race amalgamate to evoke the negative connotations of both the allegedly 'weak sex' and the 'weak native'.[31]

As well as race and gender, here, too, other concepts such as class, nation and nationalism are vitally implicated. The image of the 'effeminate Bengali' is a particularly good case in point, as it became increasingly popular during a period when members of the Bengali elite in British India had not only proved to be eminently able competitors in trade, industry and the civil service, but had also become active in anti-British, nationalist movements. The image of the 'effeminate Babu' suggests easily enforced domination and relegation to the supposedly minor concerns of the private and cultural spheres of a group of people not only competing for but also challenging political and economic power. It therefore resonated especially well with, and boosted, self-confidence among the British during a period when colonial rule became increasingly contested in a structured and organised, and thus threateningly potent, way.

Yet gender stereotypes need not be female. The grand-scale 'feminisation of the Orient' was complemented by the 'masculinisation' of some selected colonial communities – singling them out as 'martial', 'noble' and 'warrior-like'. These groups were assigned stereotypical images such as the loyal and proud native or the fierce fighter and good sport. The latter constituted a challenging match for the European soldier in the battle- as well as the sports field – although he, of course, remained inferior in character to the superior English prototype.[32] Both constructs shared a reference to quasi-scientific and, in particular, biologically, anatomically and medically grounded frameworks.

The projects of 'gendering' race and of 'race-ing' gender have developed alongside research on the gendered racialisation of colonial people (and, to a lesser extent, migrant communities) as a means of political and cultural subjugation. They also support the view that stereotypical images and representations are usually actively responded to, resisted and even turned against those who create them. Here emphasis has shifted away from an exclusive focus on the process of imposed negative identity-ascription and the disabling consequences of stigmatising discourses. As pointed out, not least by Foucault himself, 'power implies resistance': those apparently subjugated by discourses of power might resist and even reframe them in positive and empowering terms, and ultimately achieve access to the very resources and spheres of power from which they were intended to be excluded. This defiant response to Western attempts at 'othering' and subjugation is manifest in the expropriation for their own political purposes of racialised concepts by the social elite of disadvantaged groups. A striking example is the Bengali elite's attempt to make use of the racial ideologies associated with British medical theories on malaria by emphasising the prospect of a regeneration of the Bengali race by means of suitable (namely middle-class Bengali) leadership (see Arnold's contribution to this book).

An emphasis on 'complicating the categories' is relevant not only in regard to colonial formations. The delineation of different groups of peoples within Europe itself has become an equally important focus for historical and conceptual analysis. Anderson's earlier book on the construction of 'imagined communities' has helped to highlight the social fragmentation and elusive, if not illusory, boundaries around allegedly clearly delimited communities that underscore the Western dogma of a 'unitary self'.[33] The salience of the colonial project rested for a time to a great extent on the ideological premise of this undivided Western 'self', united not least by the spirit of Reason. Colonial historians and anthropologists in particular for a time fell prey to the implicit suggestiveness of an unproblematic 'Western self' and to its extension into a unified and unifying 'whiteness' that required no probing and problematising. But in fact, British society itself has been characterised not only by divisions of gender and class but also by the uneasy relationship of the English with peoples of Scottish, Welsh, Irish or Southern and Eastern European background. Nineteenth-century gentlemen such as Charles Kingsley, for example, held that they were 'haunted', during travels to Ireland, 'by the human chimpanzees' they saw 'along that hundred miles of horrible country. ... To see white chimpanzees is dreadful; if they were black, one would not feel it so much.'[34]

The dehumanisation and quasi-'Orientalisation' of the Irish, for example, is mirrored by early twentieth-century perceptions of particular immigrant communities as implicitly 'other' or 'non-European' (see Harris, Worboys, Weindling). The persistence of such transposed images and their shifting boundaries, as 'when the Irish became white',[35] has rightly been a focus of recent research that aims at exposing the processes by which whiteness is constructed as both unity and norm. A number of essays (Harris, Sawday, Thomson, Weindling) take issue with the ways in which medical science, supported by the newly emerging disciplines of anthropology and psychology, gave credence to and supported the racialised construction of boundaries between different white communities, as well as between groups of immigrants from other European countries.[36]

It would be futile to pretend that a selection of historical essays could possibly touch upon the whole range of issues relevant to the interconnections between race, science and medicine. There are obvious omissions, arising more from the practicalities of editing and the limitations imposed by the necessities of academic specialisation, than as a consequence of deliberate disregard or studied negligence. In fact, some of the themes left out of this collection had originally vitally informed the discussion of the individual papers first presented at the conference on Race, Science and Medicine in Southampton, in September 1996. Literary and visual representations of race in science and medicine, for example, played a major part in the conference debates, even though they unfortunately do not figure in the present volume.[37] Neither do accounts of the eugenics movement in Britain and abroad, or of some of the most traumatic moments in the recent history of race that affected Europe and Northern America: transatlantic slavery, the Nazi genocide and 'ethnic cleansing' in the former Yugoslavia. Despite the inclusion of accounts that focus on locations outside Europe, the 'comparative perspective' also remains restricted – with the exception of Weindling's chapter – to an almost exclusively British view of race within Britain and its empire. There is little engagement with the way in which racial categories impacted on science and medicine within other than British and British colonial national settings, nor have any contemporary Continental conceptualisations of 'race' or American preoccupations been referred to. Recent studies in the emerging subdiscipline of 'Science, Technology and Medicine Studies' have scarcely been touched on, and the intersection of race with gender and with class, in particular, would merit further elaboration. However, despite these lacunae it is hoped that this volume will further a critical engagement with issues of race in the history of science and medicine.

Individual contributions to this book have been arranged chronologically to enable readers to follow the sequential development and diverse historical manifestations of racial concepts from the eighteenth century onwards, right through to the nineteenth and the early twentieth centuries. Overlaps of time spans are, of course, unavoidable as some authors focus on the development of particular racialised disease categories and medical approaches over an extended period whilst others examine in more detail evidence for 'scientific racism' across a shorter interval.

The opening chapters by Saakwa-Mante and Augstein provide the early context on which a deeper understanding of some of the issues raised in subsequent contributions needs to be based. They also cover new ground in their assessment of the multiple conceptual considerations and geopolitical constellations that fed into eighteenth-century ideas of the origins of perceived racial difference and the construction of newly discovered diseases in the wake of the slave trade and European expansion.

In his analysis of the ideas of an early eighteenth-century naval surgeon (John Atkins) on sleepy distemper ('sleeping sickness' or trypanosomiasis), Saakwa-Mante shows that Atkins subscribed to an idiosyncratic brand of 'constitutional polygenism', anticipating developments more commonly associated with racial science only from the late eighteenth century onwards. Atkins argued that external differences (e.g. the dark skin and 'woolly hair' of African slaves) were markers and signs of hidden, inner difference (e.g. the 'constitutional immaturity' and 'natural weakness' of the African brain), so that particular kinds of bodies were prone to developing particular kinds of disease. Sleepy distemper therefore represented a disease category that was properly applied only to people of non-European racial backgrounds. The link between this disease and race was also made by subsequent generations of medical practitioners right up to the beginning of the twentieth century when the 'real' cause of sleeping sickness, a parasitic pathogen, was discovered. At that juncture medical practitioners began to see the European body, too, as potentially capable of harbouring a disease that had previously been conceptualised as intrinsically and exclusively bound up with particular racial populations. The linking of race and disease categories, and then the decoupling of this tie, suggests not only that racial preconceptions can inform and deform medical observations and practices, but it also constitutes evidence that medical theories are vitally implicated in the construction of ideas of race.

Saakwa-Mante highlights another important point that has been central to recent controversies on the periodisation and classification of various strands of racial thinking and the, at times, over-simplifying generalisations on which these are based. He traces the medley of factors, constitutional as well as environmental, that were characteristic of Atkins' construction of 'constitutional polygenism'. As Atkins suggested that cultural resources such as art and science have an impact on a people's constitution, the boundaries between 'constitution' and 'environment' became blurred in his writing. This suggests that historical accounts of 'scientific racism' that juxtapose arguments of 'constitution/heredity' with those of 'environment/culture', as if these were part of two opposed and irreconcilable sets of ideas, are too static and simplistic.

In a similar vein Augstein shows that monogenist and polygenist arguments developed alongside each other, not necessarily as a strict dichotomy. She focuses on the eighteenth century, when ideas on the geographical origins of humankind were for a time at the centre of controversy among physiologists, biologists and anatomists in Germany, France and Britain. The hypothesis of Europeans' Caucasian origin exemplifies a concept of racial origin that was based on a plethora of vague and shifting assumptions and speculative ideas and lent itself well to being incorporated into, and to giving credence to, diverse strands of ideas about race. As pointed out by Augstein, the Caucasian hypothesis 'spread precisely because it was unlikely, part of an imaginative geography rather than informed by solid factual knowledge, and hence open to all sorts of association of ideas, none of which had much to do with the original purpose of the concept: to elucidate the historical or geographical make-up of the human physique' (p. 59).

Augstein's perspective is wide-ranging in its emphasis on different national settings and she draws attention to the various scientific and philosophical traditions within Europe and to the ways in which these impacted in various different ways on the discussions about the geographic origin of the human and, more specifically, the European-born 'race'. She also traces the popularity and the appropriation of the term 'Caucasian' for racist causes in the United States, when it was variously used in support of segregation policies that privileged 'whites' over 'blacks'. In Europe, in contrast, the concept was less easily adapted to societies that were keen on finer distinctions among Europeans themselves – between Celts and Anglo-Saxons, Germans and Slavs, Gauls and Franks. Augstein's contribution underlines the importance of rigorously situating racial theories and terminologies not only within the contexts of their origins but also in relation to subsequent social and political appropriations and applications.

The issue of the spatial as well as temporal specificity of ideas of 'race' is at the centre of my own contribution on the development of psychiatric institutions in early nineteenth-century British India. The 'British Raj', with all its profusion of connotations of heat and dust, colourful indigenous diversity and splendid imperial glamour, has become synonymous with the supreme unifying imperial and military spirit and the monolithic force and rational efficiency of

British colonial administration. Yet a far less monolithic picture in fact characterised the situation in the various areas under British rule: in regard to lunacy policy and related health- and population-control measures a variety of administrative approaches and views of racial identity prevailed. These developed in response to, and in support of, diverse colonial and indigenous power structures and ethnic stratification in specific localities.

I show that psychiatric approaches and institutional policies developed both in unison with the powerful global discourse of race and in response to heterogeneous local racial discourses and indigenous social and political power structures. I conclude that it is important to pay attention to the various locale-specific manifestations and variations of 'colonialisms' and the particular 'racisms' going along with these. However, it is equally important to acknowledge the globalising and universalising tendencies inherent in Western colonising strategies and concomitant racial conceptualisations.

Deacon assesses the development of colonial psychiatry within the social and political context of the first British settler colony, the Cape. As in British India, here, too, the broader socio-economic and political contexts need to form the major setting for the study of racism and psychiatry. However, Deacon stresses that it is too simplistic to assume a straightforward translation of racist ideas and policies within colonial society at large into psychiatric theories and practices within institutions for the insane. In the Cape, measures such as the racial segregation of patients in the asylum preceded the formulation of racist psychiatric theory. In regard to institutional and psychiatric practice, therefore, 'scientific racism' appears to have lagged behind the popular racist and segregationist ideology within broader society.

Despite a high level of social stratification among European settlers as well as indigenous groups, ethnic, religious and status categories tended to be collapsed into a dichotomous racist framework which divided 'European' from 'coloured', 'civilised Christians' from 'savage heathens'. Throughout the nineteenth century the idea prevailed that 'coloured people' did not require the same sort of refined treatment and 'moral management' techniques as Europeans. According to Deacon this view echoed the stereotype of the 'coloured as savage', rather than expressing any particular conception of 'coloured insanity'. Yet, despite its apparent prescriptiveness, segregation on the basis of race alone was not always considered practical and hence less strictly applied in the day-to-day management of institutions.

Deacon suggests that the liberal roots of medical universalism opened up the space for a culturally based racism – rather than a biologically grounded racist science – to develop within Cape medicine during the course of most of the nineteenth century. It was only from the 1880s onwards that discriminatory attitudes, born out of a hardening racism among the English and the Afrikaners, came to rely on the discourse of scientific racism. Deacon concludes that 'it was not racist psychiatry or racist science more generally which formed the basis for theorising racial segregation in Cape asylums like Robben Island, but the liberal tenets of moral management which permitted the expression of racism by white staff, patients and officials in the space created by class differentiation' (p. 118).

In his chapter on malaria in colonial India, Arnold challenges some of the assumptions on which much previous research into scientific racism has been based. Arnold acknowledges that some high-profile scientific figures such as H.H. Risley did indeed promulgate a hierarchical-determinist and biologistic view of race. Yet, among the wider scientific and medical communities, as well as among the European public in British India, a number of less narrowly focused ideas on race prevailed that were more commonly based on a wide-ranging mixture of cultural and moral, as well as physical, factors. Arnold's evidence puts into question whether the commonly assumed universal shift away from cultural towards biological conceptions of race, during the period from the late nineteenth to the early twentieth century, was equally characteristic of the situation in British India.

Arnold focuses on malaria and malaria prevention as an example of a disease category that on account of its symptom-profile lent itself particularly well to developing ideas of racial decay, enfeeblement and racial regeneration. He finds that ideas of race were not exclusively confined to the British but also played a profound role in the self-perceptions and social attitudes of the European subject people. In Arnold's reading of the evidence in Bengal ideas of race and visions of racial regeneration were part of an interactive process in which not only various groups among the European communities but also Indian people were involved. The Bengali Hindu intelligentsia played a crucial role in the appropriation of particular strands of culturally based ideas of race, reinterpreting these on their own terms and for their own purposes, projecting themselves as the vanguard of Bengal's social and political regeneration, especially during a period of a heightened sense of demographic and political rivalry with Bengali Muslims. Ideas of race within colonialism, a powerful tool of stereotyping and stigmatisation in the hands of the Western colonisers, lent themselves also to appropriation by particular strata within colonial societies in search of their own political and social empowerment.

European ideas of Bengali effeminacy had been well entrenched in colonial discourse since the beginning of the nineteenth century. As many among the Bengali elite and the medically informed European public believed that the weakness and feebleness attributed to Indian people were not immutable, inherited characteristics of their race, but contingent upon poverty, deprivation and a malarious environment, Arnold concludes that medical and sanitary science 'held out the possibility of contesting the more biologically determinist interpretations of race' (p. 141).

In his chapter on 'Tuberculosis and Race', Worboys investigates the extent to which ideas of race are linked to the changing epidemiological and pathological understanding of a particular disease. He finds that concepts such as 'racial immunity' and 'primitive TB' were conflated with biological and physical, as well as social and cultural, assumptions about racial difference. He assesses in depth the reception of epidemiological evidence from a wide range of areas in Britain, North America and various colonies by Lyle Cummins, a leading authority on TB.

The collection of incidence and mortality rates for different social and cultural groups became a priority issue for public and industrial health policies during a period when immigrant groups in the United States became more visible and when contact and conflict between 'primitives' and 'civilisation' increased considerably in the wake of European imperial expansion and exploitation of African and Indian labour power. The collected data provided highly diverse and contradictory incidence and mortality rates for different groupings of people, and could thus easily be drawn on to support a wide range of different and at times conflicting views on TB. For example, data that showed that differences in mortality within the white population were as great as those between whites and non-whites were used to promulgate the view that environmental and social improvements were vital in the reduction of TB, and that TB immunity was acquired rather than racially based. Statistics collected among South African mining communities, in contrast, were interpreted as supportive of views that put emphasis on racial susceptibility – thus enabling the South African mining companies (who had commissioned the collection of statistics and medical expert advice on how to optimise labour costs) to be excused any responsibility for the high incidence of TB amongst their workers.

Worboys' study highlights the various ways in which different national and geographic contexts, and the political and economic interests within these, together with practitioners' shifting political and professional allegiances, informed and shaped the ways in which the conceptualisation of a specific disease was imbued with biologically and/or culturally based racial ideas. Worboys concludes that, before World War I, the idea that 'primitive people' were 'virgin soil', lacking immunity to TB because they had not been exposed to this disease before, seemed 'not only to make sense of the experience of disease in colonial medicine, but also was a resource in the debates about eugenics and immune theories. Between the wars, the racial theory of tuberculosis went against the wider trend in the biological sciences to question the validity of "race" as a scientific category' (p. 161).

Jackson's paper highlights the effects that racial stereotyping had not only on 'other' people 'out there', in the British Empire, but also on particular groups of people within Western societies. He discusses the changing representations and medical discourses surrounding that group of people who were for nearly a century referred to as 'mongols'. Jackson shows that in a way similar to how people in colonial countries were represented as 'having degenerated from the Caucasian pinnacle, mental defectives were frequently portrayed as the primitive products of a process of atavistic degeneration from a mental and physical norm' (p. 167). The prevalence of 'mongolism' lent itself to substantiate theories of race that suggested a link between physical form and appearance on the one hand and mental ability and state of development on the other. The concept of 'mongolism' drew on and gave credence to ideas that constructed racial hierarchies, and passed judgement on their mental abilities and stage of development on the basis of people's physical difference alone.

Jackson also investigates whether a change of medical terminology, towards seemingly purely clinico-technical terms, is bound to result in a dissociation of the clinical category from any racial allusions. He shows that the racial stereotyping of people with learning difficulties persisted even with the recognition that 'mongolism' was due to a genetic specificity subsequently referred to as 'congenital acromicria' or 'trisomy 21 anomaly'. Despite substantial variations in appearance, organic pathology and intelligence, this group of people was still regarded as different and deviant from the norm – now by virtue of their shared genetic constitution. Jackson concludes that 'novel understandings and depictions of disease failed to shake off racial assumptions evident in earlier representations, although those assumptions were now recast in the language of genotypes' (p. 183). This indicates the continuing effect and endurance of racial discourse even in the face of new gene-oriented or genomic constructions of 'race' and their apparent distance from eighteenth- and nineteenth-century scientific racisms.

In Harris' chapter the focus is on the medical profession's response to the immigration of Eastern European Jews into Britain during the late nineteenth and early twentieth centuries. Although Harris places the different ways in which racial thinking influenced debates on public health measures in relation to Jewish immigration at the centre of his analysis, he stresses that 'race was only one of the factors to influence intellectual debate at the end of the nineteenth century' and that 'we also need to examine the persistence of liberal ideas about freedom of movement, the right of asylum and free trade, together with the broader links between Jewish immigration and the politics of public health reform' (pp. 189–90) in order to understand the full range of medical responses to Jewish immigration.

Although the extent of immigration from Eastern Europe was relatively insignificant in terms of the numbers involved, East European Jews in Britain were regarded as being especially 'visible' as they tended to be geographically concentrated in particular areas of cities such as London, Manchester and Leeds. Harris argues that in late Victorian and Edwardian Britain older stereotypes of the Jewish people as Christ-killers and plain anti-Semitism still persisted, but were gradually being superseded by newer economic, moral and health-related concerns – by factors such as the perceived decline of British economic wealth and the erosion of its imperial power in the face of German and American economic competition and the early defeats of the Boer War, compounded by fears about physical degeneration, fuelled by Social Darwinism and fears that immigration put pressure on the scarce resources of a nascent welfare state.

Although there is evidence in the debates on Jewish immigration and public health that substantiates the prevalence of anti-Semitism and middle-class distaste for the poor and destitute, Harris notes that discussions were far more complex and some important factors, such as the twin principles of free trade and free movement of people, as well as liberal beliefs in the right to asylum, tended to challenge the hardening of racial attitudes and growing hostility to non-native and non-white groups.

He also highlights evidence collected by Medical Officers of Health that goes against the grain of common pre-perceptions. Harris argues: 'medical writers believed that Jews were at least as healthy as the population around them, and often more so' (p. 195). Jewish people appeared to experience higher rates of *some* physical and mental diseases, and tended to live in extreme squalor and insanitary conditions on arrival in Britain – factors that seemed to give credence to the belief in Jewish degeneracy and 'racial' susceptibility to disease. Some advocates of Jewish immigration countered this view by insisting that a 'racial habit of body' may well be implicated in regard to Jewish people – yet this did not express itself in susceptibility, but rather in 'racial immunity to disease'. Others focused more on Jewish cultural and dietary habits (such as good parenting skills, careful and abstemious diet) to explain statistical trends that affirmed that urban areas with a high percentage of resident Jewish people tended to show a more favourable health and mortality profile even than areas with more affluent, 'native' populations.

In his contribution on 'German Bacteriology as Scientific Racism', Weindling sets out to challenge the view that bacteriology, as a laboratory-based offshoot of biology, is immune to social and racial ideologies. He explores the close link between public health and sanitary policies in response to typhus, and immigration and population control procedures in Germany during the 1890s and in occupied Poland and Serbia during World War I. Weindling shows that, although towards the close of the nineteenth century anti-Semitic notions of the Jew as parasite deployed the language of bacteriology and parasitology, such rhetoric did not yet pervade bacteriology itself. This changed during the time of World War I when intolerance and apprehension towards Eastern European Jewish people changed to outright anti-Semitism. The bacteriological cleansing, segregation and hygiene measures recommended by bacteriologists in the prevention and eradication of typhus were based on centralised, authoritarian and interventionist approaches, and could therefore – in particular historical circumstances – easily be integrated into and lend credence to racist rationales. Although there was no intrinsic link between bacteriology and racial ideas, within the economic and socio-political context of Germany in the early decades of the twentieth century, a racist bacteriology could easily be elicited. Weindling concludes that at that period bacteriologists 'stood on the threshold of eradicating epidemics by eliminating the presumed carriers of the disease' (p. 231).

In his contribution on 'Savage Civilisation', Thomson assesses the reconfigurations in theories of the mind between 1898 and 1939 within the new academic discipline of psychology in response to anthropological findings that cast doubt upon the supposed link between race and mental ability. The anthropological experience (particularly in the wake of the expedition to the Torres Straits in 1898) and its reconfiguration in psychological theories appeared to demonstrate the importance of culture and the persistence of archaic mental structures, of 'savage' instincts and of the 'primitive' even within the 'civilised'. During the era leading up to and following World War I, when issues of national identity were to the fore and Britain and other nations were struggling to come to terms with the horrors and 'barbarism' of trench warfare, the idea of the omnipresence of the 'savage' captivated academic and popular thought.

Thomson raises doubts about the assumed hegemony of biologically based scientific racism in turn-of-the-century Britain, suggesting instead that culture evolved alongside biology in a more complex way during this period. He looks at popular and influential psychologists, such as McDougall, who argued that innate racial differences manifested themselves in culture over a long period, leading to distinctive national cultures that developed in harmony with a people's innate national character. This line of thinking fuelled the racialisation of national identity, as 'Englishness' and 'English character', for example, were seen to be based on innate national characteristics as well as national culture – or, as McDougall expressed it, 'the "culture species" replaced the race' (p. 244). The individual mind became a repository for a racialised national history which was both biological and cultural.

Thomson argues that as the unity and common life of all humankind were recognised, this culturalised vision of race harboured the potential to lead to the subversion of race as a category of difference. Nevertheless it could also perpetuate a racist scientific justification for colonialism as colonial subjects continued to be portrayed as childlike and driven by instinct, and therefore in need of moral guidance and civilised culture.

In his chapter on 'Arthur Keith, Race and the Piltdown Affair', Sawday invites us to unravel the story of a scientific fraud committed in 1912, by considering its importance in the construction of racially fraught scientific theories and cultural perceptions within the context of the changing political and nationalistic agenda in Britain. When the skull of a human, with an ape-like jaw, was found in a Sussex gravel-bed in 1912, British scientists were jubilant as the bones seemed to present hard evidence for the hitherto speculative Darwinian assumption that modern humans and modern apes shared the same origin. It also provided relief for those who disliked the idea of a shared origin of the human race and, in particular, the suggestion that in evolutionary terms Africa constituted the cradle of humankind. Yet Piltdown Man remained entirely out of conformity with the fossil evidence available from all over the world for about four decades. Sawday shows that while it may indeed be intriguing to expose the perpetrator(s) of the initial fraud and their particular motives, the question of why the planted evidence was accepted for so long – some forty years until the belated detection of the swindle in 1953 – is equally politically revealing and historically instructive. In fact, the importance of Piltdown Man varied over the decades with the changing scientific preoccupations and political agendas with which high-profile and public figures such as Arthur Keith, one of the protagonists in the Piltdown affair, were affiliated.

At the time of the discovery of the curious skull in 1912, when the British, like other European nations, were in pursuit of territorial expansion and still vitally implicated in the scramble for Africa, Piltdown Man bolstered the colonial disdain for 'primitive peoples' by lending credence to theories of two widely divergent branches of human lineage, and thus of different racial origins of the white and the coloured races, and the separation of the modern races in prehistoric times.

With the competing geopolitical claims of rival European powers in the colonial sphere, the focus of politics, as well as science, came to be on 'territoriality' and racial origin – of the empire as much as of evolution. In the wake of World War I, when issues of dominance and competing races at war in Europe were to the fore, Piltdown Man was at the centre of debates about racial variation within one branch of human lineage and the interrelationship of different populations belonging to the same species of men. During the 1930s the rise of fascist and eugenics movements facilitated an interpretation of the Piltdown 'evidence' both in terms of culture and biology, in the conception of race as a distinction of the spirit as much as a physical characteristic, of races struggling and fighting to preserve an archaic emotional bond to 'soil' and 'blood'. As a bearer of a biologised notion of culture, Piltdown Man became in a complex way representative both of 'Britishness' (in reference to 'race') and 'Englishness' (in reference to locality) – until discovered to be a fraud. Although the file on Piltdown Man is not yet closed, as the identity of its creator remains obscure, the fraud exerted a genuine influence on British anthropology and ideas of race, representing an example of how scientific, cultural and political assumptions may be made on the basis of what appears to be 'hard' scientific evidence.

Notes

1 J. Donald and A. Rattansi (eds), *Race, Culture and Difference*, London, Sage, 1992. F. Anthias and N. Yuval-Davis, *Racialised Boundaries: Race, Nation, Colour, Class and the Anti-Racist Struggle*, London and New York, Routledge, 1992. P. Jackson and J. Penrose (eds), *Constructions of Race, Place and Nation*, London, University College London Press, 1993. J. Rex and D. Mason (eds), *Theories of Race and Ethnic Relations*, Cambridge, Cambridge University Press, 1986. D.T. Goldberg, *Anatomy of Racism*, Minneapolis, University of Minnesota Press, 1990. D.T. Goldberg, *Racist Cultures: Philosophy and the Politics of Meaning*, Oxford, Basil Blackwell, 1993. R. Young, *Colonial Desire: Hybridity in Theory, Culture and Race*, London and New York, Routledge, 1995. J. Fabian, *Time and the Other: How Anthropology Makes its Object*, New York, Columbia University Press, 1983. L.M. Alcoff, 'Philosophy and Racial Identity', *Radical Philosophy* 75 (Jan./Feb. 1996): 5–14. P. Gilroy, *There Ain't No Black in the Union Jack: The Cultural Politics of Race and Nation*, London, Hutchinson, 1987. P. Gilroy, *The Black Atlantic: Modernity and Double Consciousness*, London, Verso, 1993. D. LaCapra (ed.), *The Bounds of Race: Perspectives on Hegemony and Resistance*, Cornell University Press, 1991. H.L. Gates (ed.), *Race, Writing and Difference*, Chicago, University of Chicago Press, 1986.

2 S. West (ed.), *The Victorians and Race*, Aldershot, Scolar Press, 1996, p. 1.

3 J. Solomos and L. Back, 'Conceptualising Racisms: Social Theory, Politics and Research', *Sociology* 28, 1 (1994): 143–61, esp. p. 143. A. Brah, 'Time, Place and Others: Discourses of Race, Nation and Ethnicity', *Sociology* 28, 3 (1994): 805–13. L.M. Alcoff, 'Philosophy and Racial Identity'. L. Lieberman, B.W. Stevenson, L.T. Reynolds, 'Race and Anthropology: A Core Concept Without Consensus', *Anthropology and Education Quarterly* 20, 2 (1989): 67–73.

4 Work in the postcolonial tradition is by now too numerous and well known to be cited. See for references to and a summary of the subaltern premises, G.C. Spivak, 'Subaltern Studies: Deconstructing Historiography', in R. Guha (ed.), *Subaltern Studies IV: Writings on South Asian History and Society*, Delhi, Oxford University Press, 1985.

5 See, for example, on the danger of reifying race or 'race', and on its shadowy companion, 'whiteness', Goldberg, *Racist Cultures*. V. Dominguez (ed.), '(Multi)Culturalisms and the Baggage of "Race" ', *Identities: Global Studies in Culture and Power*, 1, 4 (1995), special issue. Gilroy, *The Black Atlantic*. K. Mercer, *Welcome to the Jungle: New Positions in Black Cultural Studies*, New York, Routledge, 1994. R.W. Allen, *The Invention of the White Race*, London, Verso, 1994. D.R. Roediger, *The Wages of Whiteness: Race and the Making of the American Working Class*, London, Verso, 1991. R. Young, *White Mythologies: Writing History and the West*, London, Routledge, 1990. V. Ware, *Beyond the Pale: White Women, Racism and History*, London, Verso, 1992. C. Hall, *White, Male and Middle Class: Explorations in Feminism and History*, New York, Routledge, 1992.

6 A number of authors have argued against attempts to depoliticise race and have critiqued in particular race- and ethnic-relations studies and authors who insisted on the separation of research process and political action. See, for example, R. Miles, *Racism*, London, Routledge, 1989. Centre for Contemporary Cultural Studies, *The Empire Strikes Back*, London, Hutchinson, 1982. M. Banton, *Racial Theories*, Cambridge, Cambridge University Press, 1986. J. Rex, *Race Relations in Sociological Theory*, London, Weidenfeld & Nicolson, 1970.

7 D.A. Lorimer, 'Race, Science and Culture: Historical Continuities and Discontinuities, 1850–1914', in S. West (ed.), *The Victorians and Race*, Aldershot, Scolar Press, 1996, p. 12. See also Miles, *Racism*; Gilroy, *Black Atlantic*.

8 G. Myrdal, 'Der Balken in unserem Auge', *Asiatisches Drama: Eine Untersuchung ueber die Armut der Nationen*, Frankfurt, Suhrkamp, 1973, p. 13.

9 Myrdal, *Asiatisches Drama*, pp. 26–7.

> Das Problem der Objektivitaet in der Forschung laesst sich nicht einfach dadurch umgehen, dass man Wertungen auszuschalten versucht. Im Gegenteil; jede Untersuchung eines sozialen Problems ist und muss durch Wertungen bestimmt sein. Eine 'interessenfreie Sozialwissenschaft' hat es nie gegeben und wird es nie geben. Der Versuch, sich Wertungen zu entziehen, ist vergeblich and sogar schaedlich. Die Wertungen

sind in uns, auch wenn wir sie verdraengen, und sie leiten unsere Arbeit.

See also, for similar arguments, Solomos and Back, 'Conceptualising Racisms'; R. Miles and A. Phizacklea, *Racism and Political Action in Britain*, London, Routledge, 1979; Gilroy, *Black Atlantic*; Centre for Contemporary Cultural Studies, *The Empire Strikes Back*.

10 P. Gilroy, 'Race Ends Here', paper presented at Rethinking Ethnic and Racial Studies, the Ethnic and Racial Studies Twentieth Anniversary Conference in London, May 1997.

11 See, for example, the discussion surrounding the 'bell curve'. S. Fraser (ed.), *The Bell Curve Wars: Race, Intelligence and the Future of America*, New York, Basic Books, 1995. S. Jones, *In the Blood: God, Genes and Destiny*, London, HarperCollins, 1996. D. Nelkin, 'The Politics of Predisposition: The Social Meaning of Predictive Biology', in A. Heller and S. Puntscher Riekmann (eds), *Biopolitics. The Politics of the Body, Race and Nature*, Aldershot, Avebury, 1996, pp. 133–43.

12 See, on the coding of race as culture, discussion and references on pp. 6–7 of this chapter.

13 See, for example, T. Todorov, *On Human Diversity: Nationalism, Racism and Exoticism in French Thought*, Cambridge, MA, Harvard University Press, 1993. W. Kymlicka, *Multicultural Citizenship*, Oxford, Clarendon Press, 1995. K. Malik, *The Meaning of Race: Race, History and Culture in Western Society*, London, Macmillan, 1996. Goldberg, *Anatomy of Race*.

14 House of Commons Speech (1 February 1849), quoted in H. Odom, 'Generalizations on Race in Nineteenth-Century Physical Anthropology', *Isis* 85 (1967): 9, and in M.D. Biddis (ed.), *Images of Race*, Leicester, Leicester University Press, 1979, p. 16.

15 D. MacDonald – a former member of the Indian Medical Service and author of *Surgeons Twoe and a Barber: Being Some Account of the Life and Work of the Indian Medical Service (1600–1947)*, London, Heinemann, 1950 – placed in the front pages of his book Marshal H. Lyautey's epigram that 'La seule excuse de la colonisation c'est le médecin'.

16 N. Stepan, 'Race, Science and Medicine: Citizenship and the Natural' (p. 8), paper presented at the conference on Race, Science and Medicine in Southampton, September 1996. See also Section 2 (entitled 'Science Constructs "Race" ') in Sandra Harding's recent edited book, *The 'Racial' Economy of Science: Towards a Democratic Future*, Bloomington and Indianapolis, Indiana University Press, 1993.

17 See, for an analysis of the conflation of race and ethnicity in regard to citizenship and nationship, and for debates about new racism in Britain, Gilroy, *Black Atlantic*, *There Ain't No Black in the Union Jack* and 'Race Ends Here'. Donald and Rattansi, *Race, Culture and Difference*. M. Guibernau and J. Rex (eds), *The Ethnicity Reader: Nationalism, Multiculturalism and Migration*, Cambridge, Polity Press, 1997.

18 As Porter pointed out in respect to the case of history of medicine: 'the terrain of healing has always been characterized by great diversity'; R. Porter (ed.), *The Popularization of Medicine, 1650–1850*, London,

Routledge, 1992, p. 1. See also R. French and A. Wear (eds), *British Medicine in an Age of Reform*, London, Routledge, 1991; W.F. Bynum, *Science and the Practice of Medicine in the Nineteenth Century*, Cambridge, Cambridge University Press, 1992; R. Cooter (ed.), *Studies in the History of Alternative Medicine*, Houndsmill, Macmillan, 1988.

19 N. Stepan, *The Idea of Race in Science*, London, Macmillan, 1982. E. Barkan, *The Retreat of Scientific Racism: Changing Concepts of Race in Britain and the US between the World Wars*, Cambridge, Cambridge University Press, 1992. M. Kohn, *The Race Gallery: The Return of Racial Science*, London, Vintage, 1995. Much of the impetus for historical reassessments of race is due to the work of historically grounded as well as theoretically challenging authors such as H. Bhabha, 'The Other Question: Difference, Discrimination and the Discourse of Colonialism', in F. Barker *et al.* (eds), *Literature, Politics and Theory: Papers from the Essex Conferences, 1976–84*, London and New York, Methuen, 1986; R. Guha and G.C. Spivak (eds), *Selected Subaltern Studies*, New York, Oxford University Press, 1988. They have shown that ideas of race were created and disseminated by Western nations in the wake of industrial transformation, colonial expansion and the spread of the 'project of modernity'. See also Harding, *The 'Racial' Economy of Science*.

20 Barkan, *The Retreat of Scientific Racism*. H. Kuklick, *The Savage Within: The Social History of British Anthropology, 1885–1945*, Cambridge, Cambridge University Press, 1991. P. Rich, *Prospero's Return? Historical Essays on Race, Culture and British Society*, London, Hansib, 1994. G. Richards, *'Race', Racism and Psychology: Towards a Reflexive History*, London, Routledge, 1997. G. Stocking Jr, *Race, Culture and Evolution: Essays in the History of Anthropology*, New York, Free Press, 1969.

21 Furthermore, the ability to fluctuate between different perspectives has also the effect of increasing the appeal and support-base of racial discourse to a wider (and variably motivated) spectrum of people. This point is of particular relevance in respect to political mobilisation along the lines of discourses of citizenship, nation and nationalism. See, for examples, J. Wrench and J. Solomos (eds), *Racism and Migration in Western Europe*, Oxford, Berg, 1993; Gilroy, *There Ain't No Black in the Union Jack*.

22 Heller and Puntscher Riekmann (eds), *Biopolitics*. See also discussion of the contention that 'Race is irrelevant, but all is race' by Goldberg, *Racist Cultures*, p. 6.

23 Attempts by authors in the postmodern tradition to expose as contradictory and conceptually flawed the essentialism and universalism inherent in Enlightenment concepts and in theories derived from them, have themselves run the danger of over-homogenising and essentialising. See on this point, for example, the debate between G. Prakash, 'Writing Post-Orientalist Histories of the Third World', *Comparative Studies in Society and History* 32 (1990): 383–408. R. O'Hanlon and D. Washbrook, 'After Orientalism: Culture, Criticism, and Politics in the Third World', *Comparative Studies in Society and History* 34 (1992): 141–67. G. Prakash, 'Can the "Subaltern" Ride? A

Reply to O'Hanlon and Washbrook', *Comparative Studies in Society and History* 34 (1992): 168–84.

24 Solomos and Back, 'Conceptualizing Racisms', p. 156.

25 See, for example, the recent call for papers for a special issue of *International Review of Social History Supplement 1999* on the subject of 'Complicating the Categories: Gender, Class, Race and Ethnicity in Western and Non-Western Societies' (announceh-net.msu.edu).

26 V.G. Kiernan, *The Lords of Human Kind: European Attitudes towards the Outside World in the Imperial Age*, Harmondsworth, Penguin 1972, p. 33.

27 Part of the earlier academic controversies between theorists such as Banton, Miles, Rex and the Centre for Contemporary Cultural Studies, for example, can be accounted for by the relative importance attributed to class in contrast to other analytical dimensions.

28 Brah, 'Time, Place and Others: Discourses of Race, Nation and Ethnicity', p. 806.

29 R. O'Hanlon, 'Cultures of Rule, Communities of Resistance: Gender, Discourse and Tradition in Recent South Asian Historiographies', *Social Analysis* 23 (1989): 106.

30 R. Lewis, *Gendering Orientalism: Race, Femininity and Representation*, London, Routledge, 1996. E. Said, *Orientalism*, Harmondsworth, Penguin, [1979] 1985.

31 M. Sinha, *Colonial Masculinity: The 'Manly Englishman' and the 'Effeminate Bengali' in the Late Nineteenth Century*, Manchester, Manchester University Press, 1995.

32 See for gendered and racialised representations of non-Europeans in children's history textbooks and periodicals, K. Castle, *Britannia's Children: Reading Colonialism through Children's Books and Magazines*, Manchester, Manchester University Press, 1996. See for the rationales underlying such representations, A.L. Stoler, 'Rethinking Colonial Categories: European Communities and the Boundaries of Rule', *Comparative Studies in Society and History* 31, 1 (1989): 134–60. B. Anderson, *Imagined Communities: Reflections on the Origin and Spread of Nationalism*, London, Verso, 1983.

33 Anderson, *Imagined Communities*. In regard to colonial psychiatry, see W. Ernst, 'Idioms of Madness and Colonial Boundaries: The Case of the European and "Native" Mentally Ill in Early Nineteenth-Century British India', *Comparative Studies in Society and History* 39, 1 (1997): 153–81.

34 'Charles Kingsley: His Letters and Memories of His Life' (edited by his wife, 1877), vol. 2, p. 107, quoted from M.D. Biddiss, *Images of Race*, Leicester, Leicester University Press, 1979, p. 30. See also L.P. Curtis, *Anglo-Saxons and Celts: A Study of Anti-Irish Prejudice in Victorian England*, New York, New York University Press, 1968; S. Gilley, 'English Attitudes to the Irish, 1780–1900', in C. Holmes (ed.), *Immigrants and Minorities in British Society*, London, Allen & Unwin, 1978; S.B. Cook, *Imperial Affinities: Nineteenth-Century Analogies and Exchanges between India and Ireland*, New Delhi, Sage, 1993.

35 N. Ignatiev, *How the Irish Became White*, London, Routledge, 1995.

36 For literature on the later period, when the 'implosion of Empire' occurred (namely when groups from former colonial countries became resident within the core culture), see W.I.U. Ahmad, *'Race' and Health in Contemporary Britain*, Buckingham, Open University Press, 1993; W.I.U. Ahmad (ed.), *The Politics of 'Race' and Health*, Bradford, Race Relations Research Unit, University of Bradford, 1992; L. Marks and M. Worboys (eds), *Migrants, Minorities and Health: Historical and Contemporary Studies*, London, Routledge, 1997.

37 For an excellent book that focuses on discourses of race as represented in art and literature in particular, see West, *The Victorians and Race*.

Chapter 2

Western medicine and racial constitutions

Surgeon John Atkins' theory of polygenism and sleepy distemper in the 1730s

Norris Saakwa-Mante[*]

A new, natural-historical, essentially non-theological conception of race emerged in Europe and the British Isles from the mid-seventeenth to the mid-eighteenth century. Three developments at least were responsible for the emergence of this new natural-historical conception of race. First, the possibility of truly global travel following the first circumnavigation of the Earth was a social change with enormous consequences. Second, a new awareness of the different physical appearance of the world's people derived from new transcontinental population movements (e.g. the Atlantic Slave Trade and European emigration to the New World) had a major effect. Third, the application of the values and naturalising epistemology of the seventeenth-century Scientific Revolution (however defined)[1] to the different physical appearance of the human species as a whole, made possible a new theoretical vocabulary for fabricating race, or gave new meanings to old terms. These developments, among others, produced the conditions for the emergence of race.[2]

Naturalised constructions of race emerged, or were forged, as a product of very specific interaction and conflict between two intellectual traditions which have been labelled *monogenist* and *polygenist* traditions, beginning in the 1680s and 1690s.[3] Monogenism includes and is sometimes identified with the assertion that all men and women originated from a single couple. Polygenism includes and is sometimes identified with the assertion that

* I wish to thank Mark Gosbee, Mark Harrison, Christopher Lawrence, Clare Midgley, Roy Porter and Molly Sutphen for comments on earlier drafts of this paper and for their helpful criticisms.

physically diverse groups of men and women could not have originated from a single couple and that there must have been multiple original couples, or 'first parents', in the formulation sometimes given. By the second half of the eighteenth century, monogenism had become the assertion that all humans belonged to a single species and polygenism the assertion that people of diverse physical appearance belonged to different species. The idea of using species-difference to represent race is relatively rare in the mid-seventeenth- to mid-eighteenth-century period that is focused on here, rare but not unknown.[4]

Monogenism is the naturalistic version (and genealogical descendant) of the creation narrative contained in Genesis.[5] It is a natural philosophical rather than (mainly) religious viewpoint, and as such it argues (in the period before the nineteenth century) that environmental factors cause differences in physical appearance.[6] Polygenism is the naturalistic transformation (and genealogical descendant) of the 'men before Adam' or 'pre-Adamite' thesis.[7] As a natural philosophical viewpoint, polygenism denies environment has the power to cause differences in physical appearance, and argues that only differential descent from a different ancestor can account for the bodily differences that come to be called racial difference.

The principal subject of this chapter is the racial and medical theory contained in the surgical manual of John Atkins (1685–1757). This manual, *The Navy-Surgeon*,[8] is of great interest as one of the few eighteenth-century medical texts with both a clearly identifiable and formulated conception of race, and a series of ideas about disease shaped by the built-in conception of race. Atkins' view of race is a recognisable part of the polygenist tradition. Eighteenth-century polygenists are relatively little studied and John Atkins is no exception. Interestingly, this is true despite the fact that Atkins' polygenism was flagged as early as 1863–4 by the Victorian classicist, historian and member of the Anthropological Society of London, Thomas Bendyshe.[9]

In this chapter, I do not make claims for John Atkins as a major figure of eighteenth-century naval surgery/medicine, or as a dominant figure in the early eighteenth-century medicine of regions outside Europe.[10] What I do claim for John Atkins, however, is that the ideas contained in the relevant section of his surgical manual are an exemplification of a much wider cultural shift in European attitudes to race, beginning in the mid-seventeenth century. It is a shift that led to racial difference being perceived, analysed and constructed as one of the most important forms of bodily difference by the end of the eighteenth century and into the nineteenth.[11] I suggest that the ideas contributed by *The Navy Surgeon* are important for the way they signal the emergence of an independent role played by medicine in the construction of ideas of bodily difference. Medicine, as a practice and theoretical field concerned with disease, by this method contributed to constructing race in the eighteenth century. I also argue that his writing is one of the very few sites in eighteenth-century medicine where polygenist ideas and a racial constitution–construct underlying a disease aetiology come together in the same text and in the same author.

In the following section I outline one of the leading eighteenth-century trends – the neo-Hippocratic revival of environmental medicine – from which John Atkins' work constitutes a departure. Following this section I discuss in detail Atkins' polygenist ideas and their possible relationship to concepts of the racial constitution. In subsequent sections I discuss in detail Atkins' theory of the causation of sleepy distemper. I treat first his construction of its non-constitutional cause. I treat second his construction of its two constitutional causes. A final section considers John Atkins' significance for the eighteenth century.

Neo-Hippocratic theory and environmental medicine to 1730

For the 1730s and within the medical culture of the early eighteenth century more generally, John Atkins' ideas have a degree of relative novelty. They stand out and seem somewhat exceptional. While I do not wish to suggest his ideas were entirely without precedent in earlier periods, since I have no doubt precedents exist, I do wish to emphasise that John Atkins' ideas seem to be part of a new development. They were, as I have suggested, part of the wider cultural shift that has been described above, which led to the development of new naturalistic (as opposed to biblical, theological or mythological) understandings of race.[12] Within medicine itself, taken as a discrete component of intellectual culture and practice, Atkins' ideas represented a major departure from influential seventeenth-century and early eighteenth-century currents.

One of the influential currents of seventeenth-century medicine was an emphasis on environmental factors in the aetiology of disease. James C. Riley has argued that the Hippocratic view of disease and its relationship to environmental factors has exercised a large and profound influence over medicine in Western Europe, particularly since the early modern period.[13] According to Riley, in the second half of the seventeenth century, physicians still adhering to classical insights shifted emphasis away from Galen and the attribution of disease to disorder within humans, towards a revived Hippocratic notion of disease as the product of disorder between humans and their environment.[14] This aspect of seventeenth- and eighteenth-century medicine has been studied by a number of historians and I will here merely allude to some of the intellectual figures whose work most clearly embodies this 'environmental medicine' (the term used by James Riley and Ludmilla Jordanova) in the period before Atkins' own publication.[15]

Two key figures in the development of environmental medicine were Thomas Sydenham ('the English Hippocrates') and Robert Boyle. Boyle, while being a leading proponent of experimental practice and the mechanical philosophy within the Royal Society, also had a strong interest in medical cures and understanding the cause of disease.[16] Boyle endorsed the view that epidemics might be caused by emanations from the earth and from diseased persons, focusing on the idea of inorganic subterranean corpuscular emanations mixed with other atmospheric elements. Boyle, Riley argues, more generally aided the focus on the atmosphere as a possible cause of disease by investigating the properties of the atmosphere, thereby directing attention to the air as a major realm of scientific inquiry.[17]

As an admirer of Hippocrates, Sydenham accepted environmental factors as causal agents behind disease. He affirmed Boyle's ideas about emanations from the earth and from diseased persons. Indeed, Riley suggests that Sydenham, like Hippocrates, identified five phenomena as probably important aetiological elements behind manifestations of disease: heat, cold, moisture, dryness and emanations (from the earth and from pathological matter, whether human, animal or inanimate). He thought that breathing might be the method by which disease-causing agents entered the body of a healthy individual. He attributed certain diseases, such as intermittent fever and pleurisy, to climate and weather factors; other diseases, such as plague, were attributed to emanations from the earth or diseased bodies; yet other diseases, such as gout, were attributed to humoral imbalance. Riley makes the further point that there is a good deal of ambiguity about the ideas of the epidemic, atmospheric and environmental constitutions that are found in Sydenham's writings, and a great deal of ambiguity about just how environmental factors interacted to cause disease.[18]

Riley makes the point that no coherent statement of the content, aims and methods of environmental medicine existed in print until the publication of John Arbuthnot's *An Essay Concerning the Effects of Air on Human Bodies* in 1733, the year before Atkins' publication of *The Navy-Surgeon*. I am not arguing that Atkins read Arbuthnot (although he might have), or that he was steeped in the writings of Robert Boyle and Thomas Sydenham. Rather I suggest that ideas about the environmental aetiology of epidemic and endemic disease were extremely widespread in late seventeenth-century/early eighteenth-century medicine, and that they were influential both by virtue of presumed derivation from Hippocrates and through authoritative contemporary exponents. On this basis it seems likely that there would have been a strong presumption towards, or favouring of, physicians and surgeons constructing interpretations of disease which drew upon the environmental medicine developed by Sydenham, Boyle, Arbuthnot and others. John Atkins' regional medicine, in contrast, does not deploy these resources. It represents a departure from this framework.

Polygenist constructs and racial constitutions

John Atkins' regional medicine forms a part of the literature of pre-Mansonian tropical medicine which predates the adoption of germ theory and its application to tropical disease.[19] The term 'warm climates' rather than 'tropical' has been used recently by historians to designate the tropical medicine of this earlier period, partly because the phrase 'warm climates' had a strong contemporary resonance and because it underlines the fact that germ theory played no role in warm climate medical knowledge. The part of Atkins' surgical manual in which these discussions occur (to be found in the Appendix to the 1734 edition) is derived from an expedition to the Guinea Coast near the end of his naval career in 1721–2, on board HMS *Swallow* and *Weymouth*. The expedition's purpose was to protect British merchantmen trading in slaves from pirates, and to capture and hang as many of those pirates as possible.[20] The Navy mission was to make the seas off the Guinea

Coast safe for slave-traders. In the course of the expedition, one of the two navy ships engaged in an action which killed the famous pirate commander, Bartholomew Roberts. Captain Chaloner Ogle of the *Swallow* later received a knighthood, partly as a consequence of this early success. John Atkins published his journals of the voyage over a decade later, possibly stimulated by the notoriety that attached to the expedition.[21]

Atkins' surgical manual contains discussions of fevers and fluxes of the ships' crews; these were widely understood to be afflictions of warm climates. He also discusses diseases he believes to be found uniquely in the eighteenth-century African constitution or to have unique manifestations within that constitution. In particular he identifies four diseases: three diseases – yaws, chicoes, croakra – are given their eighteenth-century African names and a fourth disease – sleepy distemper – is given an English name.[22] This fourth disease he says is 'called, by Europeans the Sleepy Distemper'. This is a pointer to the fact that the English name itself predated his arrival. With all four diseases Atkins offers something new. For each he describes symptoms, suggests an aetiology and prescribes treatment. All four descriptions suggest he had direct contact with patients and attempted treatments himself. They indicate he was not just summarising local African, or locally resident European knowledge of these diseases. He was presenting knowledge based on personal experience. Nevertheless it is almost certain that he relied heavily on a local antecedent knowledge-base for identification of these clinical symptom patterns. Though some of these diseases had been described earlier, Atkins' relationship to this earlier literature is unknown.[23]

The disease we will focus on in this chapter is sleepy distemper. It is here we will seek the connections between concepts of race and concepts of disease. John Atkins describes many of the clinical symptoms of sleepy distemper in ways that are recognisable to modern observers. He also describes the course of the illness, susceptible age-groups and methods of treatment. His description is fairly full and detailed by eighteenth-century standards, but he has some of that century's tendency to therapeutic optimism. Though he believes the disease is usually fatal, he believes cure is possible in some cases:

> The Sleepy Distemper (common among the Negroes) gives no other previous Notice than a Want of Appetite two or three

> Days before; Their Sleeps are [pro]found, and Sense of Feeling very little; for pulling, drubbing, or whipping, will scarce stir up Sense and Power enough to move; and the Moment you cease beating the Smart is forgot, and down they fall again into a State of Insensibility, driviling constantly from the Mouth, as in deep Salivation; [they] breath slowly, but not unequally, nor snort.[24]

And he believes young adults are more frequent victims than the aged:

> Young People are more subject to it than the Old; and the Judgement generally pronounced is Death, the Prognostick seldom failing. If now and then one of them recovers, he certainly loses the little Reason he had, and turns Ideot.[25]

He applies the full range of eighteenth-century heroic therapeutics to the treatment of the disease, including bleeding in the jugular and, interestingly for the eighteenth century, acupuncture:

> The Cure is attempted by whatever rouzes the Spirits, bleeding in the Jugular, quick Purges, Sternutories, Vesicatories, *Acu-Puncture*, *Seton*, Fontanels, and sudden Plunges into the sea; the latter is most effectual when the Distemper is new, and the Patient as yet not attended with a driviling at Mouth and Nose.[26]

The inner core of Atkins' thinking about the causation of sleepy distemper is his view that the production of a superabundance of phlegm is the *immediate* cause of the disease. This is basically a traditional humoral approach to disease.[27] As we can see from the passage below, however, Atkins is not satisfied with the humoralist explanation, as traditionally conceived, and seeks deeper explanations. He seeks the *procatarctic* cause (defined by the *OED* as the cause that begins other causes, and in this case the cause(s) that begin(s) the immediate cause). It is in seeking these procatarctic causes that he innovates, going beyond and outside traditional humoralism.

> To return, the immediate cause of this deadly Sleepiness in the Slaves, is evidently a Super-abundance of Phlegm, or Serum,

> extravased in the Brain, which obstructs the Irradiation of the Nerves; but what the procatartick [*sic*] Causes are, that exert to this Production, eclipsing the Light of the Senses, is not so easily assigned.[28]

Turning to John Atkins' polygenist construct, it has already been noted in the introduction how Atkins articulated the doctrine of polygenism, the concept that different human racial groups, distinguished primarily by colour, have different origins.[29] It is now time to flesh out that general account of polygenism with the details of Atkins' specific account. This is how Atkins sets up the problem:

> From the River *Senega* in *Africa*, 15 [degrees] N. to almost its Southern Extremity in 34 [degrees] they are all black and woolly, the natural Cause of which, must ever perplex Philosophers. I know *Malpighius*, and from him others, ascribe these different Colours in Men to a Tinge from that reticular or mucous Substance under the Cuticle, not considering the Question as strongly returns; How even that should become so oppositely coloured as it does, in the remarkable Division of Mankind into Blacks and Whites?[30]

The problematic of monogenism that Atkins puts forward is the following: how, starting from an original white ancestor or ancestral pair (the assumption that the first human or first parents would be white is standard for much of the eighteenth century), would it be possible to arrive at black skin-colour? It is possible to see how whites might approach a 'mulatto dye', a brownish colour, but not a fully black skin-colour, so the argument goes:

> The Gradations *Europeans* make towards a Mulatto Dye, seem well enough solved from the Fineness of their Skins, and Approaches to the Sun, whose Heat, more or less, easily eliminates the thin Parts of that Mucosity, and leaves the Remainder dark; as the clearest Liquors, they say, will have some Sediment; but how so entire and opposite a Change is made, as in Negroes, is not so soon answered.[31]

Atkins has a range of arguments demonstrating the impossibility of deriving a black from an original white. They assume two mechanisms. First, that a black may be derived from a white by the direct action of the environment, principally the direct action of the sun's rays. This is the classical monogenism discussed above. Second, a subsidiary argument, that a black might be derived from a white ancestor from some sexual act of generation (and then become the ancestor of subsequent blacks). The four principal arguments Atkins makes are clearly designed to undermine these possible mechanisms. A further minor argument, listed in the text as the third, I will leave out of discussion as its logical structure and relationship to monogenism (either classical or other) is obscure and not easily interpreted. The four arguments which concern us are framed as objections to the monogenist accounts:

> There are these Objections; *First*, that the proximity of the Sun, has not the same influence on other animals in *Guiney*, nay, *their Sheep have Hair* contrary to that closer Contexture of the Skin, which is supposed to contribute to the Production of Wool in the human Species. *Secondly*, no *European* totally changes by length of Cohabitation with them, neither in Generation begets a Black, but a Mulatto, not a woolly, but hairy Race, which ever remain so.[32]

These two arguments first presuppose classical monogenism and then (for part of the second argument) the yielding of a black original by some act of sexual generation by a white ancestor. The first adopts a uniformity principle that the effects of the sun on humans and animals should be the same, yet it is not. The second is in two parts: the first asserts that the Guinea environment (i.e. cohabiting in Guinea) has never turned any living white into a black. The second part asserts that no living white has produced a black by any sexual act. The most that can be done by a sexual act is to produce a mulatto. Both parts of the second argument depend on the assumption that what is observed to be true for living whites would be true for an original white ancestor.

The last two arguments Atkins gives *both* depend on objections to classical monogenism alone. Sexual-generation monogenism does not feature. Opposition to classical monogenism clearly dominates Atkins' discourse. The direct action of the sun does not produce blacks in the Americas (this is listed as the fourth argument). Finally (i.e. the fifth), if the action of the sun causes blacks to look black, it should do so without exception. Yet it does not. There are some people in Guinea who are in every other respect negroes; but instead of being black, they are yellow. This seems to be an original argument of John Atkins and not a recycled element of discourse. It is worth underlining that the argument is not dependent on hearsay testimony. He claims the status of a direct eye-witness:[33]

> *Fourthly*, *Americans*, or other Nations in the same, or Parallels of Latitude, where the Sun equally influences, are not black: And, *lastly*, even in this *Negroland*, there are a Race of a bright yellow Colour, as though painted. I saw one of these in the next town above King *Pedro's*, in *Rio Sethos*, who was woolly, and in every Respect else a Negroe, (pardon the Impropriety,) but in Colour; and know there have others been seen (though rarely) at other Parts of the Coast.[34]

The conclusion Atkins gives to his demolition of classical monogenism and sexual-generation monogenism, is the argument from default. The remaining explanation for race, once environmental action and sex have been eliminated, can only be polygenism. Descent from a different original protoplast or different first parents causes difference, i.e. *constructs different races*. The argument is not as tautological as it first appears, once it is realised that polygenism is always a transformation *of some kind* of the concept of an original Adam (and/or original Eve) as given by Genesis. Polygenism is as empirical and no more tautological than monogenism, since it denies the efficacy of a mechanism which monogenism claims to be actually occurring. How the original protoplasts got there is removed to the realm of speculation, just as the original first human or first couple is removed to the realm of speculation in the case of monogenism. For the theologically inclined, God is the cause of the first parents; for the less theologically inclined, speculation about the first cause is omitted. Atkins is not deferential to ecclesiastical authority and does not speculate about first causes. He actually formulates his polygenist position twice, once in *The Navy-Surgeon* and once in his published journals, *A Voyage to Guinea, Brasil and the West Indies*. Therefore these statements clearly represent his views in the 1730s:

> From the Whole, I imagine that White and Black must have descended of different Protoplasts; and there is no other Way of accounting for it.[35]

> ... and tho' it be a little Heterodox, I am persuaded the black and white Race have, *ab origine*, sprung from different-coloured first Parents.[36]

Thus we see that John Atkins was a direct contributor to eighteenth-century racial, and specifically polygenist, discourse. Atkins (along with others I hasten to add) helps give naturalistic meaning to race in this period. The next question that arises for the historian is the impact of this naturalisation of race on his disease discourse. When we come to this issue, the first part of my argument is that the concept of the racial constitution is an integral part of Atkins' disease discourse. It is most strongly evident in his aetiology of sleepy distemper (and it is this disease that will be focused on in subsequent sections of this chapter). The second part of my argument is that the concept of the racial constitution depends on having some implicit or explicit notion of what a race is.

In Atkins' case there is an explicit notion of what a race is – his polygenist conception of race. It seems to me it is not simply a fortuitous coincidence that Atkins' surgical manual contains both a polygenist conceptual framework and the racial constitution construct. Polygenism *informs* the racial constitution construct and vice versa. Both comprise aspects of Atkins' thinking about differences between European and African bodies. It would be surprising if these were two completely compartmentalised notions of bodily difference occupying unconnected mental domains.[37]

I think a good case can also be made that polygenist concepts form part of the theoretical pathway to the construction of the concept of the racial constitution. If this argument were right, it would be true both generally and specifically. It would follow in John Atkins' own case, and it would follow also for subsequent generations of theorists who make use of the racial constitution construct, even though they may not remain polygenists or be committed to polygenism. But if we accept this argument, an important qualification is in order. It is unlikely that polygenism was the sole pathway to the concept of the racial constitution. Other pathways doubtless existed. However, they are not the subject of this chapter.[38]

A further point deserves emphasis. It should be stressed that the relationship between the polygenist conceptual framework and the racial constitution construct is not a logical and necessary one. Ideas about the aetiology of sleepy distemper cannot be *read off* from the fact that we know John Atkins was a polygenist. Though the two sets of ideas (the polygenist conceptual system and the racial constitution construct) *inform* each other, *we cannot derive one from the other*, in either direction.[39]

It is noteworthy that the two characteristics on which John Atkins focuses in his construction of race are skin colour (white or black) and hair texture ('hairy' or 'woolly'). And we know that he also sees mulattos and yellow-skinned Africans as separate races. Within the polygenist tradition, race was not understood to reside just on the surface. Within this tradition, skin colour was a synecdoche standing in for differences between whole bodies.[40] Once you admit the possibility that skin colour and hair texture are explained by differential descent and you allow that different groups highlighted by these external markers have different original ancestors, then the possibility arises that the original protoplasts may have been different in other ways incorporating other possible, though invisible, differences. In this way polygenism opens the floodgates to a wide range of possible differences. On this way of reading how the polygenist conceptual system might inform the racial constitution concept, external difference becomes the sign of hidden inner difference, which may be formally and explicitly traced to polygenist assumptions *or explicit linkage may simply be left open*. At a bare minimum this would legitimate the idea that particular kinds of bodies have particular kinds of diseases, as well as unspecified (and probably unknown) additional differences.

The construction of sleepy distemper

The non-constitutional basis

Something very important stands out about Atkins' aetiological analysis of sleepy distemper. He did not see it as being a straightforwardly constitutional disease, a disease in which the constitutional element was the only important cause under consideration. He saw sleepy distemper as a slave's disease (slaves were the main group of ill persons he encountered). And he built a theory of causation with the intellectual starting point that black slaves or African slaves were a demographic group with particular illnesses, in much the same way as eighteenth-century medicine considered seamen to be a demographic group with particular illnesses.

John Atkins considered all the ascribed procatarctic causes (both constitutional and non-constitutional) to be important. None acting alone could lead to illness, since he affirms quite clearly 'some or all of these causes [are] co-operating to it [i.e. the state of illness]'.[41] The underpinning concept was the notion that 'black slave' was a real, foundational and not an artifactual category.[42] That the disease seemed to affect only this group of people was not seen as, or deemed to be, an artefact of the circumstances of observation. Reconstructing the conceptual world-view that inclined him to this point of view is difficult, since in dealing with the early eighteenth century we deal with intellectual frameworks far removed from our own. But it can be done.

To emphasise the point that non-constitutional aetiology was not a secondary kind of causation for John Atkins, I will first treat his construction of non-constitutional causes. He signals early on that while he understood the slave status to be a social category, it was not the fact of being a slave or a traded commodity that was itself pathogenic. Rather the organisation of the slave trade and its geographically specific recruitment patterns provided the epidemiological key to understanding why slaves of all population groups seemed to be inextricably bound up with the sleepy distemper cases:

> In searching for the Cause of this Distemper [Sleepy Distemper], it will be necessary to repeat what I have observed, That the Bulk of Slave-Cargoes mostly consist of Country People, as distinguished from the Coast People; apparent, if the principal Way of Supply be considered. At *Whydah* more Slaves are bought, than on the whole Coast besides; And why? The King of that Country, and his next Neighbours, understand Sovereignty better than others, and often make War, (as they call it,) to bring in whole Villages of those more simple Creatures inland, to be sold at Market, and exchanged for the tempting Commodities of *Europe*, that they are fond and mad after.[43]

John Atkins' insight was that in observing slaves, one was observing inlanders as opposed to coastal groups. Enslavement did not apply to coastal populations. This was an important insight, because it meant that Atkins could then apply a life-style/cultural/behavioural factor to the interpretation of sleepy distemper, one that distinguished inlanders from coastal populations. Probably influenced by the culture of aetiological speculation within eighteenth-century *naval* medicine, Atkins put forward the theory that lack of self-discipline and inappropriate behaviour, particularly indolence, were pathogenic.[44] Diet could also be pathogenic. He applied some of these ideas to sleepy distemper and inlander populations. Atkins had no firsthand knowledge of inlander societies, though he had observed slaves. Through these observations of slaves, together with unreliable hearsay reports about inlander behaviour, he formed a portrait of the inlander populations. He concluded that inlanders were of a lower cultural level than the coastal peoples he had come to know and respect to some degree.[45] The behaviours he observed among slaves he ascribed to their inlander origin, not to the circumstances attendant on enslavement.

The theory Atkins constructed requires a bit of unpicking. First he describes the pathogenic diet and lack of civility of both inlanders (knowledge of which he derived from hearsay reports) and slaves; his descriptions show they overlap and parallel one another. The diet of the inlanders is generally roots, fruits and herbage, but eaten in its 'wild and uncultured' state. The key point of his description of the diet of slaves is their similar readiness to eat food in 'wild and uncultured' state, rather than what they are actually eating. He notes their readiness to eat meat whether 'raw or dressed', whether 'guts or a sirloin', and expressed particular disgust at this. Thus this readiness to eat 'uncultured' food itself appears to be cultural. He seems to construct the slaves (and inlanders) as being themselves wild and uncultured. The slaves may not have had much choice about what they ate, but Atkins was not particularly sensitive to this point. Atkins' first thesis seems to be that the wild and uncultured state of the slaves (and inlanders) inhibited them from distinguishing a pathogenic from a healthy diet, thus contributing to the disease. Both the wild and uncultured state and the unhealthy diet are the contributing elements to disease. Sleepy distemper thus appears as the mirror-image of a 'disease of civilisation'. It is a disease of anti-civilisation![46]

Atkins' second thesis relates to the fact that the lifestyles of slaves and inlanders also parallel and replicate each another, both slaves and inlanders displaying the same indolence and inactivity. He describes the supposed indolence of the slaves in very graphic terms, appearing to explain their lack of emotion in parting from friends and loved ones in terms of it. This also seems to be related to their low cultural level. From an eighteenth-century medical standpoint, his theory seems to be that *indolent lifestyles are pathogenic*. Atkins' second thesis, then, is that the indolent lifestyles of the slaves and inlanders, particularly when combined with unhealthy diet, were the pathogenic cause of disease. The logic of Atkins' argument requires that sleepy distemper ought also to occur in inlander societies among people not yet enslaved, though he is not explicit on this point. Here is Atkins' framing of the argument:

> *Secondly*, Promoted here *by their Diet and Way of Living*. At Home it is mostly on Roots, Fruits, and Herbage, greedily devouring such as are wild and uncultured. … Their Indolence is such, (when shipped on Board for Slaves,) as to be entirely dispassionate at parting with Wives, Children, Friends, and Country, and are scarcely touched with any other Sense or Appetite, than that of Hunger; and even in this, for want of Custom or Instinct, they cannot distinguish proper Food, … voraciously eating, though Victuals be never so dirtily cook'd; and whether the Flesh be raw or dressed, whether the Guts or a Sirloin. … By their Sloth and Idleness the Blood becomes more depauperated; and those recrementitious Humours bred from it … [47]

The constitutional basis

The principal focus of this chapter is on eighteenth-century medical ideology and aetiological theory, and within that framework the place occupied by a constitutional model of sleepy distemper. Atkins advanced two constitutional causes of this disease alongside the non-constitutional cause discussed above. The first was the constitutional immaturity of the black body, and the second the natural weakness of the African brain. I have suggested in an earlier section that we should interpret the polygenist construct and the racial constitution construct as two sets of ideas that inform each other. Here I show what this means in practice.

We can begin with the 'constitutional immaturity of the black body' argument: here the theoretical idea is simple, uncomplicated, relatively undeveloped. Atkins notes that children frequently suffer from colds and have runny noses: therefore they display in their runny noses the same excess of the humour that on his theory causes sleepy distemper.[48] The next step is to argue that African sleepy distemper victims are in some sense the physiological equivalents of children suffering colds. Thus the constitutional cause of the disease is that African bodies (of youth, middle or old age) are physiologically similar to children's bodies. It is clear he intends the idea of physiological difference because he speaks of fibres attaining their due spring and perfection in mature bodies. It is clear this constitutional immaturity is intended as a racial characteristic, since it distinguishes all Africans (young or old) from all adult Europeans. African bodies on this theory are bodies whose fibres and faculties have not attained their due spring and perfection. There is no theory of the cause of this difference in the text, but it would be consistent with his polygenism to suppose it derived from the original black protoplast or first parent:

> *First*, In *Immaturity*, or Childhood, it is a common and true Observation, that more of Phlegm and recrementitious Humour is bred; than at Manhood; because the Fibres, and consequently the Faculties resulting from their Constitution, have not attained their due Spring and Perfection; and it is only supposing the *Africans* continue longer Children than the *Europeans*.[49]

The second constitutional cause is an even more important cause of the disease; Atkins rates it the principal cause. It is the 'natural weakness of the brain' argument, and it is clearly intended as a racial characteristic. Atkins' theoretical concepts are more complex here than with the previously discussed constitutional cause, and we do see him drawing on unexpected conceptual resources. Continuing with this theory of the critical importance of excess phlegm or serum, he implies a weak brain is less able to contain or manage the excess of the dangerous phlegm that is the immediate cause of the disease. Thus bodies which have these weak brains are natural candidates for the sleepy distemper. Africans, he suggests, have the requisite weak brains, because they are 'destitute of all Art and Science, or any mechanical knowledge' to exercise the brain.[50]

This broad outline of Atkins' construction of the weak African brain is clear enough, but there is underlying it a real model of brain function, the details of which make for subtle and interesting reading. He argues that the faculties of the brain function in ways that are equivalent to the muscles of the body. By labour and exercise the muscles become strong and powerful. Without exercise they weaken and atrophy. The intellectual faculties function in similar ways. Through active participation in the 'Arts and Sciences', through the exercise of reason and logic, not only does the mind acquire learning but the brain itself strengthens its firmness of texture. The inward structure and recesses of the brain are changed by the acquisition of knowledge, by the exercise of intellectual faculties. Stupid and ignorant humans have a different brain texture from those who are learned and knowledgeable, because their faculties have been without use. Atkins appears to be reasoning within an early eighteenth-century materialist paradigm:

> The Imployment of the Soul does not only in Metaphor, but in Reality, help to strengthen the Brain; as that again, (the Condition of Mortality) by the Firmness of its Texture, and Goodness of Disposition, does the Intellectual Faculties. This is obvious in the clear, wakeful, and unclouded Understanding of Men of Learning and Genius, compared with the Stupid and Ignorant, in whom the Soul (i.e. its Operations,) and the Brain are reciprocally found strong or weak: Where Ignorance and Stupidity reign, therefore, and neither Sciences nor Mechanics are planted for exercising the Faculties, the Brain must grow weak, and such a State of Thoughtlessness and Inactivity dispose it for the Reception of Serosities.[51]

Atkins applies the same idea to groups that he applies to individuals. He sees groups as being embedded in cultures. Europeans and Africans originating in different protoplasts are so embedded. Groups may lack or possess arts and sciences, thus critically affecting the kinds of brains that exist in the group. All members of a group lacking arts, sciences and mechanical knowledge will be stupid and ignorant, and have weak brains. It will be or become a racial characteristic of that group if all members of the group belong to it by virtue of being derived from a single protoplast. Groups such as Europeans with thriving arts and sciences will have a diversity of types of men, with some men of genius and some stupid and ignorant. The nature/culture boundary on such a theory will be weak, because cultural resources affect the physical nature of the brain. This line of thought runs in the opposite direction to the anti-environmentalism that underlies Atkins' polygenism:

> Thirdly, *The natural Weakness of the Brain*, I am apt to think the principal Cause of this Distemper. Doubtless that Part gains Strength by Exercise i.e. by the Employment of our rational Faculties, as well as the Muscles and external Fibres of the Body by Labour; and since the *Africans* are hereditarily ignorant, destitute of All Art and Science, or any mechanical Knowledge to exercise the Brain, it consequently grows weaker in its inward Structure and Recesses; and fails together with the Judgement and Passions.[52]

Atkins' conception of variable brain strength is a very interesting idea because it appears potentially to be an optimistic notion. If brain strength is a quantity which is not a simple, fixed anatomical correlate of race, as it was for a number of early nineteenth-century racial determinists and craniologists, such as Samuel Morton in America, then brain weakness may turn out to be reversible.[53] A potential future of equal brains for European and African could *in principle* be envisaged. Though this is not actually stated in the text, it does seem to be the underlying tendency of the argument.

However, since Atkins' theory of weak and strong brains says little about how the arts and sciences originate, his account incorporates ambiguities which tend to qualify the straightforward optimistic interpretation. What is meant by *hereditary* ignorance? Is it ignorance that is merely historically contingent or is it ignorance intrinsically linked in some way to the original African protoplast? Is the fact that arts and sciences do not already exist a sign of a fundamental incapacity to develop and use them?

The question: can arts and sciences be implanted, accepted or adopted by groups that have been unable to create their own? is a fundamental one, and it is one that is raised by the polygenist construct. Atkins skirts around this question with his theory of weak and strong brains, and avoids it. Clearly though, the presence of phrases such as 'hereditarily ignorant' does allow the possibility of a pessimistic reading, as well as an optimistic one. My sense, however, is that John Atkins plumps for the optimistic view without quite saying so.

Concluding remarks

What is John Atkins' significance? He is significant in several different ways. One way is as a provider of an early Western account of a little-known tropical disease.[54] This is one of Atkins' important functions for eighteenth-century medicine. A second way is as a proponent of a new racialised medicine. This is his second important function for the eighteenth century.

First consider his function in providing an early modern account of a little-known tropical disease – Atkins' description of sleepy distemper is the *first* British account of the illness we now recognise as the modern disease of sleeping sickness or *African Trypanosomiasis*.[55] The function here is that of providing, for the eighteenth century, knowledge of diseases and health conditions outside Europe. There was a strong interest in knowledge of diseases of warm climate regions, but not exclusively so. Knowledge of this kind was an important aspect of the work of colonisation that had been proceeding since Columbus' discovery of the New World in the 1490s.[56]

Atkins' name appears in two normally unconnected twentieth-century bodies of historical writing – the history of polygenism[57] and the history of sleeping sickness.[58] I have tried to unite these two histories in this chapter.

The older histories of sleeping sickness that mention Atkins have tended to ignore the racial underpinnings of his construction of sleepy distemper (especially his polygenism). One reason they have treated it as unimportant and not significant is because it is so obviously false from the perspective of twentieth-century medical knowledge.[59] Behind this lies a Whig view of history in which the significance of past ideas is measured against current belief. One reason for *not* accepting this approach, however, is that it leaves us with a *caricature* of eighteenth-century medicine, and makes it impossible to understand the eighteenth- and nineteenth-century *specifically medical* (not merely popular) belief that sleeping sickness was a disease that exclusively affected 'natives'.[60]

Next consider his role as the proponent of a new racialised medicine – I have tried to argue that John Atkins embodied for the eighteenth century a new kind of medicine, one which emphasised the role of the racial, not just individual, constitution in the kinds of diseases a body might be susceptible to. This new emphasis on constitution involved the idea that different races get different diseases for reasons to do with the nature of their bodies. Framed at a high level of generalisation, it involved the idea that there were unique diseases for unique kinds of bodies. Atkins' *The Navy-Surgeon* was a part of the development of this new emphasis or approach. In more specific terms, it implied that differences in skin colour (the principal sign of race, for our period) might be the visible external sign of hidden differences between bodies, differences that caused bodies to be subject to different diseases.

Though I argue in this chapter that John Atkins participated in the construction of a new kind of medicine based on the concept of the racial constitution, I also suggest that this form of constitutional construct was not strongly entrenched when Atkins was writing in the 1730s. I argue this while acknowledging that it did become powerfully dominant at a later period within British colonial (and aspects of North American) medicine, wherever medicine dealt with racially diverse populations.[61] I suggest that handbooks such as *The Navy-Surgeon*, because they circulated among a specialised audience of mobile medical professionals (i.e. naval surgeons) and were popular enough to be reprinted in several editions,[62] may have played a particular role in increasing circulation of the new racial ideas.

Furthermore, in generating a mainly constitutional causal model of sleepy distemper, Atkins built up an idea which had powerful implications both for the construction of the strictly *medical* concept of the racial constitution, and for generating ideological conceptions of naturalised racial hierarchies.[63] Medical science is revealed here to be part of a *larger naturalising social ideology*. Medical science in the early eighteenth century cannot be separated from its social context. Via his construction of sleepy distemper, Atkins added to the central themata by which the black body came to be understood in the eighteenth century through his location of a site of racial difference in the head, or more strictly the brain.

The head was to become a fundamental site of naturalised racial difference in the later eighteenth century, and it somewhat challenges the conventional view to see it being introduced in the early part of the eighteenth. It became an important constituent of an Enlightenment science of race as developed by Petrus Camper, Johann Blumenbach and Thomas Soemmerring.[64] So Atkins' ideas look forward to and *prefigure* the later eighteenth century. Yet there is an important difference. With Atkins we have the head or brain designated as the site of difference and formulated within the context of disease theory, without the attempt to construct an anthropological system such as those of the figures named above. Atkins' exact relationship to these later developments is not known. What is clear is that the sorts of ideas he helped to create became a cultural resource for many later generations of theorists. Once invented they continue to circulate endlessly.

There is also the fact that Atkins' *The Navy Surgeon* forms part of a tradition of polygenist theorising that was represented later in the eighteenth century. Later carriers of the tradition in the 1770s include Edward Long, a British-born Jamaican planter, author and Judge of the Vice-Admiralty Court (in Jamaica),[65] and Lord Kames (a.k.a. Henry Home), a social theorist of the Scottish Enlightenment and a Lord of the Court of Sessions in Edinburgh.[66] Two decades later, the leading Manchester surgeon, male midwife and medical writer Charles White published his *Account of the Regular Gradation in Man*, further articulating the polygenist project.[67] Atkins' specific influence on these later developments is unclear and perhaps unprovable. However, there is no reason to believe that Atkins' *The Navy-Surgeon* was a lost text, unknown to these later writers, and that it played no part in constructing the eighteenth-century polygenist tradition.

Atkins' theory strongly diverges from the environmental medicine of Sydenham and Boyle which contains no concepts parallel to the racial constitution and makes no racial distinctions. Atkins did not build a model of the aetiology of sleepy distemper using the resources of environmental medicine available in the 1730s, although there was nothing to prevent him doing so. Though there is no logical inconsistency between the adoption of exclusively environmentalist models of disease-causation and the adoption of a polygenist paradigm, there may be a practical inconsistency. I have tried to argue strongly for the *contingent* element in the construction of a racial model of sleepy distemper in the early eighteenth century. I have sought to suggest that the theory of sleepy distemper could have gone in a different direction if the Sydenham–Boyle model had been still more dominant. The Sydenham–Boyle model of environmental medicine lost out to racialised constructions of disease at the imperial periphery in the early eighteenth century in the work of John Atkins. The creation of a racialised understanding of sleeping sickness was *not* an inevitable or necessary development.

Notes

1 Steven Shapin, *The Scientific Revolution*, Chicago, University of Chicago Press, 1996, is a superb introduction to the literature.

2 The idea of race is the idea that the world's peoples fall naturally into different groups. These groups are of a special kind in that the people in one group are all similar in physical appearance to one another and different from all members of other groups. These different groups, united by common external appearance, tend to be associated with different continental or subcontinental regions of the world: Europe, Africa, Asia, the Americas, and so on. Where different groups are found on the same continent, this is presumed to be the result of migration. This is the essential idea of race as it was developed in the seventeenth century. It underpins most writing about race in the eighteenth century also. A version of this conception underlies Thomas Trapham, *A Discourse of the State of Health in the Island of Jamaica*, London, R. Boulter, 1679.

3 The monogenist and polygenist paradigms themselves are naturalisations of a mid-century (mainly) theological debate over the merits of the 'pre-Adamite', or 'men before Adam', hypothesis. The most important mid-century promoter of the 'men before Adam' thesis was a French theologian, Isaac La Peyrère, although there were also less influential English exponents of the view in the seventeenth century. See R.H. Popkin, *Isaac La Peyrère (1596–1676): His Life, Work and Influence*, Leiden, E.J. Brill, 1987, for the most recent scholarly study. This work contains an excellent bibliography.

4 For a thoughtful overview, see Donald K. Grayson, *The Establishment of Human Antiquity*, London, Academic Press, 1983, pp. 139–67.

5 An early natural philosophical statement of the principle of monogenism, including a theory of the cause of differences, occurs in John Ray, 'A Discourse on the Specific Differences of Plants'. The paper was read to the Royal Society on 17 December 1674, and ordered to be registered. It was published in Thomas Birch, *The History of the Royal Society of London ... : A Facsimile of the London Edition of 1756–57*, New York and London, Johnson Reprint Corporation, 1968, vol. 3, pp.169–73, esp. p.171. Even here of course John Ray's natural history is at the service of and underpinned by natural theological considerations. But this is true too of Isaac Newton.

6 The qualifier, 'before the nineteenth century', is important because by the early nineteenth century new forms of monogenism begin to be developed which do not depend on simple direct environmental effects as understood in the eighteenth. See James Cowles Prichard, *Researches into the Physical History of Man*, Chicago, University of Chicago Press, 1973. This edition is a reprint of the 1813 edition, with an introduction and critical apparatus by its editor George Stocking.

7 A classic, very early statement of polygenism that completely lacked the baggage of defending the 'men before Adam' thesis in religious terms, was published in 1695 by an anonymous Oxford natural philosopher. See L.P., *Two Essays Sent in a Letter from Oxford to a Nobleman in London*, London, R. Baldwin, 1695.

8 John Atkins' surgical manual, *The Navy-Surgeon: or, a Practical System of Surgery*, was sufficiently popular to be published in three editions, in 1734, in 1737 and again in 1742. The 1734 edition is used for the

purposes of this chapter as it is the earliest. All passages quoted from it retain the original spellings. The 1742 edition is considerably revised and expanded. The title of the 1734 edition is:

> *The Navy-Surgeon: or, a Practical System of Surgery. Illustrated With Observations on such remarkable Cases as have occurred to the Author's Practice in the Service of the Royal Navy. To which is added A Treatise on the Venereal Disease, the Causes, Symptoms, and Method of Cure by Mercury: ... Also an Appendix, Containing Physical Observations on the Heat, Moisture, and Density of the Air on the Coast of Guiney; the Colour of the Natives; the Sicknesses which they and the Europeans trading thither are subject to; with a Method of Cure*
> (Printed in London for C. Ward and R. Chandler, 1734)

9 T. Bendyshe, 'The History of Anthropology', *Memoirs of Anthropological Society of London* 1 (1863–4): 59. Historians of race in the twentieth century have also flagged his polygenism, though without extended discussion. Histories of race that mention him include: R.H. Popkin, 'Medicine, Racism, Anti-Semitism: A Dimension of Enlightenment Culture', in G.S. Rousseau (ed.), *The Languages of Psyche: Mind and Body in Enlightenment Thought*, Berkeley, University of California Press, 1990, p. 415; L. Poliakov, *The Aryan Myth: A History of Racist and Nationalist Ideas in Europe*, trans. Edmund Howard, New York, Meridian, New American Library, 1977, p. 175; W.D. Jordan, *White Over Black: American Attitudes to the Negro, 1550–1812*, New York, W.W. Norton, 1977 (first published University of North Carolina Press, 1968), p. 17.

10 He was not – for example – comparable in influence and administrative power to the dominant figures of late eighteenth-century naval medicine, particularly James Lind, Thomas Trotter and Gilbert Blane. Atkins was a surgeon in the Royal Navy for at least twenty years, probably from 1703 (or even earlier) until 1723. For biography, see F. Tubbs, 'John Atkins: An Eighteenth-Century Naval Surgeon', *British Medical Bulletin* 5 (1947–8): 83–4, and also *Dictionary of National Biography* entry; for details of John Atkins' place within naval surgery/medicine, see C. Lloyd and J.L.S. Coulter, *Medicine and the Navy, 1200–1900*, Edinburgh, E. & S. Livingstone, 1961, vol. 3, p. 20.

11 For the late eighteenth century, see Londa Schiebinger, *Nature's Body: Gender in the Making of Modern Science*, Boston, Beacon Press, 1993, esp. pp. 115–83. For the nineteenth century, see Nancy Stepan, *The Idea of Race in Science: Great Britain, 1800–1960*, London, Macmillan, 1982. See also Ann Fausto-Sterling, 'Gender, Race and Nation: The Comparative Anatomy of "Hottentot" Women in Europe, 1815–1817', in J. Terry and J. Urla (eds), *Deviant Bodies: Critical Perspectives on Difference in Science and Popular Culture*, Bloomington and Indianapolis, Indiana University Press, 1995.

12 For biblical and/or mythological understandings of race from the medieval and early modern period see Benjamin Braude, 'The Sons of Noah and the Construction of Ethnic and Geographical Identities in

the Medieval and Early Modern Periods', *William and Mary Quarterly* 54 (1997): 103–42.

13 James C. Riley, *The Eighteenth-Century Campaign to Avoid Disease*, London, Macmillan, 1987, p. ix.

14 Op. cit.

15 In addition to Riley's study (cited above), see the following for further details of the medicine of the environment: Caroline Hannaway, 'Environment and Miasmata', in W.F. Bynum and Roy Porter (eds), *Companion Encyclopedia of the History of Medicine*, London, Routledge, 1993; Frederick Sargent, *Hippocratic Heritage: A History of Ideas about Weather and Human Health*, Oxford, Pergamon Press, 1982; L.J. Jordanova, 'Earth Science and Environmental Medicine: The Synthesis of the Late Enlightenment', in L.J. Jordanova and Roy Porter (eds), *Images of the Earth: Essays in the History of the Environmental Sciences*, London, British Society for the History of Science Monographs, 1979; Genevieve Miller, 'Airs, Waters and Places in History', *Journal of the History of Medicine and Allied Sciences* 17 (1962): 129–40.

16 For Robert Boyle, see Steven Shapin and Simon Schaffer, *Leviathan and the Air Pump: Hobbes, Boyle and the Experimental Life*, Princeton, Princeton University Press, 1985, and Steven Shapin, *A Social History of Truth: Civility and Science in Seventeenth-Century England*, Chicago, University of Chicago Press, 1994, pp. 126–92. Boyle's interests in medicine are explored in Lester King, 'Robert Boyle as an Amateur Physician', in C.W. Bodemer and L. King, *Medical Investigation in Seventeenth-Century England*, Los Angeles, William Andrews Clark Memorial Library, 1968. See also Barbara Kaplan, *'Divulging of Useful Truths in Physick': The Medical Agenda of Robert Boyle*, Baltimore, Johns Hopkins University Press, 1993.

17 Riley, *The Eighteenth-Century Campaign*, esp. pp. 7, 10, 13.

18 Riley, *The Eighteenth-Century Campaign*, esp. pp. 2, 10–12. Sydenham's co-invention with Robert Boyle of the theory of morbific particles and their production in the inward bowels of the Earth is explored in K.D. Keele, 'The Sydenham–Boyle Theory of Morbific Particles', *Medical History* 18 (1974): 240–8. See also Andrew Cunningham, 'Thomas Sydenham: Epidemics, Experiment and the "Good Old Cause" ', in R. French and A. Wear (eds), *The Medical Revolution of the Seventeenth Century*, Cambridge, Cambridge University Press, 1989, pp. 164–90.

19 A preliminary attempt to study this earlier literature is David Arnold (ed.), *Warm Climates and Western Medicine: The Emergence of Tropical Medicine, 1500–1900*, Amsterdam, Rodopi, 1996.

20 This fact goes a long way to explaining how John Atkins came to be involved in the treatment of *sick slaves*, and thus goes part way to clarifying what would otherwise be a puzzling feature of a naval expedition. But it has no bearing on his polygenist paradigm. Atkins was deeply (and unusually for the early eighteenth century) hostile to slavery. His published journals indicate this. See *A Voyage to Guinea, Brasil and the West Indies; in His Majesty's ships the Swallow and Weymouth. Giving a genuine account of the several islands and settlements. … Describing the colour, diet, language, habits … and religions of the …*

inhabitants. With remarks on the gold, ivory and slave trade, London, C. Ward and R. Chandler, 1737, pp. 61–2 and 176–9, but see also pp.119–32. An earlier edition was published in 1735, the year after the first edition of *The Navy-Surgeon*.

21 An account of the hunt for Bartholomew Roberts, his death and the capture of his crew (derived from navy records) may be found in David Cordingly, *Life Among the Pirates: The Romance and the Reality*, London, Warner Books, 1996, pp. 243–51. For a biography of Bartholomew Roberts, see Stanley Richards, *Black Bart*, Llandybie, Christopher Davies, 1966. For an overview of the rise and decline of Anglo-American piracy, see Janice Thomson, *Mercenaries, Pirates and Sovereigns: State-Building and Extraterritorial Violence in Early Modern Europe*, Princeton, Princeton University Press, 1994, pp. 45–54. For Atkins' brief description of the engagement with pirates, *naming Roberts*, see Atkins, *A Voyage to Guinea, Brasil, and the West Indies*, pp. 191–4. See also *Dictionary of National Biography* entries for Bartholomew Roberts and Chaloner Ogle.

22 Atkins states: 'This I have thought fit to premise in general: The Distempers I design to speak to, as more properly their own, are the *Sleepy Distemper, the Croakra, the Yaws, and the Chicoes*' (*The Navy-Surgeon*, Appendix, p. 17).

23 Yaws and chicoes (under the name guinea worm) are described in Thomas Trapham, *A Discourse of the State of Health in the Island of Jamaica*, London, R. Boulter, 1679.

24 Atkins, *The Navy-Surgeon*, Appendix, p. 18.

25 Op. cit.

26 Atkins, *The Navy-Surgeon*, Appendix, p. 22. Emphasis in this quotation and all other quotations from Atkins' texts are contained in the original.

27 See Vivian Nutton, 'Humoralism', in Bynum and Porter, *Companion Encyclopedia of the History of Medicine*, vol. 1, pp. 281–91.

28 Atkins, *The Navy-Surgeon*, Appendix, p. 19.

29 Op. cit.

30 Atkins, *The Navy-Surgeon*, Appendix, p. 23.

31 Op. cit.

32 Atkins, *The Navy-Surgeon*, Appendix, pp. 23–4.

33 Atkins must have observed an African albino.

34 Atkins, *The Navy-Surgeon*, Appendix, p. 24.

35 Op. cit.; the interpretation offered in this chapter applies only to the 1734 edition of *The Navy-Surgeon*. Though many of the arguments against classical monogenism remain in the 1742 edition, the sentence quoted here is omitted.

36 Atkins, *A Voyage to Guinea, Brasil, and the West Indies*, p. 39.

37 This point will not be completely transparent until we come to the section discussing the constitutional aetiology of sleepy distemper.

38 In my forthcoming Harvard University Ph.D. thesis, 'Medicine and the Construction of Race in Britain, 1660–1800', I attempt to reconstruct these other pathways.

39 This is crucial. It explains why (as we shall see) the polygenist construct and the racial constitution construct are not governed by the same anti-environmentalist reasoning.

40 Some Ovist preformationists expressed this perspective through the idea of different kinds of bodies being produced by differently coloured eggs encapsulated in the ovary of Eve. See Phillip Sloan, 'The Gaze of Natural History', in Christopher Fox, Roy Porter and Robert Wokler (eds), *Inventing Human Science: Eighteenth-Century Domains*, Berkeley, University of California Press, 1995, pp. 112–51, esp. pp. 117, 143 and n. 16 on p. 143. This example was taken from a book review in the *Journal des Sçavans* 132 (May 1742): 23–45. The idea expressed here is clearly that of far-reaching difference.

41 Atkins, *The Navy-Surgeon*, Appendix, p. 19.

42 It is worth emphasising once again that John Atkins' polygenist conception of race is completely consistent with real sympathy for anti-slavery attitudes. His hostility to slavery was based on the principle that the enslaved were worse off, not better off. This was not a trivial point, since it placed him outside British colonial norms for the period. He probably would have needed an unusual degree of courage to take this isolated position. Atkins states:

> To remove *Negroes* then from their Homes and Friends, where they are at ease, to a strange Country, People and Language, must be highly offending against the Laws of natural Justice and Humanity; and especially when this change is to hard Labour, corporal Punishment, and for *Masters* they wish at the D—l [Devil?].
>
> (Atkins, *A Voyage to Guinea, Brasil, and the West Indies*, pp.178–9)

43 Atkins, *The Navy-Surgeon*, Appendix, p. 18.

44 Eighteenth-century aetiological speculation about the causes of scurvy provides a parallel example. Christopher Lawrence has argued that indolence and indiscipline were understood to be a cause of scurvy within a multi-causal model of the disease, alongside improper diet, lack of cleanliness, and a range of other factors (all of which needed changing in order to cure the disease). Most of the medical men involved in this area of theoretical activity were naval surgeons or naval physicians. For this case study, see Christopher Lawrence, 'Disciplining Disease: Scurvy, the Navy and Imperial Expansion, 1750–1825', in D. Miller and P. Reill (eds), *Visions of Empire: Voyages, Botany and Representations of Nature*, Cambridge, Cambridge University Press, 1996. Though the particular model described by Lawrence belongs to the period 1750–1825, there is evidence that indolence and scurvy were linked in an earlier period. See Kenneth J. Carpenter, *The History of Scurvy and Vitamin C*, Cambridge, Cambridge University Press, 1986 (paperback edn, 1988), pp. 46, 60. See also C. Lloyd and J.L.S. Coulter, *Medicine and the Navy, 1200–1900*, Edinburgh, E. & S. Livingstone, 1961, vol. 3, p. 299.

45 Atkins states: '[the Inlanders] have been totally destitute of the *European* correspondence that has mended the others [the Coastal groups], and are to Appearance but a few Degrees in Knowledge above Beasts ... ' (Atkins, *The Navy-Surgeon*, Appendix, p. 17).
46 For the trope of 'disease of civilisation' within eighteenth-century medicine, see Roy Porter, 'Diseases of Civilisation', in Bynum and Porter, *Companion Encyclopedia of the History of Medicine*, vol. 1, pp. 585–600.
47 Atkins, *The Navy Surgeon*, Appendix, p. 20.
48 Op. cit.
49 Op. cit.
50 Atkins, *The Navy Surgeon*, Appendix, p. 21.
51 Op. cit.
52 Op. cit.
53 For Samuel Morton's craniological and polygenist thinking, see Stephen J. Gould, *The Mismeasure of Man*, Harmondsworth, Penguin, 1997, pp. 82–104 (first published New York, W.W. Norton, 1981).
54 Maryinez Lyons has suggested that there were also Portuguese accounts of sleepy distemper, possibly dating back to the fourteenth century, although there is no suggestion that John Atkins had knowledge of them. See Maryinez Lyons, *The Colonial Disease: A Social History of Sleeping Sickness in Northern Zaire, 1900–1940*, Cambridge, Cambridge University Press, 1992, p. 65.
55 Sleeping sickness is a disease caused by a parasitic pathogen, the protozoan haemoflagellate, known by the genus name *Trypanosome*. The protozoan cause of sleeping sickness was established in 1902–3 by Aldo Castellani and David Bruce in the course of studying a major Ugandan epidemic. Classical human sleeping sickness is restricted to those parts of sub-Saharan Africa where the insect vector – the so-called tsetse fly, which transmits the trypanosome – is prevalent, i.e. western, eastern and central Africa. Twentieth-century knowledge, therefore, declares the aetiology of sleeping sickness to be specific to certain locations but to have no relation to particular kinds of (African) bodies. See Lyons, *The Colonial Disease*, pp. 42–8. There are many accounts of the discovery of the pathogen, including H.H. Scott, *A History of Tropical Medicine*, London, Edward Arnold, 1939, vol. 1, pp. 454–83; W.D. Foster, *A History of Parasitology*, Edinburgh and London, E. & S. Livingstone, 1965, pp. 115–37; John Boyd, 'Sleeping Sickness: The Castellani–Bruce Controversy', *Notes and Records of the Royal Society* 28 (1973): 93–110; W.H.R. Lumsden, 'Some Episodes in the History of African Trypanosomiasis', *Proceedings of the Royal Society of Medicine* 67 (1974): 789–96.
56 For a view of the work of colonisation, see Stephen Greenblatt, *Marvelous Possessions: The Wonder of the New World*, Oxford, Oxford University Press, 1991.
57 See references listed in note 9.
58 Atkins' description of sleepy distemper is the only eighteenth-century British account of the modern disease of sleeping sickness. See H.H. Scott, *A History of Tropical Medicine*, vol. 1, p. 456; R. Hoeppli,

Parasitic Diseases in Africa and the Western Hemisphere: Early Documentation and Transmission by the Slave Trade, Basel, Verlag für Recht und Gesellschaft, 1969, pp. 32–4. John Atkins has been more recently referred to by Lyons, *The Colonial Disease*, p. 66; B.I. Williams, 'African Trypanosomiasis', in F.E.G. Cox (ed.), *The Wellcome Trust Illustrated History of Tropical Diseases*, London, The Wellcome Trust, 1996, p. 180; W.H.R. Lumsden, 'Some Episodes in the History of African Trypanosomiasis', *Proceedings of the Royal Society of Medicine* 67 (1974): 790. Atkins' early contribution has been honoured by modern epidemiologists by inclusion in B.H. Kean, K.E. Mott and A.J. Russell (eds), *Tropical Medicine and Parasitology: Classic Investigations*, Ithaca and London, Cornell University Press, 1978, vol. 1, p. 181.

59 J.J. McKelvey, *Man Against Tsetse: Struggle for Africa*, Ithaca, Cornell University Press, 1973, pp. 7–8, is an exception within the older literature because it does treat the racial underpinnings, albeit briefly.

60 B.I. Williams' chapter in *The Wellcome Trust Illustrated History of Tropical Diseases* begins to revise the old-fashioned approach to sleeping sickness. Racial concepts are clearly understood to underlie both eighteenth- and nineteenth-century accounts of sleeping sickness. The nineteenth-century accounts discussed there depend on *some* view of race, though not necessarily a polygenist view. Williams has argued that there is no evidence that John Atkins' aetiological ideas were influential on nineteenth-century constructions of sleeping sickness. See B.I. Williams, 'African Trypanosomiasis', in Cox, *The Wellcome Trust Illustrated History of Tropical Diseases*, pp.178–91.

61 See Mark Harrison, ' "This Tender Frame of Man": Disease, Climate and Racial Difference in India and the West Indies, 1760–1860', *Bulletin of the History of Medicine* 70 (1996): 68–93; John S. Haller, 'The Negro and the Southern Physician: A Study of Medical and Racial Attitudes, 1800–1860', *Medical History* 16 (1972): 238–53; Todd Savitt, *Medicine and Slavery: The Diseases and Health Care of Blacks in Antebellum Virginia*, Urbana, University of Illinois Press, 1978. For related ideas in the early twentieth century, see Warwick Anderson, 'Immunities of Empire: Race, Disease and the New Tropical Medicine, 1900–1920', *Bulletin of the History of Medicine* 70 (1996): 94–118. See also relevant chapters in this volume.

62 See note 8 for more details.

63 Although in Atkins' case this is qualified by brain strength not being a fixed quantity.

64 See Londa Schiebinger, *Nature's Body: Gender in the Making of Modern Science*, Boston, Beacon Press, 1993, pp. 143–60. See also chapter 3 in this volume, by Hannah Augstein.

65 Edward Long, *History of Jamaica or General Survey of the Antient {sic} and Modern State of That Island: with Reflections on its Situation, Settlements, Inhabitants, Climate, Products, Commerce, Laws, and Government*, London, Frank Cass, 1970 (facsimile edn of T. Lowndes, 1774, 3 vols). See vol. 2, pp. 351–78. See also entry for Edward Long, *Dictionary of National Biography*.

66 Lord Kames, *Sketches of the History of Man*, Edinburgh, W. Creech, and London, W. Strahan & T. Cadell, 1774, 2 vols. See vol. 1, pp. 1–43. For Kames' ideas and their context, see Robert Wokler, 'Apes and Races in the Scottish Enlightenment: Monboddo and Kames on the Nature of Man', in Peter Jones (ed.), *Philosophy and Science in the Scottish Enlightenment*, Edinburgh, John Donald, 1988, pp. 145–68. See also Ronald Meek, *Social Science and the Ignoble Savage*, Cambridge, Cambridge University Press, 1976.

67 Charles White, *An Account of the Regular Gradation in Man*, London, C. Dilly, 1799. See C.C. Cullingworth, *Charles White, a Great Provincial Surgeon and Obstetrician of the Eighteenth Century*, London, H.J. Glaisher, 1904, for a biography.

Chapter 3

From the land of the Bible to the Caucasus and beyond

The shifting ideas of the geographical origin of humankind

H.F. Augstein

The Russian province Chechnya came to sad prominence in 1994–6 when separatist parts of the population attempted to break loose from Boris Yeltsin's Russia. Images of bloodshed and bombed sites were transported by the media into the homes of the Western world. The inhabitants of the Caucasus have ever been discontented with Russian dominion: the antagonism between Russia's rulers and the Caucasus peoples forms a continuous thread through the history of the region, linking Boris Yeltsin to Peter the Great and Catherine the Great. Located on the unknown outskirts of that massive empire, little known and little noticed, the fate of the petty Caucasian fiefdoms has been determined by their distance from Russia's political centre.

In other respects, too, the geography of the Caucasus has left its stamp on history. Most notably, the division of human 'races', promulgated in the nineteenth century, brought the region into contact with the fate of the Western world. For even though the peoples inhabiting it are as varied as the topographies of their homelands, the 'Caucasian' type became the term by which Europeans and Americans were to describe themselves and 'white-skinned' people in general. In Ivan Hannaford's words, nowadays is it 'used by immigration services worldwide'.[1]

It appears somewhat striking that the far-off peoples of the Caucasus should have provided the racial identity on which all Western nations were to be modelled. As a taxonomic term for human varieties, the notion of the 'Caucasian' character is entrenched in the history of racial theory developed between 1820 and 1850. Important though the topic is, it has been neglected by scholarship.

The 'Caucasian mystery', as Thomas Huxley called it,[2] was devised by medical men, being based on anatomical and physiological comparisons. In fact, throughout Europe the emergent disciplines of anthropology and ethnology were dominated by representatives of the medical sciences who considered the study of humankind in general as philosophical and noble.[3] In the eighteenth century the term 'race' was employed as one of many synonymous translations of the Latin words 'gens' and 'genus'. Other translations included the terms 'stock' and 'tribe', 'family' and 'nation'. During the Enlightenment the word 'race' was unproblematic because the Latin texts, in which its meaning largely resided, merely distinguished between nations as political entities and tribes or families as natural entities. All this was to change, not least thanks to the medical profession who used the concept of 'race' to delineate physical classifications of human tribes. It was physicians who, in the nineteenth century, helped to base nationalism on racial theory.[4] The description of the ancestors of white Europeans and Americans as Caucasian was the result of medical men engaging with ethnology. As we shall see, it made sense within a framework of classification shared by eighteenth-century doctors and naturalists alike, who put new diseases and new organisms on the map simply by naming them.

This essay will show how the Caucasian theory was devised in the eighteenth century, how it gained ground in the European imagination and how it became accommodated to the spread of racial theory. Sometimes the course of history appears whimsical and at the mercy of contingencies; sometimes historical occurrences seem oddly improbable. In the case of the Caucasian hypothesis, we may say that it spread precisely because it was unlikely, part of an imaginative geography rather than informed by solid factual knowledge, and hence open to all sorts of association of ideas, none of which had much to do with the original purpose of the concept: to elucidate the historical or geographical make-up of the human physique.

Systems of nature, human classification

The eighteenth century witnessed conscious attempts to systematise the knowledge of the world. The fashioning of taxonomic systems, aided by empirical observation, was regarded as an advance in knowledge. Thus the naturalist Carl Linné (1707–78) conceived a *systema naturae* that aimed to encompass the whole of Creation, living and dead. The framework of the 'chain of being' was not questioned until around the beginning of the nineteenth century; to classify meant to hierarchise along a scale that ascended from the minerals, through vegetables, animals and humans, towards angelic beings.[5] Only once the chain of being was cast into doubt did systems of nature allow the possibility that white humans and people of colour were created equal. From the latter half of the eighteenth century, anatomists endeavoured to uncover intrinsic physical differences between different human sorts. Each and every aspect was considered: which was the more likely, the doctrine of monogenesis or the polygenist idea that humankind consisted of several human species? Was there an insurmountable repulsion in the human breast against racial intermarriage? What, if human varieties could mix, would their children look like? If monogenesis was true, which type of skin colour was primeval – black or white? If it was white, as most supposed, how did it turn dark? If it was black, what light did that throw on Genesis?[6] The ever-increasing body of travel literature highlighted the fact that there were all kinds of shades of skin colour, various forms of human stature, bone structure, disease, habit and custom.

Against the background of eighteenth-century universalism, environmentalist theories flourished. Yet, as the century came to a close, the theory of climate and related hypotheses were being put into doubt: the children of white settlers in the tropical zones did not acquire those physical characteristics typical of the region, nor did the progeny of black slaves in the northern hemisphere display lighter complexions and facial features softened in the European mode. The English schoolteacher and prolific writer John Bigland (1750–1832) was not a sophisticated thinker, yet as early as 1816 he suggested that 'more than is generally supposed, must be attributed to race'. 'Reason and revelation', Bigland continued, 'concur in representing the whole human species as issuing from the same stock; but experience shews, that families are often distinguished not only by certain peculiarities of external organization, but also by particular dispositions of mind, which prevail through all or the greater part of their branches.'[7] The vagueness of his notions notwithstanding, Bigland was in tune with intellectual fashions of the time. He did not merely theorise natural differences along the lines of the civilised/feral dichotomy, referring differences of national character to race, he also envisioned racial differences among Europeans, stressing for example the peculiarities of Scottish Highland clans.[8] It was no accident that racial theories started to flourish from that time. After both the French Revolution and Napoleon had been defeated, the notion of race served to create concepts of hierarchical stratification where previously social status had served as the sole classifying principle.[9] Moreover, in the age of the nation-state, racial theories reflected the political need to legitimate international antagonisms as well as allegiances. 'Race' became a scientific term, its new biological meaning gradually supplanting its loose understanding as a synonym for stock and tribe. Hand-in-hand with this development came a heightened interest in the mechanisms of heredity.

Since antiquity, outward appearances had been considered the main characteristic of varying human tribes. Around the turn into the nineteenth century, comparative anatomy, pioneered by Georges Cuvier, grew into a physiological discipline in its own right. Subsequently, bone structure became a crucial criterion – it was not only more solid than hair and horns and other integuments, but was also seemingly shielded from environmental influences. With some scholars, the make-up of the skeleton, and the shape of the head in particular, provided criteria for human classification.

At the same time there were always those physiologists and anatomists who stressed the interface between environmental circumstances and human physiology, seeing the latter as a function of the former. Georges Buffon, in France, and Johann Friedrich Blumenbach, in Germany, held that the physiological differences were to be found precisely in those modifiable characteristics which others disclaimed as meaningless and variable. It was what Blumenbach called the 'habitus' – the conglomerate of features that determined the principal laws of the animal economy which an admirer of Blumenbach described as 'those which govern the duration of life, the periods of utero-gestation, the facts which relate to reproduction'.[10] Scholars like Blumenbach and Buffon regarded the geographical habitat of animals and human tribes as the key to describing their characteristics. The habitat was determined by the prevailing climate, which in turn hinged on geographical latitude. Before the heyday of comparative anatomy, there were two main ways of classifying human tribes: if naturalists were not guided by skin colour (which applied mostly to the white/black dichotomy) they relied on geography. Most systems of human classification sought to combine the two, though matters got more complicated when the results of historical linguistics came into play as well. This is the background against which the Caucasian hypothesis unfolded.

Shifting geographies: Blumenbach and the Caucasus

From the eighteenth century, the 'Caucasian variety of humankind' became an element of anthropological classification. It implied that humankind had spread out from the tops of the Caucasus range and, more specifically, had survived the Deluge there. When first advanced in the late eighteenth century it was a rather novel viewpoint. Until then other locations had figured more prominently in geographies of the Christian imagination, for example the garden of Eden, which some theologians located close to the Mediterranean, in the southern parts of Syria, while others preferred to imagine it further towards the east, in the region of ancient Chaldaea.[11]

The shift of focus from the Mediterranean world further to the north-east was a development of the latter part of the eighteenth century. Recently, Martin Bernal has told us that this was an ideological construct. His *Black Athena* has argued that Western culture originated in Africa: more precisely in Egypt.[12] Syria, Asia, Africa – the theories shift, due to ideological factors, scientific ambition and, nowadays, feelings of political correctness. In the following we will see why it came to be believed that the origins of humankind lay in the Caucasus.

It was a doctor and an anatomist who advanced the most clear-cut 'Caucasian' doctrines. The former was the famous Johann Friedrich Blumenbach (1752–1840). A professor at Göttingen University, a man of the Enlightenment and yet not without religious beliefs, he loathed Carl Linné's classification of humankind, that is, the idea that apes and human beings constituted one genus – the bipeds. In his own endeavour to classify humankind, he argued in 1781 that there were five different human varieties: his first were the Caucasians, comprising all peoples between the Urals and the Atlantic, between Egypt and Norway. Blumenbach regarded them as the primary type of humankind; due to environmental circumstances their features deviated, on the one side, into those of the Ethiopians and the intermediary kind, the Malay; and, on the other side, into those of the Mongols and the intermediary kind, the Americans.[13] This classification was based on his analysis of different skull formations. Being the longest-lasting and most unchangeable parts of the human body, bones were regarded as the keys to human nature. Blumenbach amassed an impressive collection of human skulls which remained unsurpassed for several decades. Unlike his contemporary, the anatomist Petrus Camper,[14] he did not measure the facial angle, but the 'breadth of the horizontal section of the vertex', that is, he measured skulls as seen from above.[15]

It was known that there had been huge migrations from Asia into Europe, and Blumenbach took this into account. The skull which he deemed a prototype of the Caucasian variety belonged to a Georgian woman: Georgia is in the Caucasus – hence the term Caucasian. Blumenbach obtained the skull from an acquaintance in St Petersburg, Georg Thomas, Baron von Asch (1729–1807). Born in St Petersburg, von Asch had obtained his M.D. in Göttingen in 1750, as a pupil of Haller. Then he returned to his hometown to pursue a career as a military doctor. The pathologist who had dissected the Georgian woman gave her skull to von Asch. It was preserved, Blumenbach noted, 'for the extreme elegance of its shape', and since von Asch knew of the collection Blumenbach called his 'Golgotha' he passed the specimen on to the Göttingen anatomist.[16] Blumenbach, too, thought that the skull was the most beautiful in his collection: it was rounder, somewhat better proportioned and a little smaller than the others. As it came from Georgia, a region bordering on Europe and Asia, not too far away from the earliest known centres of human culture, Blumenbach chose it to represent the most civilised nations: Europeans, Indians and Semites. The German anatomist's opinion was backed by the Comte de Buffon, who believed that 'the most handsome and most beautiful people in the world' flourished 'between the 40th and 50th degree of latitude'. This notion in itself coincided with eighteenth-century appreciations of benevolent climates. Buffon's list of countries that fell under this description in the third volume of his *Natural History* (published between 1748 and 1788), comprised the following countries: 'Georgia, Circassia, the Ukraine, Turkey in Europe, Hungary, the south of Germany, Italy, Switzerland, France, and the northern part of Spain'.[17] As Buffon had organised his enumeration from east to west, Blumenbach was used to the idea of regarding Georgia as the first country mentioned in connection with the European type of humankind. In general,

Blumenbach's classification of human variations followed the partitions of the globe into continents. The Georgian or Caucasian variety alone was exceptional, because it encompassed Asiatic as well as European nations.[18]

Blumenbach believed that all humankind was one. In his view the cradle of the human race lay in the Caucasus whence the species had dispersed over the globe, climatic difference gradually bringing about human variations. His theory combined a classification of humankind with an account of the rise of different varieties and some rather hazy assumptions concerning the human diaspora.[19] The notion was reconcilable with the Scriptures, as the Caucasus mountains and Mount Ararat were not all that far from each other – or so, at least, Blumenbach thought.[20] His theory was monogenist, without a trace of contempt of non-European peoples. Discussing Blumenbach's classification of humankind, Londa Schiebinger has pointed out that the 'beautiful' Georgian skull lent itself to being the prototype of the Caucasian variety, as female slaves from that region were very sought after for Turkish harems.[21] But this does not explain the main question: why did Blumenbach pick the strange term Caucasian – a term that seemed to defy Scriptural tradition?

The second eminent advocate of a 'Caucasian' hypothesis was Georges Cuvier, the great Paris anatomist, palaeontologist and natural historian.[22] He, too, believed that the European variety of humankind emerged from the Deluge on top of Mount Caucasus. But, unlike Blumenbach, he suggested that the Caucasian variety became divided into two branches, namely, on the one hand, Semitic peoples (in his terminology Aramæans and Syrians), and, on the other hand, Indians, Germans as well as the ancestors of the Greeks. In 1817 Cuvier wrote that this latter branch of the 'Caucasian race' had excelled more in 'philosophy, sciences and arts' than any other.[23]

The French anatomist and Professor of Zoology at the Musée d'histoire naturelle in Paris also differed widely from Blumenbach in other respects: in his view, not all human beings had survived the Deluge on the same mountain top. The Caucasus was home of the Caucasians. By contrast the second variety, the Mongols, originated on the top of Mount Altai, situated towards the north of the Gobi Desert. In 1812 Cuvier described them as a people who wrote 'arbitrary hieroglyphics' and whose morality was merely political and devoid of religion.[24] His third type of peoples were those he called 'nègres':

> the Negroes, the most degraded race among men, whose forms approach nearest to those of the inferior animals, and whose intellect has not yet arrived at the establishment of any regular form of government, nor at any thing which has the least appearance of systematic knowledge, have preserved no sort of annals or of tradition.[25]

In 1812 he suggested they had escaped 'the great catastrophe on another spot than the Caucasians and the Mongols' – he later intimated that this might have been Mount Atlas in North Africa.[26] No wonder some of Cuvier's readers believed he was a polygenist.[27] He never said anything specific to that effect, however, though his 'Caucasian hypothesis' was explicitly designed to express his conviction that the differences between the three main human varieties were huge, too great in fact to permit one common place of postdiluvial origin.

The question I broached for Blumenbach must be repeated here: why did Cuvier come up with the notion that the Indo-Europeans and Semites originated from Mount Caucasus? The term 'Caucasian' came from Blumenbach, but Cuvier's understanding of it was so different that we must inquire into his sources as well. To explain the origins of the Caucasian hypothesis I will start with Blumenbach, from whom Cuvier adopted the term. We have to go back in history. Aspects of the problem hinge on classical mythology, on the quarrel over the Ark, on contemporary politics, on developments in geology and biblical theory, and on the accounts of travel writers.

In 1700 Louis XIV had sent Joseph Pitton de Tournefort (1656–1708) to the Levant to explore the locations mentioned in the Bible. He travelled through ancient Israel and the adjacent areas, also visiting Mount Ararat which he described as a showcase of all the plants of the world: polar ones were situated towards the top, more temperate ones lower down. But that was not all: philosophers had long asked where the ancient Paradise was to be found. The Bible said it was the source of four rivers. It was, however, more than difficult to find four river sources in the area between the Persian Gulf and the Mediterranean. Hence Tournefort turned northwards: the Tigris and the Euphrates sprang from Mount

Taurus in the Caucasus. Here also lay the source of the river Araxes and of a river called the Phasis. Tournefort asserted that the four rivers mentioned in Genesis sprang from the Taurus range. Accordingly he described the area as the site of the 'terrestrial paradise'. 'In order not to remove the terrestrial paradise from the springs of these four rivers', he wrote, 'we must place it into the beautiful valleys of Georgia'.[28] He thus moved Paradise further north than it had customarily been, transporting it into the Caucasus.

All later major naturalists read his work. Nobody, however, was obliged to think of the *northern* chains of the Caucasus. For Tournefort had added that the outliers of Mount Taurus 'occupy almost the whole of Asia Minor'.[29] That included Mount Ararat. *Zedlers Universallexicon* (1732–50), the famous German eighteenth-century dictionary, stated that Caucasus was also the name of part of the Taurus chains. At the same time Zedler affirmed that Ararat and the Taurus mountain were connected with each other.[30] The emphasis on the Caucasus was supported by classical testimonies: Herodotus had located the Scythians there, and the Roman author Strabo, too, had asserted that the Euphrates and the Araxes sprang from the Taurus.[31]

The invention of Caucasian traditions

The entire area had deep resonances for educated people because of its mythological significance. Jason had travelled to the Caucasus in search of the Golden Fleece. It was here that Prometheus was chained to a rock.[32] Prometheus' mother – other sources said his wife – was called Asia, she was the mother of a continent. There, too, had Zeus encountered Europa, mother of another continent.[33] In 1808 the German C. Rommel, a man intent on bolstering Christianity, summarised the welter of mythological evidence: the Caucasus was 'the motherland of the world, the watershed of the Earth, the gate' through which Asiatic tribes had flooded into Europe.[34]

The Caucasus owed its attraction to more than mythological connections. It is no accident that the man who devised a 'Caucasian' variety of humankind was the German Blumenbach. This was due to three factors: (1) Blumenbach's physiological evidence already mentioned, (2) new travel reports and (3) the findings of biblical critics. In the German Enlightenment, the

Scriptures were subjected to detailed philological scrutiny. At the University of Göttingen, significantly Blumenbach's hometown, biblical scholars developed the approach which became known as 'Higher Criticism' – the emphasis is on criticism. Johann David Michaelis (1717–91), Professor of Philology at Göttingen University, in particular wanted to cleanse Scriptural truth from what he held to be Jewish mysticism and metaphorical distortions.[35] In 1769 and 1780 he published two volumes on biblical geography asserting, among other things, that Paradise had been in the region comprising Kashmir and Tibet. It is important to note that this idea did not contradict what we have called the 'Caucasian hypothesis'. As Carl Ritter, revered as the founder of physical geography in Germany, was to note in 1820: 'the Caucasus range stretched as far as India'.[36]

Michaelis also maintained that Abraham's native country, Chaldaea, was actually situated on the borders of the Black Sea towards the Caucasus – rather far away from the Mesopotamia traditionally viewed as the tribal homeland from which Abraham had wandered towards the Holy Land. As a colleague of the biblical critic Michaelis at Göttingen, Blumenbach surely knew Michaelis' seminal work on biblical geography, *Spicilegium geographiae hebraeorum exterae post Bochartum* (1769–80).[37] And the theory that Abraham's homeland Chaldaea had been on the shore of the Black Sea was too original to be ignored. Blumenbach was an adherent of eighteenth-century notions concerning the original beauty of Creation. When the 'beautiful' skull of the Georgian woman fell into his hands, it might have appeared to corroborate Michaelis' theory.

Then there were expeditions, military and scientific, which brought the Caucasus to the fore. In far-away Russia, the enlightened Tsar Peter had despatched several explorers into the outskirts of his realm. Constant strife with the Ottoman Empire turned the tracts between the Black Sea and the Caspian Sea into a strategically delicate zone. The Caucasus ranges, remote as they were, came into prominence as the borderland of the Turkish enemy. Russian soldiers and explorers invaded the area. As a later reviewer was to put it: 'The importance of Georgia for operations against Persia is obvious'.[38]

At the same time, relationships between Russia and the German principalities gradually deepened. The western parts of Russia were inhabited by German enclaves, Riga and St Petersburg being two cities where German culture was thriving. The Russian–German ties became even stronger when, in 1762, a German ascended to the throne: Catharine II, daughter of the Count of Holstein-Gottorp whose foreign minister, Count Panin, forged a treaty with Prussia in 1764. In the wake of Russian–German friendship many German settlers were attracted into the country.[39] Moreover, the culturally ambitious Empress invited German scientists to undertake expeditions into those corners of her realm she never desired to see for herself – or as the traveller and philologist Julius Klaproth later put it: 'In 1767 the great Empress issued commands that the whole Empire should be visited by members of the Academy of Science, as well to describe the topography of its provinces as to examine their productions and inhabitants. Caucasus and Georgia', he added, 'fell to the share of Prof. Güldenstädt'.[40]

Johann Anton Güldenstädt (1745–81) was not the only German to explore the region. In 1768 the German naturalist Peter Simon Pallas (1741–1811) was summoned to Russia. A decade later he published a book on geology implying that the Caucasus range had been created only during or after the Flood (*Observations sur la formation des montagnes et les changemens arrivés au globe, pour servir à l'histoire naturelle de M. le Comte de Buffon*, 1779). The Caucasus was increasingly widely travelled, the list of eighteenth-century authorities on the subject comprising some two dozen names.[41]

Thus in eighteenth-century Europe the Caucasus ballooned on the map of imaginary geography. However, this did not mean that anybody had an accurate notion of the local topography. Güldenstädt himself had made his readers believe that there was hardly any distance between Mounts Caucasus and Ararat: the 'southern range [of the Caucasus]', he wrote, leads to 'the northern foothills of the Ararat'.[42] Nor, for that matter, did Blumenbach make any distinction between the (Caucasian) inhabitants of Persia and the populace of the Caucasus itself. In fact, his notion of the cultural setting of the Caucasian variety closely resembled the stereotypical image of an Eastern seraglio: the title page of his *Beyträge zur Naturgeschichte* (part I, 1790) displays the 'Caucasian variety of mankind': the lady recumbent on cushions, pampered by men – an odalisque.[43]

As late as 1808 it was said that until a short while ago 'the Caucasus was as famous as it was unknown'.[44] This completes the explanation of why Blumenbach chose the term Caucasian: the name had many cultural connotations, yet it bore no strong relations to any of the great families of nations which it included in Blumenbach's theory. His Caucasian variety comprised Saxons and Sarmatians, Goths and Gypsies, Jews and Gauls – none of them was 'more' Caucasian than the other. The Caucasus was the neverland of myth-making.

Cuvier's three centres of human development

To turn to Cuvier, his Caucasian theory was put forward in the 'Preliminary Discourse', which provided the preface to his *Researches on Fossil Bones* of 1812, and to his *Animal Kingdom* of 1817. Obviously, he had adopted the term from Blumenbach. But what made him think that the Mongols originated on Mount Altai and that the Negroes were of yet another origin?

With the Enlightenment and Higher Criticism, many philosophers maintained that the Bible contained metaphorical expressions not to be taken at face value. The Ark was one of the first items to dissolve. Everybody assumed that there had been a more or less universal flood. Yet whether humankind was saved in an Ark or whether they just headed for the nearest mountains was a different matter. In 1776 Buffon had suggested that humankind had survived the Flood not on Mount Ararat but in the vast central Asian mountain tract. This had to do with his belief that the great catastrophe was associated not only with water but also with fire. Those parts of the Earth which cooled down first, had first become habitable. Hence Buffon chose a region towards the north of Asia.[45] Other Enlightenment philosophers came to similar conclusions, although theirs were based on other assumptions: given that a Deluge had swallowed the Earth, surely humankind had fled to the highest mountain tops available? Many thought that the Himalayas were the site in question: the combined regions of Kashmir and Tibet were the original abodes of humankind. Thus contended the famous naturalist Peter Simon Pallas; similar notions were put forward by the German naturalist and Professor of Physics at Göttingen, Eberhard August Wilhelm Zimmermann, and by Johann Gottfried von Herder, the author of *Ideas on the Philosophy of the History of Mankind*.[46] Pallas, alongside the travellers Güldenstädt and Jacob Reineggs MD (1744–93),[47] asserted that all the Caucasus region was covered by seashells: obviously the entire area once had been submerged by a flood. Given that the story of the Ark went back into the shadows of mere mythology, it was clear that humankind could not have survived the flood in this region that was covered by water.

Pallas was one of those sent by Catharine into the far provinces of Russia. He believed he had discovered that, excepting the dromedary, the originally wild forms of almost all known animals were to be found in Asia.[48] Thus, Kashmir and Tibet became strong contenders for the location of Paradise, competing with Syria and a site somewhere in Asia Minor. In 1778, Zimmermann (1743–1815) argued that the dispersal of humankind could easily be explained on the assumption that they had survived the flood in the mountains stretching from the Gobi Desert, across the Himalayas up to the Altai in the north-west. Dispersing thereafter, some turned towards Europe, others towards Africa, others towards China and so forth. In Zimmermann, the Scriptural explanation of human dispersion was replaced by historical ethnography: without mentioning the biblical narrative he claimed that 'the oldest humans' had multiplied on the tableland of the Himalayas until they were so numerous that they were obliged to spread out into other territories – 'the growing number of people compelled them to turn towards greater countries, and now various families descended into different directions'.[49] All the German authors just mentioned were monogenists who believed all humankind originated in one and the same zone – even though what was known as the 'high tableland' of Asia was a lot bigger than the whole of Europe. Thus Ararat was divested of its importance: now the centre of the human origin lay in Asia proper.

In Herder's view Linnaeus had been wrong to imagine that humankind had descended from Mount Ararat: 'this mountain … exists in nature, though it is not a mountain but a wide amphitheatre, a star-shaped outcrop of mountains stretching its arms into various climates'.[50] This meant that the ethnological account of Noah and his family as stated in Genesis was a metaphor, humankind did not derive from Noah's sons, Shem, Ham and Japhet. As Herder (1744–1803) put it: 'Everywhere amidst the primeval mountains of the world peoples, languages and empires formed after the Deluge, without having waited for a delegation from a family of Chaldaea.'[51] Some such views were encouraged by the new discipline of Sanskrit studies: the Vedas seemed to many to be far older than the Bible. It is no small irony that Edward Said has castigated European Orientalists for having denigrated Eastern cultures – at that time Indian culture was so admired that a discerning Orientalist described the phenomenon as 'mania'.[52]

Herder, for one, believed that postdiluvial human culture originated in Asia because he took it for granted that the Indian civilisation and the ancient Indian languages were older than any other cultural traditions. The great enthusiasm with which the first translations of Vedic literature were received in Germany greatly added to those works of biblical criticism that tended to put the Israelites in their place: despite their role as a chosen people, in terms of civilisation the ancient Hebrews were considered nothing better than a nomadic tribe who possessed neither statecraft nor much erudition. In view of the antiquity of its languages, the philologist Johann Christoph Adelung (1732–1806) asserted that no other land but India could be considered as the cultural mother of the world. Following Michaelis' biblical geography, Adelung believed that Kashmir and Tibet were the paradise where Adam and Eve had dwelt.[53]

Cuvier's frequent references to philology indicate that he was aware of the advances the study of language had made during the first years of the new century. Yet, if we want to trace an authority for his assertion that humankind survived the Flood on different mountain tops, we must not turn to German philologists. The source was a Frenchman, the astronomer and mythographer Jean Sylvain Bailly (1736–93). In 1777 and 1779 he published two books in which he famously asserted that Indian traditions contained remnants of knowledge derived from a prediluvial people who had exceeded all others in refinement. In the Flood this people was destroyed, but parts of its wisdom, he believed, could be traced in ancient Indian traditions. The cradle of knowledge thus lay in India. Speculating on humankind's postdiluvial development, Bailly claimed 'that religious worship descended from Mount Caucasus'. He also, significantly, referred the Mongols to Mount Altai.[54]

Cuvier read Bailly's accounts very carefully. In his 'Discours préliminaire' of 1812 he vehemently rejected the vast Indian chronology endorsed by the mythographer. According to Cuvier, postdiluvial man could be no older than some 6,000 years.[55] But despite these objections we find him taking up many points raised by Bailly. Glossing him, Cuvier asserted that not only religion, but the whole Caucasian race had descended from Mount Caucasus. He did not reiterate Bailly's idea that 'religious worship' had descended from its peak, but he described the Mongols as a variety of humankind 'without any established religion' – while he obviously believed that the Caucasians possessed it.[56] Bailly had located the Mongols on Mount Altai. He had not expressly said that they had survived there, that was a detail which Cuvier added of his own accord. Thus, in Cuvier's classification, the Caucasians came from Caucasus, the Mongols came from Altai. And if he only hinted that the Negroes might have survived the Flood on Mount Atlas, without saying it in so many words, this may be due to the fact that Bailly did not relate black people to Mount Atlas. Of course Cuvier did not credit Bailly with such insights on the three varieties of humankind. After all, it had not been Bailly's intention to say anything of the kind. Disparate sources converged in Cuvier's imagination until it seemed evident to him that humankind had survived the Flood in different locations.

From natural history towards scientific racism

To conclude, through the works of Blumenbach and Cuvier the Caucasian hypothesis served as a plausible account of the original diversity of humankind. Cuvier's *Animal Kingdom* became a standard compendium for nineteenth-century naturalists. It may even have been through his *Animal Kingdom* that the Caucasian hypothesis made its way to America. Josiah Nott and George Gliddon, the United States' foremost racialist anthropologists of the 1850s, added to its currency.[57] During the remainder of the nineteenth century, and for much of the twentieth century, the concept was widely accepted in North America and provided a 'scientific' justification for numerous acts of racial segregation.

In Europe the fate of the Caucasian hypothesis proved more mixed, as it did not allow for sufficient distinctions to be made among the Europeans themselves, notably those between Teutons and Semites. In the decades following the defeat of Napoleon, European intellectuals were heartily engaged in the racial exegesis of human physiognomies. The parameter of 'race' came to be substituted for that of 'nation' – nations themselves were divided into varying racial types, distinctions were made between Celts and Anglo-Saxons in Britain, Gauls and Franks in France, Germans and Slavs in the German lands. Minute investigation of racial characteristics was meant to shed light on the darker chapters of European history; nationalist or racialist overtones were intended.

In France, the physiologist William Frédéric Edwards employed his medical knowledge to support the theories of anti-aristocratic bourgeois historians who claimed that the aristocracy, being of Frankish descent, had no right to govern the original Gallic population. Edwards aimed to delineate the laws governing the intermixture of different human stocks; he took it for granted that their racial physiognomy was unchangeably impressed upon all individuals.[58] In Britain, the notorious Dr Robert Knox advocated the idea that 'race is everything'.[59] In Germany, the physician Carl Asmund Rudolphi asserted that the existence of invariable racial traits proved polygenism.[60] Thus the Biblicist belief in the unity of humankind was superseded by the conviction that humankind was composed of different races. Cuvier's notion of different centres of human origin was increasingly more popular than Blumenbach's monogenism which had induced him to refer all humankind to Mount Caucasus.

In the second half of the nineteenth century, racialist researches focused on the indelible distinctions between Jews and Aryans. The former were associated with Asia Minor and Northern Africa, the latter were identified with that famous Indo-European tribe which, coming over from Asia, had engendered Goths, Saxons, Germans and most of the other west and central European nations. The Caucasian theory did not account for differences among Semitic and Indo-European nations, not to mention national peculiarities within Europe. It was based on physical analysis rather than on the history of linguistics which lay at the basis of the Aryan theory of race.[61] The ancient Sanskrit word *ārya*, it was said, meant 'master', or 'of good race'.[62] It is worth reflecting on the fact that the European master races were so proud of their Asiatic origins.

The story of the Aryan myth is well known: it fuelled anti-Semitism and led to the Shoah.[63] In theory, Aryanism was reconcilable with the Caucasian hypothesis; in reality, however, the Caucasian theory receded behind the more powerful new Aryan theories. This process, which took place during the nineteenth century, is the topic of another article. The same is true for attempts to exonerate the term 'Aryan' from its sordid historical charge.[64] It suffices to suggest here that the rise of Aryanism helped to prevent the Caucasian hypothesis from gaining ground in Europe. In the United States, however, it was altogether different.

The Caucasus remained a fixed point of ethnographical classification. It would be tempting to look back at the Caucasian hypothesis and see in it the essence of all the aspects of scientific racism that are nowadays repudiated, but that in itself would be anachronistic and a misreading of history, because a proper understanding of the Caucasian hypothesis shows that, while it privileged whites over blacks, in its own way it was quite universalising, as it suggested the unity of all Euro-Asian peoples. While deploring scientific racialism, we must also shun histories that oversimplify the career of racial theory.

Notes

1 Ivan Hannaford, *Race: The History of an Idea in the West*, Baltimore, Johns Hopkins University Press, 1996, p. 207.
2 See Londa Schiebinger, *Nature's Body: Gender in the Making of Modern Science*, Boston, Beacon Press, 1993, p. 130.
3 Anthropology was consciously set up as a scientific discipline in eighteenth-century Germany; see Mareta Linden, *Untersuchungen zum Anthropologiebegriff des 18. Jahrhunderts*, Bern, Herbert Lang, 1976.
4 The interplay between medicine and other disciplines in respect of racial theory has not yet been systematically studied. The mechanisms of the exchange of scientific paradigms in the nineteenth century have been described in Wolf Lepenies, *Das Ende der Naturgeschichte*, München, Hanser, 1976.
5 See W.F. Bynum, 'The Great Chain of Being after Forty Years: An Appraisal', *History of Science* 13 (1975): 1–28.
6 For a discussion of these questions, see H.F. Augstein, *James Cowles Prichard's Anthropology: Remaking the Science of Man in Early Nineteenth-Century Britain*, Amsterdam and Atlanta, Rodopi, 1999.
7 John Bigland, *An Historical Display of the Effects of Physical and Moral Causes on the Character and Circumstances of Nations*, London, Longman, and Doncaster, Sheardown, 1816, p. 76.
8 Bigland, *An Historical Display*, p. 81.
9 See Michael Biddiss, 'Arthur de Gobineau (1816–1882) and the Illusions of Progress', in John A. Hall (ed.), *Rediscoveries*, Oxford, Clarendon Press, 1986, pp. 27–45, esp. p. 41.
10 James Cowles Prichard, *Researches into the Physical History of Mankind*, 3rd edn, London, Sherwood, Gilbert & Piper, 1836, vol. 1, p. 375.
11 Arguments of these traditional opinions are outlined in Samuel Shuckford, *The Sacred and Prophane History of the World Connected*, London, printed for R. Knaplock, J. Tonson & R. Tonson, 1728–37, vol. 1, pp. 73–6. According to Withers, the 'precise location' of Paradise 'varies in early accounts', reaching as far towards the east as India, the Indus and Ganges being identified with two of the four rivers mentioned in Genesis as the boundary rivers of the garden of Eden; see Charles W.J. Withers, 'Geography, Enlightenment and the

Paradise Question', in Charles W.J. Withers and David Livingstone (eds), *Geography and the Enlightenment*, Chicago, University of Chicago Press, 1999, forthcoming. Also see Norman Cohn, *Noah's Flood: The Genesis Story in Western Thought*, New Haven, Yale University Press, 1996.

12 Martin Bernal, *Black Athena: The Afroasiatic Roots of Classical Civilization*, London, Vintage, 1991, 2 vols (first published in 1987).

13 Johann Friedrich Blumenbach, *De generis humani varietate nativa*, 2nd edn, 1781, in Thomas Bendyshe (ed.), *The Anthropological Treatises of Blumenbach and Hunter*, London, published for the Anthropological Society of London by Green, Longman, Roberts & Green, 1865, pp. 109–10. The first edition appeared in 1775, and did not refer to the 'Caucasian' variety of humankind.

14 According to Claude Blanckaert, Blumenbach was responsible for Camper's later reputation as an early racialist. As a matter of fact, however, he invented the facial angle, first of all, to teach his anatomy classes how to draw. See Blanckaert, '"Les vicissitudes de l'angle facial" et les débuts de la craniométrie (1765–1875)', *Revue de synthèse* 108 (1987): 417–53.

15 For the description, see Prichard, *Researches into the Physical History of Mankind*, 2nd edn, London, John & Arthur Arch, 1826, vol. 1, p. 172.

16 Karl Friedrich H. Marx, *Zum Andenken an Joh.* [*sic*] *Friedrich Blumenbach*, Göttingen, Dieterichsche Buchhandlung, 1840, p. 9. Blumenbach, *De generis humani varietate nativa*, in Bendyshe, *The Anthropological Treatises*, p. 162.

17 Georges-Louis Leclerc, Comte de Buffon, *Natural History, General and Particular*, trans. William Smellie, Edinburgh, printed for William Creech, 1780, vol. 3, p. 205.

18 Blumenbach, *De generis humani varietate nativa*, in Bendyshe, *The Anthropological Treatises*, pp. 268–76.

19 See Frank W.P. Dougherty, 'Christoph Meiners und Johann Friedrich Blumenbach im Streit um den Begriff der Menschenrasse', in Gunter Mann, Jost Benedum and Werner F. Kümmel (eds), *Die Natur des Menschen: Probleme der physischen Anthropologie und Rassenkunde (1750–1850)*, Stuttgart, Gustav Fischer, 1990, pp. 89–111; Frank W.P. Dougherty, 'Johann Friedrich Blumenbach und Samuel Thomas Soemmerring: Eine Auseinandersetzung in anthropologischer Hinsicht', in Gunter Mann, Jost Benedum and Werner Kümmel (eds), *Samuel Thomas Soemmerring und die Gelehrten der Goethezeit*, Stuttgart, Gustav Fischer, 1988, pp. 35–56.

20 The distance between Ararat and the Caucasus chain is *c.*200 miles.

21 Schiebinger, *Nature's Body*, p. 131. The beauty of the Georgians is attested in Julius von Klaproth, *Beschreibung der russischen Provinzen zwischen dem kaspischen und schwarzen Meere*, Berlin, Auersche Buchhandlung, 1814, p. 33, and C. Rommel, *Die Völker des Caucasus nach den Berichten der Reisebeschreiber: Nebst einem Anhange zur Geschichte des Caucasus*, Weimar, Verlag des Landes-Industrie-Comptoires, 1808, pp. 9, 16.

22 For Cuvier's anthropology, see Augstein, *James Cowles Prichard's Anthropology*, chapters 3 and 6. For a general account, see Dorinda Outram, *Georges Cuvier: Vocation, Science and Authority in Post-Revolutionary France*, Manchester, Manchester University Press, 1984.

23 See Georges Cuvier, 'Discours préliminaire', in his *Le Règne animal distribué d'après son organisation, pour servir de base à l'histoire naturelle des animaux et d'introduction à l'anatomie comparée*, Paris, Deterville, 1817, vol. 1, pp. 94–6.

24 Op. cit.; also see the English translation of the 'Discours préliminaire', which provides the preface to Cuvier's four-volume work on fossil bones: *Essay on the Theory of the Earth*, trans. Robert Kerr, ed. Robert Jameson, Edinburgh, William Blackwood, and London, John Murray, 1813, p. 160.

25 Georges Cuvier, *Recherches sur les ossemens fossiles de quadrupèdes où l'on rétablit des caractères de plusieurs espèces d'animaux que les révolutions du globe paroissent avoir détruites*, Paris, Deterville, 1812, vol. 1, pp. 105–6. The translation is by Kerr, from Cuvier, *Essay on the Theory of the Earth*, p. 164.

26 Cuvier, *Recherches sur les ossemens fossiles*, p. 105; Cuvier, *Le Règne animal*, vol. 1, p. 95.

27 Prichard, *Researches into the Physical History of Man*, 3rd edn, vol. 1, p. vii. Ludwig Schemann, an adherent of Nazi racism, thought the same: see Schemann, *Die Rasse in den Geisteswissenschaften: Studien zur Geschichte des Rassegedankens*, München, J.F. Lehmann, 1928, pp. 124–5.

28 Joseph Pitton de Tournefort, *Relation d'un voyage du Levant, fait par ordre du Roy*, Lyon, Frères Bruyset, 1727, vol. 3, p. 180.

29 Tournefort, *Relation d'un voyage du Levant*, p. 124.

30 'Caucasus', in *Zedlers Universallexikon*, Halle und Leipzig, Johann Heinrich Zedler, 1732–50, vol. 5.

31 Tournefort, *Relation d'un voyage du Levant*, p. 124.

32 See Georges Charachidzé, *Prométhé, ou, le Caucase, essai de mythologie contrastive*, Paris, Flammarion, 1986; Charachidzé, *La mémoire indo-européenne du Caucase*, Paris, Hachette, 1987.

33 'Caucasus', in *Zedlers Universallexikon*, vol. 5; Carl Ritter, *Die Vorhalle Europäischer Völkergeschichten vor Herodotus, um den Kaukasus und an den Gestaden des Pontus, eine Abhandlung zur Alterthumskunde*, Berlin, G. Reimer, 1820, p. 456.

34 Rommel, *Die Völker des Caucasus*, p. 10.

35 For Michaelis and the significance of Higher Criticism, see Luigi Marino, *Praeceptores Germaniae: Göttingen 1770–1820*, Göttingen, Vandenhoeck & Ruprecht, 1995, part II. It has been said that Michaelis advocated 'enlightened anti-Semitism' – in contrast to racial anti-Semitism. See Marino, p. 116, n. 25.

36 Ritter, *Die Vorhalle*, p. 466. It is, indeed, difficult to ascertain the exact location of placenames and geographical descriptions as lofty as 'the interior of Asia'. Eighteenth-century writers were keenly aware that such placenames as 'Armenia' or even 'Ararat' applied to various locations. Although they tried to bring order into the contradictory

information of classical texts, their own geographical understanding was less than precise.

37 The importance of Michaelis for antiquarians, theologians, historians and ethnologists cannot be overstated. Reading his books was a must for writers dealing with the biblical epochs of history (see, for example, Rommel, *Die Völker des Caucasus*, pp. 79, 86). Michaelis was recognised as the chief authority on Moses (see the entry on Moses in The Society for the Diffusion of Useful Knowledge (ed.), *The Penny Cyclopaedia*, London, Charles Knight, 1833–43, vol. 15, pp. 439–46, esp. p. 439).

38 The anonymous article 'Caucasus', *The New Englander* 9 (1851): 88–109, esp. p. 90.

39 See Hans Rothe (ed.), *Deutsche in Rußland*, Studium zum Deutschtum im Osten 27, Köln, Weimar and Wien, Böhlau Verlag, 1996. Also see several articles in Conrad Grau, Serguëi Karp, Jürgen Voss (eds), *Deutsch-russische Beziehungen im 18. Jahrhundert: Kultur, Wissenschaft und Diplomatie*, Wolfenbütteler Forschungen 74, Wiesbaden, Harrassowitz, 1997.

40 Julius von Klaproth, *Travels in the Caucasus and Georgia, Performed in the Years 1807 and 1808, by Command of the Russian Government*, trans. F. Shoberl, London, printed for Henry Colburn, 1814, p. 2. Güldenstädt died in 1781. His travel notes, written in German, were published in 1787 and 1791, highlighting once more the significance of the Caucasus region.

41 Rommel, *Die Völker des Caucasus*, p 77. For Pallas, see Folkwart Wendland, 'Deutsche Gelehrte als Mittler zwischen Rußland, Großbritannien und den Niederlanden: Peter Simon Pallas und sein Umkreis', in Conrad Grau *et al.* (eds), *Deutsch-russische Beziehungen*, pp. 225–54.

42 Johann Anton Güldenstädt, *Reisen durch Rußland und im Caucasischen Gebürge*, ed. P.S. Pallas, St Petersburg, Kayserliche Akademie der Wissenschaften, 1787, p. 437.

43 Blumenbach, *Beyträge zur Naturgeschichte*, Göttingen, J.C. Dieterich, 1790–1811, title page to part I.

44 Rommel, *Die Völker des Caucasus*, p. 433.

45 For Buffon's theory, see Jacques Roger's editorial comments in Georges Louis Leclerc, Comte de Buffon, *Les Epoques de la nature*, ed. J. Roger, Paris, Editions du Muséum, 1988 (first published in 1962); see also Peter J. Bowler, *The Fontana History of the Environmental Sciences*, London, Fontana Press, 1992, pp. 122–5.

46 Peter Simon Pallas, *Observations sur la formation des montagnes et les changemens arrivés au globe, pour servir à l'histoire naturelle de M. le Comte de Buffon*, St Petersburg, Segand, 1779, p. 26; E.A.W. Zimmermann, *Ueber die Verbreitung und Ausartung des Menschengeschlechts*, Leipzig, Weygandsche Buchhandlung, 1778, p. 114; Johann Gottfried von Herder, *Ideen zur Geschichte der Menschheit*, intro. Julian Schmidt, Leipzig, Brockhaus, 1869 (first published 1784–91), part II, p. 8.

47 After taking his M.D. degree at the University of Tyrnau (then in Hungary), Reineggs travelled through the Ottoman Empire until his good fortune led him to Tiflis, where he became the tutor to the

children of the Georgian king, Heraklius II. In 1780 he wrote an account of his travels through the Caucasus and sent it to Göttingen. Blumenbach was acquainted with him, and in 1785 Reineggs published an article in Blumenbach's periodical *Medicinische Bibliothek* (see Heinrich Schipperges, 'Jacob Reineggs (1744–1794): Arzt, Orientreisender und Abenteurer', in Wilhelm Hoenerbach (ed.), *Der Orient in der Forschung: Festschrift für Otto Spies zum 5. April 1966*, Wiesbaden, Otto Harrassowitz, 1967, pp. 586–97).

48 Pallas, *Observations sur la formation des montagnes*, p. 28.

49 Zimmermann, *Ueber die Verbreitung und Ausartung des Menschengeschlechts*, p. 114.

50 Herder, *Ideen zur Geschichte der Menschheit*, part II, p. 139. For Linnaeus, see John Hedley Brooke, *Science and Religion: Some Historical Perspectives*, Cambridge, Cambridge University Press, 1991, p. 232.

51 Herder, *Ideen zur Geschichte der Menschheit*, part II, p. 145.

52 See Edward Said, *Orientalism: Western Conceptions of the Orient*, London, Routledge & Kegan Paul, 1978. In 1823 the Orientalist August Wilhelm Schlegel deplored the fact that the Germans 'are running wild talking about Sanskrit, without knowing it'; see Wilhelm von Humboldt and August Wilhelm Schlegel, *Briefwechsel*, ed. Albert Leitzmann, intro. B. Delbrück, Halle, Max Niemeyer, 1908, p. 153.

53 Johann Christoph Adelung and Johann Severin Vater, *Mithridates oder allgemeine Sprachenkunde mit dem Vater Unser als Sprachprobe in beynahe fünfhundert Sprachen und Mundarten*, Berlin, Vossische Buchhandlung, 1806–17, vol. 1, pp. 10–11.

54 In the summer, he wrote, they inhabited 'a chain of the mountains of Altai', and in winter the banks of a river in its vicinity; see Jean Sylvain Bailly, *Letters Upon the 'Atlantis' of Plato, and the Ancient History of Asia: Intended as a Continuation of Letters Upon the Origin of the Sciences, Addressed to M. de Voltaire*, London, printed for J. Wallis *et al.*, 1801 (originally published in French, 1779), vol. 2, p. 192. Also see Bailly, *Lettres sur l'origine des sciences, et sur celle des peuples de l'Asie*, London, Elmesly, and Paris, Frères Debure, 1777.

55 Cuvier, *Recherches sur les ossemens fossiles*, pp. 87–109.

56 Cuvier, *Essay on the Theory of the Earth*, p. 160.

57 Josiah Clark Nott, George R. Gliddon *et al.*, *Types of Mankind: Or, Ethnological Researches, Based Upon the Ancient Monuments, Paintings, Sculptures, and Crania of Races, and Upon Their Natural, Geographical, Philological, and Biblical History*, London, Trübner, 1854.

58 Edwards' racial physiology is well explained in Claude Blanckaert, 'On the Origins of French Ethnology: William Edwards and the Doctrine of Race', in George Stocking (ed.), *Bones, Bodies, Behavior: Essays on Biological Anthropology*, History of Anthropology 5, Madison, University of Wisconsin Press, 1988, pp. 20–55.

59 Robert Knox, *The Races of Men*, 2nd edn, London, Henry Renshaw, 1862 (first published 1850), p. v.

60 Carl Asmund Rudolphi, *Beyträge zur Anthropologie und allgemeinen Naturgeschichte*, Berlin, Königliche Akademie der Wissenschaften, 1842, p. 167.

61 For the transformation of the linguistic term 'Indo-Iranian' into 'Aryan', see Hans Siegert, 'Zur Geschichte der Begriffe "Arier" und "arisch" ', *Wörter und Sachen*, n.s., 4 (1941–2): 84–99.

62 Adolphe Pictet, *Les origines indo-européennes ou les Aryas primitifs: Essai de paléontologie linguistique*, Paris, Joël Cherbuliez, 1859, p. 28.

63 George L. Mosse, *Toward the Final Solution: A History of European Racism*, London, Dent, 1978; Léon Poliakov, *Le mythe Aryen: Essai sur les sources du racisme et des nationalismes*, revised edn, Bruxelles, Editions Complexe, 1987 (first published 1971). For the Aryan myth, see Nicholas Goodrick-Clarke, *The Occult Roots of Nazism: Secret Aryan Cults and Their Influence on Nazi Ideology*, London and New York, I.B. Tauris, 1996; Joan Leopold, 'British Applications of the Aryan Theory of Race to India, 1850–1870', *English Historical Review* 89 (1974): 578–603.

64 'Arya', the ethnological comparatist G. Charachidzé writes, 'is the name by which, several thousand years before Christ, some peoples referred to themselves who formed one linguistic group of the Indo-European ensemble.' Charachidzé stresses that he uses the term 'Arya' instead of 'Indo-Iranian' in order to rehabilitate it. See Charachidzé, *La mémoire indo-européenne du Caucase*, Paris, Hachette, 1987, pp. 134–6.

Chapter 4

Colonial policies, racial politics and the development of psychiatric institutions in early nineteenth-century British India

*Waltraud Ernst**

This chapter focuses on the impact of 'race' on the development of institutions for the mentally ill in Calcutta, Madras (Chennai) and Bombay (Mumbai) during the time of the East India Company.[1] Diversity in institutional development in these three presidencies was closely bound up not only with different approaches to colonial administration, but also with different attitudes towards 'race' in these localities. The institutions were subject to the specific histories, social conditions and racial interactions in each of the three main presidencies. Medical institutions such as lunatic asylums could not simply be transplanted to colonial India to be imposed upon its different peoples. Rather, they had to respond and be adapted to the particular local circumstances, and thus to various racial and social sensibilities. There was no single prototype of a 'colonial madhouse', just as it would be difficult to discern one monochrome 'colonial condition' or one universal concept of 'race'. This implies a need for analysis of how the medical gaze and the discourse of colonial power acquired some of the perspectives and vernaculars extant at specific localities, and accommodated to a multitude of dialogues and discourses of resistance that articulated various social and cultural sensitivities, and commercial and political rationales. This also highlights the importance of contextualising any particular racial discourse and placing it 'in the conditions surrounding the moment of its enunciation'.[2]

* The author would like to express her thanks to the Wellcome Trust for funding this project and to M. Williams and B. Harris for helpful comments. Many thanks also to the staff at the India Office Library and Records in London.

It is crucial to be aware of the administrative and political context within which psychiatric institutions emerged during the East India Company's rule in the early nineteenth century. In contrast to most of the eighteenth century, when East India Company servants perceived themselves as merchants in pursuit of wealth and fortune, during the nineteenth century the Company concerned itself more with government than with commerce, transforming its officials into administrators, judges and diplomats, with a sizeable army and navy to provide the military backbone for a steadily expanding 'garrison state'.[3] As an eminent historian of South Asia has observed: 'The merchant was now often an official (and the official a merchant) while the whole English community gained the status of a ruling class'.[4]

Until the abolition of the Company in 1858 and the establishment of the Queen as ruler of India, the power structure was dominated by the Company's governing body, the Court of Directors, that was in turn supervised by the President of the parliamentary Board of Control. As the Company had come to India by sea, during the early part of the nineteenth century British colonial rule continued to be implemented from the main ports (Calcutta, Bombay and Madras), each the capital of a presidency (province) governed by a President and Council. The first lunatic asylums for Europeans as well as Indians were established in these main centres during the later decades of the eighteenth century by Company surgeons who ran them as part of a lucrative private practice. Following investigations into the management of these institutions during the early decades of the nineteenth century, they became subject to routine regulation by the various presidential governments.

A number of historical and literary studies on South Asia put particular emphasis on the importance of race and racial prejudice in the development of the British Raj. Philip Mason, for example, a member of the Indian Civil Service for twenty years and, following Independence in 1947, Director of the Institute of Race Relations, held that by the time of the Indian Revolts in 1857 'racial pride' had become 'more exclusive', pointing to British colonial officials' vision of themselves as, in the words of Macaulay, 'the hereditary aristocracy of mankind'.[5] Ballhatchet's important book *Race, Sex and Class under the Raj* focuses on this shift, arguing that once the spread of Western education enabled Indians to compete for posts in colonial administration, the British asserted their right to power increasingly on grounds of racial superiority.[6]

Although these authors, together with many others, rightly acknowledge the nexus between race relations and colonial power structures, they tend, at times, to look at 'race' and 'racial prejudice' as universal and conceptually sufficiently understood constructs. More recent writing of the postmodern and the 'subaltern' studies schools of thought[7] is concerned with, and has come to challenge, the alleged universality of such social constructs. Although it is not intended to fall into what could be considered the relativistic and ahistorical trap of postmodernism, some of the criticisms and insights on 'difference' derived from these recent sociological and historical studies have much to contribute to the analysis of British psychiatry in colonial India. The heterogeneity of colonial projects and experiences is one such theme which helps to shed more light on the way in which racial concepts and psychiatry were constructed within colonial settings such as British India.

Separate institutions for 'natives' and Europeans in Bengal

The institutional approach towards lunacy varied greatly in the three presidencies.[8] In nineteenth-century Bengal, the administratively supreme and rapidly expanding province, a uniquely decentralised system of asylum provision emerged. One major feature was the strictly enforced policy of keeping Europeans and Indians in different institutions. Consequently we find a European Lunatic Asylum in the capital Calcutta itself, and a Native Lunatic Asylum in each of the main districts: Benares, Bareilly, Dacca (Dhaka), Delhi, Murshidabad, Patna and Rasapagla. This racially segregative response to psychiatric institutionalisation may not strike us, even nowadays, primarily on account of its racial divisiveness. After all, the development of colonialism is commonly seen to be intrinsically linked to the unfolding of racial thinking. At the time, however, the segregative system was in fact contested on several occasions – albeit for reasons other than its inherent racialism. From the early nineteenth-century Utilitarian vantage point, the system in Bengal implied an inefficient decentralisation of institutional services resulting in a loss of what were considered the benefits of large-scale institutions. Significantly though, objections were raised not by officials in Bengal, but by Company and British government authorities in England, and others who were geographically, socially and politically remote from the idiosyncrasies of Bengal – outsiders and newcomers or 'griffins'.

Surgeon G.A. Berwick, for example, criticised the Bengal authorities for their cost-ineffectiveness soon after arrival from England in 1847. Not only, he argued, were native and European lunatics kept in several, costly-to-run, smaller-scale institutions, to the detriment of efficient large-scale management, but the asylum for Europeans was privately owned and inadequately regulated by government. Berwick's suggestion to replace the existing system with a single central panopticon-style public institution, catering for Europeans as well as Indians, did not go down well with officials in Bengal. His judgement was questioned and his ideas ridiculed.[9] Berwick had made the mistake typical of 'griffins': full of enthusiasm for the ideas of modern asylum-management then pervading medical and humanitarian circles in England, he failed to take into account the local circumstances in Bengal. For example, he failed to see that the Bengal government was then still heir to Lord Auckland's policy of *laissez-faire*, which favoured private enterprise and a hands-off attitude to the control of (civilian) medical institutions by the government.[10] More importantly, however, Berwick failed to appreciate the depth of the local community's feelings in regard to racial segregation. A major concern of the Anglo-Indian[11] community had been to maintain a degree of separation between themselves and Indians. Berwick's plan was considered therefore as plainly 'crude' and 'incongruous'.[12]

Berwick was in fact in good company as far as politically inopportune and culturally insensitive suggestions were concerned. The Company's Court of Directors in London had itself, about twenty years before, in 1820, attempted to question Bengal's disposition to costly racial segregation. The Court then suggested that mad Europeans awaiting repatriation to England should be sent to a Native Lunatic Asylum, in order to reduce the expense of a special European asylum. The reply from Bengal was then as succinct as the later response to Berwick's suggestion: 'the propriety of mixing Europeans labouring under mental derangement with natives in the same unfortunate condition' was neither 'practical' nor 'expedient'. In fact it was considered 'in itself very questionable'.[13] The Court of Directors acceded to this reasoning, becoming slowly yet increasingly attuned to the emerging imperative to keep the Anglo-Indian community aloof from the only recently subjected peoples of Bengal province.[14]

The local Anglo-Indian community's awareness of racial difference and its increasing reluctance to mix publicly with people of Indian background had emerged along with increasing territorial expansion. Although colonial historians do not on the whole elaborate on exactly how such categories as rank and class begin to slide into those of race, they tend to agree that the racialisation of colonial life had its roots in eighteenth-century class attitudes. Spear, for example, points out that in 1706 the Calcutta Council 'received a letter from Mr Arthur King, a factor ... in the Company's service who considered himself insulted because the surgeon's wife had taken her place in church above his wife. He asked the Council to order that his wife should be placed above the surgeon's wife in future.'[15]

The main concern for the Georgian English gentleman was still that of social rank – a concern which Spear describes in its extreme manifestation as a 'condition of morbid sensitiveness', as exemplified by another incident in Calcutta when a certain Captain Smith challenged Mr Hedges, chairman of the Council, to combat, because the captain considered himself insulted by not having the Fort's guns fired in his honour on his arrival.[16] However, while in the eighteenth century there was, in Spear's view, 'separation without exclusiveness' and as yet no 'very lasting colour prejudice',[17] during the early nineteenth century the steadily expanding territorial boundaries of colonial rule fostered, and were in turn maintained by, hardened racial attitudes and the social and cognitive boundaries around 'imagined communities'.[18] By the middle of the century racial segregation and exclusion had become ingrained in Bengal life.

Racial segregation and 'boarding-out' of Europeans in Madras

Things developed differently in Madras. Once the settlement of Bengal was complete and the metropolis of Calcutta began to prosper, Madras became something of a social, commercial and political 'backwater', with a European community ridden by social conservatism, parochialism and narrow provincial attitudes. Madras had developed early from an old city, Masulipatnam. It was divided into three distinct quarters: the Fort for the British, Maqua Town to the south for the boatmen, and the Black Town for the Indian merchants.[19] The local communities in Madras maintained this sort of distinct spatial segregation throughout the colonial period.

The different commercial and social development of Madras was reflected in the evolution of asylum management there. Until the 1820s asylums existed in Chittoor, Trichinopoly (Tiruchchiruppalli), Tellicherri and Masulipatnam. All of these institutions were rather small-scale, with the Madras asylum admitting as few as five to ten lunatics annually around the turn of the eighteenth to the nineteenth century.[20] In those early days both Europeans and non-Europeans had been admitted to the asylum. The place was then privately owned by a Dr Valentine Conolly, who made a living by charging exorbitant rates to whoever was willing and able to pay them.[21] Conolly's income-maximising and racially indiscriminate rationale was abandoned by the Madras authorities once he left India. Patients' maintenance charges were reduced considerably and a socially and racially selective admissions procedure was enforced. A member of the Madras Medical Board argued in 1808 in no uncertain terms that gentlemen, namely Europeans of the better classes, should not be allowed to be exposed to the 'distracting gestures and clamours of Maniacs of all Countries and of the lowest Ranks in Life'.[22] Henceforth deranged civilians were kept in private houses, hospitals or among their family, while military Europeans were looked after in cells adjacent to regimental hospitals or jails whenever practical.

Having thus disposed of any major European presence within the asylum, the Madras Medical Board busied itself devising a comprehensive scheme for classifying the remaining groups of patients. Precedence was assigned to patients' racial background rather than to their station in life prior to admission. Conveniently, and not unexpectedly, this led to considerable savings from the immediate downgrading of some long-term first-class inmates who had no independent means of support: a former Sub-Assistant Surgeon of mixed racial background was downgraded from first class because, so it was said, 'this person is a native half cast[e of] dark copper Colour'.[23] Members of the local Armenian community from respectable but recently impoverished families were referred to as 'perfect idiots, paupers, picked up in the Black Town'.[24]

The racially divisive atmosphere among Anglo-Indians in Madras emanated from a tradition of racial segregation which was highlighted by the spatial division of the Europeans in pleasant suburbs and the Fort area on the one hand and Indians in the Black Town and similarly crowded areas on the other. Unlike the authorities in Bengal, who were at times involved in prolonged policy debates about what was to be regarded as socially and racially appropriate, the Madras government managed early in the nineteenth century to clarify who was and who was not supposed to mix in an asylum. The difference in administrative thrust between Bengal and Madras owed of course much to Sir Thomas Munro, Governor of Madras from 1820 to 1827, who was well known for his general success in the implementation of clear and cost-efficient administrative structures. Yet there also prevailed a difference in the language and the arguments employed which were more outrightly discriminatory and blunt in Madras. It is this kind of bullish, condescending and unapologetically segregative racial attitude which has most frequently been associated with colonial rule. However, it was not necessarily the only way in which racial prejudice expressed itself within a colonial setting. This becomes particularly evident when the lunacy policy of Madras is contrasted with that at Bombay.

Racial segregation within institutions in cosmopolitan Bombay

Unlike Madras, whose Anglo-Indian community flourished from the mid-seventeenth century, Bombay started to prosper only much later. It was infamous for 'a thick Fog among those Trees that affects both the Brains and Lungs of Europeans and breeds Consumptions, Fevers and Fluxes'; a place epitomising the saying that 'Two Monsoons are the Age of a Man'.[25] At the turn of the seventeenth to the eighteenth century, when the European civilian population in Madras totalled 114 (in addition to 286 soldiers), Bombay sustained only 76 Europeans – as well as one horse and two oxen.[26] Nevertheless, Bombay, the eighteenth-century 'Cinderella' of the English settlements in India – the 'narrow barren island' of which Governor Charles Boone wrote in 1715 'I cannot find terms to express the misery of this island, here are great complaints' – was soon to become the bustling 'Gateway to India'.[27]

What is more important in our present context, Bombay's community became known for its cosmopolitan lifestyle and social mixing – albeit with only selected groups from the Indian communities. This special social and racial atmosphere in Bombay is to a large extent due to its peculiarly inferior position in its early days *vis-à-vis* a prospering factory at Surat. This it had to struggle to overcome by reaching out to the Indian merchants to attract them to a place which was considered a 'losing concern'.[28] Unlike Calcutta, where Indian merchants were glad to reside, Bombay had to attract them in order to create trade. It thus developed more of a spirit of 'mutual respect and necessity instead of a spirit of imperialism founded on military glory and the pride of possession'.[29]

This different historical background had an impact also in regard to the less segregated development of the European and the Indian parts of the town. Travellers would grieve, like Maria Graham who left Bombay for Calcutta in 1812, 'that the distance kept up between the Europeans and natives, both [at Calcutta] and at Madras, is such that I have not been able to get acquainted with any native families, as I did at Bombay'.[30] Statesmen, like Lord Elphinstone, noted that in Bombay Presidency every Maratha above the rank of messenger sat in his presence, while in Bengal there was hardly a native of the country permitted to sit before an Englishman.[31]

Much of the racial tolerance could be traced to Maratha self-confidence as well as to the presence of the Parsi community.[32] It was easier for the English to socialise with the Parsi because their way of life did not exclude and threaten English customs. The Parsi had no *purdah* to prohibit strangers from entering their houses; they did not insist on prohibitions of pork, beef or wine (essentials of such importance to the British in the East), and they would also frequently adopt European clothes, food and manners.[33] They were last but not least formidable traders, excelling in shipbuilding, and were renowned for their munificent philanthropy and care of their poor. The funding of medical institutions also enabled the Parsi community to nurture a mutually beneficial relationship with the colonial power, while making exclusive provision for itself.[34]

The more cosmopolitan spirit and less overtly expressed prejudice towards certain Indian communities is mirrored in the asylum system. Only in Bombay was it possible that Indians and Europeans of all social classes could be admitted to a single lunatic asylum throughout the nineteenth century. Although internal classification of patients along race, class and gender lines was enforced, this regime provides a striking contrast to the much more divisive developments in Bengal and Madras.[35] The Bombay authorities even made a point of criticising the system in Bengal, where separate asylums for Europeans and Indians were maintained.[36] It was argued that it compared very unfavourably in terms of expense to the one in Bombay. The usual range of Benthamite arguments about cost- and cure-efficiency of large-scale asylums on account of easy surveillance and availability of specialised professional expertise was advanced, unmediated by any qualms about racial desegregation. Utilitarian thinking had, of course, an impact on many projected policies in nineteenth-century Britain and India.[37] However, the decisive point here is that Utilitarian projects involving the mixing of Europeans and Indians could only be put on the agenda in a presidency characterised by a lesser degree of racial polarisation.

This does not imply that Benthamite ideas had free rein. On the contrary, just as in England itself, there were limits even in Bombay to the Anglo-Indians' tolerance of Benthamite uniformity and centralisation. In the course of the nineteenth century these limits came to be more narrowly circumscribed. In the event, a panopticon therefore was not built. However, the Bombay authorities at least went as far as seriously discussing plans and selecting potential locations for one single central institution (even though they did leave open the option for further segregation by suggesting that the small existing asylum could still be put to use to cater for particular groups, such as Europeans, criminal lunatics or the 'military insane').[38] When the project was finally dropped, it appears from the discussion that racial considerations had not been decisive. Rather, the reality of the immense geographical distance between the various districts administered from Bombay had gradually dawned on government officials. Transferring lunatics from remote districts to a central location was seen to be as inappropriate and impractical as sending deranged people for care and treatment from St Petersburg to London.[39]

The mooted Bombay panopticon was deemed impractical then, not on account of its potentially multiracial nature, but because of the vast areas from which alleged lunatics would need to be drawn. More extensive accommodation for Indian lunatics was consequently provided in Pune, Surat, Ahmadabad, Lahore and Karachi.[40] Of course, not all of Bombay's Anglo-Indian community accepted the presence of Indian patients within the compound of a European establishment. However, advocates of separate asylums for Indians and Europeans spoke up against the existing multiracial institution in Bombay Town only at a comparatively late period, towards the second half of the century. Significantly, however, Bombay retained its mixed-race lunatic asylum despite an overall tendency in all three presidencies towards increased racial segregation in the later decades of the nineteenth century. In fact, when partial segregation was finally implemented it was mainly due to the initiative of the Parsi community who was raising the money for a separate asylum, rather than the Anglo-Indian community. Even when the asylum was branded by a daily paper in 1852 as the 'Bombay Abomination' and a 'dungeon', indeed a 'disgrace to the British Government and name',[41] the main criticism was not that it allowed for racial mixing (as had been the case earlier on in Madras) but that it was overcrowded, and that the buildings and general services had deteriorated to an extent that even the then-superintendent, Assistant Surgeon W. Campbell, had to ask 'whether it be not little short of a miracle that a man ever leaves this hospital cured'.[42]

Madness and 'hybridity'

Also important in the relationship between concepts of race and colonial asylums was the way in which people of mixed parentage (Eurasians) were seen by the British.[43] Attitudes towards 'hybridity' were subject to considerable change during the colonial period. In the East India Company's early days European intermarriage with members of Indian communities was actively encouraged, not least in old Madras. In 1687 the Company's Court of Directors even informed their employees that 'the marriage of our soldiers to the Native women' was 'a matter of such consequence to posterity that we shall be content to encourage it with some expense'. A tidy sum of money therefore was to be paid to the 'Mother of any child that shall hereafter be born, of any such future marriage', with the proviso that the payment was due 'upon the day the child be christened'.[44] This favourable attitude was partly grounded in the hope that intermarriage would help to increase the Company's influence among the Indian communities, as well as provide a challenge against the French and the Portuguese Roman Catholic element in Madras. Such reasoning, however, gave way in the eighteenth century to well-grounded fears that Eurasians would, to the detriment of eager British candidates, tend to be better qualified for the Company's civil, military or marine services on account of their facility in both Eastern and Western ways. By the nineteenth century the fear of Eurasian competition for scarce jobs and the potential political threat that Eurasians might eventually pose to British rule (following events in Haiti at the turn of the century where people of mixed race were allegedly implicated in a revolt) was translated into outright contempt and discrimination.

There is ample evidence for straightforward discrimination against Eurasians inside as well as outside the lunatic asylum. While there had been few instances of discrimination against Eurasians prior to the 1780s, by 1820 they felt greatly disadvantaged in comparison to people of British descent. The petition submitted to Parliament by well-to-do members of Calcutta's Eurasian community, in 1831, just prior to the Company's Charter renewal, highlighted the predicament of Eurasian marginalisation.[45] It was particularly difficult for them to establish successful medical careers, partly because not many could afford the costly university-based training in England as income opportunities for them were restricted.[46] Consequently, Eurasians were underrepresented in medical practice, with only four Eurasians out of twenty doctors in private medical practice in Calcutta in 1831.[47]

Those who could afford a university education, like Dr Paris Dick, who qualified in Britain, returned to India only to be 'discouraged by [their] exclusion from polite society in Calcutta'.[48] Ballhatchet cites the example of Assistant Surgeon Gillies, a professionally highly qualified Eurasian who obtained his MD degree from the University of St Andrews in Britain. One of his superiors, Duncan Macpherson, the Inspector General of Hospitals in Madras, objected to Gillies' practising as a doctor, explaining that, after all, he would equally dislike to be treated by a doctor who was 'a low born or vulgar Englishman'.[49] Macpherson's objections, couched in the language of social class, indicated a refusal to acknowledge Gillies' exceptionally wealthy background and distinguished professional standing, revealing an underlying contempt for Gillies' mixed-race background.

The official approbation for the merging of considerations of race with those of social class was established in official instructions such as those by the Company Directors of 1798, conveyed in a despatch to the Madras government: 'To preserve the ascendancy which our National Character has acquired over the minds of the Natives of India must ever be of importance to the maintenance of the Political Power we possess in the East, and we are well persuaded that the end is not to be served by a disregard of the external observation of religion, or by any assimilation of Eastern manners and opinion, but rather by retaining all the distinctions of our National principles, character and usages'.[50]

In response, Eurasians began to resent the fact that the dividing line between colonial rulers on one side and all things and peoples Eastern on the other was drawn to their own hybrid community's disadvantage, relegating them to the side of the 'native race'. They developed their own ideas as to how the boundaries of race and thus of legal entitlements and professional career opportunities ought to be set, suggesting to Parliament that Eurasians ought to be regarded as 'British Subjects' rather than merely 'Natives of India'.[51]

However, discrimination against Eurasians, combining hierarchical class and racial attitudes, remained not wholly uncontested even in Madras. For example, Charles Trevelyan, Macaulay's brother-in-law, became Governor of Madras in 1859, and brought with him less narrow attitudes and a reforming spirit. On the occasion of Parliament's enquiry into the Company's affairs, before it renewed its Royal Charter in 1853, Trevelyan had spoken up against some Anglo-Indians' 'very ungenerous' language in their judgement of Eurasians' abilities, noting that 'their situation is unfortunately very equivocal, midway between the Natives and the Europeans – not owned by either – and whatever faults they have, are mainly due … to the sensitiveness caused by that unhappy situation'.[52] However, such sentiments were but rarely expressed in Madras.

The steadily increasing number of Eurasians in colonial society at large was mirrored inside the asylums. The situation in the Calcutta Asylum is particularly revealing in this regard. The proportion of Eurasians confined in the Calcutta Asylum, for example, rose from one-seventh of the asylum population in 1821 to two-thirds in 1840.[53] This over-representation of Eurasians was of course partly due to the fact that all Europeans were repatriated after one year, whereas some Eurasians would remain in institutions in India for much longer, with the result that, over time, Eurasian patients would come to predominate.[54] Whatever other reasons for Eurasians' over-representation among asylum inmates, the greater visibility of the Eurasian element tended to confirm existing fears of European officials.

In the case of mad Eurasians, the lines of segregation were, of course, less clear than in regard to Indian groups. Indians were more easily pigeon-holed as belonging to the 'other' race, to another religion, being accustomed to other habits. Eurasians, in contrast, were (using Hanif Kureishi's term) 'inbetweens'.[55] However, individual mixed-race patients could, depending on the parameters of a specific situation, conveniently be fitted into a variety of different categories. Although most Eurasian lunatics were classified as paupers or at best petty tradespeople and low-paid employees, they were usually Christians and considered as 'people of European habits'. Thus they had traditionally been seen as deserving the Company's goodwill and patronage, in particular if their immediate family was connected with the Company's services. Like the Armenians they were usually contrasted with Indians as deserving superior treatment either on account of religion or connection with the Company. For this reason both groups had qualified for admission to the otherwise exclusive European Lunatic Asylum. In the early decades of the nineteenth century it was still sufficient if a Eurasian could *potentially* belong to a 'respectable class', nurture 'European habits', or be a 'Christian'. Although paupers of Eurasian background would qualify only for admission to the Native Asylum, non-pauper Eurasians, even if in financial difficulties, were seen, on account of their European descent, religion and habits as at least the potential bearers of Europeanness. They were accordingly not excluded from the European Asylum.

During the first four decades of the nineteenth century the Company struggled to evade, whenever possible, any general, universal obligation towards its 'Native Hindoo and Mahommedan' subjects. In the best tradition of commerce-based patronage, some Company officials argued that government should be responsible only for European lunatics without independent means, employed by the Company and, in exceptional cases only, for Eurasians of reasonable social standing and with Company connections. The obligation to make institutional provision for the Eurasian community was thus curtailed and subject to a variety of, not exclusively racial, considerations. Ideas about race were conflated with those of patronage and social class, fuelled by the financial and political implications of colonial expansion.

Shortly before the demise of Company rule in 1858, a heated argument ensued between the Bengal Medical Board and the then Deputy Governor, Sir John Hunter Littler, when the latter insisted that he believed that a government servant, or any of his relations, should have no stronger title than any other class of people to the provision of institutional services.[56] It had been clear that Indians were to be excluded from the reception into the European asylum on account of their otherness. It had however been less clear-cut who was to be *in*cluded. The issue at stake was also a political one that touched upon the question of the fledgling colonial state's obligation towards its subjects: who was to be considered a subject, a citizen, with certain duties and entitlements to state protection, if not welfare. In regard to asylum provision, therefore, it was questioned whether the state really ought to be 'doing more for insane East Indians or other Christians, or people of European habits, than it does for its Native Hindoo and Mahommedan subjects when in the same lamentable condition'.[57] The message here was that rather than *extending* superior – and costly – asylum provision to Indian communities, Eurasians (and Armenians too) should in future be *excluded* from the preferential treatment hitherto enjoyed by them in the European Lunatic Asylum. Financial and political rationales and contingencies became translated into an alleged necessity of racial division.

Race, class and colonialism

Varying levels of social and commercial intercourse between the Anglo-Indian and local communities, and different degrees of sensitivity towards racial segregation, led to quite distinctive asylum systems in the three presidencies. However, although race was crucial, a variety of British philosophical and political traditions (such as Utilitarianism, Evangelicalism, *laissez-faire* or conservatism) exerted an influence. The blueprints for the various different asylum systems can of course partly be traced back to Britain, where, for example, segregation of lunatics by social class prevailed – despite Utilitarian attempts to unify and centralise asylum and poor law provision. Panopticon-style asylums in England were designed to cater predominantly for the poor, while small-scale private asylums were reserved for the richer strata of lunatics.[58] The system in Bengal could therefore be described as echoing socially segregative practices in England, by translating considerations of class into those of race. The lunatic poor in England ended up in large County, Borough and District Lunatic Asylums such as Hanwell, rather than in small and exclusive first-class establishments such as Ticehurst. In a similar vein, lunatic 'natives' in Bengal were sent to large and badly maintained Native Lunatic Asylums, with Europeans of all social classes being provided for in small, superior European establishments such as the Bhowanipur Asylum in Calcutta, also known as 'Beardsmore's Bedlam' (after its early nineteenth-century private proprietor).

But what about the Madras Lunatic Asylum, which was organised along lines of segregation quite different from those in Calcutta? Could we see the Madras model as a 'typically' colonial way of dealing with different racial and social groups? In fact, the system at Madras mirrored practices prevalent in Scotland, where 'boarding-out' had been one of the ways of dealing with lunatics that had emerged partly in rejection of the system then canvassed by the English.[59] Even the early enthusiasm and zeal for Benthamite ideas at Bombay, and the subsequent failure to put them into practice, owes something to similar affairs in England, where, even though Utilitarian doctrine reigned supreme for a while in regard to lunatic asylums and poor law institutions in some localities, it failed to be implemented in as uniform and centrally planned a way as envisaged by its proponents.[60]

What then, if anything, could be seen as specifically 'colonial' in the construction of the various asylum systems in British India? Ideological predispositions such as Utilitarianism, Evangelicalism, *laissez-faire* or conservatism would naturally have been the blueprints colonial administrators could draw on easily. However, British ideological doctrines had to be adapted to local circumstances, to the different legacies of interracial attitudes, and even to the relative economic power and social standing of particular Indian communities (such as the Parsi). These modifications may well have been more obvious to colonial officials at the time than they subsequently appeared to be in imperial propaganda, historical writing and literature. This raises the important question as to what extent colonial rule is really adequately characterised by reference only to, in the words of Homi Bhabha, the 'noisy command of colonialist authority or the silent repression of native traditions'.[61] We would need to ask whether allegedly essentialising and seemingly universal categories such as race were in fact so at the time, or whether they have been retrospectively hypostasised. Robert Young points out that if we 'look at the texts of racial theory, we find that they are in fact contradictory, disruptive and already deconstructed'.[62] In a similar vein, it could be argued that the way in which racial ideas informed the development of asylum institutions and official discussion in various colonial localities exhibits little trace of any single homogenising influence or of an all-pervasive, focused, colonial or psychiatric gaze. A rather less focused if not hazy picture emerges with repeated refocusing and accommodation dependent also upon the economic strength and political strategies of the various local communities.

There is of course some danger here that emphasis on variety merely echoes what Fanon criticised as colonialism's 'separatist and regionalist' strategies.[63] A focus on historical and geographical particularities might then run into the danger of collaborating with colonialism's partitioning strategies. If that were so, it would be important not to lose sight of the general overall pervasive effect of colonial rule and its coercive power. Regionally diverse asylum systems and racial classifications were, after all, situated firmly within a wider context of colonial domination. In regard to racialised lunacy policies we are faced with local diversity as well as all-pervasive colonial power structures. Both of these levels of racialisation need to be addressed.

Further, frequent discussions among members of the Bengal Medical Board and government officials in India and Britain bear witness to the versatility of racial and class categories and the concomitant course of inclusion and exclusion during the nineteenth century. They also indicate that the imagined and practical boundaries of race, class and hybridity were contested not only by those suffering discrimination, but also among those who were in power and keen to implement their own various different ideological orientations. Furthermore, various sets of ideas about race were employed in attempts to delineate the relationship between Europeans and Indians. Yet another set of ideas about race and categories of social class was drawn on in regard to the relationship between Europeans and Eurasians. In respect to social differentiation among Europeans, a refined and nuanced system of class categories culminated in complicated rules of social precedence.

Redefinition of the boundaries of social exclusion and inclusion, by reference to race or social class, was particularly marked in regard to people of mixed race. Race and class intersected in different ways during the nineteenth century. In the early decades Eurasians' biological connection with Company servants and their potential Europeanness, as manifested in their Christian denomination and their non-Indian habits and customs, qualified them for inclusion in a European institution. Hybridity was then crucially defined also in reference to cultural habits and customs, of which Christian religion was one vital indicator. 'European habits', even if displayed by people of mixed racial lineage, were during the early nineteenth century a matter of distinction, being indicative of superior culture and ways of life. They were an expression of 'civilisation', as expounded not least by J.S. Mill (who, together with James Mill, had been so influential in regard to Indian affairs, as well as racial theory) in his essay 'Civilisation'.[64] Cultural customs as indicative of either civilisation on the one hand, or barbarism and savagery on the other, were interconnected with ideas of racial ascent and the growing conviction of the *superiority* of European civilisation.

In the later decades emphasis came to be placed on Eurasians' potential Indianness and their biological connection with 'natives'. This implied exclusion, unless their social class background was considered adequate to prevent it. The criteria for classifying individuals oscillated, so that poor Eurasians would sometimes be admitted on account of their potentially European race, despite their low social class, while on other occasions they could be excluded from admission on account of their class background and despite their potential Europeanness. We are thus dealing not only with shifts in the racialisation of colonial subject-people over time and variously nuanced interpretations in different colonial localities, but also with situationally specific enunciations of a number of dimensions intersecting with each other.

Ballhatchet suggests that for the nineteenth-century official elite in India the 'maintenance of a proper distance between them and the populace seemed not only socially appropriate but politically necessary'.[65] Hybridity, then, tended to blur the hierarchies of appropriate distance, yet also allowed for flexibility and fluidity of definitions. Eurasians thus both constituted an inconvenience, if not a threat, to the social and political fabric of colonial rule and facilitated the establishment of links between the various communities. This dual role did not counteract the Anglo-Indian tendency to marginalise and disadvantage Eurasians. Yet, when circumstances demanded, the ways in which particular groups of people were defined could easily be shifted.

The East India Company's administration in India at some level appears to have been based on a clear-cut, linear and rigidly hierarchically organised structure of racial and social categories, but it also relied on indigenous personal agency, on individuals who carried out the routine of day-to-day administration, acted as interpreters between the colonial elite and indigenous communities, as partners in the pursuit of trade and commerce, and as willing and loyal recruits for the expansive Indian army. Categories of 'race' were thus subject not only to the influence of a single discriminatory and hierarchical colonial structure but, crucially, also had to be modified according to the diverse demands imposed by financial constraint and specific local circumstances, as well as by indigenous communities.

Notes

1 For histories of colonial psychiatry, see W. Ernst, *Mad Tales from the Raj: The Treatment of the European Insane in British India, 1800–1858*, London, Routledge, 1991; M. Lewis, *Managing Madness: Psychiatry and Society in Australia, 1788–1980*, Canberra, AGPS Press, 1988; W.H. Williams, *Out of Mind, Out of Sight: The Story of Porirua Hospital*, Porirua, Porirua Hospital, 1987; M. Finnane, *Insanity and the Insane in Post-Famine Ireland*, London, Croom Helm, 1981; J. McCulloch, *Colonial Psychiatry and 'the African Mind'*, Cambridge University Press, 1995; L.E. Fisher, *Colonial Madness: Mental Health in the Barbadian Social Order*, New Brunswick, Rutgers University Press, 1985; A. Diefenbacher, *Psychiatrie und Kolonialismus: Zur 'Irrenfuersorge' in der Kolonie Deutsch-Ostafrika*, Frankfurt and New York, Campus, 1985; J. Sadowsky, 'Psychiatry and Colonial Ideology in Nigeria', *Bulletin of the History of Medicine* 71 (1997): 94–111.

2 J. Solomos and L. Back, 'Conceptualising Racisms: Social Theory, Politics and Research', *Sociology* 28, 1 (1994): 156.

3 D.M. Peers, *Between Mars and Mammon: Colonial Armies and the Garrison State in India, 1819–1835*, London, I.B. Tauris, 1995.

4 Percival Spear, *The Nabobs: A Study of the Social Life of the English in Eighteenth-Century India*, London and Dublin, Curzon, 1980 (first published 1932), p. 28.

5 Philip Woodruff (Mason), *The Men Who Ruled India*, London, Jonathan Cape, 1971 (first published 1953), vol. 1, p. 351.

6 Kenneth Ballhatchet, *Race, Sex and Class under the Raj: Imperial Attitudes and Policies and Their Critics, 1793–1905*, London, Weidenfeld and Nicolson, 1980, p. 7.

7 For the subaltern studies approach, see G.C. Spivak, 'Subaltern Studies: Deconstructing Historiography', in R. Guha (ed.), *Subaltern Studies IV: Writings on South Asian History and Society*, Delhi, Oxford University Press, 1985. For postcolonial studies, see D. Chakrabarty, 'Postcoloniality: Careers, Disciplines and Knowledges. Minority Histories, Subaltern Pasts', *Postcolonial Studies* 1, 1 (1998): 15–30.

8 W. Ernst, 'Asylums in Alien Places', in W.F. Bynum, M. Shepherd and R. Porter (eds), *The Anatomy of Madness*, London and New York, Routledge, 1988, vol. 3.
9 India Office Library and Records, London (hereafter IOR): G.A. Berwick, MD, to Govt, 5.3.1847 (in Bg.Pub.Proc., 26.5.1847, 12) and Med.B.to Govt, 20.10.1847 (in Bg.Pub.Proc., 21.6.1848, 6, 41).
10 Lord Auckland was Governor-General from 1836 to 1842.
11 'Anglo-Indian' is used here in its nineteenth-century way, namely referring to the British in India, rather than to people of mixed European–Indian parentage (referred to here as 'Eurasians').
12 IOR: Med.B. to Govt, 20.10.1847 (in Bg.Pub.Proc., 21.6.1848, 6, 41).
13 IOR: Med.B. to Govt, 5.2.1821 (in Bg.Pub.Proc., 20.2.1821, 32, n. para.).
14 On the Anglo-Indian community's perception of Bengali people, see M. Sinha, *Colonial Masculinity: The 'Manly Englishman' and the 'Effeminate Bengali' in the Late Nineteenth Century*, Manchester, Manchester University Press, 1995; K. Castle, *Britannia's Children: Reading Colonialism through Children's Books and Magazines*, Manchester, Manchester University Press, 1996.
15 Spear, *The Nabobs*, p. 13.
16 Spear, *The Nabobs*, p. 8.
17 Spear, *The Nabobs*, pp. 13f.
18 Benedict Anderson, *Imagined Communities: Reflections on the Origin and Spread of Nationalism*, London, Verso, 1983. See also A.L. Stoler, 'Rethinking Colonial Categories: European Communities and the Boundaries of Rule', *Comparative Studies in Society and History* 31, 1 (1989): 134–60; W. Ernst, 'Idioms of Madness and Colonial Boundaries', *Comparative Studies in Society and History* 39, 1 (1997): 153–81.
19 Spear, *The Nabobs*, p. 10.
20 For details on lunatic asylums in British India, see W. Ernst, 'The Establishment of "Native Lunatic Asylums" in Early Nineteenth-Century British India', in G.J. Meulenbeld and D. Wujasyk (eds), *Studies on Indian Medical History*, Groningen, Egbert Forsten, 1987; W. Ernst, 'Out of Sight and Out of Mind: Insanity in Early Nineteenth-Century British India', in J. Melling and B. Forsythe (eds), *Insanity, Institutions and Society*, London and New York, Routledge, 1999.
21 On the 'trade in lunacy', see W.L. Parry-Jones, *The Trade in Lunacy: A Study of Private Madhouses in England in the Eighteenth and Nineteenth Centuries*, London, Routledge & Kegan Paul, 1972; W. Ernst, 'Asylum Provision and the East India Company in the Nineteenth Century', *Medical History* 42, 4: 476–502.
22 IOR: Minutes of Second Member of Med.B. (in Md.Mil.Proc., 4.3.1808, 153–83).
23 IOR: Report of Med.B., 14.3.1808, minutes of Second Member of Med.B. (in Md.Mil.Proc., 26.4.1808, 2401).
24 Op. cit.
25 Spear, *The Nabobs*, p. 5.
26 Spear, *The Nabobs*, p. 11.

27 Spear, *The Nabobs*, p. 71.
28 Op. cit.
29 Spear, *The Nabobs*, p. 72.
30 Woodruff, *The Men Who Ruled India*, vol. 1, p. 245.
31 Op. cit.
32 On Marathas, see R. O'Hanlon, *Case, Conflict and Ideology: Mahatma Jotirao Phule and Low Caste Protest in Nineteenth-Century Western India*, Cambridge, Cambridge University Press, 1985; F. Perlin, 'Of White Whale and Countrymen in the Eighteenth-Century Maratha Deccan: Extended Class Relations, Rights and the Problem of Rural Autonomy under the Old Regime', *Journal of Peasant Studies* 5, 2 (1978): 172–237; Gijsbert Oonk, 'Community, Caste or Class?', paper presented at the European Social Science History Conference, May 1996.
33 Spear, *The Nabobs*, pp. 66, 74.
34 For examples, see D. Arnold, *Colonizing the Body: State Medicine and Epidemic Disease in Nineteenth-Century India*, Berkeley, University of California Press, 1993.
35 W. Ernst, 'Racial, Social and Cultural Factors in the Development of a Colonial Institution: The Bombay Lunatic Asylum, 1670–1858', *International Quarterly for Asian Studies* 1–2 (1992): 61–80.
36 IOR: Med.B. to Govt, 19.6.1820 (in Bm.Mil.Proc., 28.6.1820, n.n., n. para.).
37 For India, see E. Stokes, *The English Utilitarians and India*, Delhi, Oxford University Press, 1982 (first published 1959).
38 IOR: Bm.Pub.L., 16.4.1851, 11; India Pub.D., 9.11.1853; Govt Bm. to Govt India, 29.11.1853 (in Bm.Publ.Proc., 30.11.1853, 8552).
39 IOR: India Pub.D., 9.11.1853.
40 IOR: Med.B. to Govt, 3.9.1853 (in Bm.Pub.Proc., 30.11.1853, 8549, 13ff.).
41 IOR: Asy.Report, 31.3.1852, in Med.B. to Govt, 24.5.1853 (in Bm.Pub.Proc., 9.7.1853, 4537, 4).
42 IOR: Asy.Supt to Med.B., 28.2.1850, n. para.
43 On Eurasians, see C. Hawes, *Poor Relations: The Making of a Eurasian Community in British India, 1773–1833*, Richmond, Curzon, 1996; V.R. Gaikwad, *The Anglo-Indians: A Study in the Problems and Processes involved in Emotional and Cultural Integration*, London, Asia Publishing House, 1967.
44 Ballhatchet, *Race, Sex and Class under the Raj*, pp. 96f.
45 IOR: Report of proceedings connected with the East Indians' petition to Parliament, Calcutta, 1831.
46 The most a Eurasian qualifying for any position in the government service could expect to earn was officially set at the minimum a newly arrived civil servant from Britain would receive. Hawes, *Poor Relations*, p. 53.
47 Hawes, *Poor Relations*, p. 49.
48 Op. cit.
49 Ballhatchet, *Race, Sex and Class under the Raj*, p. 108.
50 IOR: Pub.L. to Md, 15.5.1798, 12299.
51 Hawes, *Poor Relations*, p. 135.

52 Ballhatchet, *Race, Sex and Class under the Raj*, pp. 99f.
53 W. Ernst, 'Psychiatry and Colonialism: The Treatment of European Lunatics in British India, 1800–1858', University of London (SOAS) Ph.D. thesis, 1987, p. 76.
54 The policy of repatriating Europeans who did not recover from mental illness in India within one year was introduced in 1818. On the repatriation policy, see Ernst, *Mad Tales* and 'Out of Sight'.
55 Hanif Kureishi, *My Beautiful Laundrette and The Rainbow Sign*, London, Faber & Faber, 1986, quoted in R.J.C. Young, *Colonial Desire: Hybridity in Theory, Culture and Race*, London and New York, Routledge, 1995, p. 3.
56 IOR: Note by Sec. to Govt, 9.6.1852 (in Bg.Pub.Proc., 24.6.1852, 9, n. para.).
57 Op. cit.
58 On segregation, see L.J. Ray, 'Models of Madness in Victorian Asylum Practice', *European Archive for Sociology* 22 (1981): 229–64; A.T. Scull, 'Madness and Segregative Control: The Rise of the Insane Asylum', *Social Problems* 24, 1 (1976): 337–51. On private lunatic asylums, see C. MacKenzie, *Psychiatry for the Rich: A History of Ticehurst Asylum, 1796–1914*, London, Routledge, 1992. On asylums for the poor, see P. Bartlett, *The Poor Law of Lunacy: The Administration of Pauper Lunatics in Mid-Nineteenth-Century England*, University of London Ph.D. thesis, 1993.
59 On the various Scottish approaches to lunacy, including the 'boarding-out system', see H. Sturdy, 'Boarding-out the Insane, 1857–1913: A Study of the Scottish System', paper presented at the Third Triennial Conference of the European Association for the History of Psychiatry, Munich, September 1996.
60 In regard to the Poor Law in Britain, see Derek Fraser, *The Evolution of the British Welfare State*, London, Macmillan, 1984 (first published 1973); A. Digby, *The Poor Law in Nineteenth-Century England and Wales*, London, Historical Association, 1982; B. Forsythe, J. Melling and R. Adair, 'The New Poor Law and the County Pauper Lunatic Asylum', *Social History of Medicine* 9, 3 (1996): 335–55.
61 Homi Bhabha, 'Signs Taken for Wonders: Questions of Ambivalence and Authority under a Tree outside Delhi, May 1817', *Critical Inquiry* 12, 1 (1985): 154.
62 Young, *Colonial Desire*, p. 27.
63 Frantz Fanon, *Black Skin, White Masks*, London, Pluto, 1986 (first published 1952), p. 74.
64 James Mill entered the Company's executive government in 1819, followed by his son John Stuart in 1823. J.S. Mill wrote *Civilisation* in 1836.
65 Ballhatchet, *Race, Sex and Class under the Raj*, p. 121.

Chapter 5

Racial categories and psychiatry in Africa

The asylum on Robben Island in the nineteenth century

Harriet Deacon

Colonial psychiatry in Africa was, as Fanon pointed out, part of the system of colonial control – a set of myths about the native's laziness and brutality which justified and perpetuated settler colonial rule, and which were codified in the science of ethnopsychiatry.[1] McCulloch describes how the theory of African psychiatric inferiority was expanded in the first half of the twentieth century, relying first on supposed biological differences (size of brain) and then cultural differences (upbringing of children), and used to model a discrepancy between ruler and ruled: whites were perceived as virtuous, and blacks as savage, lazy, promiscuous and violent.[2] Ethnopsychiatry thus justified the continuation of white colonial rule at a time when African nationalists and European anti-colonialists were pressing for change: Africans needed colonialism. Theories about the 'primitive mind' had already begun to play a role in colonial psychiatry during the late nineteenth century. Before the 1880s, however, 'scientific' psychiatry was in its infancy, there were few colonial asylums and no clearly recognisable psychiatric profession. Empire was still riding on the self-congratulatory back of abolition and liberal paternalism; the 'African insane', not yet an established discursive construct, were sometimes thought to be merely 'African' (and therefore 'primitive') or sometimes merely insane (and therefore susceptible to treatment).

In the Cape Colony, the concept of 'the African insane', a violent, criminal, incurable group more affected by physical than psychological therapy, was consolidated during the latter part of the nineteenth century.[3] In understanding the origins of a racist psychiatry at the Cape it is essential to take seriously the content of racist and medical ideologies and conditions within the asylum, as well as the broader socio-economic and institutional context.[4] These factors did not have an equal or consistent influence on the formulation of racist psychiatric theory and practice, nor was there a simple correspondence between racist medical theory and practice. Popular racist ideology and socio-economic and political conditions outside the asylum were major influences on the emergence of racial segregation in asylums, which, notably, preceded the formulation of racist psychiatric theory. But increased racial tensions in colonial society did not inevitably result in calls for the racial segregation of asylum inmates, and when they did they were dependent on the political and financial will to implement segregation. They entered the institutional context filtered through the political and professional interests of staff and patients, expressed in terms which sat most comfortably with ideas about medical treatment and asylum management.[5] Medical ideas were in turn influenced by the diverse and changing relations in the colony at large between settlers and those they described as 'Kaffirs', 'Hottentots', 'Bushmen' and ex-slaves. Particularly significant for the events analysed in this chapter is the relationship between ideas about class and race in both popular and medical discourse.

The most important stimulus for the emergence of a racist psychiatry at the Cape was not the sudden formulation or acceptance of racist theory, medical or scientific, by asylum doctors and officials, but the consolidation of racist social practices outside the asylum and the application of these ideas within asylums which had to accommodate more wealthy white patients alongside poor black ones. Bickford-Smith has explained the emergence of systematic racial segregation in urban Cape Town during the 1880s by pointing to a convergence of social, economic and political factors.[6] He argues that, by the late 1870s, the dominant (exclusively white) class in Cape Town promoted an assertively English ethnic identity, defining black Capetonians as 'other' in order to further their political agenda.[7] Thereafter increased economic competition threatened to disrupt the particular class-structure that had formerly protected middle-class Cape Town from association with blacks. White Capetonians responded to these changes with plans for racial segregation and, from the 1880s, blacks were actively excluded from public facilities used by the Cape Town middle class.[8] At the same time, the expansion of the Cape economy, fuelled by the discovery of gold and diamonds, allowed an expansion of the institutional network which provided a window of opportunity for segregationist practice in asylums. This opportunity arrived at a time when more white middle-class families had begun to see the asylum as an appropriate place to send their insane relatives.

When systematic racial segregation became common practice, a racist theory was not always on hand to justify it 'scientifically'. At the Cape, the formulation of racist psychiatric theory lagged behind the implementation of racial segregation in its asylums, which began in the 1870s. But both segregationist practice and the various factors that had encouraged its emergence provided fertile conditions for the development of a racist psychiatry in the 1880s. The specific formulation of racist psychiatry at the Cape, the emergence of the concept of the 'African insane', owed much to popular colonial understandings of race. As Russell has pointed out in relation to English psychiatry,[9] Cape asylum doctors did not get their theoretical approach from research on their patients – many black patients, in particular, spoke languages incomprehensible to the staff. A racist interpretation of admission patterns in asylums and colonial racial stereotyping[10] were more important than patient data in formulating the psychiatric profile of the black insane as less curable and more violent than whites. While racism defined what was new about theories of madness in Africa, however, there was no one-to-one mapping from colonial racism to racist theories about madness and racial discrimination within medical institutions. Racist psychiatry at the Cape had to maintain its authority by straddling both local prejudice and universalist science.

Perhaps local prejudice was not entirely incompatible with universalist science: some of the literature on racism in the West[11] and a recent thesis on racism at the Cape[12] have suggested that the biological sciences – phrenology, comparative anatomy, physiology – played a crucial role in the development of a scientific racism embedded in biological rather than cultural difference. The epistemological foundation of racist psychiatry at the Cape should, however, be located within liberal psychiatric theory, and its first expressions interpreted as depending on cultural rather than biological explanations of racial difference. As Malik and others have argued, the liberalism of the European Enlightenment, which 'introduced a concept of human universality which could transcend perceived differences', made the modern concept of race possible.[13] The fact that racial difference was recognised and elaborated within liberal discourse created a space for the paternalism of 'civilisation';

the construction of an egalitarian moral economy created the opportunity for exclusions from it.[14] By the 1890s both racism and universalism had been firmly established within Cape psychiatry. As Swartz has commented, it deployed a universalising discourse which reduced 'diverse histories and symptoms to small numbers of categories' but also insisted upon 'race and gender as organising principles of classification, [which] asserted and naturalised biological difference'.[15]

This analysis of Cape psychiatric discourse between about 1850 and 1890 suggests that the development of a racist psychiatry at the Cape was more deeply influenced by treatment and theories of insanity born out of mid-nineteenth-century liberalism (represented by the 'moral management' system in asylums and based on markers of cultural difference) than by racist science concerned with biological difference. The moral management approach assumed insanity was everywhere identical but allowed for cultural differences between classes and differentiated between the treatment of the insane on the basis of social position and type of insanity. The recognition of class-difference among the insane under the moral management system paved the way for the recognition of racial difference within a nascent colonial psychiatry at the Cape by the 1880s. Before about 1900, racist psychiatry at the Cape also used a definition of racism which depended on cultural rather than biological difference. Without seeking any physical differences in brain size or function as justification for differential treatment, racist psychiatric theory represented the black insane as more responsive to physical than mental treatment because they were less refined and less civilised than whites.[16]

This chapter will use an asylum case-study to explore the liberal foundations of the racist concept of 'the African insane' in the nineteenth-century Cape, the earliest British settler colony in Africa. While there was never a 'great confinement' of the insane at the Cape, the Robben Island asylum, established on an island just off the coast of Cape Town in 1846, was the earliest separate institution for the insane at the Cape, the largest for much of the century and the only Cape asylum until 1875. The history of Robben Island asylum provides a fascinating insight into the provision of colonial asylum care in Africa over a period when the framework of a racist colonial psychiatry was being constructed. A key focus of this chapter will be the origins of racist psychiatric theories at the Cape in the 1880s when the concept of the 'African insane' first emerged. In particular we shall examine the way in which liberal medical universalism created the space for racism within 'medical science'.

Racial categorisation, racism and the political economy of the Cape

Although racist psychiatry developed 'scientific' arguments it drew deeply from colonial prejudice, from understandings of the group rather than the individual. Racial stereotyping of Muslims in the Cape meant that their madness was interpreted in the nineteenth century as the Dutch East Indian habit of running 'amok', even though only about a fifth of slaves had ever come from there. Jock McCulloch has shown how important settler expectations of *servants* were in defining the insane African in colonial Kenya.[17] As Vaughan has argued, when the African madman was brought into colonial discourse in the twentieth century, he was brought in as an African, his insanity caused by his racially determined incapacity to cope with the stresses of civilisation and urbanisation.[18] The identification and stereotyping of racial groups was not a constant because it was not a natural consequence of innate difference, but there were also certain commonalities in the local, national or imperial context which produced enduring racial categorisations, although the ethnic composition of the racial categories might have changed. The broad socio-economic and political context thus forms an important backdrop to the study of racism and psychiatry at the Cape.

The colonial order at the Cape was one in which there were many social layers. After the first permanent Dutch settlement was established in 1652, to provide fresh food and water for trading ships on their way to the Dutch East Indies, the existing Cape population of indigenous Khoisan and Nguni-speaking African inhabitants had been augmented by immigration from continental Europe and enforced immigration of slaves from Africa and the East Indies. Close connections, social and cultural, grew up between slaves and Khoisan, and between frontier farmers and their Khoisan servants. The European settlers did not form a homogenous social or economic group by the end of the eighteenth century either – officials and wealthy businessmen who lived in Cape Town, farmers in the wealthy wine- and wheat-growing areas of the Western Cape hinterland and poorer stock farmers in the interior had little in common. British settlers who arrived at the Cape in greater numbers after 1820 added a further layer to the cosmopolitanism that was the Cape and, in particular, was Cape Town. Visitors and settlers differentiated between 'Kapenaars' (Capetonians) and 'Afrikanders' (rural people who spoke the local creole, Afrikaans), Dutch and English settlers, 'Hottentots', 'Bushmen' and 'Kaffirs' (Africans from the Eastern Cape), slaves of different nationalities and free blacks.

In settler discourse, these ethnic, racial and status categories were often collapsed into a racist framework which divided 'European' from 'coloured'. In part this was because 'European' had come to define those with certain socio-economic, legal and political advantages in colonial society (whether or not they had actually been born in Europe). Andrew Bank argues that, during the eighteenth century, Dutch-speaking settlers carved out a *colonial identity* predicated on differences drawn between them and the black slaves and Khoisan indigenes at the Cape.[19] These differences were represented in terms of Christian/heathen and civilised/savage dichotomies; there was little interest in evangelising slaves or Khoisan. Although some slave or free black and Dutch intermarriage had occurred in the early eighteenth century, interracial marriages became less socially acceptable and less frequent by the end of the century. By 1806, when the British captured the Cape from the Dutch for the second time, the colony's whites were almost always richer and of a higher status than blacks. After slave emancipation in 1838, there was an increasing tendency among the British as well to divide the heterogeneous Cape population into 'European' and 'coloured'.[20] In the eyes of the dominant class, the differences among black groups were reduced by the emancipation of slaves and the slow destruction of African independence on the Eastern Frontier: their common role as 'free' labourers for whites was what united them.

This conception of colonial society was broadly shared by various liberal and anti-liberal groups in Cape society. British rule at the Cape before 1820, in spite of abolition of the slave trade in 1807, essentially accommodated the forms of colonial racism that had developed under the Dutch.[21] During the 1820s, a local humanitarian liberalism, which grew out of an alliance between missionaries and a rising middle class dominated by merchants, presented the first major challenge to the racist traditions of the Cape. The liberal movement was supported by the amelioration of slavery laws in the

1820s, slave emancipation in 1838 and the refusal of the British parliament to sanction explicit racial discrimination in Cape law. Cape liberalism was itself deeply ambiguous, however, characterised by an uneasy tension between evangelical humanitarianism and Utilitarian political economy.

As Goldberg has pointed out, both Enlightenment egalitarian liberalism and Utilitarian liberalism, which denied the immutability and moral relevance of race while admitting the possibility of racial difference, only tolerated such difference with the presumption of reform to the European rational ideal.[22] Early Cape liberals, while influenced by the egalitarianism of the abolitionist movement and monogenicist ideas, called for the assimilation of blacks to the civilised ideal. The assimilatory ideal in the nineteenth-century Cape was represented as a fixed endpoint on a developmental scale from hunter-gathering savagery to European civilisation. The 'noble savage' was in need of Christian improvement through judicious paternalism, subjection to the rule of law and education.[23] This approach did not exclude racial segregation. The dominance of a broad liberal tradition has been used to explain why Cape Town was tardy in instituting racial segregation within the town itself, but Bickford-Smith has suggested that this tardiness was due in part to a well-established system of *de facto* racial segregation based on the exclusion of blacks from the social space of the middle class before the 1880s. Systematic segregation began in earnest in Cape Town after a black middle class began for the first time to cross this boundary and white settlers, anxious about their status and more sure of their identity as 'Englishmen', opposed them.[24]

Developing in opposition to this humanitarian Cape liberalism were two political positions: one coming from slave-holding wine and wheat farmers of the Western Cape and the other from Eastern Cape settlers. These 'anti-liberal' discourses were formulated in opposition to the liberalism of the British in Cape Town. Central to both anti-liberal approaches was the desire to create a subjugated, disciplined labour force from a forcibly crushed indigenous polity and a totally reformed African character.[25] Where they differed was in the identification of the enemy – for the Western Cape farmers it was the slave within the homestead, for the frontiersmen it was the savage outside the bounds of civilised society.[26] What Bank sees as the central difference between liberal and anti-liberal ideologies is the liberal belief in common origins and the ease of racial 'development' or assimilation compared to anti-liberal pessimism.

Unlike anti-liberalism, whose proponents embraced phrenology and other racist science in the 1840s, liberalism tended towards cultural rather than biological definitions of race.[27]

While both liberal and anti-liberal ideology at the Cape called for the reform of the 'native', they differed in their optimism as to its success, the method (encouragement or force) and the rationale (civilisation or self-protection). The gap between Utilitarian political economy and racist anti-liberalism could be bridged, however. All it required was (a) a group who were placed outside the moral economy that prohibited the exercise of force on its members, (b) the domestication of force by institutionalisation, and (c) an ideology which reconciled a general notion of improvement with the protection of the interests of certain groups of society. This reconciliation worked well when legislation could be used to represent black independence from white employment as vagrancy. John Montagu, Colonial Secretary from 1843 to 1855, planned a scheme for reforming such 'criminals' through hard labour on public works, thus improving the colonial infrastructure cheaply, reducing government demand for scarce free labour and training new labourers for work on white farms. While Montagu followed humanitarian prison reforms in prohibiting hanging or scourging and providing a system of rewards for good behaviour, his main focus remained the creation of a new pool of forced labour, people who were predominantly marked as black.

Racism and liberal reform at Robben Island

The relationship between humanitarian liberalism, medical universalism and racism has a long and interesting history at the Robben Island asylum. During the early years of the nineteenth century the Cape administration, eager to reform the old-fashioned Dutch laws of the Cape, supported changes in the treatment of prisoners and institutionalised lunatics consistent with Enlightenment humanitarian reforms in Europe. Cape doctors also pressed for such reforms: the Medical Committee condemned the beating of lunatics by Somerset Hospital staff in 1825 and 1826, and compiled new regulations for the operation of the Hospital (the only civilian hospital at the Cape).[28] In Britain a medical moral-management system based on humanitarian principles of 'non-restraint' was defined and popularised by Dr John Conolly in the 1830s, just in time for a massive expansion of state-sponsored medical provision for the insane after 1845. Cape doctors were not unaware of these developments, although they had fewer opportunities to act on them. Dr Laing, of the Colonial Medical Committee at the Cape, visited England in the late 1830s and was introduced to the methods of moral management. He said later,

> I was perfectly thunderstruck to find ... how differently [the patients] were treated to what had been the case in my younger days.[29]

Doctors became increasingly important in the treatment of the insane both in Britain and the Cape. In the early 1840s, the Cape Medical Committee pressed for greater medical control over hospital and asylum management. Increased accommodation for and admissions of lunatics to the Hospital during the 1830s and the establishment of the Robben Island asylum in 1846 strengthened the association between doctors, hospitals and the care of the insane. But until the 1890s the Somerset Hospital lunatic wing and the Robben Island asylum were managed by the general surgeon in charge of the institution. This only changed with the expansion of psychiatric institutions and the emergence of a psychiatric profession in the latter part of the nineteenth century.

While Britain and some of her colonies provided extensive provision for the insane, the Cape did not. Most of the colonial insane were cared for at home or through private boarding arrangements: only the most desperate resorted to the asylum. In 1890, the proportion of registered white insane to the white population at the Cape was 1:1,180, about three times lower than that in Ireland, New Zealand, New South Wales, Victoria and Britain (from 1:294 to 1:380). There was also a much larger proportion of those identified as criminally insane in the Cape than in Britain or New South Wales (13 per cent compared to 1 per cent or less).[30] At Robben Island, most of the criminal insane were black. This was partly a result of the colonial criminal justice system, which was mainly used to control a black labour force, and partly a result of committal patterns among black communities at the Cape.[31] The asylum, which had no simple counterpart in these communities, was viewed (perhaps rightly) as a type of prison and it did not attract many black patients for voluntary care.

Although it was born out of a system focused on humanitarian reform and the medicalisation of insanity, the Robben Island lunatic asylum was thus no simple echo of the British asylums of the period. It was established by the colonial government in 1846 as part of a General Infirmary designed to house lepers and the chronic sick, as well as lunatics. The Infirmary rationale, a spin-off from Montagu's convict labour-scheme and emerging out of middle-class attempts to clean up Cape Town after emancipation, was custodial rather than curative. For the colonial government, medical care for the poor was not a right but a privilege which they tried to restrict to emancipated slaves and recent British immigrants. The island asylum, initially conceptualised within a system of state medical relief designed more for social sanitation than support of the poor, was thus at first more a place of banishment from polite society rather than of healthy rural isolation.

In the 1850s the Robben Island asylum was criticised by Montagu's political enemies as inhumane and old-fashioned, a symbol of the autocratic and conservative colonial government. The subsequent reform of the asylum along humanitarian lines was embraced by the middle class as representing colonial maturity and modernity. By the early 1870s the asylum was represented as a curatively oriented institution, managed under a modern and humane system that reflected the use of moral management and non-restraint methods in British asylums. It attracted many more middle-class patients than before – especially women – who were housed in a new asylum building built during the 1870s. When the Grahamstown asylum was opened in 1876 many of these clients left Robben Island and, especially after the opening of another middle-class asylum, Valkenberg, in Cape Town in 1891, it became a second-tier institution, home to those classified as violent, black and criminal patients.[32] Tainted with therapeutic pessimism over moral management and increasing doubts that mental illness was 'everywhere the same', the Robben Island asylum was no longer a suitable model of Cape 'modernity'.

Classification within the asylum

One of the issues informing the debate about Robben Island as a site for the asylum, and the reform of the asylum itself, was a concern about the proper place for persons of various social statuses and racial classifications within the social space defined by the colony's boundaries and those of the institution itself. Robben Island was used to imprison criminals, to keep them outside the moral and physical boundaries of the colony, from the very beginning of white settlement at the Cape. Its use as a prison, and a prison mainly for East Indian prisoners-of-war and African indigenes, gave it a clear association with the 'other' in colonial society, which from the very beginning was linked with blackness. It was separate from the colony and unsullied by indigenous control, having never been settled by indigenous South Africans before Europeans came to the country. Robben Island was thus a safe dumping ground for elements causing disruption to colonial control on the mainland.

Within the island institutions, social distinctions between inmates were an important means of control (discouraging them from seeking common cause with each other) and served as a prototype of 'correct' social behaviour on the mainland (discouraging allegations of institutional anarchy). Within the Robben Island asylum, men and women were separated from the very beginning, although initially they shared a common roof. This was too close for comfort for the reformers of the 1850s, for whom gender segregation was an important measure of the middle-class morality and reformative potential of the institution. So too was the provision of separate accommodation for 'better class' patients. As L. Smith has suggested, there was some debate in British asylums as to whether insanity was a leveller of social rank in the late eighteenth century, but asylum managers became 'steadily more conscious of the perceived desirability of replicating and reinforcing within the asylum the [class] norms ... of the wider society'.[33] Differential privileges were also often insisted upon by higher-status inmates. There were no 'better class' blacks, but the few lower-class whites were not initially given accommodation separate from that given to black patients. The allocation of asylum accommodation thus matched the situation of *de facto* racial segregation in Cape Town at the time.

Before the reforms, 'European' lunatics were explicitly differentiated from 'coloured' lunatics. Defending Birtwhistle to a Government Commission in 1852 against the accusations of harsh treatment of lunatics at Robben Island, the Surgeon of the Somerset Hospital said that most of the lunatics transferred to Robben Island in 1846 were 'coloured people of various races, many of them in a wild semi-savage state, and from their habits not requiring the same degree of close attention and refined treatment' as Europeans would.[34] Here the 'habitual savagery' of the 'coloured' was advanced to justify the absence of humanitarian treatment in the asylum. This argument, unlike those advanced after the 1880s, did not rest on any specific analysis of 'coloured' insanity, just a stereotype of the 'coloured' as savage. While the 'coloured' was also considered more savage than the European within the liberal humanitarian discourse, humanitarian treatment still held out the possibility of their reform. As the humanitarian reforms brought with them a more detailed concern about insanity and its cure, the difference between European and coloured insanity was expressed in new ways.

Racial difference was now also expressed in terms more usually employed for class difference so as to fit into the moral management discourse, even by those most pessimistic about the possibility of cure for the coloured insane. The problems at Robben Island were represented in these new terms in 1859, when the *Cape Monthly Magazine* commented:

> it is impossible, in all respects, to assimilate an asylum at the Cape with all first-class asylums in Europe or America. The class of patients is essentially different. A very considerable portion of them are from the very lowest orders of society, and incapable of appreciating or benefiting by many of the refinements practised in Hanwell or Gartnavel [asylums in Britain].[35]

In the philosophy of moral management it was essential to tailor asylum treatment to the social status of patients. W.A.F. Browne had noted in 1837 that 'the pauper [lunatic] could not appreciate ... nor derive benefit from the refinement and delicacies essential to the comfort and instrumental in the recovery of the affluent'.[36] Cape doctors were aware that patients at Crichton Asylum in England under Dr Browne were classified and treated first according to social status and then according to the kind of case,[37] and they were interested in duplicating this situation. The assumption was that while coloured patients might not appreciate 'refinements' within asylums, they could still benefit from moral management. In India, where there were explicit differences in privilege and accommodation for white and Indian asylum patients,[38] plans to establish a Hanwell-style asylum for both Europeans and Indians were rejected in the late 1840s because of the undesirability of social proximity, not because the Indian authorities thought Indians would not respond to moral management.[39]

At the Cape, the term 'coloured' had connotations of social class: its function was centrally concerned with identifying and maintaining social status. Most of the black patients in the asylum were members of the urban underclass, referred through the criminal justice system; the same was true of poorer whites. Yet the difference between European and coloured was recognised to go deeper than class. The Surgeon Superintendent claimed in 1861 that

> The European poor are more likely to ['admire' the comforts of a 'decent' British asylum in the boarding home style] than the other [i.e. the coloured poor]. ... Some of the better class of coloured people are quite as intelligent as our Europeans, but they have not the same tastes.[40]

These 'tastes' and the gap in 'education' were used to justify the existence of differential treatment in the asylum to Government Commissioners in 1861. Europeans 'who could not carry the heavy loads on their shoulders as well as the coloured people' did not generally take out night tubs or collect water. They got the newest clothes, the cleanest bedding, the luxury of bedsheets and were buried in coffins rather than blankets.[41]

The discourse of 'savagery' continued to inform asylum practice, however. In 1860, the Robben Island Surgeon had proposed a systematic separation of white and black inmates for the first time, but this did not get financial support because of proposals to remove the asylum altogether. But black male lunatics (and a few of the most 'dangerous' white males) were consigned to a separate section, called the 'kraal', while most white males (and a few 'respectable' black lunatics) were kept in the 'lunatic square'. This *de facto* segregation placed most black lunatics within the space of violent and savage animals (a kraal is an animal pen) and most white lunatics within the rational, square, European-style asylum courtyard.

There was not absolute agreement on the permissible degree of racial discrimination within the asylum, however, especially as the British government forbade racist legislation. Government Commissioners retreated to managerial rather than moral judgements in 1862:

> We beg to call attention to the fact that there exists in the General Infirmary a distinction in the treatment of persons of colour and Europeans, or persons of European descent. We refrain from expressing any opinion on the propriety of such a practice; but so long as such a distinction exists it ought to be carried out under definite rules; so also ought it to be in respect to the treatment of those who defray the expense of their board and those who do not.[42]

Edmunds, the new Surgeon Superintendent appointed after the Commission's report, saw no reason to differentiate between the races because he considered 'the treatment of insanity ... everywhere identical'.[43] His 'constant aim {was} to assimilate the condition of patients, their mode of treatment and their everyday life to the system of treatment that is carried out in European asylums'.[44] He reported in 1862 that several 'improvements' had been made: black patients were now also buried in coffins and received sheets and clothes from the central store rather than cast-offs from white patients.[45] As humanitarian medical discourses of treatment and asylum practice dominated the official discourse, racial segregation was mentioned less often. Edmunds suggested that the lunatics should be divided into four sections, separating the refractory, quiet, incurable and dirty cases. Up to two-thirds of the patients could be in separate rooms.[46] This behavioural rather than diagnostic division was common in asylums abroad.[47] The division of the men into three sections on the basis of conduct in March 1867[48] interrupted the effective racial division, as all three sections now contained black and white. Section One contained 'better class' or convalescent patients, Section Two violent or noisy ones and Section Three held idiotic, epileptic, 'dirty' (incontinent) or working ones.[49]

But, in practice, there was continued racial segregation of sorts. In part this was because most 'better class' patients were white. A room was set aside for six of the 'better class' male patients within the asylum,[50] and 'better class' women had their own sitting room by 1866, continuing the tradition of exclusionary segregation. In Section One of the female asylum, the 'Ladies' Room' (containing mainly white patients) was distinguished from the 'Large Room' (containing mainly coloured patients).[51] A new female asylum, called the Gallery and used for the 'quieter' and 'better class' patients, was in use by 1867, where many had their own rooms.

Still in the old building, the other female patients were described as 'kafirs [*sic*] and others' (spelling varied), and as epileptic, idiotic and violent, although they seem to have done most of the needlework and washing.[52] But class was not the only criterion. It appears that white male lunatic patients were usually admitted to Section One of the asylum, and were only briefly sent to Section Two[53] (still largely coloured) or Section Three[54] when they were violent or 'troublesome' respectively. This use of reclassification as part of the punishment and reward system was common in asylums such as Utica in New York.[55] Patients themselves seem to have requested more segregation. The white patient Walsh complained in 1872 of the 'mixture of the races and of the want of quiet' in Section Three.[56] And in the following year, Mr de Villiers in Section One complained of the 'mixture with coloured men' when men from all three sections were brought into Section One for reading sessions with the Chaplain.[57] The Chaplain sympathised with both men.[58]

De facto racial segregation was thus maintained under the moral management system within a framework that stereotyped whites as quiet and tractable while blacks were violent and problematic. This system seems to have produced the desired effect for in 1880 the Surgeon Superintendent, Dr Biccard, thought more systematic racial segregation was 'desirable' but prioritised the more 'practicable' separation of noisy and quiet patients, paying and non-paying.[59] As we have seen, both classifications would have produced a considerable degree of racial segregation. Asylum staff were reluctant to abandon the discourse of class and its association with the moral management system. Rev. Wilshere noted that, although most coloured lunatics should not be mixed with white patients because of their swearing and 'coarse habits', there were 'some coloured people ... as amenable to treatment as the Europeans' who could not be excluded from the new asylum.[60] His colleague Canon Baker said, 'I should divide the white [lunatics] from the black if expense were not an insuperable objection; but I would not draw a strict line'.[61] Biccard explained:

> The separation of the whites from the blacks might be regarded as much as possible in the asylum, but you must have some regard to the class [of patients] you are treating. Some would do well enough together, while others are of a class that would be better apart.[62]

The argument that members of different social classes required different conditions for recovery was more acceptable than explicit racism within moral management medical discourse, but it allowed (as we have seen) a considerable degree of *de facto* racial segregation.

By 1880 there was, however, growing social pressure among white Capetonians for explicit racial segregation of all social classes. A more explicit racism was born out of a hardening of white colonial identity (both English and Afrikaans) during the 1870s and a removal of the British brake on racist legislation after responsible government was granted in 1872. This paved the way for asylum staff to express their doubts about medical universalism. Rev. Wilshere mused that

> It would be very desirable to separate the European from the coloured patients. I think some higher and different course of treatment would be required to produce an amelioration of the condition of Europeans.[63]

Biccard's opinion that the European patients 'had a larger proportion amenable to treatment' and produced 'more cures'[64] was generally accepted. The argument that black patients did not respond as well to moral management was used to justify the low cure rate for black patients, and to promote the building of new institutions which would concentrate resources on more promising white subjects. The Inspector of Asylums from 1889, Dr Dodds, was instrumental in furthering explicit racial segregation within asylums and encouraging racially specific asylums.

A new asylum on the mainland was planned for 'the paying and better-class lunatics' in 1880 – this was to be Valkenberg which opened in 1891. Criminal lunatics would remain on Robben Island as they should not be mixed with 'ordinary' lunatics on the mainland.[65] It was no coincidence that ordinary (i.e. non-criminal), paying and 'better class' patients, most of whom were white, would be kept in the newest and best asylum. In the symbolic geography of the Cape, the 'native' had to be placed furthest from Cape Town as the epicentre of civilisation: either in the Eastern Cape or on Robben Island. Captain Mills, as Under Colonial Secretary, claimed that

> With regard to the Kafir, the closer you can assimilate his condition to that of his normal state the better. I think it

> would be a mistake to confine Kafirs to a house and tie them to one spot. For that reason I think the asylum on Robben Island is particularly suited for natives.[66]

Negative representations of the black insane now often referred not to the 'coloured' but to the 'Kafir' and the 'native' (Nguni-speaking Africans from the Eastern Cape and Natal). Eastern Cape Africans had come to the island in greater numbers after the cattle-killings of the late 1850s (when whole communities slaughtered their cattle in an unsuccessful millenarian protest against colonial rule) and their defeat in various frontier wars accelerated their entry into the wage-economy of the Cape. Asylum staff had even fewer linguistic and cultural affinities with these patients than they had had with descendants of slaves from Cape Town. These more obvious differences were coupled with the existing stereotype of the criminal, dangerous and incurable 'coloured' lunatic and used to elaborate a racist psychiatry which claimed that blacks exhibited a fundamentally different, less sophisticated, form of insanity to whites.[67]

Conclusion

The pseudo-scientific racist discourse about insanity which had begun to emerge by the 1880s drew on social prejudices that had affected medical practice at the Robben Island asylum as early as the 1840s but not been articulated as medical theory. There had been no need to discuss treatment or cure in an essentially custodial environment. The grand tradition of Cape liberalism which lay behind the pressure for reform at Robben Island was not free of racial bias, but nevertheless stressed assimilation of the black person to the British ideal, recognising the potential for 'civilisation' rather than innate and unalterable difference. All lunatics should thus be treated using the same (European) methods. The universalist liberal discourse of medico-moral treatment therefore challenged to some extent the openly racist ideas and practices that had already become part of the fabric of the Island asylum by the 1860s, based on notions about 'place in society' rather than 'place in a hospital'.

Nevertheless, the idea that all patients could respond to moral management was qualified, in the Cape as in Britain, by the notion that moral treatment and facilities in the asylum had to be adapted to take account of a patient's class in order to have the maximum effect. Allowing the recognition of racial differences, represented in the same way as class differences, thus ensured that some forms of racial discrimination were maintained. 'Respectable' blacks who enjoyed some privileges alongside white lunatics in the 1860s were gradually pushed into the lower-class black wards by the 1870s. As patients were segregated along lines of tractability, they were also segregated along lines of race. By the 1880s, only Europeans were thought to truly benefit from moral management, justifying separate institutions and explaining low recovery rates among black patients.

There was some reluctance to wholly abandon the universalism of medical knowledge about madness in the official and legal literature, however. The tension between racism and universalism was to remain in Cape psychiatry even after 1890, because of the need to embrace both white and black insanity in lunacy legislation and medical discourse (and thus protect the profession), while differentiating between them on grounds of diagnosis, prognosis and treatment. In 1892, Dodds expressed this ambiguity when he remarked,

> While colour should not be a dividing line in medicine, and every effort should be made to render happy coloured as well as white, I do not think it right that these two races should mix as they often have to do at present [in Cape asylums].[68]

Ultimately, it was not racist psychiatry or racist science more generally which formed the basis for theorising racial segregation in Cape asylums like Robben Island, but the liberal tenets of moral management which permitted the expression of racism by white staff, patients and officials in the space created by class differentiation. Pressure for racial segregation outside the asylum, together with a growing proportion of white patients being admitted to Cape asylums, brought a more self-confident racism into the nascent discipline of Cape psychiatry after the 1880s. The recognition of class as a basis for social differentiation in the liberal discourse of asylum management and the close association between class and racial divisions at the Cape provided Cape psychiatry with an opportunity to develop universalist psychiatric theory in the direction of colonial racism. By the 1890s Cape psychiatry had sketched out the pattern it was to follow during the next century, straddling both colonial racism and admiration for the universalism of science.

Notes

1 J. McCulloch, *Colonial Psychiatry and the African Mind*, Cambridge, Cambridge University Press, 1995, p. 134.
2 McCulloch, *Colonial Psychiatry*, pp. 139, 141.
3 On the subject of Cape psychiatry after 1890, see for example S. Swartz, 'Colonialism and the Production of Psychiatric Knowledge in the Cape, 1891–1920', University of Cape Town Ph.D. thesis, 1996; D. Foster, 'Historical and Legal Traces, 1800–1900', in S. Lea and D. Foster (eds), *Perspectives on Mental Handicap in South Africa*, Durban, Professional Publishers, 1990, pp. 21–70.
4 On the importance of this approach, see S. Dubow, *Racial Segregation and the Origins of Apartheid in South Africa, c.1919–1936*, Basingstoke, Macmillan, 1989.
5 H.J. Deacon, 'Racial Segregation and Medical Discourse in Nineteenth-Century Cape Town', *Journal of Southern African Studies* 22, 2 (1996): 287–308, contains a more extended discussion of this point.
6 J.V. Bickford-Smith, *Ethnic Pride and Racial Prejudice in Victorian Cape Town: Group Identity and Social Practice, 1875–1902*, Cambridge, Cambridge University Press, 1995.
7 Bickford-Smith, *Ethnic Pride and Racial Prejudice*, p. 39.
8 Bickford-Smith, *Ethnic Pride and Racial Prejudice*, pp. 23–5, 70–2.
9 R. Russell, 'Mental Physicians and Their Patients: Psychological Medicine in the English Pauper Lunatic Asylums of the Later Nineteenth Century', University of Sheffield Ph.D. thesis, 1983, p. 298.
10 More of the black patients were classified as severe and criminal cases at Robben Island (see H.J. Deacon, 'A History of the Medical Institutions on Robben Island, 1846–1910', Cambridge University Ph.D. thesis, 1994, Table C7, Appendix C). The preponderance of criminal insane among black patients at Robben Island came about because most black patients came through the criminal justice system or employers rather than being referred by their families. Where black families could, they usually chose to care for the insane within the community. There was also a racist tendency for black patients to be perceived as dangerous by white asylum staff.
11 For example, see N. Stepan, *The Idea of Race in Science: Great Britain, 1800–1960*, London and Basingstoke, Macmillan, 1982; A. Smedley, *Race in North America: Origin and Evolution of a Worldview*, Oxford, Westview Press, 1993, chap. 10.
12 A. Bank, 'Liberals and Their Enemies: Racial Ideology at the Cape of Good Hope, 1820 to 1850', Cambridge University Ph.D. thesis, 1995.
13 K. Malik, *The Meaning of Race*, Basingstoke, Macmillan, 1996, p. 42.
14 D.T. Goldberg, *Racist Culture: Philosophy and the Politics of Meaning*, Oxford, Blackwell, 1993, p. 6.
15 Swartz, 'Colonialism and the Production of Psychiatric Knowledge', p. 99.

16 The same kind of argument was made in prisons: black prisoners were put to manual labour and given more beatings because it was felt that this was the only way to punish and reform the savage criminal. See Deacon, 'Racial Segregation and Medical Discourse'.
17 McCulloch, *Colonial Psychiatry*, pp. 117, 145.
18 M. Vaughan, *Curing Their Ills: Colonial Power and African Illness*, Cambridge, Cambridge University Press, 1991, pp. 101, 112.
19 A. Bank, 'Liberals and Their Enemies', chap. 2.
20 P. Scully, 'Liberating the Family? Gender, Labor and Sexuality in the Rural Western Cape, South Africa, 1823–1853', University of Michigan Ph.D. thesis, 1993, p. 393.
21 Bank, 'Liberals and Their Enemies', chap. 1.
22 Goldberg, *Racist Culture*, p. 6.
23 Bank, 'Liberals and Their Enemies', chap. 2.
24 Bickford-Smith, *Ethnic Pride and Racial Prejudice*, p. 39.
25 Bank, 'Liberals and Their Enemies', chap. 3.
26 Bank, 'Liberals and Their Enemies', p. 192.
27 Bank, 'Liberals and Their Enemies', pp. 313–14.
28 Dr Wehr to Burgher Senate, 4 August 1826, Cape Town, Cape Archives Division (CA), Medical Committee Miscellaneous Papers, MC 19.
29 Dr Laing, Minutes of evidence, 'Report of the Select Committee appointed to take into consideration the papers laid on the table referring to Somerset Hospital', Cape Parliamentary Papers (CPP), A27–1865, p. 9.
30 Report of the Inspector of Asylums for 1890, CPP, G37–1891, p. 14.
31 Deacon, 'A History of the Medical Institutions', Table C7, Appendix C.
32 For more details about this process, see Deacon, 'A History of the Medical Institutions', chaps 3 and 5. See also Swartz, 'Colonialism and the Production of Psychiatric Knowledge'; S. Marks, ' "Every Facility that Modern Science and Enlightened Humanity have Devised": Race and Progress in a Colonial Hospital, Valkenberg Mental Asylum, Cape Colony, 1894–1910', in J. Melling and B. Forsythe (eds), *Insanity, Institutions and Society in the United Kingdom and Its Colonies, c.1800–1914*, London, Routledge, 1999.
33 L. Smith, ' "Levelled to the Same Common Standard"? Social Class in the Lunatic Asylum, 1780–1860', in O. Ashton, R. Fyson and S. Roberts (eds), *The Duty of Discontent: Essays for Dorothy Thompson*, London, Mansell, 1995, p. 149.
34 Bickersteth to Commissioners, 23 June 1852, in papers relating to the 'Report of the Select Committee on and documents connected with the Robben Island Establishment', CPP, A37–1855, p. 41. In this context, the word 'coloured' referred to black patients in general rather than a subset of the black population later distinguished from 'Africans' or 'natives'. The use of an umbrella term ('coloured') helped to identify all non-Europeans as 'savage', while at the same time 'of various races' indicates the differences among them were still perceived to be significant.
35 'A Visit to Robben Island', *Cape Monthly Magazine* 6 (1859): 238.

36 W.A.F. Browne, in A. Scull (ed.), *The Asylum as Utopia: W.A.F. Browne and the Mid-Nineteenth Century Consolidation of Psychiatry*, London, Routledge, 1991, p. 199.
37 Ebden, Minutes of evidence, 'Report of the Commission of Inquiry into the General Infirmary and Lunatic Asylum on Robben Island' (hereafter 'Commission of 1861–2'), CPP, G31–1862, p. 245. This was in fact the case, see Browne in Scull, *The Asylum as Utopia*, p. 199.
38 W. Ernst, *Mad Tales from the Raj: The European Insane in British India, 1800–1858*, London, Routledge, 1991, p. 80.
39 W. Ernst, 'The Establishment of "Native Lunatic Asylums" in Early Nineteenth-Century British India', in C.J. Meulenbeld and D. Wujastyk (eds), *Studies in Indian Medical History*, Groningen, Egbert Forsten, 1987, p. 190.
40 Dr Minto, Minutes of evidence, 'Commission of 1861–2', CPP, G31–1862, p. 14.
41 Rev. Kuster, Minutes of evidence, 'Commission of 1861–2', CPP, G31–1862, p. 54.
42 Report, 'Commission of 1861–2', CPP, G31–1862, pp. xiii–xiv.
43 Edmunds to Colonial Secretary, 31 August 1864, CA, Letters received by the Colonial Engineer, CO 837.
44 'Report on the General Infirmary, Robben Island, for the Year 1866', CPP, G9–1867, p. 4.
45 'Report on the General Infirmary, Robben Island, for the Year 1862', CPP, G3–1864, p. 3.
46 Edmunds to Colonial Secretary, 31 August 1864, CA, Letters received by the Colonial Engineer, CO 837.
47 E. Dwyer, *Homes for the Mad: Life Inside Two Nineteenth-Century Asylums*, London, Routledge, 1987, p. 13.
48 Rev. Baker, March 1867, Johannesburg, University of the Witwatersrand Manuscripts Collection (UWMC), Chaplains' Diaries, AB 1162/G2.
49 Chaplain's report, 'Report on the General Infirmary, Robben Island, for the Year 1868', CPP, G2–1869, p. 25.
50 Chaplain's report, 'Report on the General Infirmary, Robben Island, for the Year 1868', CPP, G2–1869, p. 25.
51 Kuster, August 1866, Johannesburg, UWMC, Chaplains' Diaries, AB 1162/G2.
52 Chaplain's report, 'Report on the General Infirmary, Robben Island, for the Year 1868', CPP, G2–1869, p. 25.
53 Rev. Baker, 16 February 1869, Johannesburg, UWMC, Chaplains' Diaries, AB 1162/G2.
54 Rev. Baker, 25 September 1868, Johannesburg, UWMC, Chaplains' Diaries, AB 1162/G2.
55 At Utica classification was not related to race, although ethnic factors played a part in diagnoses; see Dwyer, *Homes for the Mad*, pp. 5, 14.
56 Rev. Baker, 7 May 1872, Johannesburg, UWMC, Chaplains' Diaries, AB 1162/G2.
57 Rev. Baker, 10 October 1873, Johannesburg, UWMC, Chaplains' Diaries, AB 1162/G2.

58 Rev. Baker, 7 May 1872, 10 October 1873, Johannesburg, UWMC, Chaplains' Diaries, AB 1162/G2.

59 Dr Biccard, Minutes of evidence, 'Report of the Commission appointed to inquire into and report upon the best means of moving the asylum at Robben Island to the mainland' (hereafter 'Commission of 1879'), CPP, G64–1880, p. 9.

60 Rev. Wilshere, Minutes of evidence, 'Commission of 1879', CPP, G64–1880, p. 8.

61 Canon Baker, Minutes of evidence, 'Commission of 1879', CPP, G64–1880, p. 19.

62 Dr Biccard, Minutes of evidence, 'Commission of 1879', CPP, G64–1880, p. 9.

63 Rev. Wilshere, Minutes of evidence, 'Commission of 1879', CPP, G64–1880, p. 8.

64 Dr Biccard, Minutes of evidence, 'Commission of 1879', CPP, G64–1880, p. 9.

65 Captain Mills, Minutes of evidence, 'Commission of 1879', CPP, G64–1880, p. 2.

66 Captain Mills, Minutes of evidence, 'Commission of 1879', CPP, G64–1880, p. 3.

67 Swartz, 'Colonialism and the Production of Psychiatric Knowledge', p. 113.

68 Dr Dodds, quoted in R.C. Warwick, 'Mental Health Care at Valkenberg Asylum, 1891–1909', UCT B.A. (Hons) thesis, 1989, pp. 31–2.

Chapter 6

'An ancient race outworn'

Malaria and race in colonial India, 1860–1930

David Arnold

Much recent discussion of race has been concerned with racial theories advanced in Europe and North America from the mid-eighteenth century onwards and with what appear from the perspective of the West to be the defining moments in the history of race – Atlantic slavery and Nazi genocide against the Jews. With the exception of South Africa, relatively little consideration has been given, by contrast, to how ideas of race were evolved and enacted in various extra-European locations. Scholarship has thus tended to reinforce the notion of race as a relatively homogeneous set of ideas and practices, driven by material greed and social anxieties in the West, and capable of delivering social power and political authority to whites across the globe. Race was, however, a far more nebulous and often self-contradictory concept, and rather than being the voice of white authority alone, could form part of an interactive process by which ideas of race were internalised and reworked by the subjects of European racial discourse and practice, in search of their own empowerment.

This chapter seeks to capture the diverse uses of the concept of race in British India in the late nineteenth and early twentieth centuries, and to locate race alongside debates about science, disease and environment. It focuses on one disease (malaria) and one locality (Bengal) in order to provide a specific set of geographical, cultural and historical parameters for a discussion of race, science and colonialism.

Slaying the dragon

It would be difficult to embark on a discussion of malaria, race and British India without referring to Ronald Ross. In the words of one obituary, it was Ross who, by his pioneering work on malaria in the 1890s, 'slew the dragon and delivered mankind from immemorial bondage'.[1] He gained international renown (including in 1902 a Nobel prize) for his discovery of the role of anopheles mosquitoes in the transmission of malaria, and for several decades his advice was widely sought as a leading expert on the disease and its eradication. But Ross, it should not be forgotten, was a child of the imperial age, born into an army family in India in May 1857 (the month the Mutiny erupted) and returning there after completing his medical training in Britain. He spent eighteen years (1881–99) in the Indian Medical Service before leaving India and the service at the age of forty-one. Ross's view of malaria, and its relationship with race and empire, was necessarily informed by his Indian background, even if, paradoxically, his malaria eradication schemes were more readily adopted elsewhere in the tropics than in the land of his birth.

In his memoirs, Ross observed that Europeans visiting India for the first time were 'always much struck' by the weak and sickly nature of the people. Indians appeared 'hard-working … , faithful, docile, and intelligent', yet in many parts of the country they had an 'amazingly delicate physique combined with great timidity and a habit of unquestioning obedience'. What, Ross asked, was the cause of this weakness? Was it due to climate, diseases connected with climate, 'or have we here merely the picture of an old civilisation fallen into decay?'[2] Ross believed that malaria was a primary cause of Indians' physical weakness, and had done much over the centuries to make them 'an ancient race outworn'. This situation need not, however, continue indefinitely: it ought to be possible, through modern medical and sanitary science, to rescue Indians from a disease that had so incapacitated their race. In freeing Indians from malaria, the British would also be fulfilling their own imperial destiny, simultaneously delivering their subjects from the thraldom of disease while ensuring that members of their own race, sojourners in the tropics, would not fall prey to the same affliction.[3] As will be seen, the idea of malaria as a site both of racial decay and of potential regeneration was not confined to Ross, but was common among many of his British and Indian contemporaries.

Ross's comments about malaria, published in his memoirs in 1923, were intended to reflect his sentiments in the early 1880s. In fact, the linking of race with malaria was most prominent in medical and social discourse in India between about 1890 and 1920, though its antecedents can certainly be traced back two or three decades earlier. In *The Prevention of Malaria* (1910), Ross made little explicit reference to race and sought to situate the malaria problem within a wider context, though his principal reference point remained India. Malaria, 'perhaps the most important of human diseases', was, he wrote, most prevalent in the tropics, where it accounted for between a quarter and a half of the total sickness.[4] It was thus a blight on precisely those tropical territories that Europeans and Americans were most actively seeking to colonise and exploit in the late nineteenth and early twentieth centuries. As Ross wrote in his memoirs, malaria had probably 'done more than anything else to prevent the settlement and civilisation of the vast areas which would otherwise be most suitable for the human race'.[5] His work on malaria helped give scientific specificity to what Europeans had long felt to be dangerous about the tropics but had hitherto been able only to conceive in terms of fatal miasmas and the effects of hot climates on temperate constitutions. Malaria was both a burden to the 'coloured' races that lived in the tropics and a challenge to the white races that sought to establish their moral and material ascendancy there.

> Very malarious places cannot be prosperous [Ross wrote]: the wealthy shun them; those who remain are too sickly for hard work; and such localities often end by being deserted by all save a few miserable inhabitants. Malaria is the great enemy of the explorer, the missionary, the planter, the merchant, the farmer, the soldier, the administrator, the villager and the poor; and has … profoundly modified the world's history by tending to render the whole of the tropics comparatively unsuitable for the full development of civilisation.[6]

Having invested so much personally and professionally in the disease, Ross might be considered somewhat partisan in elevating malaria to a position of such importance in the health and history of the tropical world, and to have overlooked the competing claims of yellow fever or sleeping sickness (neither of which existed in India). But he was not alone in his convictions. Patrick Manson, his former mentor, similarly saw malaria as 'by far the most important disease agency in tropical pathology' and devoted to it almost a quarter of his manual of tropical diseases.[7] In India malaria dominated discussion of tropical medicine, even before the cause was known. And yet, though Ross and others repeatedly pointed out that malaria was the largest single cause of death in India, it is in some ways remarkable that it came to assume such exceptional prominence. India was afflicted by so many other fatal diseases – the 1890s and 1900s alone saw major epidemics of cholera, plague and kala-azar – that it is surprising that malaria should have been afforded such importance in debates about health and race, among Indian as well as British commentators. Elsewhere in the colonial world other diseases – tuberculosis, syphilis, ankylostomiasis – occupied a similar role in discussions of race. These diseases were not absent from the Indian debates, but they seldom commanded the same degree of concern. Why was malaria so important to India?

An imperial disease

Ross's discovery of the role of the anopheles came at a critical juncture in the political economy of health in India. In line with the first priorities of colonial state medicine, malaria (and the broad category of 'fevers' in which it was statistically subsumed) was seen to constitute a particular threat to Europeans, both soldiers and civilians. This was met by evasive measures – relocating barracks to more salubrious locations, the establishment of fever-free hill-stations and sanatoria – and by partial recourse to quinine prophylaxis. Although the idea of settling substantial numbers of whites in India had been abandoned by the 1870s, European health remained a primary concern of the colonial state. The size of the British garrison in India (55–70,000 men in the late nineteenth century) alone made malaria a high priority, and the annual reports of India's sanitary and medical officers continued to stress the importance of 'fever' as a threat to European soldiers and a cause of high levels of hospitalisation, even though there had been a marked fall in European mortality from malaria since the 1850s.[8] The implications of European exposure to malaria were seen to range well beyond India itself. C.F. Oldham in 1871 stressed the continuing threat fevers posed to army health there and also noted 'their powerful effect in checking the spread of the white race over a large portion of the globe'. He believed that there was 'scarcely a family in Britain but sends forth some of its members to the regions in which these diseases constantly prevail, and where few escape their attacks'.[9] Malaria contracted in the tropics might thus menace the health and well-being of families at home. Ross, too, saw the dangers posed to the British through exposure to a disease that had already enfeebled Indians. Would the 'vigorous populations of Europe also sink some day to the same level', he asked himself, or could science save them?

> Here from my lonely watch-tower of the East
> An ancient race outworn I see —
> With dread, my own dear distant Country, lest
> The same fate fall on thee.[10]

Malaria, to Ross, was the great sapper of civilisations, the destroyer of imperial races, and, historically, not just in the tropics. With encouragement from Ross, W.H.S. Jones argued that malaria had been instrumental in the decline and fall of ancient Greece and Rome.[11] Since the Victorians regarded Rome as a worthy model for their own rule in India, this was a worrying precedent. In recent times malaria had been driven back to the southern backwaters of Europe, but, in becoming a largely tropical disease, it presented a new threat to the white races in an age of imperial expansion. India, in disease terms an eminently 'tropical' country, was in the front line of the white races' battle against malaria.

The urgent need to protect European lives in the tropics also informed the control measures Ross advised. In addition to 'malaria brigades' to eradicate mosquitoes and destroy their larvae, Ross favoured the segregation of whites so as to minimise infection from 'native' populations. He was struck by the importance of this on moving from India, where the military, administrative and residential zoning of towns and cities created a system of *de facto* racial segregation, to West Africa where the practice was rare. As evidence for the sanitary value of segregation, he cited India's cantonments where malaria was 'certainly much less rife than in the crowded native quarters in the neighbourhood'. Segregation alone would not eliminate malaria, but 'it should always be adopted until sanitation in general arrives at a much higher degree of development in the tropics than it has hitherto attained'.[12]

But protecting white health was not the sole criterion. By the 1880s a plantation economy (based mainly on tea and coffee) had grown up in India and it had become a major source of migrant labour to other colonial territories. In the mid-nineteenth century cholera had appeared the main threat to Indian labour, but a few decades later malaria was being identified as 'one of the most important economic and industrial problems' India had to face. The eradication of malaria from India would, Patrick Hehir claimed, 'in a single generation, convert that country into one of the most prosperous in the world'.[13] After leaving India in 1899, Ross set himself the dual objective of making the tropics safe for whites, and improving the economic efficiency and productivity of Indians and other tropical races. Following the apparent failure of the Mian Mir 'experiment' in the early years of the century,[14] one of the principal applications of Ross's ideas of malaria control was to the tea estates of north-eastern India. It was indicative of the importance attached to improving the productiveness of tropical labour that in 1928 the Ross Institute in London established an Industrial Anti-Malarial Advisory Committee to 'keep industry in touch with science, to make the tropics healthy, and expand the markets of the world'.[15] The Indian branch of the Ross Institute in Calcutta, set up in 1930, further exemplified the resolve of its parent-body, for its advisory committee was drawn almost entirely from British tea companies and agency houses.[16]

The practical concern with race among those who ran India's tea industry was threefold. There was, first, a desire to protect the health of white planters and their families living in heavily malarious areas of Assam and north Bengal; but second, and of increasing importance, there was a need to curb the economic cost of malaria in terms of high morbidity levels, absenteeism and mortality among estate workers. By the 1920s, as the recruitment of fresh labour became practically and politically more difficult, the planters had to rely more and more upon keeping and reproducing the labour force they already had. The high incidence of miscarriages and stillbirths, and the deaths of infants and children from 'fever and convulsions' threatened the planters' immediate and long-term interests and directed unprecedented attention to the health of estate women and children. The importance of malaria as a disease that adversely affected reproduction was one reason for its prominence in debates about health and race. The third area of management interest lay in utilising the supposed natural immunity to malaria among certain 'races' of estate workers. This was a local variant of an old imperial theme – manipulating the supposedly innate characteristics of non-white races to serve European economic and military ends. A large proportion of Indian tea-estate labourers were recruited from 'tribal' populations (such as the Santhals and Oraons) and the possibility that these 'jungle coolies' had a natural immunity to malaria was a convincing argument for their preferential recruitment and retention. Although there appeared to be some initial advantage in this strategy, accumulating evidence suggested, disappointingly from the planter perspective, that any acquired or inherited immunity was soon lost and second generation tribal workers were as liable to malaria as anyone else.[17]

The meanings of race

But what did 'race' signify? Among physicians like Ross, as among a wider public, the term was often used without technical precision and in a bewildering variety of ways. By 'race', Ross in his memoirs variously indicated Indians, Britons, Europeans, or simply the entire 'human race'. Nonetheless, concepts of race were widely employed in both British and Indian writing of the period and these more specific usages require comment.

One of the most authoritative usages was in colonial anthropology, where 'race' nestled alongside 'caste', 'tribe' and 'nation', sometimes as a synonym, sometimes as a generic term encompassing smaller collectivities. The idea of race assumed particular prominence in the anthropometry of the 1890s and 1900s, where it was given a seemingly precise biological significance and where the sanction of science was explicitly invoked. The most influential representative of anthropometry in India was H.H. Risley, a leading civil servant as well as anthropologist, who believed that the caste system was the embodiment of racial divisions. He took to task the work of J.C. Nesfield, who claimed that castes were essentially occupational categories and argued for the essential unity of the 'Indian race'. Nesfield conceded that India had been conquered thousands of years earlier by Aryan invaders, who had settled down and imposed their language and religion upon an indigenous population, but he saw no evidence that racial differences had survived or formed any part of the existing caste system. The 'blood of this foreign race became gradually absorbed into the indigenous, the less yielding to the greater, so that almost all traces of the conquering race eventually disappeared'. For the past 3,000 years, 'no real difference of blood between Aryan and aboriginal … has existed'. Hence, 'the question of caste' was 'not one of race at all, but of culture'.[18]

Risley, by contrast, argued that physical differences were, in fact, visually apparent among the Indian population and represented the survival of ancient racial differences between Aryan invaders and Dravidian indigenes. They had been preserved because of the race-consciousness of the fair-skinned Aryans and the taboos on intermarriage enforced through caste endogamy. The physical characteristic of each caste, representing different degrees of racial purity of the Aryan, Dravidian and (in eastern India) Mongoloid 'types', were thus retained intact from generation to generation. These physical differences were so pronounced that they could be measured through 'leading physical characters, such as the stature and proportions of the head, features and limbs', the 'nasal index' being a particularly sensitive means of determining racial identity. Anthropometry thus enabled the researcher to work backwards to the 'probable origins of the various race-stocks'. Risley was confident that 'race sentiment' in India, 'so far from being a figment of the intolerant pride of the Brahman', rested upon 'a foundation of fact which scientific method confirms' – that race had 'shaped the intricate groupings of the caste system' and 'preserved the Aryan type in comparative purity throughout Northern India'.[19]

Even at the time Risley's work came in for criticism, not least for its claims to scientific exactitude, but his opinions about the existence of distinctive racial 'types' and the scientific value of anthropometric techniques enjoyed the support of the Government of India and were repeated, largely unchanged, in his ethnographical essay for the Indian census of 1901 and in *The People of India* in 1908. For twenty years Risley's anthropometric approach dominated colonial anthropology in India and informed not just a large body of ethnographical studies of 'castes and tribes' but also the work of provincial census commissioners, army recruitment officers and police superintendents, for all of whom racial 'types' and anthropometric indices seemed to offer a convenient guide to India's complex social order. However, anthropometry as a 'test of race' had already begun to fall out of favour by the time of Risley's death in 1911.[20] Though his account of the 'tribes and castes' of Bengal incorporated earlier research by a civil surgeon, James Wise of Dhaka, there is little evidence that subsequent medical writers found Risley's racial typology and anthropometry useful in their own work. In this respect at least, medicine and anthropology seem to have been rather different colonial species. For his part, Risley's anthropology had little to say about health and disease. Indeed, the idea of races remaining virtually intact over many generations largely denied a role to disease and environmental factors in the fashioning of racial 'types'. There is, too, little evidence that Indian intellectuals, in an era of growing nationalist self-assertion, took favourably to the anthropometric understanding of race and the remorseless emphasis upon India's diverse physical 'types' as the antithesis to a single national identity. At a time when middle-class Indians were acutely conscious of the racial discrimination practised against them in government service and public life, they were understandably wary of the more divisive or hierarchical implications of colonial race ideology, and particularly the suggestion that 'coloured races' were physically and mentally inferior to white ones.[21] That did not mean, however, that European ideas of race were entirely rejected. By contrast with Risley's biological version, a more generalised notion of race – in which culture and environment figured far more prominently – circulated widely among Indians and Europeans.

The idea that India's environment, and particularly that of 'tropical' Bengal, had moulded the characteristics of its people, had a long history in colonial discourse. Influential statements of the supposedly negative effects of climate, soil and vegetation on the moral and physical qualities of Bengalis can be found in the writing of Robert Orme in the 1760s and T.B. Macaulay in the 1840s. Both emphasised the extent to which the natural abundance of the region, combined with a hot and humid climate, had made Bengalis as a race indolent and cowardly, feeble and 'effeminate'.[22] The disdainful nature of these stereotypes, and the blend of cultural and environmental typologies that accompanied them, were discursive tropes that persisted well into the 1870s and beyond. As will be seen shortly, they were intensified and given a new specificity by the malarial 'Burdwan fever' epidemic of the 1850s and 1860s and further metamorphosed through the explicit language of race in the 1880s and 1890s. One example of how these multiple strands of thought were brought together can be found in the report of the Bengal Census Commissioner, H. Beverley, in 1872. He declared:

> In Bengal Proper we have a people physically distinct from any other race in India. Whether, on the one hand, they are to be attributed to climatic influences and the natural characteristics of the country, or, on the other, to the greater infusion of aboriginal blood, this people represents national peculiarities sufficient to identify it in any part of the world. Living amidst a network of rivers and morasses, and nourished on a watery rice diet, the semi-amphibious Bengali in appearance belongs to a weak and puny race, yet he is able to endure an amount of exposure to which the up-country Hindustani would soon fall a victim. In active pursuits the Bengali is timid and slothful, but in intellect he is subtle and sharp-witted ... [23]

Explaining the physical and moral character of Bengalis by reference to their environment was not a trope confined to British writers. As the region of India where Western ideas had their earliest and greatest impact, and where, at the same time, the colonial typification of race and environment was at its most censorious, Bengal was a critical site for the presentation, internalisation and reformulation of Western race ideology. The power of such ideas, not least when they were proclaimed in official publications, could hardly be ignored. In addition to the widely circulated views of men like Macaulay and Beverley, colonial policies actively discriminated against Bengalis through their exclusion from the Indian Army in favour of the 'martial races' of northern and north-western India. Ideas of race not only divided Bengali from Briton; they also differentiated between 'manly' and 'effeminate' races within India itself.[24] The claim that they were a peculiarly weak and effeminised race had a profound impact on the self-representation and social anxieties of the Bengali intelligentsia (the *bhadralok*), and generated a powerful autocritique into which many of the elements of British racial abuse and environmental scorn were incorporated.

In an article published under the pseudonym 'Arcydae', R.C. Dutt explained how the soil and climate of the province had shaped the character of its people. Borrowing heavily from the environmental determinism of H.T. Buckle, Dutt observed:

> All those physical causes which enfeeble and enervate, and make man incapable of having mastery over Nature, are found to exist and work in this country to an alarming extent. The

> damp heat of Bengal, unlike the dry heat of western India, disposes the people to be inactive and averse to labour; while the alluvial soil of the land, moistened and softened by periodical rains and inundations, produces an exuberance of crops almost without the toil of man, and denies him that salutary exercise which is absolutely necessitated in more hilly countries. Rice, too, which is the chief produce of the land, affords nourishment rather than strength. ... All these causes have acted with combined force on the physique of the Bengali, and have made him the weak and inactive creature that he is.[25]

That much of the Bengali countryside abounded with 'malarious fevers' and was full of 'swamps and malarious lakes teeming with rank vegetation and animal life', only added to this picture of sickness, weakness and gloom.

Interleaving with ideas about race generated by physical anthropology and environmental determinism was a further conceptual ingredient – that of an Aryan race. This, too, had a long ancestry. The discovery made by the British Orientalist William Jones in the 1780s that Sanskrit shared a common origin with Greek, Latin and other European languages, was later extended to encompass a wider claim that there was a close racial, and not merely linguistic, connection between Indians and Europeans: Indians (at least north Indians) were descendants of the southern branch of the Aryan race and thus distant kin to the Aryans who had settled in Europe.[26] The idea of the Aryans having entered India from the north was adopted by Indian writers as well, including the Hindu nationalist Bal Gangadhar Tilak in *The Arctic Home of the Vedas* in 1903.[27]

For many European writers the Indo-Aryan idea had a convenient duality. On the one hand, the invasion by a 'superior' race akin to Europeans helped to explain why ancient India had been able to produce such a remarkable civilisation; on the other, however, it also helped to explain why these early achievements had not been sustained and leadership had passed to the Western Aryans. In India a long process of cultural decline and racial degeneration had set in, whether as a result of 'miscegenation' with dark-skinned aboriginals and the corrupting effects of their religious beliefs and social practices, or as a result of the debilitating effects of the heat, humidity and diseases of tropical India. This was not only a useful explanation for an awkward historical fact – it also had a contemporary relevance in sounding a warning to the latter-day Aryans of

Britain and the United States, if they attempted to settle among 'inferior' races in life-sapping climes. An American geographer, Ellen Semple, thus alluded in 1911 to the time when 'the Aryans descended to the enervating lowlands of tropical India, and in that debilitating climate lost the qualities which first gave them supremacy'.[28] Twenty years later, George MacMunn, in an account of India's 'martial races', asked why it was that so many Indians had 'neither martial aptitude nor physical courage', despite being descended from 'a white race akin to our British selves'. One answer, he believed, was the effect of 'a thousand years of malaria and hookworm, and other ills of neglected sanitation in a hot climate and the deteriorating effects of aeons of tropical sun on races that were once white and lived in uplands and on cool steppes'.[29]

By the 1870s the term 'Aryan' was being widely employed by Indian writers and publicists, and, through the title and programme of the revivalist Arya Samaj, formed by Dayananda Saraswati in 1875, it acquired powerful associations with resurgent Hinduism. Largely shorn of any implications of racial affinity with the West, Hindu nationalists used the term 'Aryan' 'to promote … Indian self-esteem, not Indo-European solidarity'.[30] In Bengal the idea of Aryan descent became central to a 'new Bengali sense of a national heritage'. It gave a 'heightened sense of antiquity and pedigree', and became 'the most powerful metonym of the nation's lost, ancient glory'.[31] In place of the English word 'race', Bengali writers commonly used the term *jati* to signify community or nation, whether referring to Aryans, Indians, Bengalis or tribal Santhals. Significantly, when they spoke of their own race or *jati* they almost invariably excluded the Muslim population.[32] 'Race' took on strongly religious connotations in Bengal and the intensity of the debate about malaria in the province partly needs to be understood in terms of this increasingly communalised context.

'A dying race'

Since the mid-nineteenth century there had been a marked growth in statistical as well as sanitary awareness in middle-class Bengal. The use of statistics was one of the principal ways in which science, as both method and matter, manifested itself and made its claim to authority among the Western-educated elite. The annual reports of the Provincial Sanitary Commissioners from the mid-1860s, and the decennial censuses from 1871–2 onwards, gave detailed and seemingly incontrovertible evidence that malaria was the greatest single threat to health in rural Bengal. It was not just the large numbers who died that caused concern, but the many more who were incapacitated. Malaria was seen as an emasculating disease that threatened reproduction, produced weakly and sickly individuals, and further accentuated the division between the 'manly races' of the north-west and the 'effeminate' inhabitants of Bengal.

In 1899, the Provincial Sanitary Commissioner calculated that in Bengal 'malarial fever' accounted for three-quarters of all deaths or almost 1,000,000 a year. He urged local authorities to do more to check the disease, not only to curb the death rate but also to bring better health to the living:

> Where now are to be seen wretched beings of sallow and ghastly countenance, looking twice their real age, with attenuated frames, shrunken limbs, muscles thin and powerless, tongues of silvery whiteness ... , pulses feeble and irregular, spleens and livers enormously enlarged, and pitiable languid gait, would be found men well-knit, with their muscles developed, and their vital organs sound – altogether powerful, vigorous, healthy and happy.[33]

Four years later, in the 1891 census report, C.J. O'Donnell provided the most pessimistic picture yet of malaria's desolation of rural Bengal. From Calcutta northwards, almost to Darjeeling, there existed 'a large area of decaying or nearly stationary population'. In Jessore District the population had fallen by 2.5 per cent since 1881, in Rangpur by 1.6 per cent. In Rajshahi 'the spectacle of whole villages depopulated by a brooding mortality' was 'almost universal'. In Nadia District 'the great fever epidemic' had caused 73,196 deaths, a loss of 3.6 per cent, in a single year. In Burdwan 'ruined houses and abandoned sites were everywhere visible'. The effects of fever were so widespread that 'the sickly physique is the ordinary physique ... the healthy physique is the exceptional one'.[34] Over the next thirty years, census commissioners repeated much the same story. Year by year, L.S.S. O'Malley remarked in his 1911 census report, malaria was 'silently and relentlessly at work. ... Not only does it diminish the population by death, but it reduces the vitality of the survivors, saps their vigour and fecundity'.[35]

The devastating impact of malaria on Bengal was seen to have commenced with the 'Burdwan fever' epidemic of the 1850s and

1860s. The cause of the outbreak was a matter of contention in medical circles, as to whether it was malaria, kala-azar or some combination of the two; later opinion favoured malaria. But its psychological and demographic significance was beyond dispute. It dramatically brought to the attention of the Bengali intelligentsia what appeared to be a specific reason for the decline of their *jati* and firmly established the identification of race with environment. 'Burdwan fever' was the Bengali Black Death. Perceptually it marked a precipitous decline, within two or three generations, from a rural golden age to pervasive poverty, hunger and disease. Though malaria was by no means confined to Bengal – there was heavy mortality, too, in Punjab and the North-Western Provinces – nowhere does it appear to have made such a profound cultural impression as in Bengal. This was not just because Bengal was demographically hard hit; it was also because malaria epitomised ideas of Bengali enfeeblement and emasculation that were already current in colonial discourse and mirrored in the internalised self-doubts of the Bengali elite.

One of the most vivid accounts of 'Burdwan fever' was given by a physician, Gopaul Chunder Roy, in the 1870s, who remarked how districts that once 'smiled with peace, health and prosperity' had been turned into 'hotbeds of disease, misery and death'. Villages that 'once rang with the cheerful, merry tone of healthful infants', now resounded 'with loud wailings and lamentations'.[36] Like many other early commentators, Indian as well as British, Roy did not explicitly invoke the language of race. But the pathos of his descriptions, and the fact that they were written by a Bengali rather than a foreigner, made them particularly resonant for subsequent Bengali writers. Within a few decades, however, the idea of a countryside, once prosperous, now disease-ridden and impoverished, had become closely identified with the idea of the Bengalis as a 'dying race'. Speaking in 1912, Motilal Ghosh, a newspaper proprietor, echoed Roy when he remarked that sixty years earlier the Bengali countryside had been largely free of disease. Villages in those days teemed with 'healthy, happy and robust people', untroubled by the 'bread question or the fear of being visited by any deadly pestilence'. But, Ghosh claimed, those days were now long gone. Dating the 'deterioration of the [Bengali] race' to 'Burdwan fever' in the 1850s, he observed, citing official reports and statistics: 'Within the last 60 years, malaria and cholera have swept away tens of millions of people from Bengal. Those who have been left behind ... are more dead than alive'. Villagers were 'dying like flies' from malaria and malnourishment, and the Bengali race would ultimately disappear, 'like the old Greeks', unless 'vigorous steps' were taken to 'save them from extinction'.[37]

But while the 'Bengali race' as a whole was often invoked, it was the fate of Bengali Hindus that constituted the main focus of concern. Again, the census reports were influential in this. In his 1891 census report, O'Donnell not only detailed the impact of malaria, but also produced statistics to chart the 'decline of Hinduism' over the previous twenty years. Since 1872 'out of every 10,000 persons Islam has gained 100 persons in Northern Bengal, 262 in Eastern Bengal, and 110 in Western Bengal', or 157 across Bengal as a whole. 'The Musalman increase is real and large', he averred. 'If it were to continue, the faith of Muhammad would be universal in Bengal proper in six and a half centuries whilst Eastern Bengal would reach the same condition in about four hundred years'. Because malaria was particularly destructive in the western and central districts, where Hindus formed the majority, they suffered most from the disease, while the eastern, Muslim-majority districts were far less affected. But O'Donnell was not satisfied that malaria was the sole cause of Hindu decline, arguing that, in addition to numbers gained by proselytisation, Muslims also had a more varied and nutritious diet and followed marriage practices (including widow remarriage and polygamy) that promoted a higher birth rate.[38]

Against a background of growing tension between Hindus and Muslims, accentuated by the partition of Bengal in 1905, malaria figured as one of several factors reputedly making Bengali Hindus an imperilled race. The most influential statement of this view was a tract entitled *A Dying Race* by U.N. Mukherji, first published in 1909. Mukherji drew extensively from census data to show that the number of Bengali Hindus was falling sharply compared to the Muslims and he followed O'Donnell in attributing this decline to conversion, a lack of vigour among Hindus and a high death rate combined with a low birth rate. 'We are a dying race', Mukherji declared. 'Every census reveals the same fact. We are getting proportionately fewer and fewer.'[39] Despite being a member of the Indian Medical Service, Mukherji's proposed solution was not primarily a medical or sanitary one. Instead, he argued for the need for Hindus to reform themselves, by showing less discrimination against the low castes and untouchables, and so saving them from being driven into the arms of Islam. Having compared Bengali Hindus to other 'dying races' like the Maoris, Mukherji concluded:

> The Mohammedans have a future and they believe in it – we Hindus have no conception of it. Time is with them – time is against us. At the end of the year they count their gains, we calculate our losses. They are growing in number, growing in strength, growing in wealth, growing in solidarity, we are crumbling to pieces. They look forward to a United Mohammedan world – we are waiting for our extinction.[40]

Mukherji's widely disseminated tract – it was twice reprinted in English and 50,000 copies of a Bengali translation were distributed free – did not go unchallenged. Some writers were more willing to accept malaria as the cause of Hindu decline than to face the need for caste reform. S.G. Deuskar, a prominent nationalist, recalculated the census statistics to show that malaria was one of the most significant threats to the health and numerical strength of the Hindu community and to argue that there was accordingly no need to jettison established religious and social attitudes.[41] The *Amrit Bazar Patrika* put the argument bluntly: 'When malaria is such a potent factor for mischief and is ever present in our midst, why blame the social system?'[42] But Mukherji's identification of the Bengali Hindus as a 'dying race' was widely accepted and, extended to apply to all Hindus not just those in Bengal, became a rallying cry for Hindu militancy and reconversion movements throughout India. The reference to malaria, one of Mukherji's starting points, was, in the process, almost entirely dropped.[43] In Bengal itself, however, malaria remained a vital issue. Other members of the *bhadralok*, while making no specific appeals to Hindu identity, concentrated on the menace of disease itself. Malaria and other fevers, observed G.K. Mitra in 1925, were 'the greatest scourge of Bengal'. The vitality of the people had been lowered, and there had been an appalling increase in the death rate over the birth rate. 'It is literally true', he concluded, without differentiating between Hindus and Muslims, 'that the Bengalis are a dying race.'[44]

Response to the malaria problem

By the 1910s and 1920s it was widely recognised that malaria was not race-specific. Hehir in 1927 stated that there was 'no true racial immunity to malaria' – except possibly among Africans. Indian children acquired some degree of immunity through frequent exposure to malaria, but economic circumstances were far more important than race in explaining the severity and distribution of malaria in India. The rural poor suffered most because of their 'improper and scanty food, miserable housing, insufficient clothing [and] excessive work'.[45]

The Bengali *bhadralok* saw malaria as a disease that had profound implications for their race, but did not accept that it was an inseparable part of their racial identity. An article in Calcutta's *Modern Review* in 1909 captured this belief. The author argued that three factors had contributed to the growth of ill-health and high mortality in Bengal – the hot, moist climate and 'pestilential soil', the harmful effect of social customs (such as early marriage), and the poor nutritional value of the Bengali diet. Fortunately, while it took 'years and centuries to produce degeneration', it took a 'much shorter time in the other direction'. Little could be done to alter Bengal's climate, but diet and social customs could be changed, and the British had recently shown in their own country how the health of a race could be improved.[46]

By the early twentieth century, the response of the *bhadralok* was to see malaria as a threat that could be met and tackled in ways which challenged colonial assumptions about Bengali weakness and passivity while at the same time furthering its claims to rural leadership. By forming their own anti-malaria brigades *à la* Ross but on a voluntary basis rather than waiting for the state to act, Bengalis believed that they could revitalise the ailing countryside and eradicate disease. In 1917 N.K. Sirkar advocated combating malaria through a combination of village sanitation and quinine, a campaign in which the *bhadralok* would provide leadership for the masses, educating them out of their 'prejudice, ignorance and apathy'.[47] In 1925 G.K. Mitra urged a similar self-help programme to tackle rural malaria. He, too, believed this would reverse rural depopulation, educate the masses in hygiene and disease-control and enable the *bhadralok* to assert its hegemonic authority over the poor and backward villagers.[48] There was a class agenda here, not just a racial score to settle.

The rural anti-malarial movement, launched in two villages in Bengal in 1917, had by 1932 spread to more than a thousand villages. Though C.A. Bentley, the Director of Public Health, believed that far more capital-intensive measures than cleaning up villages were needed to resolve the malaria problem in Bengal, he believed the self-help movement was 'full of promise'. Quite apart from the immediate effects of the committees' work, they were 'a valuable means of educating the public and gradually enlisting their help against the common enemy'.[49] The village committees also won praise from the Ross Institute in London and its Calcutta branch. Neither Ross nor his followers apparently found anything incongruous about a Bengali self-help programme.[50] Indians might have seemed to Ross half a century earlier to be an 'ancient race outworn' and, like other tropical races, dependent on European leadership and expertise for their salvation. But the *bhadralok* did not intend to wait for outsiders for deliverance. They could slay the dragon themselves.

Conclusion

This chapter has tried to show the complex intermingling of ideas of race and disease in colonial India. As much by its 'emasculating' effect on an afflicted population as by the actual mortality it caused, malaria was deeply implicated in discussions of racial identity, decay and regeneration. This was particularly so in Bengal where environmental determinism had long informed racial stereotyping and where ideas of an 'enfeebled' race were strongly entrenched in indigenous as well as European discourse. The outbreak of 'Burdwan fever' in the 1850s, the resulting mortality and widespread debility, helped make malaria a specific focus for fears of population decline and racial decay, especially among Hindus, and in ways which heightened a sense of demographic and political rivalry with Bengali Muslims. Clearly, then, ideas of race were not confined to the British (who themselves held widely differing views of what it signified), but also had a profound role in Indian self-perceptions and social attitudes.

It is evident, too, that while some anthropologically minded civil servants like Risley stressed the immutability of race (as embodied in caste) and gave prominence to the physical dimensions of race, race was more commonly regarded as a combination of cultural (as well as physical) traits and environmental influences rather than simply as a set of biological signs and anthropometric indices. The significance of this for the discussion of race and malaria was the belief, shared by Ross and many of Bengal's elite, that the weakness attributed to Indians in general and Bengalis in particular was not inherent to their race, but was contingent upon poverty, ignorance and a malarious environment. Medical and sanitary science thus held out the possibility of contesting the more biologically deterministic interpretations of race.

Notes

1 *The Times* (London), 17 September 1932, quoted in the Ross Institute and Hospital for Tropical Diseases, *Annual Report and Accounts for 1932*, p. 21.
2 Ronald Ross, *Memoirs*, London, John Murray, 1923, p. 43.
3 Ross, *Memoirs*, p. 4.
4 Ronald Ross, *The Prevention of Malaria*, London, John Murray, 1910, p. vii.
5 Ross, *Memoirs*, p. 115.
6 Ross, *The Prevention of Malaria*, pp. vii–viii.
7 Patrick Manson, *Tropical Diseases: A Manual of the Diseases of Warm Climates*, London, Cassell, 1898, p. 1.
8 Joseph Fayrer, *On the Climate and Fevers of India*, London, J. & A. Churchill, 1882, p. 53.
9 C.F. Oldham, *What is Malaria? And Why Is It Most Intense in Hot Climates?*, London, H.K. Lewis, 1871, p. 2.
10 Ross, *Memoirs*, pp. 43–4.
11 W.H.S. Jones, *Malaria: A Neglected Factor in the History of Greece and Rome*, London, Macmillan & Bowes, 1907.
12 Ross, *The Prevention of Malaria*, p. 287.
13 Patrick Hehir, *Malaria in India*, London, Oxford University Press, 1927, p. 246.
14 W.F. Bynum, 'An Experiment That Failed: Malaria Control at Mian Mir', *Parassitologia* 36 (1994): 107–20.
15 Ross Institute, *Annual Report and Accounts for 1931*, p. 5.
16 Ross Institute, *Annual Report and Accounts for 1932*, p. 15.
17 G. Strickland, *Abridged Report on Malaria in the Assam Tea Gardens*, Calcutta, Indian Tea Association, n.d., pp. 2–7, 27–9, 41–2.
18 John C. Nesfield, *Brief View of the Caste System of the North-Western Provinces and Oudh*, Allahabad, North-Western Provinces and Oudh Government Press, 1885, pp. 3–4.
19 H.H. Risley, *The Tribes and Castes of Bengal: Ethnographic Glossary*, vol. 1, Calcutta, Bengal Secretariat Press, 1891, pp. i–ii, xxvi, xxx.
20 L.S.S. O'Malley, *Census of India, 1911, Volume V: Bengal, Bihar and Orissa, and Sikkim, part I, Report*, Calcutta, Bengal Secretariat Book Depot, 1913, p. 519.
21 Anon., 'The So-Called Inferiority of the Coloured Races, II', *Modern Review* (Calcutta) February 1909: 136–44; Bipin Chandra Pal, 'Race-Equality', *Modern Review* April 1911: 319–24.
22 Robert Orme, *A History of the Military Transactions of the British Nation in Indostan*, vol. 2, London, F. Wingrave, 1803, p. 5; Thomas Babington Macaulay, *Critical and Historical Essays*, vol. 1, London, Dent, 1907, pp. 503, 562.

23 H. Beverley, *Report on the Census of Bengal, 1872*, Calcutta, Bengal Secretariat Press, 1872, p. 152.
24 Mrinalini Sinha, *Colonial Masculinity: The 'Manly Englishman' and the 'Effeminate Bengali' in the Late Nineteenth Century*, Manchester, Manchester University Press, 1995.
25 'Arcydae' (R.C. Dutt), 'The Past and Future of Bengal', *Bengal Magazine* January 1873: 251.
26 Thomas R. Trautmann, *Aryans and British India*, Berkeley, University of California Press, 1997.
27 Christophe Jaffrelot, 'The Ideas of the Hindu Race in the Writings of Hindu Nationalist Ideologues in the 1920s and 1930s: A Concept Between Two Cultures', in Peter Robb (ed.), *The Concept of Race in South Asia*, Delhi, Oxford University Press, 1995, pp. 329–32.
28 Ellen Churchill Semple, *Influences of Geographic Environment on the Basis of Ratzel's System of Anthropo-Geography*, London, Constable, 1911, p. 37.
29 George MacMunn, *The Martial Races of India*, London, Sampson, Low, Marston, 1933, p. 2.
30 Joan Leopold, 'The Aryan Theory of Race', *Indian Economic and Social History Review* 7 (1970): 273–4.
31 Tapati Guha-Thakurta, 'Recovering the Nation's Art', in Partha Chatterjee (ed.), *Texts of Power: Emerging Disciplines in Colonial Bengal*, Minneapolis, University of Minnesota Press, 1995, p. 69.
32 Indira Chowdhury-Sengupta, 'The Effeminate and the Masculine: Nationalism and the Concept of Race in Colonial Bengal', in Robb, *Concept of Race*, pp. 284–7.
33 W.H. Gregg, 'Malarial Fever in Bengal', *Calcutta Review* 88 (1889): 384.
34 C.J. O'Donnell, *Census of India, 1891, Volume III: The Lower Provinces of Bengal: The Report*, Calcutta, Bengal Secretariat Press, 1893, pp. 2, 64, 88, 92.
35 O'Malley, *Census of India, 1911*, vol. 1, part I, p. 69.
36 Gopaul Chunder Roy, *The Causes, Symptoms and Treatment of Burdwan Fever or the Epidemic Fever of Lower Bengal*, 2nd edn, London, J. & A. Churchill, 1876, p. 1.
37 *Proceedings of the Second All-India Sanitary Conference Held at Madras, November 11th to 16th, 1912*, Simla, Government Central Branch Press, vol. 2, pp. 514–23.
38 O'Donnell, *1891 Census*, p. 146.
39 Quoted in Anon., 'Are the Bengali Hindus a Dying Race?', *Modern Review* January 1911: 39.
40 Quoted in Papia Chakravarty, *Hindu Response to Nationalist Ferment: Bengal, 1909–1935*, Calcutta, Subarnarekha, 1992, p. 33.
41 'Are the Bengali Hindus a Dying Race?', pp. 39–40.
42 Quoted in Chakravarty, *Hindu Response*, p. 37.
43 Shraddhananda, *Hindu Sangathan: Saviour of the Dying Race*, Delhi, published by the author, 1926.

44 Girindra Krishna Mitra, *Skeleton of a Scheme to Combat Malaria and Other Prevalent Febrile Diseases in Bengal*, 2nd edn, Calcutta, Department of Public Health, 1925, pp. 2–3.
45 Hehir, *Malaria in India*, pp. 34–9.
46 Indu Madhab Mallick, 'Growing Ill-Health and Increasing Mortality in Bengal and How to Prevent It', *Modern Review* May 1909: 449–54.
47 Nalini K. Sirkar, *Malaria: Its Causation and Means of Preventing It*, Calcutta, K.L. Ghoshal, 1917, pp. 5, 11.
48 Mitra, *Skeleton of a Scheme*.
49 C.A. Bentley, *Malaria and Agriculture in Bengal: How to Reduce Malaria in Bengal by Irrigation*, Calcutta, Bengal Book Depot, 1925, p. 120.
50 Ross Institute, *Annual Report and Accounts for 1932*, pp. 41–3.

Chapter 7

Tuberculosis and race in Britain and its empire, 1900–50

Michael Worboys

The history of tuberculosis in twentieth-century America or Germany could not be written without considering race. However, historians of the disease in Britain have largely ignored the issue and have only considered this great 'social disease' in terms of class, occupation, urbanisation and welfare policy.[1] Race was to the fore in the United States for obvious reasons: the differential incidence of tuberculosis among immigrants from Europe, the exceptionally high mortality rates among Native Americans and fears about the rising toll among African Americans after 1870. [2] In Germany, the disease was spoken of as a 'racial poison'.[3] Yet British work and campaigning with tuberculosis was not completely insulated from race. The country had its own 'races' and immigrants, and was at the centre of an empire of many 'peoples', among whom the incidence of tuberculosis rose rapidly in this century. In this chapter, I argue that discussion of the relationship between tuberculosis and race was integral to the changing epidemiological and pathological understanding of the disease in Britain and its colonies. I focus on the dominant discourse developed by doctors in Britain and Africa, and only briefly mention the different patterns of ideas current in Australasia, India and the West Indies. Indeed, it was the alliances of medical specialists, rather than national or physical geographies, which defined the relevant communities. In general, colonial medical officers interested in tuberculosis found a more receptive audience in metropolitan medicine than they did among their peers, who were preoccupied with tropical diseases.[4] In an earlier article, Mark Harrison and I discussed how tuberculosis in Africa and India was constructed as a 'disease of civilisation'; here I focus on race and explore in detail ideas of 'racial immunity' and 'primitive tuberculosis'.[5]

The notion that different races had differing immunities to disease is long-standing. It was only too evident to European explorers in the contrast between their vulnerability to the diseases they encountered in new environments, and the seeming immunity to these conditions among local peoples. The stability of such vulnerabilities was an important practical question in European settlement, where there was ambivalence about whether acclimatisation could be achieved to a sufficient level in a matter of years by the 'seasoning' of individuals, or whether it would take many generations and need to be 'fixed in the blood'. The vulnerability of non-Europeans to the diseases brought by explorers and settlers was understood in the same terms and expressed in the notion that these were 'virgin soil' populations.[6] 'Racial immunity' as a term emerged after 1900 as a synthesis of ideas of race, evolutionary theories and immunology.[7] Within twentieth-century medicine the term 'race' was used quite loosely, referring both to groups with shared physical/biological characteristics and to groups defined by social/cultural differences. As in other spheres, such divisions were often blurred, confused and combined, not least when biology seemed to determine culture and culture to shape biology. Such conflations were particularly prevalent in discussions of immunity, because of uncertainties about the extent to which resistance to specific diseases was acquired or inherited. All these issues were illustrated in discussions of the decline of leprosy in Europe. Had this been due to cultural practices, such as isolation of sufferers and improved hygiene, or had Europeans become habituated to the disease? If the latter, was resistance being lost, now that Europeans were no longer exposed to the disease, and to what extent would modern Europeans be vulnerable again as they met the disease in the tropics? In these discussions, Lamarckian ideas of the inheritance of acquired immunities were as influential as Darwinian notions that implied 'survival of the immunest'.[8]

During the first half of this century, especially in the wake of the work of eugenists, there was a move to reserve the term 'race' for groupings that were biologically, if not genetically, distinct. In the field of immunology, this ought to have led to the reservation of the term 'racial immunity' for inherited as opposed to acquired resistance. However, things were not that simple, as the discourse of tuberculosis and race illustrates. In medicine, the importance accorded to acquired and inherited immunity varied over time and between different groups of practitioners. There was also disagreement about the balance of disease-specific and general immunities, and whether specific immunities had to be acquired whereas general ones could only be inherited. The issue was further complicated because health policy regarded tuberculosis as a social disease. However, the environmental, cultural and behavioural factors that were believed to determine the incidence of the disease were thought to interact with the biology of individuals and groups, and perhaps inheritance. This was evident in the idea of 'primitive tuberculosis' developed in the 1930s by S. Lyle Cummins.[9] In many ways this was constructed as the mirror image of the pathological and epidemiological position in advanced or civilised countries. People in 'primitive societies' were supposed only to produce 'primitive' responses to tuberculosis in two senses: rudimentary immune responses that failed to combat infection and the complete absence of any preventive health measures. Against this, what might be called 'civilised tuberculosis' was a disease in decline as effective immunity developed in individuals and populations, while hygienic practices prevented infection and allowed controlled tubercularisation. Of course, such ideas gave medical and scientific authority to the construction of non-European peoples as physiologically weak, diseased, backward and ignorant: in other words, as biologically and culturally inferior.

This chapter is based around the ideas on tubercular immunity developed by Lyle Cummins, who became one of the leading British authorities on the disease in the first half of this century. After training at Cork and Netley, Cummins joined the Royal Army Medical Corps (RAMC), serving in Egypt and the Sudan from 1899 to 1908, the latter posting leading to his first work on tuberculosis among 'primitive' tribes. Between 1908 and 1913 he worked in the RAMC's Vaccine Department in London, before becoming Assistant Professor of Pathology at the Army Medical School (AMS) in 1914.[10] Service in World War I, after which he penned the official history of the pathology services, was followed by appointment as full professor at the AMS. In 1922, he left the army to take up the new Chair of Tuberculosis at the Welsh National Medical School, Cardiff, a post he held until his retirement in 1938. He became a leading authority on tubercular disease among miners, continued to investigate tuberculosis in the Empire, and was active in the National Association for the Prevention of Tuberculosis (NAPT), steering it towards becoming an imperial rather than merely British agency.[11] In 1945, the NAPT published a pamphlet, written by Cummins, entitled 'A New Empire and Colonial Vista'. This set out a vision of medically planned and controlled colonial development which would bring the backward peoples of the Empire into the modern world more slowly and more hygienically than previously.[12] Cummins' changing views about race and tuberculosis both reflected wider medical assumptions and at times challenged them. His first statement of his 'virgin soil' theory in 1908 assumed that immunity was inherited, though by 1912 he had switched to an exclusively acquired model. In the mid- to late 1920s, Cummins again accepted there was a role for inheritance, only to abandon this again in the 1940s. My main concern in what follows is to explain how and why Cummins changed his views, and to explore the impact of his work in Britain and its empire, in order to reach an understanding of not only tuberculosis but also the changing ideas of race.

'Virgin soil'

Cummins first published on tuberculosis and race in 1908, in an article on the disease among Egyptian and Sudanese troops. He concluded, in line with Karl Pearson's eugenic views, that the high incidence of the disease in regiments recruited from remote Sudanese tribes was because they had 'no hereditary resistance' and hence were 'virgin soil'.[13] He observed that in their 'natural' conditions the primitive Sudanese were not exposed to the disease so there was no selection pressure from the *Tubercle bacillus*. Their 'biology' only became a disadvantage when they moved to new environments, such as those of army garrisons and towns. Cummins noted that a similar fate befell monkeys brought to the London Zoo! He also used reports from military surgeons in Africa and India on tuberculosis in native regiments; all of these showed a high incidence among troops from remote areas and lower rates in those recruited from towns.[14] In the Indian Medical Service (IMS) mortality among the Gurkhas was four times that of Sikhs; however, IMS officers linked this to climate and 'racial habits', such as diet, cleanliness, chewing and spitting, rather than inherited features.[15]

In 1912 Cummins gave a paper to the Society of Tropical Medicine and Hygiene (STMH) in which he addressed the general issue of high mortalities from tuberculosis suffered by 'primitive tribes' when they came into contact with 'civilisation'.[16] However, he now expressed his 'virgin soil theory' in different terms, arguing that such peoples 'were not victims of an inevitable and invincible racial susceptibility' but were vulnerable because of their lack of previous exposure to the *Tubercle bacillus*. This meant they had been unable to develop any acquired immunity. His key point was that primitive peoples, like new-born children everywhere, were non-immune until able to develop immunity after exposure to the disease. To develop his case Cummins drew on current aetiological ideas in Britain, and reports on ethnic and racial differences in North America. In making tuberculosis a 'disease of civilisation', he was in part following the dominant idea that tuberculosis was a 'social disease', but adding a new immunological dimension. It was widely assumed that the incidence of tuberculosis in Europe had increased with urbanisation and industrialisation, more specifically with overcrowding, overwork, poor hygiene, intemperance and poverty. Yet in Europe at the turn of this century, as urbanisation and industrialisation continued apace, tuberculosis mortality rates were in decline. Why? There were two main explanations. First, that sanitary reform had improved urban and working environments, while industrialisation had produced higher standards of living. Second, better understanding of the causes of tuberculosis had allowed infection to be reduced and treatments to be improved. Put another way, tuberculosis may have been a 'disease of civilisation' but the answer to the problem was more not less civilisation.[17] The additional factor Cummins added was tubercularisation. He maintained that European populations were now exposed to low levels of infection in increasingly hygienic conditions. Thus from birth onwards individuals were able to build up immunity, as long as levels of infection were sufficient to evoke an immune response but not large enough to overcome immunity and produce the disease. Put another way, tubercularisation was a form of natural immunisation, where individuals had to be diseased in order to be healthy.

After Koch's announcement of the *Tubercle bacillus* in 1882, medical views on the aetiology of the disease had been divided on how much to attribute to 'seed' and how much to the 'soil'.[18] At one extreme were those, mostly in public health medicine, who focused almost exclusively on the 'seed' and wanted tuberculosis categorised as a contagious or 'catching' disease, so that it could be controlled by notification, isolation, disinfection and hygienic education. At the other pole were those, mostly clinicians, who continued to use a modified version of the older notion that the disease arose from an inherited tubercular diathesis or acquired vulnerability. The holders of such views were able to draw support from laboratory work, especially marked interspecies differences in susceptibility to tuberculosis; indeed, inoculation of suspected tubercular matter into non-immune guinea pigs was adopted as a diagnostic test. Also, clinical and epidemiological evidence had shown considerable variation in susceptibility between individuals, some of whom took the disease quickly and severely, while others remained unaffected in the same conditions. The notion of vulnerable and non-vulnerable individuals was extrapolated to families, communities, nationalities and races, and, of course, chimed with interspecies differences. However, when anti-tuberculosis campaigners discussed the aetiology of tuberculosis in the early decades of this century, any idea of inherited or racial susceptibility was considered a minor factor. The rapid fall in mortality in the previous half-century was thought to have been simply too rapid for inheritance or natural selection to have played a large part. Childhood infections might have been seen to be eliminating the 'unfit', but as tuberculosis mainly killed adults who had already had children, little hereditary advantage was accruing in the population. Besides, campaigners were very keen to counter traditional fatalism towards the disease and to emphasise that the disease was preventable and curable.

In his 1912 paper, Cummins also referred to the American literature on tuberculosis in European immigrants, in Native Americans and in African Americans. The mortality from tuberculosis in East Coast cities among different immigrant communities was a major campaigning theme of the American anti-tuberculosis movement.[19] The disease-specific mortality rate for American-born whites in the 1900s was 210 per 100,000 population, whereas that of the Irish-born was 400 per 100,000 across the country and as high as 600 in certain districts in New York and Boston. However, the group that was the focus of most comment was Polish Jews, whose tuberculosis mortality rate was only 170 per 100,000 despite living in very crowded conditions in inner-city areas.[20] Their ethnic advantage, which allowed them to escape the influences of occupation and socio-economic class, was explained by their long experience of urban living. Had evolution led to the selection of a race carrying an inheritable non-susceptibility, or was their advantage due to their dietary and hygienic practices, sobriety and healthcare systems? The priority given to hygienic measures in anti-tuberculosis propaganda makes it clear that Jewish advantage was seen to be cultural rather than racial. Nonetheless, the ways that cultural variables (such as dietary choices) supposedly worked with immunological and evolutionary mechanisms (say, by giving greater physiological strength) made the biological and social dimensions of Jewishness constitutive of each other. The Irish were, of course, the opposite of everything Jewish. They were a previously non-urban 'race' meeting the *Tubercle bacillus* for the first time, who still had a rural sanitary mentality and were intemperate and indifferent to health. Italian experience (and to a lesser extent that of Scandinavian immigrants) was similarly explained, as was the difference between Chinese and the previously urban Japanese immigrants.[21] However, notions of racial and ethnic difference could not be pushed too far – tuberculosis still killed many thousands of American-born whites every year, so any non-susceptibility was relative.

In comparative terms, the experience of Native Americans was off the scale. In 1912 their tuberculosis mortality was estimated at up to 3,000 per 100,000 population per year, nearly fifteen times the rate for American-born whites. Their 'virgin soil' status was confirmed for Cummins and others in the rapid progress and disseminated character of the disease, a pathology very similar to that common in children. However, their weakness was believed to be compounded by alcoholism, insanitary living conditions and poverty. Observers were unclear why Native American mortality rates were now so high. Why had tuberculosis not affected them earlier? Could it be changes in lifestyle rather than 'virgin soil' status that was to blame? Their fate was a tragedy that few addressed and about which those who commented felt powerless to act.

This was not the case with the group with the second highest mortality in America – 'coloreds', 'negroes' or blacks, whose fate drew increased attention during the 1900s. The average mortality of African Americans was around 500 per 100,000 population, though it was higher in cities (up to 600 per 100,000) and much lower in rural districts (300 per 100,000). The American medical community was divided, mostly on geographical and racial lines, about the causes of black disadvantage. White physicians, especially in northern cities, assumed that the mix of biological and cultural variables that was favouring white immunity had been and was still denied to African Americans. However, anti-tuberculosis campaigners were concerned about blacks as sources and spreaders of the *Tubercle bacillus*, particularly as their occupations (particularly domestic work) brought them into close contact with whites. Their migration to northern cities brought added anxiety; indeed, racial fears were a factor that made the American anti-tuberculosis movement more contagionist than its British counterpart.[22] Elements in the movement certainly used these fears to promote segregation and to confirm racial stereotypes, yet the disease among African Americans was not approached with the same resignation as that among Native Americans.

Black physicians, especially in the South, used the improving ideology of the national anti-tuberculosis movement to counter fatalism and promote practical measures. The movement's propaganda had focused on how environmental and social improvements had reduced mortality rapidly in recent decades, and how such principles could be systematically extended. This rhetoric gave powerful support to the claim that tubercular immunity was acquired and non-racial. Black physicians argued that differences in mortality levels within the white population were as great as those between races. They also pointed out that the fall in the mortality rate of whites, which only two generations ago had been as high as that among African Americans, was also claimed as a triumph of sanitary reform and was too rapid for heredity to have played any part. Indeed, the majority medical position was that the influences of poverty, poor housing, overcrowding, illiteracy and overwork were primary, a view which some extended to the view that these factors 'totally eclipse[d] any racial predisposition'.[23]

While making use of American and imperial sources to help make his case, Cummins' immediate working environment was perhaps a greater influence on his new view of 'virgin soil' non-immunities. When he delivered his 1912 paper, Cummins had been in charge of the RAMC's anti-typhoid inoculation programme for three years. This preventive measure had been controversially pioneered by Almroth Wright and Cummins was regarded as one of an influential group of military medical officers known as 'Wright's Men'.[24] In the 1900s Wright also introduced therapeutic vaccines and articulated elaborate immunological models that stressed the power of acquired immunity. These ideas were reflected in Cummins' work. In 1912 he explicitly linked 'virgin soil' populations to those who 'present to the tubercle bacillus a soil that is other than virgin', in other words, modern adult Europeans.[25]

Observations from across Europe had long shown that up to 90 per cent of adults had healed or arrested tubercular lesions, whereas less than 10 per cent ever showed clinical signs of the disease. Anti-tuberculosis campaigners used this data to argue the disease was 'curable', but for Cummins the important point was that resistance was as important as – if not more important than – infection in determining the development of tuberculosis.

Cummins speculated that in everyone exposed to the bacillus there was a struggle between *infection* and *resistance*, and that in most cases bodily resistance gained a 'victory' over bacterial infection. He supposed that this happened when levels of infection were low enough for the body to resist the bacillus and yet still have the capacity to build 'relative immunity'. How this occurred was revealed by research that showed the percentage of people with positive skin tests to tuberculin increased with age. It seemed, therefore, that low-level infection from birth onwards, as long as resistance continued its victories over infection, was actually beneficial as it enabled individuals to build up immunity. On this model, the full-blown disease only occurred when high levels of the bacilli overwhelmed the immunity that had built up, and in those individuals who, for whatever reason, had not developed effective immunity. The extreme case in the latter category were 'the children of our own race' and primitive peoples.[26] The implications of this view were profound. They suggested that each new generation across the world was 'virgin soil' and that resistance had to be built up anew in every individual and every generation. As mentioned already, he was also read as saying people had to be diseased in order to be healthy; indeed, the decline of tuberculosis in Europe posed dangers, as tubercularisation would cease to be effective.

Cummins offered three possible prescriptions for avoiding the rapid spread of tuberculosis among 'primitive' tribes. The first was to stop, by inspection and the regulation of migration, the disease reaching 'virgin soil' populations and gaining a foothold. A second was that research might produce a protective vaccine so that all the peoples of the world might be given artificial immunity rather than having to acquire natural immunity. The third (and in Cummins' view the only practical option) was that imperial powers in Africa and elsewhere should slow down the 'civilising mission' and ensure that it did not move ahead of the tubercularisation process. The ideal was to achieve conditions that would assist Nature's campaign against the disease, where people received small 'immunising dose[s]' in childhood and after, in the hygienic conditions that ensured resistance always beat infection. Such views assumed and gave naturalistic authority to social evolutionary models which suggested that Africans had childlike bodies as well as minds. It might be expected that the notion of 'virgin soil' ideas would support the idea that 'primitive people' were feminine. However, I have no evidence of the term being gendered, except implicitly in lack of toughness in male African mineworkers.[27]

Cummins was not alone in articulating such views. In 1917 another of Britain's tuberculosis experts, Louis Cobbett, published a major study on *The Causes of Tuberculosis*.[28] Cobbett had undertaken experimental work for the Royal Commission on Bovine Tuberculosis and was particularly interested in the susceptibility of different animal species and variations within a species. This approach carried over into his views on the incidence of tuberculosis in different human groups. He had no doubt that high and low resisting powers were inherited, but had found this hard to prove. However, he was also clear that the decline in tuberculosis in Britain since the early nineteenth century was too rapid for the natural selection of any inherited resistance. Like Cummins, he was more impressed with the contribution of 'another kind of racial immunisation', namely that which developed from the 'minimal immunising infections' people received in industrial and urban conditions. Some read Cobbett as suggesting that bovine tuberculosis, spread in milk, might be a form of natural immunisation similar to the way cowpox protected against smallpox. Nonetheless, he supported the dominant view that social and economic conditions had been – and still were – the major determinants of the incidence and mortality rates from the disease.

World War I and the movements of peoples it produced created a series of large epidemiological experiments. Among the most notable were the arrival of colonial troops in northern Europe and the experience of American troops of different origin in theatres across the world. The Army Surgeon, George Bushnell, reflected in 1920 on how the American experience at home, in the tropics and in Europe confirmed the theories of 'virgin soil' and tubercularisation.[29] He maintained that liability to tuberculosis was entirely due to social and economic causes, largely because effective tubercularisation depended on appropriate socio-economic conditions.[30] Given his role as the official historian of pathology, Cummins was well placed to assimilate the disease experience of colonial troops, most notably 'Cape Boys', 'Kaffirs', Indians and Chinese, into his 'virgin soil' theory.[31] He reflected on the experience in a major article in 1920, in which he stated unequivocally that '[t]he newly born infant is virgin soil to the tubercle bacillus. Like the natives of central Africa, he is completely devoid of resistance', and that '[n]o theory of inherited disposition is necessary'.[32] Cummins now incorporated into his theory the age-specific mortality of different regions within Britain. Differences in mortality levels between regions, and between towns and the countryside, had long fascinated epidemiologists and pathologists. Of particular significance were the many reports of health migrants from rural districts, who went down with tuberculosis promptly and severely in cities. In line with this, Cummins pictured the remote Shetland Islands as the nearest Britain had to a 'virgin soil' area and noted the preponderance of the 'young adult' type of tuberculosis with peak mortality between 20 and 35 years of age. He supposed that these deaths occurred among young adults who had not developed effective immunity in childhood and who then received infection for the first time when they began work or left their village. Urbanised London (the most civilised place and with most infection) showed 'normal' middle-age type, a chronic condition that waxed and waned, seemingly with immunity and infection. Cummins also saw Snowdonia in Wales as possessing near to 'virgin soil' status.

This work was valuable ammunition in the battle against those doctors and eugenists who continued to argue that an inherited vulnerability was an important factor in tubercular pathology.[33] Indeed, it was none other than Karl Pearson who first responded to Cummins' post-war work. Pearson said that his views had been misinterpreted. He was not suggesting the existence of an inherited predisposition, in the sense of a positive tendency to develop the disease, rather that the genetic factor was essentially negative, a biological absence of the ability to acquire immunity.[34] The epidemiologist, Major Greenwood, also attacked Cummins for confusing inherited and acquired resistance. Greenwood maintained that Cummins and others had assumed that 'virgin soil' populations would become tubercularised in a couple of generations, implying that acquired immunity would quickly be built into the physiology and genes of a population. Greenwood pointed out that such a phenomenon would require a Lamarckian mechanism rather than a

Darwinian one. The larger significance of this work was that notions of race, as well as mixing the cultural and the biological, also still embraced both inherited and acquired characteristics.

'Virgin soil' and after

It was Louis Cobbett who reopened the question of the balance between inherited and acquired immunity in 1925.[35] He made a distinction between the acclimatisation of an individual, which he saw as acquired immunity, and the racial immunity that was 'deeply fixed in the blood'.[36] Cobbett now interpreted epidemiological evidence from New York's different racial groups, living in similar conditions, as evidence of 'a true racial and inheritable capacity'.[37] He believed acquired individual immunity was 'superimposed' on the racial type and warned his fellow doctors not to disregard either determinant. Cobbett's views signalled a growing tendency from the mid-1920s to reassert the role of inherited racial factors in susceptibility to tuberculosis. Practically this represented no more than a change of emphasis, as the major focus in aetiological thinking and preventive schemes remained on social and cultural factors. Cobbett was impressed by new evidence from pathological anatomists which showed that tuberculosis in 'civilised races' was chronic and localised in the lungs, while in the 'primitive and dark races' it tended to be acute and generalised.[38] These differences had been reported during World War I and were confirmed by reports throughout the 1920s.[39] Among the most influential post-mortem studies were those performed in the British colony of Jamaica by Eugene Opie, a leading American tuberculosis specialist. These emerged from the interest of American eugenists in racial mixing in the colony.[40] The studies were backed up by more extensive surveys of autopsies in the United States, the majority of which showed that tuberculosis in black Americans tended to affect the lymph nodes and was more generalised than among whites.[41] It also seemed the lungs of blacks lacked the specific ability to produce the fibrous tissue necessary for localising the disease.[42] This evidence was interpreted as suggesting that it was not just the immune system that determined responses to tuberculosis, there were other, perhaps deeper, differences that were set in the structure of organs and tissues.

From the mid-1920s Lyle Cummins also began to argue that there was an inherited racial element in immunity to tuberculosis and that African natives were not the exact equivalent of European infants. He told the Annual Conference of the NAPT in 1928 that this racial factor depended on 'not an inherited resistance or an inherited susceptibility, but *on an inherited faculty to develop resistance when brought into contact with infection*' (italics as original).[43] Cummins' change of mind coincided with his involvement with the Tuberculosis Research Committee (TRC) in South Africa and the three visits he made to Africa after 1926. The TRC, supported by the South African Government and mining companies, was charged with determining the causes of the high mortality rates among black migrant workers in the gold mines of the Rand. The patterns of incidence were complex and did not seem to fit any simple 'virgin soil' hypothesis. In particular the high number of deaths in the very early months of employment suggested many migrant workers already had the disease when they arrived and that mine conditions merely 'reawakened' or accelerated prior infections. The waters were further muddied by migration itself, as sick miners returned home and 'recuperated' in what were said to be the sanatorium-like conditions of African villages. Once they were well again, these men returned to the mines, but as disease-carriers with latent infections, hence not only did the disease reappear quickly in a more intense form, it spread more readily to other workers.

Cummins now began to reflect that perhaps the historical moment of 'virgin soil' had passed. In his South African work he began to differentiate types of primitive community; especially between those few tribes who remained true 'virgin soil' and the great majority of humankind who had now been exposed to the *Tubercle bacillus* from travellers and migration for decades, if not centuries.[44] He began to argue (largely from pathological and epidemiological evidence) that Africans and other 'primitives' who had been exposed to the *Tubercle bacillus* did not show the same immune response as European children or adults. African responses to infection were said to be 'slighter and transitory', and this was taken to follow from their 'imperfect individual and racial adaptation to the tubercle bacillus'.[45] Cummins' views on acquired and now inherited immunity in tuberculosis were not uncontroversial. Many doctors thought that he relied on a false analogy with acute infectious diseases, like scarlet fever and smallpox, where permanent antibody protection was established after one attack.[46] There was no laboratory evidence of this, in large part because the methods which had supported such claims before 1914 had been discredited along with Wright's vaccine therapy. However, his changed views may have owed something to the pressure from the synthesisers of Darwinian natural selection and Mendelian genetics to be more rigorous in distinguishing inherited and acquired characteristics.

Cummins set out his new position in an article entitled ' "Virgin Soil" – and After' in July 1929.[47] He still maintained that '[a]ll of us were once virgin soil to the tubercle bacillus', but said that the crucial factor in developing immunity was the extent to which the small infections were successfully localised and arrested. 'Localisation' and 'arrest' were now said to be different things: 'arrest' meant there were no longer any germs present, whereas 'localisation' meant merely that infection had been halted and possibly remained latent. Hence a positive tuberculin test could no longer be read as indicating resistance, it might simply be an allergic reaction to a localised but unarrested infection. Cummins developed a new metaphor, suggesting that localised lesions were 'larval', in the sense of being dormant but ready to burst into action again. Larval lesions were also said to be unstable, liable to break down and erupt if the person became physiologically or perhaps emotionally stressed.

As with his earlier work he linked these views to the immunology of peoples in civilised societies. He suggested that larval lesions could be developed by European children and might explain typical adolescent disease, which was often sudden and intense. Nonetheless, he was confident that most people in Europe would develop what he called fully 'compensated' lesions, that were both arrested and gave effective immunity. All this led Cummins to argue that adult migrant African workers were no longer childlike in their immune status. A better parallel might be that they were like other animal species who lacked 'immunity potential'.[48] In 1930 he said that '[h]e found himself increasingly sympathetic to the view that there existed differences in racial susceptibility. After some generations of intense endemicity, no appreciable evidence of increased resistance was found in some races'.[49] Critics suggested that such views helped excuse the mining companies of any responsibility for the incidence of tuberculosis among their workers, as not only did they bring the disease on themselves, the high death-toll was because of their racial susceptibility. In this context, it is interesting that to my knowledge Cummins never offered a racial account of tuberculosis in Wales, though there was potential in purported differences between the purer Celts in the north and the mixed-race south.[50]

Following the publication of the South African Tuberculosis Report published in 1932, Cummins continued to elaborate his new racial ideas in immunological terms, increasingly utilising the work of American authorities such as Arnold Rich.[51] Soon he suggested that African migrant workers represented a newly discovered phenomenon in tuberculo-allergy – 'hyper-allergic soil' – exploiting new ideas on the relationship between allergy and immunity.[52] His explanation of this state relied on socio-cultural conditions (migration, poverty and dust pollution) shaping the development of both acquired and inherited immunity. All this was spelt out in his speculation about the development of so-called 'primitive tuberculosis' in the 'homelands' of the mineworkers. Their larval lesions signalled that their immune systems had only produced a weak allergic reaction, not a strong immune response. While this phenomenon was commonest in Africans, it was also found in Europeans, which made positive tuberculin skin tests more difficult to read. The weak physiological responses led Cummins to conclude that 'many generations might be necessary for the acquisition of enhanced powers of developing resistance by African natives'. He drew support from new British and American studies on pathological and tissue differences between blacks and whites that were said to point to 'a true genotypic difference between the two races'.[53] In Britain such views were championed as an alternative to 'virgin soil' theory by H. Harold Scott, who was consultant pathologist at London Zoo.[54] Scott developed his views after working in the West Indies and Far East, and observed with regard to the United States that, after hundreds of years in another continent, African Americans still remained more susceptible to tuberculosis than whites.[55] By 1935 Cummins was writing that 'native races' lacked 'toughness' and would only develop resistance to infection on a historical timescale.[56]

Without a figure like Cummins to disseminate information and connect with metropolitan discourses, the experience of the disease in the rest of the Empire did not have the same impact in Britain as African studies. However, this may also have been because pathology and policy in these countries was developing on different lines. Turbot's influential 1935 study of tuberculosis among the Maoris of Waiapu County emphasised social factors, especially poverty and changes in lifestyle, although this had to be set against the wider perception of Maoris as an exhausted race.[57] In Australia 'virgin soil' ideas still prevailed, largely because the disease in Aborigines was only encountered in towns and cities, and because of their presumed vulnerability on abandoning open-air lifestyles.[58] By the 1930s, many cities in India had limited tuberculosis services, including sanatoria and dispensaries, and ran anti-tuberculosis health campaigns, all of which stressed how the disease could be prevented by behavioural changes. Race was seen to be one factor, but as Indian groupings were also linked with social class, cultural and religious mores, geography and climate, it was rarely singled out for special comment.

While tuberculosis specialists on the Britain–Africa–America triangle were referring increasingly to inherited racial differences, they still regarded environmental factors as more potent determinants of morbidity and mortality.[59] Also, environmental improvements and behavioural changes were the only available preventive policy options.[60] Questions of policy, rather than speculative pathology and immunology, became important in British colonial territories in the 1930s as the growing incidence of tuberculosis was recognised. The problem was first noticed in mines, towns, jails, prisons and factories, where it threatened expatriates, but began to be addressed more widely after 1930. It was a particular problem in the context of the new policy of 'trusteeship', for – while tropical diseases could be blamed on climate and environment – tuberculosis was a disease that the British had seemingly brought with them and then helped spread by encouraging urbanisation and other social changes. By the 1930s the rising toll became an example of colonial development and welfare working against each other. If so, what type of development was appropriate for Africa? As far as tuberculosis was concerned, Western people had evolved into 'an immune civilisation', but the conditions that had produced this would be 'unsuitable for a susceptible race' and, if introduced quickly into Africa, would perhaps be its death warrant.[61] Some worried that black Africans might suffer the same fate as Native Americans, while others returned to Cummins' ideas about slowing development and changing its direction to allow for effective tubercularisation. One part of this would be to spare Africans the dangers of urbanisation and to ensure as far as possible the maintenance of their sanatorium-like lifestyle: outdoor living, wearing few clothes to give high exposure to disinfecting sunlight, plus rest or steady exercise. In this context it is interesting to speculate about the extent to which the creation of 'townships' in Africa was first encouraged on health grounds.[62]

By the late 1940s, the 'fact' (from pathology if not immunology) that there were degrees of inborn racial resistance was incorporated into the major tuberculosis textbooks.[63] This point was always included in sections on resistance and linked to variations among individuals, species and, of course, age-groups.[64] Indeed, the refutation of the 'virgin soil' theory was cited as the best evidence for racial resistance. However, doubts about the importance of any racial factor began to emerge from within medicine and from outside. There were scientists who denied that 'races' had any biological reality, especially when skin colour was the main criterion in determining 'race'.[65] In 1948, the famous Australian immunologist, Macfarlane Burnet, wrote of racially based hyper-susceptibility of Maoris and Aborigines, but saw this as a historical phenomenon that had been already lost in the very few generations since the arrival of Europeans.[66]

The wider political scene also mitigated against stressing racial susceptibilities. Nazi racial policies and the manner in which medical practitioners had been a party to some of the worst atrocities made doctors wary of anything that might appear eugenic. Besides, the idea of a genetic factor that might take many generations to mitigate did not fit with the temper of the times. The introduction of streptomycin and then combined antibiotic therapy gave anti-tuberculosis programmes new impetus and optimism. The control of tuberculosis was one of the earliest priorities of the World Health Organisation. The head of its Tuberculosis Section told the Annual Conference of the NAPT in 1952 that the incidence of the disease was due to malnutrition, housing, poverty, spitting and the presence of other debilitating diseases. He went on to state there was 'no convincing evidence that susceptibility to tuberculosis, or the course of tuberculosis, is dependent on the degree of pigmentation of the skin or any other racial factor'.[67] The whole tenor of post-war aid and development initiatives was about what could be done with modern science and technology, not about impediments to progress. At the same time, in newly independent countries such as India and colonies with growing nationalist movements, anti-tuberculosis campaigns took on a new symbolism as righting the wrongs of imperialism, one of which had been the importation of tuberculosis and creation of the conditions in which it could flourish.

Conclusion

One of the increasing number of colonial medical officers working on tuberculosis in Africa in the 1930s was Charles Wilcocks, who eventually became a distinguished metropolitan expert on tropical diseases, editing a later edition of Manson's *Tropical Diseases*. In his Heath Clark Lectures in 1960, he reminisced about tuberculosis in Africa in the 1930s and 1940s, saying that '[t]he racial theory ... and the virgin soil theory, though commonly held and expressed, were not seriously entertained by research workers without reference to environmental factors'.[68] Indeed, I would go further and say that environmental factors were always primary in policy and practical measures. However, this should not divert us from the conclusion that 'virgin soil' and racial theories of tuberculosis were influential both in Britain and its empire. They were an integral part of the developing understanding of the epidemiology, pathology and immunology of the disease; indeed, it is revealing the extent to which immunological ideas depended on comparative epidemiology and old-style pathological anatomy rather than laboratory studies. The rise and fall of both 'virgin soil' and racial theories has been shown to be shaped by many factors. Among the most decisive were ways in which changes in the recorded patterns of the disease were used to construct histories of the disease, despite the known unreliability of the data for comparative purposes. Similar uncertainties pervaded the production and use of pathological evidence, not least the changing significance of tuberculin skin tests. However, to complain about the unreliable categories and the misuse of evidence would be to miss the point: what mattered was the use of the data to construct or deconstruct categories. Before World War I the 'virgin soil' theory was developed not only to make sense of the experience of disease in colonial medicine, but also as a resource in the debates about eugenics and immune theories. Between the wars the racial theory of tuberculosis went against the wider trend in the biological sciences to question the validity of 'race' as a scientific category.[69] However, those working on tuberculosis began to distinguish inherited and acquired characteristics in novel ways. For example, pathologists suggested that differences in the response of tissues to disease revealed genetic differences, whereas those found in immune systems did not. The latter was seen as interacting with the external world and to be more labile, whereas tissues were internal and fixed. Whatever their role in medicine, both theories sustained notions of racial difference, albeit on different and shifting ground.

In 'virgin soil' theory non-Europeans were childlike, a view which not only resonated with wider racial stereotypes, but carried implications for colonial development. Cummins assumed that all societies would follow the path of Western civilisation but argued that colonial development would require a historical timescale and have to be carefully planned and monitored. The implications doctors drew from the racial theory were that colonial development could only occur on an evolutionary timescale, or would have to follow new trajectories adapted for peoples who had particular constitutional weaknesses. In the 1930s, such notions were easily reconciled with the policy of complementary development which was originally designed to support British industry and end colonial indebtedness. The policy proposed that colonial societies would remain non-urban primary producers of agricultural goods and raw materials that would be exchanged for British products. However, any hope that what might be good for the British economy would also benefit the health of colonial peoples was exploded in the recession of the 1930s. Falling commodity prices and other problems damaged colonial economies and the fall in standards of living was seen to produce a rapid deterioration in the health of colonial peoples. Whatever immunities and non-immunities different peoples possessed, these were seen as insignificant in the face of the scale of the health problems that emerged in colonies and former colonies, and the new political imperative to meet these problems.

Notes

1 F.B. Smith, *The Retreat of Tuberculosis*, London, Croom Helm, 1988; L. Bryder, *Below the Magic Mountain*, Oxford, Oxford University Press, 1988.

2 M. Teller, *The Tuberculosis Movement: A Public Health Campaign in the Progressive Era*, Westport, Greenwood Press, 1988; B. Bates, *Bargaining for Life: A Social History of Tuberculosis, 1876–1938*, Philadelphia, University of Pennsylvania Press, 1992; K. Ott, *Fevered Lives: Tuberculosis in American Culture*, Cambridge, MA, Harvard University Press, 1997; R. and J. Dubos, *The White Plague: Tuberculosis, Man and Society*, 1952, repr. New Brunswick, Rutgers University Press, 1987, pp. 190–5.

3 P. Weindling, *Health, Race and German Politics between National Unification and Nazism, 1870–1945*, Cambridge, Cambridge University Press, 1989.

4 J. Farley, *Bilharzia: A History of Imperial Tropical Medicine*, Cambridge, Cambridge University Press, 1991.
5 M. Harrison and M. Worboys, '"A Disease of Civilisation": Tuberculosis in Africa and India', in L. Marks and M. Worboys (eds), *Migrants, Minorities and Health: Historical and Contemporary Studies*, London, Routledge, 1997, pp. 93–124.
6 J.B. Huber, *Consumption: Its Relation to Man and His Civilisation: Its Prevention and Cure*, Philadelphia, Lippincott, *c.*1906, p. 69.
7 W. Anderson, 'Immunities of Empire: Race, Disease and the New Tropical Medicine', *Bulletin of the History of Medicine* 70 (1996): 94–118.
8 P.J. Bowler, *The Non-Darwinian Revolution*, Baltimore, Johns Hopkins University Press, 1988.
9 S.L. Cummins, *Primitive Tuberculosis*, London, John Bale Medical Publications, 1939.
10 *British Medical Journal* i (1949): 1,054; *Lancet* i (1949): 983–4.
11 NAPT, Meeting of the Council, 1 June 1945. Minute Books held at Stroke Association, London. The NAPT had written to the Colonial Office as early as January 1945 offering 'to devote increased attention and resources to the Colonies and Dependencies'.
12 NAPT Pamphlet, 'A New Empire and Colonial Vista', London, October 1945; S.L. Cummins, *Empire and Colonial Tuberculosis*, London, NAPT, 1945.
13 S.L. Cummins, 'Tuberculosis in the Egyptian Army', *British Journal of Tuberculosis* 2 (1908): 35–46.
14 F. Smith, 'Tuberculosis Amongst Civilised Africans: Special Prevalence and Fatality', *Journal of Tropical Medicine and Hygiene* 7 (1905): 88.
15 C.A. Johnston, 'Tuberculosis in the Indian Army: Its Incidence as Affected by Locality, Racial Proclivity and Service Generally', *British Journal of Tuberculosis* 2 (1908): 20–34.
16 S.L. Cummins, 'Primitive Tribes and Tuberculosis', *Transactions of the Society of Tropical Medicine and Hygiene* 5 (1912): 245–55.
17 Robert Philip wrote in 1902 that tuberculosis was 'a vicious by-product of an incomplete and ill-formed civilisation', *British Medical Journal* i (1902): 873.
18 G. Feldberg, *Disease and Class: Tuberculosis and the Shaping of Modern North American Society*, New Brunswick, Rutgers University Press, 1995.
19 A.M. Kraut, *Silent Travellers: Germs, Genes and the 'Immigrant Menace'*, New York, Basic Books, 1994.
20 F.P. McCarthy, 'The Influence of Race in the Prevalence of Tuberculosis', *Boston Medical and Surgical Journal* 166 (1912): 207–11.
21 Kraut, 'Southern Italian Immigration to the United States at the Turn of the Century and the Perennial Problem of Medicalised Prejudice', in Marks and Worboys, *Migrants*, pp. 228–49.
22 M.M. Torchia, 'The Tuberculosis Movement and the Race Question, 1890–1950', *Bulletin of the History of Medicine* 49 (1975): 152–68.
23 T.J. Jones, 'Tuberculosis Amongst the Negroes', *American Journal of Medical Science* 132 (1906): 598.

24 Z. Cope, *Almroth Wright: Founder of Modern Vaccine Therapy*, London, Nelson, 1966, p. 7.
25 Cummins, 'Primitive Tribes', p. 249.
26 Cummins, 'Primitive Tribes', p. 255.
27 R.M. Packard, *White Plague, Black Labor*, Pietermaritzburg, University of Natal Press, 1989, *passim*.
28 L. Cobbett, *The Causes of Tuberculosis*, Cambridge, Cambridge University Press, 1917.
29 G.E. Bushnell, *A Study in the Epidemiology of Tuberculosis – With Especial Reference to Tuberculosis in the Tropics and of the Negro Race*, London, John Bale, Sons & Danielsson, 1920.
30 For Maurice Fishberg, a leading American expert, the clinching evidence was the primacy of social and economic factors in mixed-race communities; see M. Fishberg, *Pulmonary Tuberculosis*, Philadelphia, Lea & Febiger, 1919, pp. 69, 154. In 1922, a report in the *British Medical Journal* stated that 'heredity in tuberculosis had been practically dismissed'. This referred to direct hereditary causation not predisposition; see *British Medical Journal* ii (1922): 208.
31 Table of morbidity and mortality from tuberculosis of different troops (1914–19), showing the different rates of sickness and death among the different forces:

Source of troops	*Cases per 100,000*	*Deaths per 100,000*
British and dominions troops	60	4
Chinese Native Labour Corps	364	134
Indian troops	934	173
Indian Native Labour Corps	1420	534
South African Native Labour Corps	2906	2219
Cape Colony Native Labour Corps	4441	1036

Source: S.L. Cummins, *Medical History of the War: Pathology*, London, HMSO, 1923, p. 480.

32 S.L. Cummins, 'Tuberculosis in Primitive Tribes and Its Bearing on the Tuberculosis of Civilised Communities', *International Journal of Public Health* 1 (1920): 158.
33 K. Pearson, *The Fight Against Tuberculosis and the Death Rate from Phthisis*, London, Dulau & Co., 1911; Pearson, *Tuberculosis, Heredity and Environment*, London: Dulau & Co., 1912; W. Weinberg, *Die Kinder der Tuberkulösen*, Leipzig, S. Hirzel, 1913; R. Pearl, *Studies in Human Biology*, Baltimore, Williams & Wilkins, 1924, chap. 10; Pearl, 'On the Incidence of Tuberculosis in the Offspring of Tuberculous Parents', *Zeitschrift für Rassenkunde* 3 (1936): 301–7.

34 See the discussion in D.S. Davies, 'An Enemy of the People – Tuberculosis and Natural Selection', *Bristol Medico-Chirurgical Journal* 30 (1912): 135–41.
35 S.L. Cobbett, 'The Resistance of Civilised Man to Tuberculosis: Is it Racial or Individual in Origin?', *Tubercle* 6 (1925): 577–90.
36 Cobbett, 'The Resistance of Civilised Man to Tuberculosis', p. 590.
37 Cobbett, 'The Resistance of Civilised Man to Tuberculosis', p. 589.
38 S.L. Cummins, 'Laboratory Research on Clinical Conceptions of Tuberculosis', *British Medical Journal* i (1927): 762.
39 A. Borrel, 'Pneumonie et Tuberculose des Noirs', *Annals de l'Institut Pasteur* 34 (1920): 105; H.C. Clark, 'Observations on Tropical Pathology', *American Journal of Tropical Diseases and Preventive Medicine* 3 (1915): 331.
40 E. Opie and E.J. Isaacs, 'Tuberculosis in Jamaica', *American Journal of Hygiene* 12 (1930): 1; C.B. Davenport and M. Steggerda, *Race Crossing in Jamaica*, Washington, Carnegie Institution of Washington, 1929.
41 A. Krause, 'Immunity and Allergy in the Pathogenesis of Tuberculosis', *Tubercle* 10 (1928): 256.
42 M. Pinner and J.A. Kasper, 'Pathological Peculiarities of Tuberculosis in the American Negro', *American Review of Tuberculosis* 24 (1932): 463; F.R. Everett, 'The Pathological Anatomy of Pulmonary Tuberculosis in the American Negro and in the White Race', *American Review of Tuberculosis* 27 (1933): 411.
43 S.L. Cummins, 'Tuberculosis Among the Indians of the Great Plains of Canada', *Annual Report of the NAPT*, London, NAPT, 1928, p. 92.
44 *Bulletin of Hygiene* 3 (1928): 314; 4 (1929): 582.
45 *Bulletin of Hygiene* 4 (1929): 311, 317.
46 *Lancet* i (1933): 315.
47 S.L. Cummins, ' "Virgin Soil – and After": A Working Conception of Tuberculosis in Children, Adolescents and Aborigines', *British Medical Journal* ii (1929): 39–41.
48 Cummins, 'Primitive Races and Epidemiology', *British Medical Journal* ii (1930): 529–30.
49 Cummins, 'Primitive Races and Epidemiology', p. 529.
50 S.L. Cummins, 'Tuberculosis in Wales', *British Medical Journal* i (1922): 340.
51 A.R. Rich, *The Pathogenesis of Tuberculosis*, Springfield, C.C. Thomas, 1944.
52 S.L. Cummins, 'Tuberculosis and the South African Native', *Lancet* i (1933): 251–2, also see p. 100.
53 L.S.T. Burrell, 'Reinfection in Tuberculosis', *Tubercle* 16 (1934): 150.
54 H.H. Scott, 'Tuberculosis in Man in the Tropics', *Proceedings of the Royal Society of Medicine* 28 (1935): 134–40.
55 E.R. Long, 'Present Concepts in Tuberculous Infection and Disease', *Tubercle* 17 (1935–6): 170. Long admitted that he was calling attention to factors 'less stressed in recent years than environment, … namely constitution and heredity'.

56 S.L. Cummins, 'Studies of Tuberculosis Among African Natives: General Introduction', *Tubercle* supplement (1935): 13; C. Wilcocks, *Tuberculosis in Tanganyika*, Dar-es-Salaam, printed privately, 1938.
57 A. Wells, 'Tuberculosis in New Zealand', in A.J. Proust (ed.), *The History of Tuberculosis in Australia, New Zealand and Papua New Guinea*, Canberra, Brolga Press, 1991, pp. 97–102.
58 N. Thomson, 'Tuberculosis Among Aborigines', in Proust, *The History of Tuberculosis*, pp. 61–78.
59 P.P. McCain, 'Tuberculosis Among Negroes in the United States', *American Review of Tuberculosis* 35 (1937): 25–35.
60 R.C. Wingfield, *A Textbook of Pulmonary Tuberculosis for Students*, London, Constable, 1929, pp. 47–54.
61 J.A. Young, 'Tuberculosis and the Development of the Native African', *West African Medical Journal* 7 (1934): 128–32.
62 Op. cit.; Young writes of the health virtues of townships.
63 G.G. Kayne, W. Pagel and L. O'Shaughnessy, *Pulmonary Tuberculosis*, Oxford, Oxford University Press, 1939, p. 59.
64 F. Heaf and N.L. Rusby, *Recent Advances in Respiratory Tuberculosis*, London, J. & A. Churchill, 1948, pp. 19–21.
65 H.M. Payne, 'The Problem of Tuberculosis Control Among American Negroes', *American Review of Tuberculosis* 60 (1949): 332–42.
66 F.M. Burnet, 'The Natural History of Tuberculosis', *Medical Journal of Australia* 1 (1948): 57.
67 J. Holm, *NAPT Annual Conference*, London, NAPT, 1952.
68 C. Wilcocks, *Aspects of Medical Investigation in Africa*, London, Oxford University Press, 1962. See also Wilcocks, *A Tropical Doctor in Africa and London: An Autobiography*, Leatherhead, Surrey, published privately, 1977.
69 E. Barkan, *The Retreat of Scientific Racism*, New York, Cambridge University Press, 1992.

Chapter 8

Changing depictions of disease

Race, representation and the history of 'mongolism'

Mark Jackson

Historically, descriptions of people with what has variably been referred to as mental deficiency, mental handicap or learning difficulties have been heavily laced with racial imagery.[1] In the late nineteenth and early twentieth centuries, for example, when mental deficiency initially became seen as a pressing social problem, racial metaphors and analogies were routinely employed to capture the pathological and deviant nature of defectives. In the same way that different races were construed by many anthropologists as having degenerated from the Caucasian pinnacle, mental defectives were frequently portrayed as the primitive products of a process of atavistic degeneration from a mental and physical norm.[2] As the perpetrators of crime, the receptacles of disease and the propagators of mental and physical weaknesses, such degenerates were portrayed not only as the root cause of many social problems but also as an unremitting menace to the future health and wealth of the nation – as an explicit threat to the pursuit of racial purity and pre-eminence.[3]

In this climate, a variety of social reformers (many of whom were doctors) pressed for measures to reverse the 'racial damage'[4] that was being effected by the uncontrolled propagation of mental defectives. As Robert Rentoul made clear in his book, *Race Culture; Or, Race Suicide?*, published in 1906, the consequences of failing to implement appropriate measures (such as sterilisation, segregation, birth control or marriage regulation) were immense – in short the inevitable destruction of healthy national stock and the collapse of racial supremacy.[5]

Racial metaphors also defined the form of institutional provisions established for mental defectives. In a manner akin to efforts to tame the savage 'other' by imperialistic measures imposed on the colonies, the minds and bodies of the idiotic, the imbecilic and the feeble-minded were also to be subdued and domesticated in the safe, segregated environment of purpose-built 'colonies' for defectives. As a result of this geographical isolation and marginalisation, mental defectives became literally, as well as metaphorically, a race apart.[6]

The relationship between representations of defectives and images of racial difference and racial danger was not straightforward. Doctors involved in classifying defectives and in capturing the distinctive degenerate pathologies that were thought to set defectives apart from the normal population around the turn of this century certainly borrowed contemporary understandings of racial difference from other disciplines, especially from physical and criminal anthropology.[7] However, the transfer of knowledge was not a one-way process. The subsequent categories of pathology developed by doctors not only reinforced stereotypes of racial inferiority but were also employed as evidence in continuing debates about racial unity and the aetiology of racial difference. Thus representations of mental defectives were not only drawn *from* but more importantly were drawn *into* contemporary debates about racial inferiority.

There is a particularly striking example of the ways in which understandings of race and representations of mental deficiency became closely connected in the last half of the nineteenth and the first half of the twentieth century, and that is in the identification and depiction of what is now most commonly referred to as Down's syndrome. The syndrome was first identified as 'mongolism' by John Langdon Down in 1866 as part of his attempt to develop a broad 'ethnic classification' of idiots and imbeciles.[8] Since Down's initial description, medical accounts of the syndrome have consistently addressed not only clinical issues of classification, prognosis and treatment, but also the racial connotations implicit in Down's original account.

In this chapter I want to explore changing depictions of people with Down's syndrome from a particular perspective. I do not propose to provide a comprehensive medical history of the syndrome. Lilian Zihni's excellent doctoral thesis offers an extensive survey of the various ideas about and treatments of the syndrome on both sides of the Atlantic since Langdon Down's original classification.[9] Instead I want to exploit a variety of published and unpublished textual and photographic sources to examine in depth a number of related facets of the history of 'mongolism' that have not been addressed fully in previous historical accounts.[10] In the first instance this chapter will explore the manner in which understandings of racial difference were incorporated into depictions of mental deficiency, but more particularly it will examine the ways in which those understandings influenced the visualisation of people with Down's syndrome. This chapter will also explore the corresponding impact of medical knowledge on debates about racial unity and about the origins and biological basis of racial difference. In addition it will assess the extent to which changing scientific constructions of the aetiology and pathology of mental deficiency, and changing sensitivities to the language of racial difference and deficiency, encouraged transformations in visual representations in medical texts of people identified as having Down's syndrome.

The first section of the chapter explores the roots and essence of Langdon Down's ethnic classification of idiots and, in particular, the form and content of his depiction of 'mongolian idiots'. The second section traces the contours of late nineteenth- and early twentieth-century medical representations of 'mongolism' in the light of more sophisticated explanations of aetiology, more detailed clinical and post-mortem examinations of the bodies of 'mongols', and the increasing use of photographs to visualise the anatomical features of deficiency. I shall argue that in spite of widespread objections to the superficiality of Down's ethnic analogies, the racial assumptions inherent in his work persisted in many medical discussions. The final section charts the emergence in the middle decades of this century of what appears to be a major transformation in the medical understanding of Down's syndrome (that is, as a chromosomal abnormality) and examines the implications of this new understanding both in generating novel medical depictions of the syndrome and as provoking vigorous debates about the racial implications of nomenclature.

Langdon Down's ethnic classification of idiots

In 1862, John Langdon H. Down, physician to the Asylum for Idiots at Earlswood, published a preliminary report of his investigations into the 'structure and function of the various organs' in idiots and imbeciles. The investigation had been motivated both by Down's 'conviction of the importance of a study of the physiological manifestations of idiocy' and by his hopes of dividing the residents at Earlswood into 'natural groups, by simple reference to their physical state'. His 1862 paper focused exclusively on the various conditions of the mouth in idiocy and, having described the significance of anomalies of the palate, teeth, tongue, tonsils, mucous membranes and flow of saliva, Down concluded not only that anomalies of the mouth could be used in the diagnosis of idiocy but also that 'the psychical condition of these unfortunates should be specially sought to be ameliorated by an improvement in their physical condition'.[11]

Buried in the heart of Down's short report is a significant reference to a particular group of patients with apparently shared features:

> In 16 cases the tongue presented a soddened appearance, and exhibited deep transverse furrows on its dorsal surface; in all these patients one is able to trace a marked physiological and psychological agreement, and so much do they resemble one another in these respects that they might readily be taken for members of the same family.[12]

Four years later, it was this 'family' of patients that provided the cornerstone of Down's attempt to classify idiots on the basis of their resemblance to particular ethnic groups. In his 'Observations on an Ethnic Classification of Idiots' (published in 1866) Down suggested that by 'arranging them [idiots] around various ethnic standards', asylum doctors could develop a 'natural system' of classification that would facilitate diagnosis, treatment and prognosis. Although he noted that many Caucasian asylum residents and out-patients resembled members of the Ethiopian, Malay and American families or races, the focus of his attention was particularly directed to the superficial facial features and behavioural attributes of those idiots that he referred to as 'typical Mongols'.[13]

In the absence of photographs[14] Down offered a detailed verbal description of the characteristic physical appearance of his 'mongolian idiots':

> The face is flat and broad, and destitute of prominence. The cheeks are roundish, and extended laterally. The eyes are obliquely placed, and the internal canthi more than normally distant from one another. The palpebral fissure is very narrow.

> The forehead is wrinkled transversely from the constant assistance which the levatores palpebrarum derive from the occipitofrontalis muscle in the opening of the eyes. The lips are large and thick with transverse fissures. The tongue is long, thick, and is much roughened. The nose is small. The skin has a slight dirty yellowish tinge, and is deficient in elasticity, giving the appearance of being too large for the body.[15]

Down also paid careful attention to the 'typical' behavioural attributes of 'mongolian idiots', recounting their apparent powers of imitation, their 'lively sense of the ridiculous', their indistinct speech and their abnormal coordination.[16] Although he recognised slight differences between his 'mongolian idiots' and 'real Mongols', Down nevertheless regarded the similarities between the two as unmistakable and considered the combined physical and mental features that he described as pathognomonic of a distinct and prevalent class or type of idiocy. 'A very large number of congenital idiots', Down wrote, 'are Mongols. So marked is this, that when placed side by side, it is difficult to believe that the specimens compared are not children of the same parents.'[17]

In Down's opinion the 'ethnic features' of 'mongolian idiots' were largely the result 'of degeneracy arising from tuberculosis in the parents'. Such speculation about cause was not merely of practical clinical importance. As Down emphasised, it also held broader philosophical implications. According to Down the existence of Caucasian defectives with the physical and behavioural attributes of Mongols offered substantial evidence to refute polygenist beliefs that the 'great racial divisions are fixed and definite'. 'These examples of the result of degeneracy among mankind,' he concluded, 'appear to me to furnish some arguments in favour of the unity of the human species.' Importantly for Down the various races were 'merely varieties of the human family having a common origin' and any differences between races were to be regarded as 'not specific but variable'.[18]

In many ways Down's detailed formulation of 'mongolian idiocy' was unremarkable. His belief in degeneration as an explanation for human differences, his ethnic classification in general and his creation of the 'mongol type' of idiot in particular, clearly borrowed from a number of contemporary understandings and stereotypes of both mental deficiency and racial difference. From the middle decades of the nineteenth century, alienists were attempting to capture the physiognomical features of insanity and mental deficiency, either in extensive verbal accounts or, increasingly, in line drawings and photographs. Attempts to visualise mental instability in this way were predicated on a belief that there were strong correlations between the mental and the physical manifestations of insanity and idiocy.[19]

The construction of close associations between appearance and mental ability was supported by parallel and influential developments in physical and criminal anthropology, according to which distinct physical attributes were to be read as signs of particular constitutional tendencies, and physical and mental differences were seen as the product of degeneration.[20] Depictions of idiots and imbeciles as the primitive products of degenerative processes also derived from comparative anthropological studies of race. As Zihni and others have clearly argued, Down's vision of the 'mongolian idiot' as racially degenerate drew strongly on monogenist explanations for the origins of racial difference and should be understood in the light of contemporary debates about racial inferiority and, in particular, slavery.[21]

Significantly Down's representation of certain idiots as examples of racial degeneration did not constitute a passive incorporation of anthropological theories into a system of medical classification. Down's arguments in their turn clearly reinforced (as well as reflected) broad assumptions about both the superficial physical appearance, and the intellectual and behavioural attributes of members of the Mongolian race.[22] Furthermore, as will become apparent later in this chapter, Down's explicit use of his observations and classification of idiots to support a particular philosophy of racial difference was emulated by later medical authors who sought to exploit changing scientific and clinical accounts of 'mongolism' to substantiate particular theories of race. In this way medical constructions of idiocy were not merely derived from debates about racial inferiority and the origins of racial difference but were also a principal ingredient of those debates.

Early responses to Down's ethnic classification of idiots

Langdon Down was not the only late nineteenth-century medical practitioner to draw distinct parallels between the appearance and behaviour of certain people identified as mentally deficient and those of particular racial groups. In 1876 John Fraser and Arthur Mitchell published clinical details with autopsy findings from a number of cases of what they referred to as 'Kalmuc idiocy'.[23] Their detailed description of the facial features of a 'Kalmuc idiot' (so called because of supposed similarities to the appearance of people from the region of the Caspian Sea) was accompanied by lithographic illustrations of appearance, anatomical anomalies and brain configuration, and rehearsed many of the features recounted by Down ten years earlier. In spite of certain objections to Fraser's use of the term,[24] 'Kalmuc idiocy' persisted. In the last two decades of the nineteenth century 'mongolism' and 'Kalmuc idiocy' were subsequently recognised by both George Shuttleworth, Medical Superintendent of the Royal Albert Asylum in Lancaster, and George Sutherland, physician to the Children's Hospital at Paddington Green, to constitute the same degenerate condition.[25]

The stereotypical ethnological bias adopted by Down and by Fraser and Mitchell was strongly reinforced in these late nineteenth-century studies by Shuttleworth and Sutherland. In 1886 Shuttleworth recounted the supposedly typical facial features and behavioural characteristics of the 'Mongol' or 'Kalmuc' type of idiot, emphasising (as Down had done) 'a certain family resemblance' shared by all 'mongolian idiots' even though they came 'from widely distant parts of our district'.[26] Although Shuttleworth acknowledged the prevalence of tuberculosis in this group of idiots, he believed the cause of the condition to be 'a defect of formative force' resulting in the production of 'unfinished children'.[27]

According to Sutherland, the arrested development of the brain in 'mongolian imbecility' was more likely to be caused by syphilis than tuberculosis and he took greater pains than previous authors to differentiate the condition from 'cretinism', with which 'mongolian imbecility' had sometimes been confused.[28] However Sutherland also emphasised the particular constellation of mental and physical characteristics that not only set 'mongolian imbeciles' apart from other infants but also served to group them together, like members of the same race, as 'members of the same family'.[29] Although Sutherland recognised that Down's 'classification of idiots on an ethnological basis' had not been generally accepted, he acknowledged that the particular term 'mongolian' had been adopted as 'happily descriptive'.[30]

As Sutherland had correctly noted, by the turn of the twentieth century, a number of factors had combined to undermine Down's ethnic classification of idiots and, indeed, to challenge the validity of the term 'mongolian idiot'. An increasing focus on mental defectives as the root cause of most social problems was associated with extensive statistical surveys of asylum and school populations, and with more detailed and penetrating studies of the various organic and mental pathologies to be found in mental defectives. This process, part of a powerful crusade to portray the feeble-minded as diseased and pathological and thus worthy of permanent segregation or sterilisation, led to increasingly sophisticated classifications of mental deficiency according to its presence or absence at birth (congenital or acquired), its supposed aetiology (primary or secondary) or its severity (idiocy, imbecility, feeble-mindedness).[31]

In the light of this more profound approach to the pathology of deficiency and in a climate in which appearances were recognised to be deceptive,[32] Down's ethnic classification (including his portrayal of the 'mongolian idiot') appeared at best superficial and at worst inaccurate. Ironically, one of Down's sons, Reginald Langdon Down, was among the first to draw attention to problems with his father's account in a paper delivered in 1906:

> It would appear, however, that the characters which at first sight strikingly suggest Mongolian features and build are accidental and superficial, being constantly associated, as they are, with other features which are in no way characteristic of that race, and if this is a case of reversion it must be reversion to a type even further back than the Mongol stock, from which ethnologists believe all the various races of men have sprung.[33]

Three years later the superficiality of Down's original comments was further challenged by George Shuttleworth, who, in presenting his clinical observations from approximately 350 cases, emphasised the 'striking divergences between the physical characters of the real Mongol or Kalmuck and these Mongoloid specimens of the Caucasian race'. In particular Shuttleworth pointed to differences in the prominence of the cheek bones, the texture of the hair and skin, and the shape of the head and hands. In essence, 'the most notable signs of similarity' were simply the shape of the eyes and the flat-bridged nose.[34]

More detailed depictions of 'mongolian imbecility' were associated with the development of a more systematic scrutiny of possible aetiological factors, a process which also served to distance early twentieth-century accounts of 'mongolism' from Down's earlier work. Down's conviction that 'mongolism' was the product of degeneration due to tuberculosis was gradually abandoned. Instead doctors focused on syphilis, hormonal imbalances, neuropathic heredity or (increasingly) maternal age and uterine exhaustion as the major causative factors.[35] In the scientific rhetoric of the period, these factors operated by arresting the development of the foetus *in utero*, thereby producing 'unfinished children, bearing permanently the imprint of a phase of foetal life'.[36]

Although Down's ethnological and aetiological understanding of 'mongolism' was contested by early twentieth-century doctors, it is significant that many of the prejudices inherent in his descriptive approach persisted in medical writings. In the first instance it is clear that, in spite of doubts about the meaning of appearance, most medical authors continued to focus on the external physical features shared by this class of defectives. Thus major medical texts by Alfred Tredgold, George Shuttleworth and William Potts, and Charles Paget Lapage (as well as many journal articles) reproduced photographs depicting the supposedly characteristic physiognomical and anatomical anomalies of 'mongols' (Figure 8.1 on p. 176).[37] This persistent propagation of visual images served a significant purpose. In the light of medical preoccupations with diagnosing mental deficiency on the basis of extensive clinical examination, 'mongolism' served as an exemplar of the perceived link between physical form and mental ability. The visualisation of deficiency in these cases was therefore critical to medical claims of diagnostic and managerial expertise.[38]

Early twentieth-century medical authors also reiterated and extended Down's initial behavioural stereotype of the 'mongolian idiot' as humorous, imitative, lacking coordination and able to speak only indistinctly. According to Shuttleworth, for example, 'mongols' possessed 'certain common mental characteristics, such as general backwardness, want of originality but remarkable imitativeness, retarded speech, often a taste for musical rhythm, and usually a placid disposition'.[39] Similarly for Tredgold 'mongols' exhibited 'a very considerable power of mimicry, as well as a remarkable sense of rhythm and love of music, and many of these children are adepts at drilling and dancing'.[40] As a number of authors have suggested, such descriptions reflected profound contemporary stereotypes not only of 'mongolian imbeciles' but also of members of the Mongolian race.[41]

PLATE XIV.

FIG. 1.—" MONGOL " PROFILE.

FIG. 2.—" MONGOL " TONGUE.

Figure 8.1 Mongolian type

Source: G.E. Shuttleworth and W.A. Potts, *Mentally Deficient Children: Their Treatment and Training*, London, H.K. Lewis and Co., 1916, facing p. 119.

Inherent in these persistent stereotypes was a belief in the constancy of the group and in the enduring descriptive force of the term 'mongol'. Most medical writers continued to stress strong resemblances between 'mongols', to play down individual differences in ability or personality, and to endorse the use of 'mongolian imbecility/idiocy' to capture the supposedly peculiar pathology of this type of mental defective. According to Stevens, writing in 1915, the 'group is constant and typical; the name is characteristic'.[42] Even Shuttleworth, who had highlighted evident dissimilarities between 'mongolian imbeciles' and members of the Mongolian race, acknowledged both his own and the general public's preoccupations with racial parallels:

> Allowing, however, for the differences I have named, the fact remains – as I think will be obvious from a scrutiny of the photographs I submit to you of so-called Mongolian imbeciles of European parentage – that their physiognomies recall in many particulars those of Asiatic Mongols, and it is remarkable how they all bear, though unrelated, of very varying social class, and natives of far-distant places, a sort of family resemblance to each other. Even lay people recognise the Mongolian physiognomy; and Dr Still mentions that the mother of a Mongol imbecile under his care in London stated that the neighbours called her child 'the Chinese baby', and I have myself known one of this type attending a special school nicknamed by his schoolfellows 'John Chinaman'.[43]

Langdon Down's legacy is also conspicuous in the persistent conceptualisation of 'mongolism' as an anthropological problem, and in the use of 'mongolian imbecility' as a disease category furnishing evidence for theories of racial origins and difference. In 1919, for example, in a paper delivered to the Anthropological Section of the British Association for the Advancement of Science, Arthur Keith argued that both racial differences and certain pathological conditions (including mongolism) could be explained as the product of the differential maturation of the endocrine system.[44] Although many contemporary medical writers discounted pathology of the thyroid gland as a causative factor in the aetiology of 'mongolism',[45] Keith and a number of other authors continued to explore the possible contribution of thyroid imbalance.[46] What is immediately remarkable about Keith's account, however, is that the origins of mental deficiencies were considered to be the same as (rather than just like) the origins of racial difference and inferiority. Explanations of racial and mental inferiority were part of the same intellectual and political quest for an overarching aetiology and pathology of difference.

At a more extreme level some authors, notably Crookshank and Herrman, continued to argue that 'mongolism' was to be explained as 'a reversion to a primitive type' and maintained that 'mongolian imbeciles' displayed characteristics shared not only with 'racial mongols' but also with orang-utans.[47] Although Herrman was eager to equate his reversion theory with Shuttleworth's concept of arrested foetal development (via the doctrine that ontogeny recapitulated phylogeny),[48] his views demonstrate that the transformation from Down's ethnic classification to a more detailed aetiological and pathological approach was more apparent than real.

Chromosomes and changing representations of 'mongolism'

Down's ethnic classification of idiots, and subsequent understandings of 'mongolism' as some form of atavism, gained some crude plausibility from beliefs that 'mongolian imbecility' occurred only in Caucasians. This conviction remained unchallenged until the 1920s, when two American paediatricians, I. Harrison Tumpeer and Adrien Bleyer, published separate reports (with photographs) of 'mongolism' occurring in Chinese and Ethiopian children respectively.[49] Critically it was Bleyer's contribution to the debate, together with increasingly intricate analyses of the possible causes of the condition (notably those based on twin studies), that provoked a transformation in medical understandings and representations of the origins and nature of 'mongolism'.

In the 1920s a number of doctors attempted to resolve debates about the aetiology of 'mongolism' (particularly whether it was 'germinal in origin or acquired')[50] by surveying its occurrence in twins. In 1923 T. Halbertsma, a Dutch physician, discussed details of fifteen cases of 'mongolism' occurring in one twin only and two cases occurring in both twins. Evidence that all the cases in which only one twin was affected were 'two-egg' pregnancies, while those cases in which both twins were affected were 'one-egg' pregnancies, convinced Halbertsma that 'mongolism has to be regarded as the result of defects inherent in the germ plasm'.[51] Five years later

Hubert Armstrong, senior honorary physician to the Royal Liverpool Children's Hospital, similarly used twin studies to argue that the cause of 'mongolism' was already present in the ovum (or possibly sperm) 'before fertilization has followed and segmentation started'.[52]

The implications of these earlier surveys and case reports were explored extensively by Bleyer in two seminal papers published in the early 1930s. In the first of these articles, on the frequency of 'mongolism', Bleyer addressed 'the question of race'. He mobilised various types of evidence (including reports of 'mongolism' occurring in thirty-one different nationalities) to distance himself carefully both from Down's ethnic classification of idiots and from Crookshank's more recent theory that 'mongolism' constituted an example of reversion to 'a former type of being, in effect, to a mongolian or premongolian race'. In addition to emphasising that 'this disease has not the slightest relation to any race', Bleyer suggested that it would be best to 'reserve the terms Mongol and Mongolian for their ancient and accepted meaning indicating race rather than disease' and proposed that the term 'mongolian imbecility' should be replaced by 'mongoloid imbecility'.[53]

Two years later Bleyer addressed the vexing question of aetiology. Drawing on contemporary theories of genetics (including the 'mutation theory of de Vries') and on twin studies, Bleyer offered a number of critical insights. First, he argued that 'no part of the entire body is spared its own particular distortion by this disease; that no organ or tissue whatever may not reveal evidence of it'.[54] Accordingly he insisted that imbecility was only 'incidental' to 'mongolism'. Second, Bleyer echoed the theories of Halbertsma and Armstrong by suggesting that 'mongolism' was the product of 'a deviation which was present at the time of fertilization or even before fertilization which would involve the entire structure of the new being'.[55] Consequently he suggested that answers to questions concerning aetiology were more likely to be provided by cytologists than clinicians.[56]

Bleyer's discussion of the 'gametic origin' of 'mongolism' went further. Basing his arguments on genetic understandings of chromosome separation during the maturation of ova and sperm and of their subsequent fusion during fertilisation, and citing specific examples of recognised disturbances in these processes (such as unequal migration of the chromosomes), Bleyer suggested that 'mongolism' might be the product of 'an alteration in the normal number of chromosomes'. Having dismissed previous aetiological explanations (such as syphilis, endocrine disturbances, parental age, race and so on) as mistaken or unproven, Bleyer concluded that 'mongolism' was caused by a 'degressive mutation'.[57]

Although Bleyer's focus on inheritance was not entirely new,[58] his arguments signalled the emergence of a new vision of the 'mongol', one no longer preoccupied with tracing superficial facial appearances or with charting the limits of intelligence but with visualising and analysing the extensive pathology of the internal constitution. There is no space here to explore in detail the complicated (and frequently contested) cytological train of events that substantiated many of Bleyer's beliefs, or indeed to examine the extent to which these scientific developments were influenced by the shifting politics of racial difference. It is sufficient for present purposes to note that in 1959, three years after the chromosome complement of normal human cells had been set at 46, Lejeune and his colleagues declared that people with 'mongolism' possessed 47 chromosomes (a phenomenon accounted for by the presence of an extra chromosome number 21).[59]

As Jean-Paul Gaudilliere has persuasively argued, 'the transformation of "mongolism" into a chromosomal disorder in the late 1950s and early 1960s' was not straightforward and was marked by extensive disputes about the clinical importance of cytological findings.[60] Nevertheless it is possible to identify marked shifts in the visual representation of 'mongolism' in medical texts from this period. This shift is exemplified in the work of Clemens Benda, a leading American author on 'mongolism' through the middle decades of this century. In contrast to earlier twentieth-century attempts to capture the superficial physical anomalies of 'mongolism', Benda focused on utilising a variety of bio-scientific techniques to depict an extensive range of internal, as well as external, pathologies, which he carefully catalogued in the text and in line drawings.[61] His books consequently included illustrations of X-ray findings,[62] diagrams of skull development, graphs and plates of haematological and biochemical characteristics, and slides illustrating the gross and microscopic appearances of the nervous system, endocrine glands and gonads.[63] More tellingly, in a chapter on cytogenetics Benda reproduced karyotypes demonstrating what for many physicians had replaced the 'mongolian' faces as the pathognomonic feature of 'mongolism': an abnormal genotype with a trisomy in the 21–22 group of chromosomes.[64]

Changing understandings of aetiology, culminating in this transformation in the conceptualisation and representation of 'mongolism', were both a product of and a stimulus for conscious efforts on the part of some clinicians to distance themselves from earlier racial explanations of the condition.[65] In a letter to the *Lancet* in 1961, for example, a group of eminent physicians and scientists (including Benda, Lejeune, Penrose, Polani and W. Langdon Down, one of John Langdon Down's descendants) argued, on a number of grounds, that the term 'mongolism' was no longer appropriate:

> Sir, – it has long been recognised that the terms 'mongolian idiocy', 'mongolism', 'mongoloid', &c., as applied to a specific type of mental deficiency, have misleading connotations. The occurrence of this anomaly among Europeans and their descendants is not related to the segregation of genes derived from Asians; its appearance among members of the Asian population suggests such ambiguous designations as 'mongol Mongoloid'; and the increasing participation of Chinese and Japanese investigators in the study of the condition imposes on them the use of an embarrassing term. We urge, therefore, that the expressions which imply a racial aspect of the condition be no longer used.
>
> Some of the undersigned are inclined to replace the term 'mongolism' by such designations as 'Langdon Down anomaly', or 'Down's syndrome or anomaly', or 'congenital acromicria'. Several others believe that this is an appropriate time to introduce the term 'trisomy 21 anomaly' which would include cases of simple trisomy as well as translocations. It is hoped that agreement on a specific phrase will soon crystallise if once the term 'mongolism' has been abandoned.[66]

In spite of such forceful rejections of the ethnological and aetiological approach adopted by Langdon Down nearly 100 years earlier, many clinicians in the middle decades of this century continued to repeat many of the racial assumptions of earlier authors, albeit carefully reframed in the language of genotypes and multisystem pathologies. Although most medical practitioners increasingly regarded karyotyping as diagnostic, clinicians continued to reproduce superficial physical features for diagnostic and classificatory purposes.[67] In addition, although Benda had acknowledged in the 1950s that individuals could differ substantially in appearance, organic pathology and intelligence,[68] 'mongols' remained a recognised 'type' or 'family' identifiable now by virtue of their shared genetic constitution.

More critically it is clear that clinicians continued regularly to use 'mongolism' as a descriptive term in articles and books published throughout the 1960s and 1970s.[69] Indeed, at a Ciba Foundation Study Group on 'mongolism' held in 1966 to commemorate John Langdon Down's work, clinicians and scientists (including many of those who had signed the letter to the *Lancet*) offered only weak and unconvincing apologies for their continued use of a term that they acknowledged carried misleading and racist connotations.[70] Although 'Down's syndrome' and 'trisomy 21' gradually replaced 'mongolism' in both medical and non-medical literature during the 1980s (a phenomenon perhaps related more to the emergence of increasingly vocal patient and carer pressure groups than to developments in scientific knowledge), persistent use of the term 'mongolism' in medical and popular discourse highlights clear continuities in depicting disease in the face of decisive transformations in scientific understandings.

Conclusion

In this chapter I have explored the relationship between racial ideas and the classification and representation of disease, by focusing on changing depictions of what was originally defined as 'mongolism' by John Langdon Down in 1866. Down's original formulation of the condition not only borrowed heavily from contemporary understandings of race but also contributed to tense debates about racial unity and the origins of racial difference. By the early years of this century more detailed surveys of the cause and pathology of 'mongolism' encouraged clinicians to reject Langdon Down's ethnic classification of idiots and to challenge the superficiality of his depiction of 'mongols'. However, in spite of objections to Down's racial analogies, the racial assumptions inherent in his work persisted. Clinicians continued to depict the physiognomical and behavioural attributes that were thought to characterise this particular 'family' of mental defectives. In addition some researchers continued to use 'mongolism' as a means of substantiating particular theories of racial difference.

It is clear that dramatic changes in medical understandings of 'mongolism' occurred in the middle decades of this century. In particular 'mongolism' became defined as a chromosomal abnormality, a transformation which generated new ways of depicting the condition. From the 1960s medical texts focused increasingly on deeper macroscopic and microscopic abnormalities (especially the possession of an abnormal karyotype) rather than on superficial physical features. However, these novel understandings and depictions of disease failed to shake off racial assumptions evident in earlier representations, although those assumptions were now recast in the language of genotypes. Most tellingly, in spite of increasing sensitivities to racial implications, clinicians continued to use the terms 'mongol' and 'mongolism' to describe what was still believed to be a recognisable disease type.

Notes

1 Throughout this chapter I shall adopt the terminology employed during the period under discussion. In the late nineteenth and early twentieth centuries, mental deficiency was used as a generic term to describe people regarded as unable to benefit from ordinary elementary education or to manage their own affairs. This group was subdivided in that period (according to perceived differences in ability) into idiots, imbeciles and the feeble-minded. In the middle decades of the twentieth century, mental deficiency was replaced by the term 'mental handicap' and subsequently by 'people with learning disabilities/difficulties'.

2 See, in particular, the discussion in Daniel Pick, *Faces of Degeneration: A European Disorder, c.1848–1918*, Cambridge, Cambridge University Press, 1989.

3 For a contemporary exposition on the dangers of allowing mental defectives to breed and spread their taint, see Robert Reid Rentoul, *Race Culture; Or, Race Suicide?*, London, The Walter Scott Publishing Co., 1906. For further discussion of contemporary representations of mental defectives as a threat to social order, see Mark Jackson, 'Images of Deviance: Visual Representations of Mental Defectives in Twentieth-Century Medical Texts', *British Journal for the History of Science* 28 (1995): 319–37.

4 This particular phrase was used in the report of a paper, entitled 'Feeble-Mindedness in Its Racial Aspects', delivered by Leonard Darwin at a conference organised by the National Special Schools Union in 1915; see 'Physically and Mentally Defective Children', *The Medical Officer* 14 (1915): 178.

5 Rentoul, *Race Culture; Or, Race Suicide?*. On early twentieth-century debates about appropriate measures to control the spread of mental defectives, see David Barker, 'How to Curb the Fertility of the Unfit: The Feeble-Minded in Edwardian Britain', *Oxford Review of Education* 9 (1985): 197–211.

6 On the emergence of specific colonies for mental defectives in the early twentieth century, see Mark Jackson, 'Institutional Provision for the Feeble-Minded in Edwardian England: Sandlebridge and the Scientific Morality of Permanent Care', in David Wright and Anne Digby (eds), *From Idiocy to Mental Deficiency: Historical Perspectives on People with Learning Difficulties*, London, Routledge, 1996, pp. 161–83; M. Thomson, 'Sterilisation, Segregation and Community Care: Ideology and Solutions to the Problem of Mental Deficiency in Interwar Britain', *History of Psychiatry* 3 (1992): 478–88; Thomson, ' "Though Ever the Subject of Psychological Medicine": Psychiatrists and the Colony Solution for Mental Defectives', in Hugh Freeman and German E. Berrios (eds), *150 Years of British Psychiatry, Volume II: The Aftermath*, London, Athlone, pp. 130–43.

7 See Pick, *Faces of Degeneration*; Stephen Jay Gould, *The Mismeasure of Man*, London, Penguin Books, 1981; Jackson, 'Images of Deviance'.

8 J. Langdon H. Down, 'Observations on an Ethnic Classification of Idiots', first published in *Lectures and Reports from the London Hospital for 1866*; repr. C. Thompson (ed.), *The Origins of Modern Psychiatry*, Chichester, John Wiley & Sons, 1987, pp. 15–23.

9 Lilian Zihni, 'The History of the Relationship between the Concept and Treatment of People with Down's Syndrome in Britain and America from 1866 to 1967', unpublished University of London Ph.D. thesis, 1989. Some of the specific issues raised in this thesis have been subsequently published. See Zihni, 'Raised Parental Age and the Occurrence of Down's Syndrome', *History of Psychiatry* 5 (1994): 71–88; Zihni, 'Obstinacy and Down's Syndrome: A Misunderstanding of Behavior in the Past', *History and Philosophy of Psychology Newsletter* 18 (1994): 10–16; Zihni, 'Imitativeness and Down's Syndrome', *History and Philosophy of Psychology Newsletter* 19 (1994): 10–17; Zihni, 'Mongolism, Down's Syndrome and Trisomy 21: Damning Diagnoses in the Twentieth Century', *History and Philosophy of Psychology Newsletter* 21 (1995): 20–5.

10 Apart from Zihni's work, the history of Down's syndrome has not been extensively explored, although textbooks on the management of people with Down's syndrome have sometimes incorporated historical chapters. For an excellent overview of the changing use of names, see Tony Booth, 'Labels and Their Consequences', in David Lane and Brian Stratford (eds), *Current Approaches to Down's Syndrome*, London, Holt, Rinehart & Winston, 1985, pp. 3–24.

11 Down, 'On the Condition of the Mouth in Idiocy', *Lancet* 18 January 1862: 65–6.

12 Down, 'On the Condition of the Mouth', p. 66. Interestingly Down was subsequently accused of having stolen some of the ideas that he presented in this paper by the surgeon Thomas Ballard, who had visited the asylum at Earlswood during October 1860. Down and his assistant, A. Brown, strongly refuted the accusation. See the correspondence on this in the *Lancet* 8 February 1862: 160 and 15 February 1862: 186.

13 Down, 'Observations on an Ethnic Classification of Idiots', pp. 15–16.

14 Although Hugh Diamond had been attempting to capture the faces of madness on camera since the 1850s, it was unusual for medical texts to include photographs of mental defectives until the last decade of the century. Until then medical authors relied on extensive verbal descriptions. On the emergence of photography as a tool for accurately and objectively recording insanity and mental deficiency, see Sander L. Gilman (ed.), *The Face of Madness: Hugh W. Diamond and the Origin of Psychiatric Photography*, New York, Brunner/Mazel, 1976; Gilman, *Disease and Representation: Images of Illness from Madness to AIDS*, New York, Cornell University Press, 1988; John Tagg, *The Burden of Representation*, London, Macmillan, 1988; Jackson, 'Images of Deviance'.
15 Down, 'Observations on an Ethnic Classification of Idiots', pp. 16–17.
16 Down, 'Observations on an Ethnic Classification of Idiots', p. 17.
17 Down, 'Observations on an Ethnic Classification of Idiots', p. 16.
18 Down, 'Observations on an Ethnic Classification of Idiots', pp. 17–18.
19 See the discussion in Jackson, 'Images of Deviance'.
20 See, in particular, Pick, *Faces of Degeneration*.
21 Zihni, 'The History of the Relationship between the Concept and Treatment of People with Down's Syndrome', esp. pp. 20–61; Booth, 'Labels and Their Consequences'.
22 See discussions in Booth, 'Labels and Their Consequences'; Gould, *The Mismeasure of Man*, p. 135; Zihni, 'The History of the Relationship between the Concept and the Treatment of People with Down's Syndrome', pp. 72–103, p. 104 n.4.
23 'Case and Autopsy of a Kalmuc Idiot', *Journal of Mental Science* 22 (1876): 161–2; John Fraser and Arthur Mitchell, 'Kalmuc Idiocy: Report of a Case with Autopsy with Notes on Sixty-Two Cases', *Journal of Mental Science* 22 (1876): 169–79.
24 Fraser's adoption of the epithet 'Kalmuc' did not pass unchallenged. In the discussion after Fraser's initial presentation of his case ('Case and Autopsy of a Kalmuc Idiot', p. 162), Dr Jamieson from Aberdeen insisted that 'the term Kalmuc was a very objectionable term. He thought there was nothing marked about the Kalmuc, and there was no reason for nicknaming an idiot by calling him a Kalmuc. He thought this uncalled-for-term should be departed from. Why did they call such an one a Kalmuc? The idiot is no more a Kalmuc than any other human being.'
25 G.E. Shuttleworth, 'Clinical Lecture on Idiocy and Imbecility', *British Medical Journal* i (1886): 183–6; G.A. Sutherland, 'Mongolian Imbecility in Infants', *The Practitioner*, n.s., 10 (1899): 632–42.
26 Shuttleworth, 'Clinical Lecture', p. 185.
27 Ibid.
28 Sutherland, 'Mongolian Imbecility', pp. 640–1; G.A. Sutherland, 'The Differential Diagnosis of Mongolism and Cretinism in Infancy', *Lancet* i (6 January 1900): 23–4. For a discussion of Sutherland's syphilis theory, see Zihni, 'Sutherland's Syphilis Hypothesis of Down's Syndrome', *Journal of the History of the Neurosciences* 4 (1995): 133–7.
29 Sutherland, 'Mongolian Imbecility', p. 632.

30 Sutherland, 'The Differential Diagnosis', p. 23.
31 See, for example, the classifications adopted in Alfred Tredgold, *Mental Deficiency (Amentia)*, London, Baillière, Tindall & Cox, 1908; Charles Paget Lapage, *Feeble-Mindedness in Children of School-Age*, Manchester, Manchester University Press, 1911; G.E. Shuttleworth and W.A. Potts, *Mentally Deficient Children: Their Treatment and Training*, 4th edn, London, H.K. Lewis & Co., 1916.
32 See, in particular, Lapage's comments in his *Feeble-Mindedness in Children*, pp. 60–1.
33 Langdon Down's paper, presented to a meeting of the South-Eastern Division of the Medico-Psychological Association, is reported in *Journal of Mental Science* 52 (1906): 187–90.
34 G.E. Shuttleworth, 'Mongolian Imbecility', *British Medical Journal* 11 September 1909: 661–5.
35 Sutherland, 'Mongolian Imbecility', 1899; W. Bertram Hill, 'Mongolism and Its Pathology: An Analysis of Eight Cases', *Quarterly Journal of Medicine* 2 (1908): 49–68; Tredgold, *Mental Deficiency*, pp. 182–5; Shuttleworth, 'Mongolian Imbecility'; H.C. Stevens, 'Mongolian Idiocy and Syphilis', *Journal of the American Medical Association* 64 (1915): 1,636–40; Charles Herrman, 'The Etiology of Mongolian Imbecility', *Archives of Pediatrics* 34 (1917): 494–503.
36 This comment is from Shuttleworth's response to Reginald Langdon Down's paper and appears in *Journal of Mental Science* 52 (1906): 189. According to Dr D. Hunter, 'all the characteristics of the condition could be paralleled in the foetus, and ... the Mongolian idiot was a grown-up foetus'; see *Lancet* ii (1909): 1,501.
37 See, for example, Shuttleworth, 'Mongolian Imbecility'; Tredgold, *Mental Deficiency*, plates xii–xiv, pp. 184–8; Shuttleworth and Potts, *Mentally Deficient Children*, plates xiv–xv, pp. 119–20.
38 For further discussion of this, see Jackson, 'Images of Deviance'.
39 Shuttleworth, 'Mongolian Imbecility', p. 664.
40 Tredgold, *Mental Deficiency*, p. 189.
41 Stephen Jay Gould, 'Dr Down's Syndrome', *New Scientist* 86 (1980): 252; Gould, *The Mismeasure of Man*, p. 135; Zihni, 'Imitativeness and Down's Syndrome'; Booth, 'Labels and Their Consequences'.
42 Stevens, 'Mongolian Idiocy and Syphilis', p. 1,637.
43 Shuttleworth, 'Mongolian Imbecility', p. 662.
44 Arthur Keith, 'The Differentiation of Mankind into Racial Types', *Lancet* 27 September 1919: 553–6.
45 Sutherland, 'The Differential Diagnosis'; Shuttleworth, 'Mongolian Imbecility', p. 664; Bertram Hill, 'Mongolism and Its Pathology', p. 67.
46 An exhaustive argument for pathology of the thyroid gland as causative in 'mongolism' was presented in a series of papers published between 1928 and 1933 by R.M. Clark, Medical Superintendent at Whittingham Mental Hospital in Lancashire. See R.M. Clark, 'The Mongol: A New Explanation', *Journal of Mental Science* 74 (1928): 265–9; Clark, 'The Mongol: A New Explanation', *Journal of Mental Science* 74 (1928): 739–47; Clark, 'The Mongol: A New Explanation', *Journal*

of Mental Science 75 (1929): 261–2; Clark, 'The Mongol: A New Explanation', *Journal of Mental Science* 79 (1933): 328–35.

47 F.G. Crookshank, 'Handprints of Mental Defectives', *Lancet* 5 February 1921: 274; Crookshank, 'The Fissured Tongue of Mongolian Idiots', *The Medical Press and Circular* 13 April 1921: 297; Charles Herrman, 'Mongolian Imbecility as an Anthropologic Problem', *Archives of Pediatrics* 42 (1925): 523–9. For a further discussion of Crookshank's theories, see Zihni, 'The History of the Relationship between the Concept and the Treatment of People with Down's Syndrome', esp. pp. 251–75.

48 Herrman, 'Mongolian Imbecility', pp. 527–8.

49 I. Harrison Tumpeer, 'Mongolian Idiocy in a Chinese Boy', *Journal of the American Medical Association* 74 (122): 14–16; Adrien Bleyer, 'The Occurrence of Mongolism in Ethiopians', *Journal of the American Medical Association* 84 (1925): 1,041–2.

50 T. Halbertsma, 'Mongolism in One of Twins and the Etiology of Mongolism', *American Journal of Diseases of Children* 25 (1923): 350–3.

51 Halbertsma, 'Mongolism in One of Twins', p. 353.

52 Hubert Armstrong, 'The Etiology of Mongolism; With a Case of Mongol Twin', *British Medical Journal* 30 June 1928: 1,106–7.

53 Adrien Bleyer, 'The Frequency of Mongoloid Imbecility', *American Journal of Diseases of Children* 44 (1932): 503–8.

54 Ibid., p. 344.

55 Ibid.

56 Ibid.

57 Ibid., p. 348. For further information on Bleyer, see Zihni, 'The History of the Relationship between the Concept and the Treatment of People with Down's Syndrome', pp. 312–76.

58 In 1917, for example, Herrman ('The Etiology of Mongolian Imbecility') had argued strongly for the inherited nature of the condition.

59 For an account of these discoveries, see Daniel J. Kevles, *In the Name of Eugenics*, London, Penguin, 1986, pp. 244–9; Jean-Paul Gaudilliere, 'Whose Work Shall We Trust? Genetics, Paediatrics and Hereditary Diseases in Postwar France', in P. Sloan (ed.), *Controlling Our Destinies*, Notre-Dame University Press, forthcoming.

60 Gaudilliere, 'Whose Work Shall We Trust?'.

61 Clemens Benda, *Down's Syndrome: Mongolism and Its Management*, New York, Grune & Stratton, 1969, pp. 42–3.

62 Benda, *Down's Syndrome*, pp. 48–65.

63 Benda, *Down's Syndrome*, pp. 134–208 *passim*.

64 Benda, *Down's Syndrome*, pp. 121–33.

65 Of course the factors contributing to this move away from the racial implications of 'mongolism' were complex and by no means confined to developments in science. For example it is likely that clinicians were responding to heightened concerns about race relations in this period and to more strident discourses about disability, generated in part by patient and carer support groups such as Mencap.

66 'Mongolism', *Lancet* 8 April 1961: 775.

67 See Gaudilliere's comments in 'Whose Work Shall We Trust?'.

68 Benda, 'Mongolism: A Comprehensive Review', *Archives of Pediatrics* 73 (1956): 391–407.

69 Note, for example, Margaret I. Stern, Valerie A. Cowie and Alec Coppen, 'Dehydroepiandrosterone Excretion in the Mothers of Mongols', *Acta Endocrinologica* 53 (1966): 79–83; Valerie Cowie and E. Slater, 'The Fertility of Mothers of Mongols', *Journal of Mental Deficiency Research* 12 (1968): 196–208; Benda, *Down's Syndrome*, 1969; George F. Smith and Joseph Berg, 'The Biological Significance of Mongolism', *British Journal of Psychiatry* 125 (1974): 537–41.

70 Ciba Foundation Study Group, *Mongolism*, London, J. & A. Churchill, 1967, pp. 88–90.

Chapter 9

Pro-alienism, anti-alienism and the medical profession in late-Victorian and Edwardian Britain

Bernard Harris[*]

The chapters in this book have been broadly concerned with the interaction between racial ideas, medicine and science. They have highlighted the different ways in which racial thinking influenced the development of medicine and science, and the ways in which medicine and science gave added 'legitimacy' to racial stereotypes. The current chapter seeks to add to this discussion by examining the medical profession's response to the immigration of Eastern European Jews into Britain during the late nineteenth and early twentieth centuries. In contrast to some earlier accounts, this chapter seeks to give equal weight to both pro-alien and anti-alien discourses.[1]

It is now widely accepted that the attitudes and ideas of medical and scientific figures are deeply embedded in the social-cultural contexts of their times, and Nancy Stepan has argued that 'in an atmosphere … [where] theories of difference and exclusion … seemed almost necessary for social identification and moral orientation, scientific racism no longer appeared an aberration of Western intellectual traditions, but its very essence'.[2] However, it is important to remember that race was only one of the factors to influence intellectual debate at the end of the nineteenth century. In order to understand the full range of medical responses to Jewish immigration, we also need to examine the persistence of liberal

* This chapter draws on research conducted for an earlier paper, entitled 'Anti-alienism, health and social reform in late-Victorian and Edwardian Britain', published in *Patterns of Prejudice* 31, 4 (1997): 3–34. I should like to thank Waltraud Ernst and Tony Kushner for comments on the earlier paper, as well as the current one. I am also grateful to Lisa Schuster for helpful comments on the history of asylum policy.

ideas about freedom of movement, the right of asylum and free trade, together with the broader links between Jewish immigration and the politics of public health reform.

The background to anti-alienism

It is something of a truism (albeit a necessary one) that Britain has always been a country of immigration. During the first two-thirds of the nineteenth century the country provided both a home and a staging post for large numbers of European migrants and transmigrants fleeing hardship or persecution. If one discounts the Irish, who were (at least technically) regarded as internal migrants, moving from one part of the United Kingdom to another, the largest single group of 'foreign-born' residents on the mainland of Britain were the Germans, who numbered just under 33,000 at the time of the 1871 census.[3] However, by the end of the century they had been overtaken by the large number of Jewish immigrants fleeing economic and religious persecution in Eastern Europe. It is notoriously difficult to put a precise figure on the scale of this influx, but it has been estimated that between 120,000 and 150,000 Jews settled in Britain between 1880 and 1914.[4]

The majority of the Jews who settled in Britain were extremely poor, and some historians have doubted whether many of them originally intended their stay to be permanent.[5] Although the total number of immigrants was small when compared with the size of the population as a whole, they were regarded as being particularly 'visible' because they concentrated in particular areas and particular trades. In 1894 Geoffrey Drage told the Royal Statistical Society that 'the recent publication of the Board of Trade … has placed it beyond question that alien immigration into the United Kingdom is both absolutely and relatively insignificant, and that, were it not for the fact that the immigrants congregate in three centres – London, Manchester and Leeds – and engage mainly in one branch of industry, we should hear little of the "displacement of native labour by the lower-priced labour of aliens" '.[6] The most important 'immigrant trades' were garment-making, boot- and shoe-making, furriery, cane-making, cabinet-making and the making of tobacco products.[7] In Leeds, it was estimated that 67 per cent of all male employees and 70 per cent of female employees were engaged in tailoring, while 13 per cent of employed Jewish men worked as boot- and shoe-makers.[8]

In order to understand the response to Jewish immigration, it is necessary to look beyond the immediate context and to examine the full range of social, economic and cultural factors which helped to shape attitudes to Jews and immigrants in the late nineteenth and early twentieth centuries. In his study of *John Bull's Island: Immigration and British Society, 1871–1971*, Colin Holmes suggested that 'the centuries-old image of Jews as Christ-killers, a source of much historical antipathy and discrimination, had lost much of its force' by the 1880s, but it had been replaced by new (or newer) stereotypes which could often be equally damaging. One image, which was sometimes seen as complimentary to Jews but which was more often associated with hostility, was the notion of the Jew as 'economic man' or '*homo œconomicus*'. In 1889 Beatrice Potter (the future Beatrice Webb) wrote:

> We need not seek far for the origin of the antagonistic feelings with which the Gentile inhabitants of East London regard Jewish labour and Jewish trade. ... The immigrant Jew ... seems to justify ... those strange assumptions which figured for *man* in the political economy of Ricardo – an Always Enlightened Selfishness, seeking employment or profit with an absolute mobility of body and mind, without pride, without preference, without interests outside the struggle for the existence and welfare of the individual and the family.[9]

Although Victorian attitudes to Jewish immigration focused partly on the image of the immigrant as Jew, they were also influenced by broader concerns about the position and status of Britain itself. During the second half of the nineteenth century many observers became increasingly concerned about what they saw as the decline of British wealth and power.[10] At the end of the century Britain still enjoyed the highest levels of income *per capita* of any country in the world, but its status as the world's leading economic power was coming under increasing threat from countries such as Germany and the United States of America.[11] These fears were compounded by the erosion of Britain's imperial power and, in particular, by the humbling of the British army during the early stages of the Boer War of 1899–1902. As the imperialist writer Leo Amery observed in 1900: 'The war has not only shaken our military organisation. It has profoundly affected the whole nation in many ways'.[12]

The anxieties associated with the loss of military and economic power were compounded by fears about 'physical deterioration'. During the early years of the twentieth century a growing number of writers became convinced that the average standard of public health in Britain was deteriorating, and this led to calls for the establishment of a national enquiry into 'physical deterioration'.[13] The majority of these writers believed that the main reason for the decline in public health standards was an increase in the proportion of the population residing in towns, but some observers thought that the problem was being exacerbated by the increase in alien immigration. First, it was claimed that the immigrants themselves came from 'inferior stock' and that their presence would therefore tend to depress the standard of vitality in the population as a whole. Second, it was also claimed that the immigrants' willingness to work for low wages would drive down the living standards of native workers and make it more difficult for them to purchase the necessities for a healthy life.[14]

The increasing importance of racial issues was also underlined by the growth of Social Darwinism and the revival of scientific racism. In recent years both Greta Jones and Mike Hawkins have argued that the term 'Social Darwinism' encompassed a variety of meanings and could be applied to a range of ideas, but the majority of Social Darwinists continued to believe that competition was the governing factor in international relationships, and many of them also argued that nations and races were engaged in a bitter 'struggle for existence'.[15] These ideas were given added importance during the latter part of the nineteenth century by the continuing growth of 'scientific racism'. José Harris has recently argued that 'most expert anthropological opinion continued to resist the idea that there were any innately inferior races, but ... anthropologists increasingly endorsed the view that there was an immense evolutionary gulf between the "backward" and "advanced" races, which the former could only cross by following in the footsteps of the latter'.[16] However, as Douglas Lorimer has shown, even though expert opinion may have taken a step back from racial typologising in the 1870s and early 1880s, explicitly racist thinking experienced a revival in the decades which followed this.[17]

It is also important to place the debate about alien immigration in the context of broader debates about the growth of state intervention and the changing nature of 'citizenship'.[18] In 1898 the *Lancet* published two separate reports attacking individual Jews who had refused to serve on coroner's juries, and claiming that 'in a country where the Jews properly enjoy perfect freedom and protection they should take their share in discharging the duties imposed on all citizens by law'.[19] The *Lancet*'s concern with the rights and responsibilities of citizenship was heightened by the growth of state welfare provision during the early years of the twentieth century. In 1911 it asked:

> If the indigent alien comes here because he considers that our indigent classes are better off than himself, do we not increase the attractions for him every time we improve conditions for them; and, if we seek to raise the masses now engaging our attention to a higher level of living, shall we not find the space thus left vacant below incessantly replenished, and more than replenished, by fresh and increasing arrivals from abroad?[20]

While many of the most important social, economic and cultural tendencies of the late nineteenth and early twentieth centuries moved in the direction of a hardening of racial attitudes and a growing hostility to non-native and non-white groups, it is also important to recognise that there were many other aspects of British life which tended in the opposite direction. Following the repeal of the Corn Laws in 1846 it had become axiomatic on the part of Liberals and Conservatives that the foundations of Britain's wealth were built on free trade, and this argument was frequently extended to include the free movement of people as well as the free movement of goods. In 1894 Geoffrey Drage told the Royal Statistical Society that 'England can still safely adopt at home that liberal policy of leaving her doors open to those who desire to enter and those who desire to leave her, which has so materially contributed to her greatness in the past'.[21] In 1905, when Joseph Chamberlain told the House of Commons that 'this Bill [i.e. the Aliens Bill] ... is an effort to protect the working classes of this country against ... the underpaid labour of ... immigrants', the Liberal MP for Oldham, Alfred Emmott, responded:

> The Right Honourable Gentleman appears to have let the cat out of the bag, in words which cannot be palatable to the Government, or to free-traders on that side of the House, or to my Honourable Friend the Member for Poplar, who has declared his intention of supporting the Bill, which we are now told is a

> protectionist Bill, founded on the principle of protection which the Right Honourable Gentleman, the Member for West Birmingham, desires to introduce into the country.[22]

The campaign to impose restrictions on the immigration of 'aliens' also offended against another sacred principle in the canon of Liberal beliefs: the principle of asylum.[23] In 1887, when the Conservative MP for Tower Hamlets and Bow, Captain J.C.R. Colomb, asked what steps the Government was taking to deal with the problem of destitute aliens, the Conservative Leader in the House of Commons, W.H. Smith, replied that 'Her Majesty's Government was fully alive to the importance of placing some restrictions on the importation of destitute aliens into this country, but there were many serious difficulties in the way of dealing with it, among them the right of asylum in this country'.[24] The rights of immigrants continued to be a major factor in the debates over the introduction of the Aliens Bill in 1905. The Radical Member for the Forest of Dean, Sir Charles Dilke, complained that the Bill would 'interfere with the principle of asylum in this country without any proved necessity for taking any such step', and Herbert Samuel protested that the Government had 'no right to shut out oppressed people merely because they are poor'.[25] The MP for the Isle of Wight, Major J.E.B. Seeley, said that the Bill 'marked the abandonment of a great and high principle which, if not immemorial, had been slowly and laboriously built up – the principle that to keep out people because they were miserable and without means was neither wise nor right'.[26]

Doctors and anti-alienism

Although the agitation against 'alien immigrants' took many forms, many of the issues raised by 'anti-aliens' were directly related to public health, and the whole question of alien immigration was of considerable interest to the medical profession. As the *Lancet* observed at the beginning of 1906, '[t]o the manner in which foreigners of all sorts and conditions have been allowed free ingress into Great Britain have been attributed many ills by many people. Questions of morality, questions of public health, and questions of political economy have all been imported into the debates on the modification of the laws relating to alien immigration, and all are germane to such debates. It follows, therefore, that all medical men, at any rate for the first two reasons, must be interested in the workings of the Aliens Act.'[27]

In looking at the history of medical anti-alienism, it is important to recognise that the vast majority of the immigrants were not only Jewish, but also poor, and it can be difficult to separate attitudes to race from attitudes to poverty. Nevertheless, anti-alien writers did pay considerable attention to questions of race and ethnicity. Some of these ideas were clearly directed at Jews as a whole, and were concerned with the position of Jews as a distinct racial grouping. However, most were more concerned with the specific attributes of those Jews who happened to be migrating to Britain from Eastern Europe, and in particular with the habits and morals which they were supposed to possess.

It is important to recognise that in the last years of the nineteenth century most medical writers believed that Jews were at least as healthy as the populations around them, and often more so. In 1881 Dr Louis Henry told the Health Section of the Social Science Congress in Melbourne that Jews experienced lower rates of typhoid fever, cholera, consumption, intermittent fever, syphilis and puerperal fever, and that their standards of health and longevity were very high; in 1882 M. Gustave Lagneau told the Paris Academy of Moral and Political Science that Jews had the lowest death rates in all the countries for which statistics existed.[28] In 1896 F.L. Hoffman reported that in New York 'scarlet and typhoid fevers and diphtheria are almost as prevalent among the Jews as among the Germans and Irish', but Jews experienced much lower rates of mortality from phthisis, pneumonia, accidents and liver diseases.[29] These findings were echoed in a large number of international studies. In 1911 Dr Maurice Fishberg concluded:

> When compared with the non-Jewish population of the countries in which they live, the Jews have a much lower mortality. In Algeria their death rate is less than 89 per cent of that of the Europeans in that colony; in Poland it is less than 75 per cent; in Bavaria, about 58 per cent; while in European Russia less than one half the number of Jews die proportionately than Christians. In other words, the death rates of the Jews are from 11 to 52 per cent less than those of the Christians.[30]

However, while most observers believed that Jews were at least as healthy as non-Jews and often healthier, this was not true of all health indicators. In 1885 Joseph Jacobs claimed that 'Jews are nowadays the shortest and narrowest of Europeans (excepting, perhaps, Magyars as regards the former)' and in 1891 an American study found that, even though Jews experienced lower rates of tuberculosis than other groups and about the same ratio of deaths from cancer, they were more likely to be affected by diphtheria, diarrhoeal diseases, diseases of the nervous system (especially the spinal cord), diseases of the circulatory and urinary systems, of the bones and joints, and of the skin.[31] In 1901 the *British Medical Journal* reported that in Prussia and Bavaria Jews experienced high rates of puerperal psychoses and general paralysis, and that the incidence of blindness, deaf-mutism and insanity was twice that of 'native' Germans. The unhealthiness of Jews was also indicated by the fact that they experienced higher rates of myopia and trachoma than other groups in the Russian Empire.[32]

Although the medical press was concerned about the existence of high rates of physical disease, it is arguable that the most alarming statistics were those relating to insanity. In 1891 the *British Medical Journal* reported that 'the number of Jewish patients in Prussian lunatic asylums has nearly quadrupled in sixteen years. In the German Empire, the proportion of insane persons among Jews is 389 in every 100,000, the corresponding ratio among Protestants being 241, and among Roman Catholics, 237.'[33] In October 1900 the Superintendent of Colney Hatch Lunatic Asylum, C.F. Beadles, said that Jews tended to be admitted at younger ages than non-Jews, that they were more likely to suffer relapses and that they furnished 'the most troublesome, degraded and refractory of chronic and incurable cases'. He attributed the high rate of insanity among Jews to a wide range of possible causes, including sexual excess, heredity, early marriage, overcrowding, malnutrition and 'the worry, anxiety and excessive zeal in acquiring riches'.[34] Dr Maurice Fishberg also found that Jews experienced higher rates of puerperal insanity, amaurotic family idiocy and hysteria. In contrast to Beadles, he attributed the disproportionate incidence of these conditions to the prevalence of consanguineous marriages, to the effects of 2,000 years of persecution and to the fact that 'the Jew has for centuries been an urban resident, only rarely living in the country or engaged in agricultural pursuits'.[35]

The fact that Jews appeared to experience higher rates of some physical and mental diseases provided a rich hunting ground for those who wished to exclude Jewish immigrants on racial grounds.

In 1902 Dr Francis Tyrrell told the Royal Commission on Alien Immigration that Jews were uniquely susceptible to trachoma, which was one of the symptoms of chronic granular ophthalmia, and that the introduction of such a vulnerable population had led to a significant increase in the incidence of the disease among the 'native' inhabitants.[36] In 1905 the Medical Officer of Health for Glasgow, Dr Archibald Chalmers, reported that 'trachoma … is not a disease of fulminating activity … [and] the introduction of a few cases into a district is not … sufficient to ensure a wide extension of the malady', but the *Lancet* declared that such statements 'can only be accepted with much reserve'. It concluded that 'the secretion of trachoma which is brought into this country by aliens may be more virulent than that of the home-grown disease and [its] importation … may assume a very formidable character. It should, we think, be an instruction to the port authorities under the expected Aliens Act that all persons suffering from the disease should be refused permission to land and that information as to the prohibition should be widely circulated.'[37]

In addition to concerns about ophthalmic diseases, other observers focused attention on the racial constitution of the Jews and, in particular, on their alleged susceptibility to insanity. In 1895 the *Lancet* complained that 'the landing of foreign insane paupers, who almost immediately go to swell the numbers in our own county asylums and have to be maintained at the county's expense, is a matter which should surely be inquired into by the Government'.[38] Dr John Gray, the Secretary of the British Association's Anthropometric Committee, believed that ' the Jews … have been shown to be an exceedingly degenerate type in Europe, and there is a high percentage of insanity amongst the Jews, much higher than among the surrounding Gentile races. This seems to point to the conclusion that the insanity is connected with degeneration.'[39] In 1903 he told the Interdepartmental Committee on Physical Deterioration that 'the history of Poland is an awful example of national ruin brought about by the unrestricted immigration of degenerate aliens. About six hundred years ago, the Jews were invited to settle in Poland at a time when they were cruelly persecuted in every other country in Europe. At that time the Poles still possessed the high average stature which the other races of northern Europe still possess. Poland now contains the largest percentage of Jews and the lowest average stature in northern Europe.'[40]

Although many observers opposed Jewish immigration on the grounds of the supposed inferiority of the immigrants, it is worth noting that these complaints existed side-by-side with the apparently contradictory notion that the Jews were better adapted to the strains of urban life and therefore able to sustain themselves on a lower standard of living than their non-Jewish neighbours. In 1889 the Parliamentary Select Committee on Emigration and Immigration reported that 'the mode of living of these immigrants is wretched in the extreme. … Their food is of a poor nature, and they are able to maintain existence on much less than an English workman.'[41] In 1894 the Marquess of Salisbury complained that 'there is a very general belief among working men … that the introduction of these aliens, who are content with the very lowest conditions of existence, has a tendency to drive our own population out of employment and to increase the hardness of that battle which they have to fight in finding the means of living'.[42] In 1903 Ralph Neville told the Interdepartmental Committee on Physical Deterioration that 'these people can live, and are accustomed to live, on what will not support an English person in health. … I am satisfied that one of the reasons why wages in the clothing trade are so pitiable is because of the influx of these people who … are crushing our unhappy natives and bringing down wages to starvation point.'[43]

It is clear from the preceding paragraphs that many of the arguments used to oppose alien immigration were influenced by deep-seated beliefs about the susceptibility of Jews to various diseases and the 'inferiority' of the Jewish race, but very few writers were as openly anti-Semitic as Joseph Banister, or as happy to refer to a 'degenerate race' as John Gray.[44] Most of the arguments in favour of anti-alienism were not concerned with the status of Jews as Jews, but with the particular condition of those Jews who wished to settle in Britain as immigrants. Nevertheless the supporters of these views often expressed their concerns in language which seemed to reflect a deeper hostility. In 1903, when the *Lancet* published an account of the problems faced by the out-patient clinics of London's voluntary hospitals, it seemed to go out of its way to highlight the strangeness of the immigrants and the 'foreignness' of their sanitary habits:

> To anybody unfamiliar with the *clientèle* of a large general hospital in London the extent to which foreigners prevail there

> would provide no little surprise if he were to investigate the question. If such an inquirer were to spend a Saturday among the out-patients of an East End hospital – the London Hospital, let us say, or the Children's Hospital in the Hackney Road – his surprise would amount to nothing less than amazement. He would find himself surrounded by a crowd whose language was unknown to him, whose faces were strange, whose clothing was scarce, and whose odour was indescribable. … From an educational point of view, no doubt, it may be a fine thing that our students and young physicians should behold the filth diseases, the infectious disorders, and the skin lesions of other countries. From the point of view of the general charitable public, however, who support the hospitals to which these pauper aliens are driven by their bodily misfortunes, it may give us some food for reflection upon the trite theme that 'charity begins at home'.[45]

One of the most important claims made by the anti-aliens was the argument that the immigrants were drawn from the poorest sections of their own societies and that Britain was therefore being used as a 'dumping ground' for the unfit.[46] In February 1903 the Conservative MP for Stepney, Major William Evans-Gordon, told the Royal Commission on Alien Immigration (of which he was also a member) that the problem of Jewish immigration was compounded by the fact that 'the emigrant to England … comes from the lowest stratum of Jewish society in the congested towns'.[47] When Evans-Gordon published an extended account of his travels in Eastern Europe later in the same year, the *Lancet* noted sympathetically:

> In the main, the emigration to England comes from the lowest stratum of the Jewish society in the congested towns. From Poland the emigrants to England are, as a rule, drawn from the most necessitous class and from Roumania from the poor and incapable. … Of the other aliens who come to our shores from different countries many are merchants and skilled craftsmen whom no sane person proposes to impede, but concurrently there proceeds a systematic incursion of criminals and vicious persons for purposes of criminality and vice. The cost of maintaining these alien criminals is a serious burden to the community.[48]

For many observers the threat posed by the selective nature of Eastern European emigration was made even worse by the absence of effective immigration controls in the United Kingdom and the presence of such controls in the United States. This led to repeated claims that the least healthy and least desirable emigrants settled in Britain, whilst the more healthy and more desirable continued on their way to America. In 1896 the *British Medical Journal* complained that, as a result of the persecution of the Jews in Russia, 'hundreds of thousands of wretched paupers ... are crowded together in the cities of the Pale [i.e. the Jewish Pale of Settlement] until life there becomes intolerable. Then they escape in hordes in the hope of reaching the free West. The stronger and more able-bodied manage to reach America, but the less fit stay behind in England.'[49] In 1905 the *British Medical Journal* reviewed a pamphlet by Dr Robert Rentoul on 'The Undesirable Alien from the Medical Standpoint'.[50] It concluded:

> The numbers which Dr Rentoul quotes as debarred from entry at ports in the United States and Canada are particularly striking when it is remembered that aliens who actually ship to America and arrive there are only those who have succeeded in passing through the meshes of the medical net set to catch undesirables at the port of departure. To the best of our belief, such a precaution is not taken in the case of those who are bound for England only.[51]

In addition to concerns about the 'quality' of the 'stock' from which the immigrants were derived, many observers also chose to highlight the often poor condition of the ships on which they arrived. In 1893 the *British Medical Journal* reported that 'on September 11 the SS *Eilida* was boarded at Gravesend by the Medical Officer to the Port Sanitary Authority, who found 26 passengers from Libau [Liepaja] in Russia, a place infected with cholera ... in a filthy condition'. The paper condemned the leniency of the fine imposed on the captain when it was discovered that he had allowed the passengers to disembark without giving any forwarding addresses, thus exposing 'London to the risk of cholera, and set[ting] at naught regulations framed especially for cases such as this'.[52] In February 1906, after the implementation of the Aliens Act, the *Lancet* claimed that 'practically all the vessels which come into the Port of London with immigrants are foreign vessels, and it is certain that some of them are in a very insanitary condition and offer the most inadequate accommodation to their wretched freight'.[53] On 17 February the paper reported:

> It appears ... that in a vessel sailing from St Petersburg with 305 aliens on board, an especially filthy state prevailed. Both air space and floor space were palpably insufficient, and no provision was made for the separation of the sexes. ... The state of affairs in the reports received by Dr Williams cannot have been exaggerated. The lavatory accommodation for females in one ship which our representative inspected is not fit for description even in a medical journal.[54]

Many of the complaints which were made about the condition of immigrant ships were directed at the owners of the ships and their captains, but the *Lancet* was anxious to ensure that blame was evenly shared. It claimed that 'the nationality of the incomers must be borne in mind and too much blame must not be attributed to those responsible for the state of the vessels [*sic*]'. It continued:

> The majority of those who come to London are Polish Jews from Eastern Europe. ... They are, as a rule, of indifferent physique, wretchedly poor, and unclean in their habits, and however good the quarters offered them might be at the beginning of the voyage, short as that voyage usually is, they may be trusted to foul their nest.[55]

This concern with the sanitary habits of Jewish immigrants also played an important part in debates about the sanitary condition of immigrant workplaces. In 1884 the *Lancet* conducted a special enquiry into what it called 'the Polish colony of Jew tailors' in East London. It argued that 'the foreign Jews, who for many years have been flocking to the East End of London, are so numerous that their presence seriously affects the social and sanitary condition of this part of the Metropolis' and that 'the principal grievance to be brought against these Jew tailors is that they work in unwholesome, overcrowded houses, where girls and women are kept toiling long after the hours prescribed by the Factory and Workshops Act'.[56] The paper was anxious to emphasise that 'it is, unfortunately, not merely the foreign workmen, but dirty habits foreign to our ideas of salubrity, that are being introduced into our midst'.[57] In 1888 it noted:

> Manchester, as an abode for sweaters, possesses some notable advantages over London. The town is comparatively new; the streets are therefore wider, and there is more air and more light. Further, it so happens that the greater number of Jew sweaters have settled in the district of Strangeways, where they have found houses in some instances built for an altogether different and higher class of tenants. Somehow the higher-class tenants did not think fit to live in this quarter, and this, so far as public health is concerned, is a fortunate circumstance, for thus many of the Manchester sweaters are located in a better class of houses than those generally occupied by the sweaters of, for instance, London or Liverpool. Nevertheless, grave sanitary defects exist. The sweating dens we inspected in Manchester, though sometimes possessing the advantages we have mentioned, did not in any way reconcile us to the evils of the system.[58]

The *Lancet*'s attacks on the condition of the immigrants' work-places reflected a broader concern with their overall standard of hygiene and, in particular, with their housing conditions. In 1889 Dr William Clayton, a surgeon and Chairman of the Leeds Board of Guardians, told the Select Committee on Emigration and Immigration that 'many of them do stop, and some go away; but they spend no money, and they have no idea of domestic comfort; I should think that many of the floors [in the district in which they live] … have never been washed for years'.[59] In 1905 the Conservative Home Secretary, Aretas Akers-Douglas, told the House of Commons that 'the evils which these aliens bring in their train – overcrowding, living in insanitary conditions, the lowering of the general standard of life and morality, and crime – have also … increased'.[60] The Government's spokesman in the House of Lords, Lord Belper, argued that even though the Royal Commission on Alien Immigration had found that there was no great amount of disease among the immigrants on arrival, 'it is a fact that the insanitary conditions under which some of them live have introduced new diseases of a very disagreeable character'.[61]

Doctors and pro-alienism

The opponents of Jewish immigration claimed that the immigrants were drawn from the most unhealthy sections of the Eastern European population; that they travelled on dirty and insanitary ships; that they were the source of new and unpleasant diseases, and that after they had arrived in Britain they lived and worked under the most insanitary conditions. However, it is important to recognise that these were not the only ways in which public health issues interacted with the anti-alien debate. Many observers argued that the anti-alienists' claims were not only untrue, but that the immigrants were often healthier than the rest of the population in the districts in which they lived. They argued that the immigrants set standards of parenthood and sobriety which the native population should be encouraged to emulate.

One of the most alarming features of the anti-alien debate was the claim that the Jews were in some way a 'degenerate' race or that they were uniquely susceptible to certain diseases. However, several of the expert witnesses who gave evidence before the Royal Commission on Alien Immigration argued that these allegations were unfounded. Dr Shirley Forster Murphy, the Medical Officer of Health for London, thought that trachoma (the disease referred to by Dr Tyrrell) was common to all overcrowded districts, whether occupied by Jews or non-Jews,[62] and the President of the Ophthalmological Society of the United Kingdom, William Lang, told the Commission that Jewish children were no more susceptible to granular ophthalmia than any other children living under comparable circumstances, while the condition itself was in any case entirely treatable.[63] Charles Mansfield, the head teacher at Settles Street Board School in Stepney, said that even though Jewish schoolchildren suffered from a higher incidence of short-sightedness, this was more closely related to cramped and overcrowded living conditions than to any 'racial' susceptibility.[64]

In addition to questions about the incidence of specific diseases, some observers argued that, far from being a degenerate race, Jews might even possess some degree of racial immunity to disease. The Medical Officer of Health for Whitechapel, Dr Joseph Loane, believed that mortality rates had declined in his area as a direct result of Jewish immigration, and that 'there is no doubt that the foreign Jew has far less tendency to diseases which carry off a large number of the Whitechapel people ... constitutional disease, consumption, and diseases of that kind'.[65] Dr Robert Hutchison thought that the greater robustness of the Jewish population was partly racial and partly cultural. He told the Interdepartmental Committee on Physical Deterioration that Jewish mothers had greater reproductive powers than other groups, and that this 'may be partially racial and partly the indirect consequence of the Jewish code'.[66]

The supporters of Jewish immigration also challenged the view that Jewish immigrants were, in some sense, a 'selection of the unfit'. Dr Herbert Williams, the Port of London Medical Officer, told the Royal Commission on Alien Immigration that the people who disembarked from emigrant ships looked as though they had been 'overworked and underfed, and ... harassed a great deal', but there was no evidence that their physique had been ruined in any way: 'I think you might assume that it is a sort of survival of the fittest, and it is some of the best who come over'.[67] The Medical Officer of Health for Glasgow, Dr Archibald Chalmers, told the Interdepartmental Committee on Physical Deterioration that 'the immigrant is a vigorous man, with a definite intention of bettering himself, and that is why he comes here, and forms an incentive which probably does not exist in the case of his neighbour, who is a native'.[68] The MP for Oldham, Alfred Emmott, also challenged the view 'that it was the best who went away and the worst that remained with us'. He argued that 'there is a good deal of evidence telling in another direction, because the reports of the Jewish schoolmasters show how well the children of these aliens are doing in the schools, and the returns of lunatics and paupers show that the aliens are proportionately only one-third or one-fourth of the natives who come upon them'.[69]

The immigrants' supporters also sought to defend them against many of the other allegations which were made against them. Dr Williams said that 'the number of cases of infectious disease ... that I have detected among these people has not been numerous, speaking as a whole. I cannot say that much infectious disease has come to this country among these people'.[70] The Assistant Medical Officer of Health for London, Dr William Hamer, found that the incidence of overcrowding in Whitechapel and Mile End was significantly lower than the incidence of overcrowding in Lambeth and St Pancras, where the number of immigrants was much smaller.[71] The Medical Officer of Health for Manchester, Dr James Niven, thought that although the level of overcrowding was heavier in immigrant areas, there was little evidence to show that this was reflected in higher levels of infectious disease. There were some indications that Jewish children suffered from a higher incidence of diphtheria, but the Jewish population was entirely free of both typhus and smallpox.[72]

Many of the witnesses who gave evidence to the Royal Commission on Alien Immigration devoted considerable attention to the question of whether the sanitary habits of the immigrant population were better or worse than those of their neighbours. Dr Shirley Murphy said that immigrants 'were like most English populations – they have got good people, and they have got fair people, and they have got indifferent people amongst them, but taking them as a whole … I should certainly not have picked out their houses as being amongst the worst'.[73] Other witnesses thought that when the immigrants first arrived, their sanitary habits left a lot to be desired, but they showed a considerable capacity for improvement and were extremely responsive to official pressure. Dr Daniel Thomas told the Royal Commission that 'for the first year or two … their condition of life is very much below that of the native population [but] after that they improve very rapidly'.[74] Dr Niven thought that 'the people when they first come over have a different standard of cleanliness to what exists in this country, but … the fact is that they are amenable to the ordinary methods of sanitary administration, and … the defects have, in fact, been largely remedied, partly by persuasion, and partly by pressure'.[75]

In addition to the direct rebuttal of anti-alien claims, the immigrants' supporters also sought to highlight what they saw as the positive aspects of immigrant life. Several of the witnesses who gave evidence before the Royal Commission on Alien Immigration affirmed that Jewish parents took better care of their children and were more responsive to suggestions for improvement than their non-Jewish neighbours. William Ward, the Bethnal Green Vaccination Officer, said that he was sure that 'we run no danger of disease from these foreigners, and if our natives were only as conscientious in obeying the laws as to vaccination, there would be much less risk of smallpox getting a hold'.[76] Shirley Murphy thought that the immigrants were 'a very abstemious people … they were very careful of their children, and … led more regular lives than it is generally the habit of people living in the same class of house over here to lead'.[77] The Medical Officer of Health for Liverpool, Dr Edward Hope, noted that the Jewish mothers 'devote a great amount of care and attention to their children' and that, in contrast to the native children, 'the infants are almost always breast-fed'.[78] Dr James Niven praised the good sense and economy which the immigrants showed in their choice of food: 'I think they feed pretty well as far as their means will go, and as far as I have been able to judge by going into their houses'.[79]

Many of the favourable comments made during the deliberations of the Royal Commission on Alien Immigration were reiterated in the evidence presented to the Interdepartmental Committee on Physical Deterioration. Shirley Murphy repeated his view that the Jewish population spent less money on drink and took better care of its children.[80] The Chairman of the Manchester and Salford Sanitary Association, Thomas Horsfall, said that 'the Jewish mothers as a rule have a strong sense of duty towards their children … and … there is not nearly so much drinking amongst them'.[81] Dr Eustace Smith thought that the Jewish mothers took much better care of their children and that they spent more time at home than other mothers, with the result that they were able to supervise their children more closely.[82] The Secretary of the Charity Organisation Society, Charles Stewart Loch, agreed that 'the Jewish mothers feed their children much better, and not only know what is best for them, but know how to cook it, and are more thrifty and … abstemious [than] … our own people'.[83]

The belief that Jewish children were more healthy than non-Jewish children living under comparable circumstances was not based entirely on anecdotal evidence. In 1903 Dr William Hall, a retired general practitioner living in Leeds, conducted a series of investigations into the comparative health of Jewish and non-Jewish children attending Board schools in different parts of the city. He found that Jewish children were both taller and heavier than non-Jewish children attending schools in the same part of the city, and that they were even larger than children attending schools in the city's more affluent districts. He also examined the children's teeth and bone structure, and found that, while 51 per cent of the non-Jewish children had bad or badly developing teeth, the incidence of defective teeth among the Jewish children was only 27 per cent. The incidence of rickets among the non-Jewish children was 45 per cent, as opposed to only 17 per cent among the Jewish children.[84]

The apparent healthiness of Jewish children was reflected in the population's mortality statistics. In 1902, Joseph Loane told the Royal Commission on Alien Immigration that the decline of infant mortality in Whitechapel was directly attributable to the influx of Jewish immigrants who were inherently healthier than the native population.[85] Dr Murphy also used the mortality statistics to show that infant mortality had declined in Whitechapel and St George-in-the-East while increasing in London as a whole.[86] However, as S. Rosenbaum noted in 1905, the best evidence of Jewish healthiness appeared to come from Manchester.[87] Dr James Niven found that mortality rates were lower among people living in 'Jewish districts' than in the city as a whole. The general mortality rate was lower at all ages from 0 to 64 and the mortality rate from phthisis, or pulmonary tuberculosis, was lower at all ages except for those aged 15–24.[88]

In evaluating these statistics, it is important to recognise that not all public health workers believed that Jewish children were healthier than non-Jewish children, or that their parents necessarily took better care of them. Dr James Kerr, the Medical Officer to the Education Committee of the London County Council, told a meeting of the Society of Medical Officers of Health that the apparent healthiness of Jewish children was probably attributable to a 'racial habit of body', and Dr Algernon Wear claimed that even though 'a good deal has been published from time to time as to the physical superiority of Jewish children over Gentile children ... a study of the returns in [the Leeds school medical] report does not show that the comparison is as favourable to the former as has been thought'.[89] However it is clear that the majority of public health officers were convinced of the facts of Jewish healthiness, and they showed little hesitation in attributing this to the higher standards of domestic care associated with Jewish families. In 1908 the Medical Officer of Health for Sheffield, Dr Harold Scurfield, wrote that 'in our arrogance ... we have established a society for converting the Jews. It would be much more to the point if we induced the Jews to establish missions for the teaching of good motherhood in our big towns.'[90]

Conclusions

The majority of accounts of the campaign against alien immigration have tended to focus on the part played by arguments about the impact of foreign immigration on the labour market and the 'displacement' of native-born inhabitants by foreign immigrants.[91] However, it is clear that arguments over public health also played an important part in the contemporary debate. Newspapers such as the *British Medical Journal* and the *Lancet* sought to highlight the supposedly injurious effects of Jewish immigration on health standards, while many Medical Officers of Health argued that the immigrants were often healthier than the population in whose midst they settled.

In the context of this book, it is particularly important to examine the role played by assumptions about 'race' in these debates. It is clear that although newspapers such as the *British Medical Journal* and – especially – the *Lancet* may well have been affected by a degree of anti-Semitism, most writers appear to have believed that differences between the health of Jews and non-Jews owed more to differences of culture and behaviour than to any innate 'racial' differences. This was true of both pro-alien and anti-alien camps. Even though some commentators, such as Francis Tyrrell and John Gray, insisted that Jews were uniquely susceptible to particular diseases, most anti-alien campaigners preferred to highlight the 'foreignness' of the immigrants and their reluctance or inability to observe the sanitary standards of British society.[92] The question of behavioural differences was even more important to the pro-alien supporters. They argued that the Jews were naturally no more healthy than any other group, but that they made themselves healthier by their adherence to fundamental hygienic values.

In making these arguments both pro- and anti-alien lobbies were clearly influenced by a much broader range of ideas than those associated exclusively with questions of public health. In 1893 the *Lancet* pointed out that the case for excluding foreign immigrants could be broken down under three main headings, namely moral grounds, sanitary grounds and economic grounds. However, although it insisted that these issues needed to be treated separately for administrative reasons, it recognised that in practice there was a high degree of overlap between them.[93] The development of medical attitudes to anti-alienism was also influenced by a wide range of other factors, including the persistence of anti-Semitism, the rise of Social Darwinism, the fear of national and racial decline, and the belief that the influx of foreign immigrants threatened the foundations of Britain's nascent welfare state. In 1903 the *British Medical Journal* welcomed the formation of the Immigration Reform Association on the grounds that 'most English people will be inclined to wish it success, for, with emigration societies actively engaged in exporting to new colonies as many of the best of the true British stock as they can catch, and immigration from the East continuing unchecked, the outlook is not reassuring for those who set some store on the preservation of the characteristics which have hitherto been regarded as the source of England's strength'.[94]

There are a number of reasons why Medical Officers of Health may have been more favourably disposed towards Jewish immigrants. One possibility is that they were anxious to play down the case for immigration controls because of the extra work which this might impose on them as Port Medical Officers.[95] However, in other cases Medical Officers of Health were more than anxious to expand their range of responsibilities in order to strengthen the case for the creation of full-time appointments and the introduction of full security of tenure.[96] In the case of the health problems associated with Jewish immigrants, the Medical Officers of Health argued strongly that the best way to address these issues was not by introducing immigration restrictions, but by strengthening the existing machinery of sanitary administration.[97]

The Medical Officers of Health's attitudes may have been more closely related to their general political sympathies. During the second half of the nineteenth century Medical Officers of Health became increasingly divorced from general practice, especially in London, and this may have led them to take a rather different view of social and political questions.[98] In 1862 the Medical Officer of Health for Bermondsey, Dr John Challice, was elected to Parliament as a Liberal,[99] and the leading sanitarian, Sir Lyon Playfair, represented the Liberal constituencies of Edinburgh and St Andrews and, subsequently, Leeds, between 1868 and 1892.[100] During the early years of the twentieth century the Society of Medical Officers of Health played an increasingly important role in the campaign for social reform.[101] In 1909 the Medical Officer to the Local Government Board, Arthur Newsholme, told the members of the Society that:

> With wider and more exact knowledge of hygiene, it is being increasingly realised that the whole range of the physical, mental and to a large extent … moral life of mankind may be brought within the range of preventive medicine; and that as medical knowledge grows, the number of diseases that can be regarded as preventable will increase, and public administration will extend beyond its present limits.[102]

It is also important to place Medical Officers of Health's attitudes to Jewish immigrants in the context of broader debates within the public health movement. During the 1890s and early 1900s public health officers had begun to place increasing emphasis on the need for improvements in personal hygiene to build upon earlier improvements in environmental conditions, and the apparent healthiness of the Jewish population provided an important illustration of the benefits which would follow from this.[103] In 1907 Shirley Murphy told the Education Committee of the London County Council that:

> Enquiries into the causes of mortality had brought the Medical Officer of Health into touch with the personal factor in relation to disease. The destitution of the poor, the intimate association of their diseases with want of cleanliness [and] the part played by ignorance and neglect in fostering ill-health necessarily impressed upon him the knowledge that it was not external environment alone which determined ... the health of the community, and hence ... he had allied himself with movements which have had as their aim the improvement of the personal hygiene of the people.[104]

The apparent healthiness of the Jews also provided Medical Officers of Health with an important weapon in their contest with members of the eugenics movement. During the early part of the twentieth century the supporters of eugenics argued that the sources of ill-health were rooted in heredity and that the health of the population could only be improved by a campaign for 'racial hygiene'.[105] In contrast the Society of Medical Officers of Health argued that the best way to improve the standard of public health was by improving the environment and by persuading the individual that 'when he has put his house in order, it is then his duty to fit himself to live in it'.[106] The apparent healthiness of Jewish immigrants, in both London and New York, reinforced the message which Medical Officers of Health wished to convey. As *Public Health* observed in 1896:

> The Jew ... proves that it is possible for man to overcome the bad effects of his environment, and that he is practically in control of a long span of his duration of life. The Jew proves that a man can add from fifteen to twenty years to his average

duration of life if he will implicitly obey the dictates of his moral nature. It is his temperate mode of living, his high respect for domestic virtues, his belief in the gospel of life worth living, and his attention to matters of personal hygiene, that are the secret of his exceptional longevity.[107]

Notes

1 See, for example, B. Gainer, *The Alien Invasion: The Origins of the Aliens Act of 1905*, London, Heinemann, 1972; C. Holmes, *Anti-Semitism in British Society, 1876–1939*, London, Edward Arnold, 1979. The pro-alien case is discussed in J. Garrard, *The English and Immigration, 1880–1910*, London, Oxford University Press and Institute of Race Relations, 1971, esp. pp. 85–153.

2 N. Stepan, *The Idea of Race in Science: Great Britain, 1800–1960*, London and Basingstoke, Macmillan, 1982, p. 84.

3 The exact number of German-born residents was 32,823, out of a total 'European-born' population of 89,829. For further information, see C. Holmes, *John Bull's Island: Immigration and British Society, 1871–1971*, Basingstoke, Macmillan, 1988, pp. 3–35; see also D. Baines, 'Population, Migration and Regional Development, 1870–1939', in R. Floud and D. McCloskey (eds), *The Economic History of Britain since 1700. Volume 2: 1860–1939*, 2nd edn, Cambridge, Cambridge University Press, 1994, pp. 55–6; D. Feldman, 'Nationality and Ethnicity', in P. Johnson (ed.), *Twentieth-Century Britain: Economic, Social and Cultural Change*, London, Longman, 1994, p. 128.

4 L. Gartner, *The Jewish Immigrant in England, 1870–1914*, London, Simon Publications, 1973, p. 30; V.D. Lipman, *A History of the Jews in Britain since 1858*, Leicester, Leicester University Press, 1990, p. 45.

5 G. Alderman, *Modern British Jewry*, Oxford, Clarendon Press, 1992, pp. 102–51.

6 G. Drage, 'Alien Immigration', *Journal of Royal Statistical Society* 58 (1895): 12.

7 Gartner, *The Jewish Immigrant in England*, p. 64.

8 B. Harris, 'Anti-Alienism, Health and Social Reform in late-Victorian and Edwardian Britain', *Patterns of Prejudice* 31, 4 (1997): 16.

9 B. Potter, 'The Jewish Community (East London)', in C. Booth, *Life and Labour of the People in London. First Series: Poverty*, vol. 3, *Blocks of Buildings, Schools and Immigration*, London, Macmillan, pp. 190–2.

10 G.R. Searle, *The Quest for National Efficiency: A Study in British Social and Political Thought, 1899–1914*, Oxford, Blackwell, 1972, p. 27.

11 R. Floud, 'Britain, 1860–1914: A Survey', in Floud and McCloskey, *The Economic History of Britain since 1700. Volume 2: 1860–1939*, p. 1.

12 L. Amery, *The Times History of the War in South Africa*, vol. 1, London, Sampson Low, Marston, 1900, p. 11.

13 See B. Harris, *The Health of the Schoolchild: A History of the School Medical Service in England and Wales*, Buckingham, Open University Press, 1995, pp. 6–25.
14 See, for example, *Parliamentary Debates*, 4th series, vol. 145, col. 740.
15 G. Jones, *Social Darwinism and English Thought: The Interaction between Biological and Social Theory*, Brighton, Harvester, 1980; M. Hawkins, *Social Darwinism in European and American Thought, 1860–1945: Nature as Model and Nature as Threat*, Cambridge, Cambridge University Press, 1997, esp. pp. 184–215.
16 J. Harris, *Private Lives, Public Spirit: Britain, 1870–1914*, Harmondsworth, Penguin, 1994, p. 235.
17 D. Lorimer, 'Theoretical Racism in Late Victorian Anthropology, 1870–1900', *Victorian Studies* 31 (1987–8): 405–30, esp. p. 421.
18 See also D. Feldman, *Englishmen and Jews: Social Relations and Political Culture, 1840–1914*, New Haven and London, Yale University Press, 1994, pp. 263–4.
19 'A Jew's Objections to Serve on a Coroner's Jury', *Lancet* 12 November 1898: 1,282; 'A Jew's Objections to Serve on a Coroner's Jury', *Lancet* 19 November 1898: 1,347–8.
20 'Indigent Aliens and the Public Health', *Lancet* 29 April 1911: 1,147.
21 Drage, 'Alien Immigration', p. 2.
22 *Parliamentary Debates*, 4th series, vol. 145, cols 764–8. The MP for Poplar was Sydney Buxton, the leading supporter of immigration controls on the Liberal side.
23 See B. Porter, *The Refugee Question in Mid-Victorian Politics*, Cambridge, Cambridge University Press, 1979; B. Porter, *The Origins of the Vigilant State: The London Metropolitan Police Special Branch before the First World War*, London, Weidenfeld & Nicolson, 1987.
24 *Parliamentary Debates*, 3rd series, vol. 321, col. 490; see also 'Destitute Aliens', *Lancet* xvii (September 1887): 599. Smith, who was Deputy Leader of the Conservative Party, had originally stood for Parliament in 1865 as a 'Liberal-Conservative', and his strong educational interests brought him close to the Liberal politician, W.E. Forster. See M. Bentley, *Politics Without Democracy, 1815–1914*, London, Fontana, 1984, p. 389.
25 *Parliamentary Debates*, 4th series, vol. 145, cols 472, 732.
26 *Parliamentary Debates*, 4th series, vol. 145, col. 1,261. Seeley added that 'it was because they believed that humanity could be regarded as a great commonwealth that [members on his side of the House] … opposed the policy of the exclusion of the poor and miserable'.
27 'The Alien Question and the New Aliens Act', *Lancet* 3 February 1906: 331.
28 'Special Correspondence: Melbourne. Proceedings of the Health Section of the Social Science Congress', *British Medical Journal* 26 February 1881: 319; 'Comparative Longevity of the Jews', *British Medical Journal* 13 May 1882: 723.
29 'The Duration of Life of the Jew', *Public Health* 8 (1895–6): 308–10.

30 M. Fishberg, *The Jews: A Study of Race and Environment*, London, Felling-on-Tyne, New York and Melbourne, Walter Scott Publishing, 1911, pp. 256–7; see also the sources cited in L. Marks, *Model Mothers: Jewish Mothers and Maternity Provision in East London, 1870–1939*, Oxford, Clarendon Press, 1994, pp. 52–9.
31 J. Jacobs, 'The Racial Characteristics of Modern Jews', in Jacobs, *Studies in Jewish Statistics: Social, Vital and Anthropometric*, p. xi; 'The American Climate and the Jews', *British Medical Journal* 24 January 1891: 190–1.
32 'The Pathology of the Jew', *British Medical Journal* 21 September 1901: 828.
33 'Insanity among German Jews', *British Medical Journal* 20 June 1891: 1,366.
34 'The Insane Jew', *Lancet* 27 October 1900: 1,219. Mr Beadles declined to say what effect his evident lack of sympathy for his Jewish charges may have had on their recovery rates.
35 'The Jew as a Study in Racial Pathology', *British Medical Journal* 1 June 1901: 1,356.
36 PP 1903 Cd 1742 ix, Royal Commission on Alien Immigration, Minutes of evidence, QQ 3,676–84.
37 'Trachoma among Aliens', *Lancet* 3 June 1905: 1,525. See also 'Use of Adrenalin by Immigrants to Conceal Trachoma', *Lancet* 7 January 1905: 62; 'Aliens and Trachoma', *Lancet* 13 May 1911: 1,298–9. For reports of references to the disease in Parliament, see 'Aliens and Trachoma', *British Medical Journal* 17 April 1909: 975; 'Aliens and Trachoma in London', *British Medical Journal* 31 July 1909: 293; 'Aliens and Trachoma', *Lancet* 22 April 1911: 1,111; 'Aliens and Trachoma', *Lancet* 29 April 1911: 1,181.
38 'The Importation of Foreign Lunatics', *Lancet* 21 May 1895: 1,327.
39 PP 1904 Cd 2210 xxxii, Interdepartmental Committee on Physical Deterioration, Minutes of evidence and list of witnesses, Q 3,371.
40 Interdepartmental Committee on Physical Deterioration, Minutes of evidence and list of witnesses, Q 3,257.
41 PP 1889 (311) x, 265, Report from the Select Committee on Emigration and Immigration (Foreigners), together with the proceedings of the Committee, Minutes of evidence and appendix, p. ix.
42 *Parliamentary Debates*, 4th series, vol. 26, col. 134.
43 Interdepartmental Committee on Physical Deterioration, Minutes of evidence and list of witnesses, Q 4,876.
44 For Banister, see Holmes, *Anti-Semitism in British Society*, pp. 39–42; for Gray and Banister, see Harris, 'Anti-Alienism, Health and Social Reform', pp. 6–7.
45 'Pauper Aliens and London Hospitals', *Lancet* 31 January 1903: 320–1.
46 These arguments were invoked frequently in the Houses of Parliament. In 1905 the Conservative peer, Lord Belper, told members of the House of Lords that 'this country … is rapidly becoming the sink of the undesirable class of aliens on the Continent'. See *Parliamentary Debates*, 4th series, vol. 145, cols 761, 797; vol. 150, col. 752.

47 Royal Commission on Alien Immigration, Minutes of evidence, Q 13,349.
48 W. Evans-Gordon, *The Alien Immigrant*, London, William Heinemann, and New York, Chas Scribner's Sons, 1903; 'Reviews and Notices of Books: *The Alien Immigrant*', *Lancet* 7 November 1903: 1,304–5.
49 'Consumption among East End Jews', *British Medical Journal* 12 September 1896: 700.
50 Robert Reid Rentoul, 'The Undesirable Alien from the Medical Standpoint', Liverpool, Cornish, 1905. I have been unable to locate a copy of this publication, but there is a more detailed account in Holmes, *Anti-Semitism in British Society*, pp. 36–7, 46–7.
51 'The Undesirable Alien', *British Medical Journal* 15 April 1905: 842. See also 'The Aliens Act', *British Medical Journal* 24 February 1906: 453–4. The author argued that 'the class of aliens who have ousted sections of our native population and forced them into already overcrowded neighbourhoods has been a class selected as fit for shipment to England on account of their unfitness for any other country'.
52 'The Importation of Filthy Aliens', *British Medical Journal* 23 September 1893: 716.
53 'The Alien Question and the New Aliens Act', *Lancet* 3 February 1906: 331–2.
54 'The Insanitary Condition of Immigrant Ships', *Lancet* 17 February 1906: 467–8; see also 'Sanitary Administration in the Port of London', *Lancet* 12 May 1906: 1,330–1. Dr Williams was the Port of London Medical Officer.
55 'The Alien Question and the New Aliens Act', *Lancet* 3 February 1906: 331.
56 'Report on the *Lancet* Special Sanitary Commission on the Polish Colony of Jew Tailors', *Lancet* 3 May 1994: 817.
57 'The *Lancet* Special Sanitary Commission on "Sweating" among Tailors at Liverpool and Manchester', *Lancet* 21 April 1888: 793.
58 'The *Lancet* Special Sanitary Commission on "Sweating" ', *Lancet* 21 April 1888: 792.
59 Report from the Select Committee on Emigration and Immigration (Foreigners), together with the proceedings of the Committee, Minutes of evidence and appendix, Q 1,132.
60 *Parliamentary Debates*, 4th series, vol. 145, col. 465.
61 *Parliamentary Debates*, 4th series, vol. 150, col. 750.
62 Royal Commission on Alien Immigration, Minutes of evidence, Q 4,918.
63 Royal Commission on Alien Immigration, Minutes of evidence, QQ 20,595–601.
64 Royal Commission on Alien Immigration, Minutes of evidence, QQ 18,428–42.
65 Royal Commission on Alien Immigration, Minutes of evidence, Q 4,541.
66 Interdepartmental Committee on Physical Deterioration, Minutes of evidence and list of witnesses, QQ 10,018, 10,036–8.

67 Royal Commission on Alien Immigration, Minutes of evidence, QQ 6,185–6.

68 Interdepartmental Committee on Physical Deterioration, Minutes of evidence and list of witnesses, Q 6,090. Ironically, Chalmers believed that this was true of all areas except his own. In 1905 he told a meeting of Medical Officers of Health 'that Jewish children turned out better physically on inspection he understood was the case in all places except Glasgow. He did not think they had a worse type of alien than the Jews in Glasgow. They were not physically better in comparison with the Christian children, and he found that Jews were very much worse as regards eyesight.' See L. Brunton, 'The Report of the Interdepartmental Committee on Physical Degeneration', *Public Health* 17 (1904–5): 288.

69 *Parliamentary Debates*, 4th series, vol. 145, col. 772.

70 Royal Commission on Alien Immigration, Minutes of evidence, Q 6,113.

71 Royal Commission on Alien Immigration, Minutes of evidence, QQ 18,112–21.

72 Royal Commission on Alien Immigration, Minutes of evidence, QQ 21,791–3. See also 'Dr Niven on Sanitation amongst the Manchester Jews', *Lancet* 6 June 1896: 1,594; 'Manchester Jewish Board of Guardians', *Lancet* 18 July 1896: 216–17; Interdepartmental Committee on Physical Deterioration, Minutes of evidence and list of witnesses, Q 5,575.

73 Royal Commission on Alien Immigration, Minutes of evidence, Q 4,076.

74 Royal Commission on Alien Immigration, Minutes of evidence, Q 5,775.

75 Royal Commission on Alien Immigration, Minutes of evidence, Q 21,810.

76 Royal Commission on Alien Immigration, Minutes of evidence, Q 18,311.

77 Royal Commission on Alien Immigration, Minutes of evidence, Q 3,693. See also Royal Commission on Alien Immigration, Minutes of evidence, Q 4,884; Interdepartmental Committee on Physical Deterioration, Minutes of evidence and list of witnesses, QQ 9,408–14; PP 1904 Cd 2186 xxxii, Interdepartmental Committee on Physical Deterioration, Appendices and index, p. 55.

78 Royal Commission on Alien Immigration, Minutes of evidence, Q 21,412.

79 Royal Commission on Alien Immigration, Minutes of evidence, Q 21,674.

80 Interdepartmental Committee on Physical Deterioration, Minutes of evidence and list of witnesses, Q 9,408–14; Interdepartmental Committee on Physical Deterioration, Appendices and index, p. 55.

81 Interdepartmental Committee on Physical Deterioration, Minutes of evidence and list of witnesses, Q 5,700.

82 Interdepartmental Committee on Physical Deterioration, Minutes of evidence and list of witnesses, QQ 8,482–4, 8,524–7.

83 Interdepartmental Committee on Physical Deterioration, Minutes of evidence and list of witnesses, Q 10,356.

84 W. Hall, 'Christian and Jew: A Remarkable Comparison', *Yorkshire Post* 2 May 1903: 12. See also Hall, ' "Where Men Decay", and How', *Yorkshire Post* 28 March 1903: 10; 'Christian and Jew: The Case of the Girls', *Yorkshire Post* 9 May 1903: 9; 'Gentile and Jew: The Care of the Children', *Yorkshire Post* 19 May 1903: 8.

85 Royal Commission on Alien Immigration, Minutes of evidence, Q 4,538–46.

86 Royal Commission on Alien Immigration, Minutes of evidence, QQ 3,960–3; Interdepartmental Committee on Physical Deterioration, Minutes of evidence and list of witnesses, QQ 9,412–14.

87 S. Rosenbaum, 'A Contribution to the Study of the Vital and Other Statistics of the Jews in the United Kingdom', *Journal of the Royal Statistical Society* 68 (1905): 550. See also Gartner, *The Jewish Immigrant in England*, pp. 158–9.

88 Royal Commission on Alien Immigration, Minutes of evidence, Q 21,872. See also Interdepartmental Committee on Physical Deterioration, Minutes of evidence and list of witnesses, Q 5,575 and Table 1.

89 A. Wear, 'Physical Condition of Jewish Schoolchildren in Leeds', *Public Health* 23 (1909–10): 339. For a more detailed examination of the Leeds results, see Harris, 'Anti-Alienism, Health and Social Reform', pp. 15–34.

90 Untitled, *Public Health* 21 (1908): 22.

91 See, for example, Garrard, *The English and Immigration*, pp. 51–4; Gainer, *The Alien Invasion*, pp. 15–59; Feldman, *Englishmen and Jews*, pp. 268–76. Holmes, *Anti-Semitism in British Society*, pp. 36–48, does discuss the impact of alien immigration on 'the health and morals of the nation', but his account focuses on the views expressed by individual campaigners. He makes little attempt to examine the dissemination of anti-alien arguments in the mainstream medical press.

92 See, for example, 'The Immigration of Undesirable Aliens', *British Medical Journal* 22 August 1903: 423–4.

93 'Alien Immigration', *Lancet* 7 October 1893: 833–4 and *Lancet* 14 October 1893: 950–1.

94 'The Immigration of Undesirable Aliens', *British Medical Journal* 22 August 1903: 423–4.

95 For description of the burdens which the Aliens Act did impose on Medical Officers of Health, see 'The Aliens Act', *British Medical Journal* 24 February 1906: 453–4; 'The Alien Question and the New Aliens Act', *Lancet* 3 February 1906: 331–2; 'Medical Inspector under the Aliens Act at the Port of Hull', *Public Health* 18 (1905–6): 159.

96 See B. Harris, 'Medical Inspection and the Nutrition of Schoolchildren in Britain, 1900–50', University of London Ph.D. thesis, 1989, pp. 71–2.

97 See, for example, Royal Commission on Alien Immigration, Minutes of evidence, QQ 3,908–4,116, 4,722–5,155.

98 See D. Watkins, 'The English Revolution in Social Medicine, 1889–1911', University of London Ph.D. thesis, 1984, pp. 83–5.

99 Watkins, 'The English Revolution in Social Medicine', p. 68; Challice died before he could take his seat.

100 J. Brand, *Doctors and the State: The British Medical Profession and Government Action in Public Health, 1870–1912*, Baltimore, Johns Hopkins Press, 1965, p. 14. For further information, see *Who Was Who. Volume 1: 1897–1915*, London, A. & C. Black, 1920, p. 566.

101 Brand, *Doctors and the State*, pp. 114–33.

102 A. Newsholme, 'Some Conditions of Social Efficiency in Relation to Local Public Administration', *Public Health* 22 (1908–9): 403–14; quoted in Searle, *The Quest for National Efficiency*, p. 64.

103 See, for example, Brunton, 'The Report of the Interdepartmental Committee on Physical Degeneration', pp. 274–92, esp. comments by Sir John Gorst and Dr H. Franklin Parsons on pp. 284–5.

104 London County Council, Education Committee, Day-Schools Sub-Committee, Agenda, 21 January 1908, p. 55.

105 See D. Porter, ' "Enemies of the Race": Biologism, Environmentalism and Public Health in Edwardian England', *Victorian Studies* 34 (1990–1): 147–78.

106 W.L. Mackenzie, *The Health of the Schoolchild*, London, Methuen, 1906, p. 50.

107 'The Duration of Life of the Jew', *Public Health* 8 (1895–6): 310.

Chapter 10

A virulent strain

German bacteriology as scientific racism, 1890–1920

Paul Weindling

The bacteriology of imperialism

'Gentlemen, I forget that I am in Europe' was Robert Koch's comment on the conditions in Hamburg during the cholera epidemic of 1892.[1] The new science of bacteriology offered powers of intervention into the darkest recesses of foul living-conditions, as well as into the fluids and fibres of the human constitution. The stigma of the sick person was compounded by the sense that disease was implanted by alien species of bacteria. Epidemics were deemed to be a throwback to a more primitive era when Europeans stood at a cultural level similar to the 'lower' colonial races. Bacteriology as advanced by Koch was imbued with the sense of a civilising mission. It offered a comprehensive causal explanation for the occurrence of disease: Koch and his disciples were scientific empire-builders, as they demanded hygiene institutes and facilities for surveillance of micro-organisms harboured by people, animals and the natural environment.

The state authorities readily invested funds into bacteriology as a means of offering technical solutions to controlling diseases that could otherwise contribute to social unrest and dislocation during a period of rapid growth of German cities and industry. Although the history of bacteriology has traditionally been conceived of in value-neutral terms as the discovery of new pathogens and improvements in laboratory techniques, the place of bacteriology in German imperialist ideology merits consideration. The support for imperialism by Koch and his colleagues meant that bacteriology became susceptible to more racist formulations. This chapter examines the extent to which bacteriology became racialised as part of medical responses to transmigrants crossing from the East in the 1890s, and culminating in the German occupation of eastern territories during World War I.

While Koch encountered the cholera epidemic at its last gasp in Western Europe, bacteriologists were aware that other 'Asiatic' diseases threatened the vigour of imperial powers. Koch noted that leprosy was resurgent on the Baltic fringes of Germany and the new corps of microbe-hunters dreaded the importation of typhus, smallpox and especially plague by transmigrants from the East. Urban sanitary experts for their part feared tuberculosis and sexually transmitted infections as 'racial poisons'. Bacteriologists were imbued with imperialism and militarism, or with ideas of a patriotic cleansing of the civic environment. Diseases came to be associated with such ethnic undesirables as Gypsies/Romanies and Jews.

The political cultures nurturing the growth of bacteriology have often been overlooked in favour of more value-neutral explanations. Being grounded in experimental biology, bacteriology and the rise of germ theory have been seen as antithetical to social and racial ideologies. Historians of social medicine have played down bacteriology as merely offering technical solutions in the form of disinfectants and vaccines: Dorothy Porter makes the point that bacteriology had a negligible effect on the rhetoric and practice of English public health. Yet bacteriologists – or lapsed bacteriologists – pressed for an ambitious social programme of sanitary improvements and preventive measures.[2] This can be seen in the cases of two disillusioned bacteriologists who looked to biological theories to make good the limitations of bacteriology. Ferdinand Hueppe in Prague stressed the notion of an inherited predisposition to disease, while conceding that exercise and diet could improve a person's constitution; Adolf Gottstein as a municipal doctor in Berlin developed theories of social medicine which incorporated eugenic ideas. For prevention involved not only vaccines and quarantine, but also positive improvements to the domestic and social environment.

Bacteriology gave diseases a new and more objective specificity by proving that a disease was caused by a species of micro-organism. If susceptibility to specific pathogens could be shown to be a racial attribute, then such specificity could give biological objectivity to the idea of different human species. The stigmatisation of disease carriers thus followed from the identification of particular pathogens. It was possible for the animal vector to be discovered before the pathogen, as with the body louse in spreading typhus. In this way anyone harbouring parasitic vermin represented a lethal threat. Ethnicity and contagion might be confused as the concept of an invasive parasitic organism was extended to supposed human parasites. Notions of the susceptibility of particular races to particular diseases began to gain currency.

While Koch's strict laws of causality were not inherently racist, bacteriologists subscribed to a concept of eradication or *Ausrottung* of disease by eliminating the species causing the infection. Bacteriology was in many ways an outgrowth of parasitology – disease was not so much a physiological malfunction, but the result of species of invasive parasites. Here the historian has to distinguish between the containment of disease, its eradication in a locality and the extinction of the pathogen so eliminating the disease. Robert Koch considered wholesale eradication of anthrax (*gänzlich auszurotten*) by preventing the reproduction of the bacilli and the spread of the spores. But he regarded destruction of all substances containing the bacilli as impracticable, and so suggested ways of hindering the bacilli from developing spores – a type of bacteriological eugenic sterilisation. In this sense the transition from sterilisation in its conventional sense to eugenic sterilisation is quite direct. Koch and Louis Pasteur were inspirational figures for the founders of German racial hygiene, who searched for the germs of inherited diseases; the racial hygiene movement had entrenched support from the hygiene institutes in Berlin and Munich. Yet bacteriologists did not envisage the wholesale extermination of a species of bacteria – and beyond this of the host species of carriers – as Koch spoke idealistically of liberating the human race (not, it should be noted, races) from an 'angel of death'. Such a strategy of emancipation from an invasion by a primitive plant-like parasite occurred repeatedly in Koch's work. But it is doubtful whether rallying cries for bacteriologically based programmes of disease control can be read as a call for exterminating an animal species – let alone a human ethnic group.[3] Koch was uninterested in whether there was an ethnic predisposition to certain diseases, as his sole concern was to identify bacterial pathogens. However, some of his disciples became increasingly concerned with ethnicity and disease, stressing the need to defend Germany's eastern borders.

These issues can be examined through the case-study of typhus as (primarily) a louse-borne disease. Retrospectively it is clear that, being caused by a class of micro-organisms called *rickettsiae*, the disease was neither truly bacteriological nor was it readily treatable by drugs or preventable by vaccines as a viral disease. Typhus illustrates the transition to a racial understanding of disease partly because of connections made between the disease vector – mainly but not exclusively body lice – and the human traits of those infested. Shula Marks and Warwick Anderson observed how de-verminisation procedures inflicted on African migrants were racist and coercive.[4] While delousing was a highly specific set of routines, it has a prehistory in the more generalised medical screening of transmigrants from the East, as they made their way via Bremen and Hamburg, Antwerp and Liverpool to Ellis Island: here we find a sequence of routines imposed under different state regulatory systems on suspect ethnic carriers of 'Asiatic' epidemics like cholera, trachoma and typhus. These diseases became demonised as a potential Black Death, as if they were poised to eradicate European civilisation.[5] Such traumas meant that alarmed politicians increased resources for bacteriologists as guardians of civilisation.

Much attention has been lavished on the US immigration station at Ellis Island as demonstrating the combination of nativist, sanitary and bacteriological rationales underlying the increasingly rigorous screening procedures.[6] The coincidence between bacteriology and racism is striking and suggests that sanitary science reinforced measures to exclude racial undesirables. More neglected – at least from the point of view of the specificities of the imposed medical procedures – is how the Prussian medical authorities guarded against migrants sparking off outbreaks of disease among those in transit or igniting a major epidemic in Germany itself. Although the liberal constitution of imperial Germany meant that it was far removed from the 'racial state' of the Nazis, it nonetheless contained a spectrum of racist ideologies from the entourage of Kaiser Wilhelm II to popular anti-Semitism.

The question arises as to whether policy towards transmigrants was in any way racist. It was in line with the liberal structures of imperial Germany that the state allow free movement in terms of emigration. Transmigrants could cross from the East, but were increasingly subject to police and medical controls. Border stations functioned as collecting centres for migrants and were the portals for a hygienically controlled route which terminated at Ellis Island: the more modern control stations incorporated bathing, disinfecting and medical facilities. Procedures began on Germany's eastern frontiers as a prelude to transfer in segregated carriages or sealed trains via the 'Central Control Station' at Ruhleben on the outskirts of Berlin, ensuring that the migrants did not defile the metropolis.[7] Sick migrants were weeded out at the border control stations and a central hub at Ruhleben near Berlin had large-scale facilities for washing and disinfecting baggage.[8] The border stations regulated the through-flow of migrants like the valves in a sewage system, so that travellers would not have to stay more than the required five days at the port emigration camps, where overcrowding could be a health hazard. The hygiene institutes of Breslau (now Wrocław) and Posen (now Poznan) trained disinfectors and oversaw medical facilities at the migration stations (financed by the shipping companies) to ensure that these were up to standard.[9] Sanitary authorities dragooned Eastern populations into expecting disinfection as part of the experience of migration.

Because of German indignation at the draconian requirements of US immigration inspectors it is difficult to assess the impact of the bacteriologically based US regulations. The Hamburg Institute for Maritime and Tropical Diseases, founded in 1901, agitated for more effective (but not necessarily severe) hygienic controls on migrants. This Institute linked tropical medicine for the colonies to establishing quarantine and other medical procedures for transmigrants. The wave of support for tropical medicine derived from the German Colonial Society, the Reich, port and municipal authorities, and the army and navy. The Colonial Society agitated for improved tropical medicine during the 1890s, and Koch (who in 1896 worked on cattle plague in Africa) was sympathetic. Bernhard Nocht, a former naval doctor and assistant to Koch, remained in Hamburg after the cholera epidemic of 1892 in a new position as Port Medical Officer. With support from the Colonial Society, Nocht succeeded in establishing a tropical institute in Hamburg: at the national level, this was a response to the opening in 1899 of the Liverpool School of Tropical Medicine and the London School of Tropical Medicine, as well as being, at the regional level, a triumph over Koch's scheme for a Berlin Institute of Tropical Medicine.[10]

The Hamburg Institute formulated regulations to eradicate parasites aboard ships. The Reich Health Office backed Nocht's experimental studies of different poisonous gases to kill rats. The aim was to replace, on an organised basis, the vagaries of rat-catchers and other traditional pest-control methods by scientific strategies.[11] Nocht advocated highly toxic carbon monoxide gas, for which he devised generator equipment. The Hamburg Institute was crucial in the development, as a means of securing Germany's borders, of regimes of disinfection and pest-eradication by gassing. The International Sanitary Convention of 1912 required the fumigation of ships at least once a year. The term 'deratisation' made its debut in the vocabulary of international hygiene in 1912 – the term 'delousing' was soon to follow.

The various stages of medical screening were designed to weed out carriers of epidemic diseases. The hygienic routines provided a general cleansing, rather than targeting a specific health hazard. In 1905 it was decreed that, at times of typhus epidemics, migrants could only cross Germany in special carriages without upholstery, and all towelling had to be burned as part of disinfecting routines.[12] Until 1912 there was no special delousing procedure as a typhus-control measure. The Balkan Wars aroused fears that diseased Serbian migrants might travel through Germany bringing an epidemic of typhus. Regulations were introduced in the event of a case of typhus occurring within twenty kilometres of a military barracks.[13] By May 1913 delousing was on the medical agenda for the Hamburg migration station.[14]

The system of medical controls on transmigrants often broke down because of the large numbers of people involved, the economic interests of the shipping companies and the off-putting draconian procedures which prompted evasion. Having escaped Czarist repression and terrifying pogroms, migrants could expect prison-like regimentation by German medical personnel, border guards and officials. The control centres were guarded and encircled by walls. After disembarking from the packed trains, disinfection involved the separation of male and female passengers and consequent breaking up of families, the confiscation of all clothing and possessions, rubbing down with strange, slippery substances, and a shower (hopefully of a tolerable temperature). The 'dirty' and 'clean' sides of the sanitary circuit were rigorously policed by coarsely behaved attendants. An immigrant reflected on being transmuted into 'dumb animals, helpless and unresisting'. Mothers were separated from sick children who were taken to the new but remote city hospital of Eppendorf, where visits were forbidden and no information was provided to relatives.[15]

Each of the control stations had its own idiosyncratic medical routine. Where baths were compulsory there were inspections of the naked body, but at Myslowitz only eyes, hair and forearms were examined. In Bajohren, Insterburg and Tilsit, throats were inspected, but only at Posen was the temperature taken. Compulsory baths involved being rubbed down with various bactericidal soaps and disinfectants. Most stations had only the older steam disinfection equipment rather than the more modern hot-air chambers. Some stations disinfected all clothing and personal effects, some exempted clean clothes and at others the doctor selected items for disinfection. Different substances – like carbolic or creosote – were sprayed or painted on clothing. Despite the pressure from the authorities to improve hygienic conditions for steerage passengers, the problems of overcrowding, lack of sanitation and washing facilities, and infestation persisted. A Russian Jewish emigrant of 1908 recalled that 'the atmosphere was so thick and dense with smoke and bodily odours that your head itched and when you went to scratch your head … you got lice in your hands.'[16]

Whether such varied procedures actually protected the health of the German population was dubious. In 1906 the Bremen Medical Officer, Heinrich Tjaden, and the Hamburg Port Medical Officer, Nocht, inspected the control stations on the eastern border. They had no confidence in the haphazard medical screening on the frontiers as capable of detecting persons incubating diseases and they condemned the hygienic procedures for being so severe as to encourage 'wild transmigrants' illegally to make their own way across Germany. The medical measures often went beyond what was scientifically necessary – Nocht and Tjaden considered that the germs were inside rather than on the body and that even after bathing such vermin as head lice remained. They condemned the rituals of chemical disinfection as useless and steam disinfection as only partially effective.

At some stations the transmigrants were held in the control stations and at others they were allowed to lodge in the vicinity. Arrangements differed with regard to the provision of food and whether or not alcohol was allowed. In order to remove the sheer terror from the procedures, Nocht and Tjaden recommended that baths ought to be voluntary and only soiled underclothes ought to be disinfected. They singled out the system at the control station of Ratibor as ideal, with medical inspection of eyes, hair, skin, arm movements, breathing and temperature, while recognising that extensive medical personnel and thermometers would be necessary. They argued that if the sanitary controls were relaxed, more transmigrants would comply with them, thereby minimising contact with the German population. The Prussian authorities accepted that control-station doctors should have discretionary powers over baths and disinfection procedures, and that only in exceptional cases should there be total nudity.[17]

The system was criticised as exploiting migrants for commercial ends. Socialists argued that there was greater leniency at German control stations for migrants who had booked passages with German shipping companies than for those intending to embark from the Netherlands, Belgium or Britain.[18] The Hamburg medical authorities criticised the facilities as overcrowded and the procedures as too lax.[19] The herding of immigrants into dirty, prison-like conditions while undergoing disinfection routines or medical examinations increased the risks of infection from typhus. Tjaden warned that a mysterious 'infective substance' was invading the overcrowded migration halls.[20] The original barracks in Hamburg, designed for 150 passengers, were inadequate and new pavilions were constructed with dormitories, each for 22 passengers. Complaints against poor-quality food and overcrowding erupted into violent protests. Facilities designed to cope with 5,000 people at one time were flooded with thousands of extra persons – a situation that was profitable to the shipping company but which was constantly criticised by the Port Medical Officer. For those unfamiliar with modern medical routines, medical inspections could be terrifying, arousing fears of robbery and murder. Medical attention was reduced to mechanically applied systems designed to protect external society, rather than personal welfare.[21] The medical controls and forced removal to insanitary quarantine facilities were hated by migrants as severing ties of kinship and violating the personal sanctity of the body.[22] Despite the anxiety concerning epidemics, of the 5,272 (from around 112,000 passengers) turned back at the control stations on the German–Russian border and at Ruhleben in 1905, most had eye problems, 98 were refused passage because of the condition of their hair and 146 were deemed to be too decrepit, but only 40 persons were denied passage for having contracted infectious diseases like cholera, plague and typhus.[23]

Although the German and American press sensationalised how Eastern European Jews imported infections, such was the official disinterest in religious background that regulations and statistics did not generally record religion. There were special facilities for Jews in the Hamburg migration halls, but this was a functional requirement to cope with Jewish dietary customs. Bacteriologists during the 1890s were largely unconcerned about religious categories.[24] What mattered was the contact with infectious pathogens, and race and notions of constitutional susceptibility were irrelevant to the Koch school of bacteriologists.

Yet public prejudice against Russian Jewish refugees fleeing from the Eastern European pogroms increased during the 1890s: racial biology reinforced stereotypes of Eastern Europeans as living in filth and squalor and as clothed in dirty and verminous rags. Hereditary biology and bacteriology cross-fertilised with hatred of Jews as an alien culture and religion – albeit for a restricted set of groups – to generate a stereotype of the biologically immutable Jewish race as pathogenic. The Hamburg cholera epidemic of 1892 generated a poisonous atmosphere of anti-Semitism, but such prejudices had not yet infected expert opinion. Although Koch identified Russian migrants as the source of the epidemic, ethnicity and religion were irrelevant. Koch's views were controversial, as other sanitary experts stressed the effects of local insanitary conditions or considered that cholera came from the Middle East via France. Jews were in an overall minority among Eastern European migrants during the 1890s and, even if in 1892 numbers of Jewish migrants were high (and possibly exceeded other ethnic groups), there was no proof that Jewish migrants were the carriers of cholera. Given that transmigrants did not 'cause' cholera in other port cities, notably Bremen, to accept that Russian Jews had to be the primary cause and carriers of cholera would be to swallow the anti-Semitic prejudices of the time. While Koch demonstrated that the cholera epidemic was caused by contaminated drinking water from the river Elbe, Russian Jews were scapegoated for the failure of the Hamburg authorities to provide filtration. Because there were cholera outbreaks in Russia in 1892, it did not mean that Russian Jews (as opposed to other ethnic groups among Russian migrants) were necessarily the carriers of the germs which caused the Hamburg epidemic; moreover, there was cholera in other parts of the world that were in contact with Hamburg.[25]

Beyond the legal and empirical world of officials and medical officers there were sporadic attempts to gain acceptance for anti-Semitic notions of the Jew as a parasite by deploying the rhetorical force of bacteriological discoveries. It is tempting to construct an identikit picture of a scientised anti-Semitism by taking sporadic outbursts and presenting these as a coherent movement. I shall take two much-cited instances. First, it is said that in 1892 the Italian physiologist, Paolo Mantegazza, published in the liberal Austrian newspaper, *Neue Freie Presse*, a characterisation of Jews as alien 'tubercular growths' in 'our European body'. However, scrutiny of the original text shows that while Mantegazza outlines the opinions of anti-Semites, he does not endorse their prejudices.[26] Second, in 1895 the Reichstag debated whether 'those Jews who were not German citizens' – a euphemism for *Ostjuden* (or 'Eastern Jews') – could be allowed to cross frontiers. Anti-Semites condemned Jews as 'parasites on the German oak', a 'deathly enemy', bringers of 'misfortune or *Unheil*', and threats to 'the spiritual and moral health of the German *Volk*'. These outpourings from virulent racists culminated in Jews being denounced as 'cholera germs'.[27] Nationalists attributed exterminatory sentiments to one of their inspirational propagandists, Paul Lagarde: 'One does not negotiate with trichinia and bacillus … they will be annihilated as quickly and as thoroughly as possible'.[28] Outbursts of anti-Semitic rhetoric reinforced pressures to seal borders against undesirables from the East. Yet such rhetoric did not pervade bacteriology itself during the 1890s. Indeed there were attempts to refute the allegations of Jews as corrupters of blood and to present Jewish traditions as in keeping with modern hygienic laws.[29]

Initially designed to safeguard migrants and to ensure a smoothly running system of mass emigration, the medical controls became steadily more restrictive. At times isolation and accompanying rituals like the compulsory showers exceeded what made sense in terms of contemporary medical theories. Migrants found the experience of quarantine bewildering, but as disease and vermin became welded together by medical science, migrants in time became conditioned to expect sanitary controls and disinfection. Emigration from persecution and starvation in Europe prompted doctors and state bureaucrats to prevent the importation of diseases by ever more stringent medical screening and disinfection. Stringent controls on migrants culminated in immigration quotas and international agencies adopted policies of intervention in Eastern Europe to impose the rigorous disease-control measures of quarantine, health checks on migrants and delousing.

World War I battles against bacteria

Delousing and sanitary provision in World War I similarly indicate the ambivalent situation concerning bacteriology and race. German medical officers in occupied Poland sought to convert priests, teachers and rabbis to the gospel of cleanliness. A policy of cooperation with Jews was in keeping with the German and Austrian armies' promise of civic rights to Jews. Rabbis were summoned to Warsaw where they were addressed by a German military doctor on the importance of cleanliness; he persuaded them that delousing was not against religion and showed them greatly enlarged photographs of lice. Anti-lice posters, produced by a military entomologist, were issued with a Yiddish text, and adorned the antechambers of synagogues, baths and schools. A Bavarian rabbi cooperated with the German medical officer, Gottfried Frey, in producing the Yiddish pamphlet outlining the dangers of 'Fleckentyphus' (i.e. typhus), aimed at persuading Jews, 'aso [*sic*] reinlich Volk', that they should abide by the hygienic commandments of the delousing regulations: they were urged to shave hair and beards and burn the wigs of Orthodox women when infested, and not to offer hospitality to wandering beggars. Although hundreds of thousands of copies were issued for discussion by rabbis and teachers, Frey considered that the 'primitive' religious culture of the Jews meant that the pamphlet had no impact.[30]

German medical officers condemned ritual baths, describing the water as brown, stinking and rarely changed, and the associated washing and sanitary facilities as covered with decades of filth: the medical officers encouraged Jewish councils to improve the water quality and the sanitary installations, and to add showers and delousing facilities. Modernisation of the baths involved cleaning the walls, central heating, electric lighting, new benches, steam sterilisation of basins, hot-air delousing ovens and electrically driven water pumps. The German sanitary authorities were proud that 188 delousing centres were opened in Polish towns, the cost being borne by municipalities in the hope of overcoming popular resistance and engendering a new hygienic culture among Jewish schoolchildren, who were forced to bathe weekly. As the epidemics spread, so the throughput was increased from a couple of hundred to 1,500 people per day at a large new delousing installation in Warsaw in 1917. Between 1915 and 1918 official statistics claimed that three-and-a-half million people and 418,000 dwellings were deloused.[31]

Jews might resent the medically administered rituals of bathing and haircutting, domestic intrusions to enforce alien 'German hygiene', the closing of Jewish schools and synagogues, and of shops, markets, foodstuffs and the prohibiting of rag collecting. Delousing was perceived as a collective punishment by local communities. The hatred of delousing installations meant that some were burned down as acts of local resistance. German medical officers condemned the ritual washing and laying out of corpses, as well as traditional burial customs in which coffins were not sealed. Hygiene violated religious and personal sanctity: Orthodox Jews were shaved and women were violated by enforced haircutting. The Germans insisted that no Jewish-owned shop could open unless the owner's family was deloused, and accused the Jewish shop owners of sending their children a number of times rather than going themselves. The Germans compiled lists of Jews who were to be forcibly washed and deloused every week. Pedlars and other peripatetic occupations were denounced for spreading typhus. Wilhelm His, Professor of Internal Medicine at the University of Berlin, denounced Jews as natural spies, smugglers and swindlers, and Poles joined in the prejudice against Jews as responsible for epidemics of cholera and typhus.[32] Heroisation of medical researchers was accompanied by demonisation of Eastern European Jews as an alien species carrying lethal germs.

The need to remedy labour shortages at harvest time led to the import of Eastern European workers into Germany. Since the winter of 1915 the War Ministry and the Warsaw Government General had agreed that all workers from occupied Poland and Russia should be deloused, but delousing was not fully effective and typhus was often misdiagnosed as influenza by inexperienced German doctors. The Prussian medical authorities complained in 1917 that Russian agricultural workers arrived louse-infested and that their barracks were filthy. Between September 1916 and March 1918 over 11,000 Polish-Jewish workers were transferred to Germany. Outbreaks of typhus among the civilian population were attributed to these workers. A mild epidemic of typhus in Warsaw in 1916 was disregarded as primarily affecting the Jewish population, but a severe epidemic of typhus in Warsaw during 1917 had a radicalising effect on the German authorities, arousing racist hostility against Jews.[33]

Sanitary reconstruction measures were also undertaken by the Austro-Hungarian military government in occupied Serbia from 1916, which was (like Russian Poland) characterised as 'a Land drenched in epidemic poison'. The civilian population, characterised by a medical officer as 'awfully filthy and lousy', was subjected to rigorous delousing and education about the dangers of *Ungeziefer* or 'vermin'. *Salubritätskommissionen* (sanitary commissions) established typhus isolation wards and delousing installations. The military doctors saw their role as apostles of civilisation, engaged on a sanitary *Kulturarbeit* (cultural task) to achieve sanitary 'rebirth' by means of steam and baths. A highly sensitive problem was to locate typhus among Muslims, especially women, because of religious prohibitions against medical inspection by male doctors. The government arranged for immune Serbian women to undertake such inspections. The military medical officers took pride in respecting local piety, improving the overall health of the Serbian population, and thereby defending the health of the occupying troops and preventing the spread of epidemics to the Fatherland.[34] The tone of the Austrian military doctors tended to be moralistic and they were often more moralistic and indeed religious than racial in spreading their gospel of hygiene.

By 1918 prejudice against Polish Jews as typhus carriers infected the German and Austrian civilian authorities, who linked supposed Jewish indolence to the spread of typhus. As Eastern European refugees poured into Vienna, the Austrian authorities feared pogroms – because Jews were accused of spreading typhus – and held refugees in what at the time were called 'concentration camps'. Sanitary conditions in these camps were so atrocious that they caused deaths among those incarcerated. In March 1918 there was a Reich conference on preventing typhus imported by Polish-Jewish unskilled workers. The Director of the Prussian Medical Department, Martin Kirchner (schooled in bacteriology by Koch) denounced Jewish workers as dirty, unreliable, lazy and opportunistic, and as possessed of 'a special number of morally degenerate characteristics' they were vilified as the worst possible type of worker. This outburst indicates that Kirchner was infected by the virus of racial anti-Semitism. The medical official, Frey, while denying anti-Semitism, reported that typhus was considered in Poland to be a *Judenfieber*, because of its very high incidence among the Jewish population (95 per cent of all cases in 1915–16) even though Jewish mortality rates were lower. Medical advice that

Polish Jews constituted an epidemic risk meant that the Reich authorities decided to close the borders to these workers. The medical staff of the Warsaw Government General denounced the Polish Jews as depravedly filthy, so accounting for the greater prevalence of typhus among them. By 1918 it was wearily admitted that it was pointless to delouse Polish Jews, as they very quickly became reinfested.[35]

Racial pathogens

World War I triggered a transition from relative tolerance of other races to virulent hostility. Before the war, bacteriologists sought to correct the worst excesses of sanitary procedures imposed on transmigrants. Initially the attitudes to Polish Orthodox Jewish males and Muslim women in Serbia sought to blend hygienic requirements with tolerance. Sanitary provision was fuelled by a fervent sense of enthusiasm for modern scientific medicine as a civilising mission. But as the military situation deteriorated, racial rhetoric increased. Jews were to be cleansed, deloused and herded into 'concentration camps' as they represented a lethal sanitary threat to the central powers. Bacteriology became increasingly racialised as the need to control and prevent typhus led to attempts to seal the borders against ethnic undesirables from the East.

While there was no internal necessity for any linkage between race and bacteriology, the historical contingencies in German society elicited a virulent strain of bacteriological racism. Such a view is confirmed by an analysis of the views of eugenicists who were also concerned with infectious diseases, suggesting that socio-cultural factors shaped bacteriology. The bacteriological cleansing measures suggest an authoritarian and interventionist potential. Given dire historical contingencies, measures could be radicalised and take on racist rationales. Bacteriologists stood on the threshold of eradicating epidemics by eliminating the presumed carriers of the disease.

Notes

1 *Hamburger Freie Presse*, 26 November 1892, cited in R.J. Evans, *Death in Hamburg: Society and Politics in the Cholera Years, 1830–1910*, Oxford, Oxford University Press, 1987, p. 313.

2 D.E. Porter, 'Biologism, Environmentalism and Public Health in Edwardian England', *Victorian Studies* 34 (1991): 159–78; G. Göckenjan, *Kurieren und Staat machen*, Frankfurt am Main, Suhrkamp, 1985,

p. 56; 'Ferdinand Hueppe', in L. Grote, *Die Medizin der Gegenwart in Selbstdarstellungen*, Leipzig, Felix Meiner, 1923, vol. 2, pp. 73–138; M. Stuerzbecher, 'Aus der Geschichte des Charlottenburger Gesundheitswesens', *Bär von Berlin* 1980: 43–113.

3 R. Koch, 'Die Aetiologie der Milzbrand-Krankheit, gegründet auf die Entwicklungsgeschichte des Bacillus Anthracis', *Beiträge zur Biologie der Pflanzen* 2 (1877): 277–310. For the language of extermination, see *Medical Classics* 2, 8 (1938): 777, 815.

4 S. Marks and W. Anderson, 'Typhus and Social Control: South Africa, 1917–1950', in R. MacLeod and M. Lewis, *Disease, Medicine and Empire*, London, Routledge, 1988, pp. 257–83.

5 More fully explored in P.J. Weindling, *Epidemics and Genocide in Eastern Europe, 1890–1945*, Oxford, Oxford University Press, forthcoming.

6 For example, H. Markel, *Quarantine: East European Jewish Immigrants and the New York City Epidemics of 1892*, Baltimore, Johns Hopkins University Press, 1996.

7 D. Dwork, 'Health Conditions of Immigrant Jews on the Lower East Side of New York, 1880–1914', *Medical History* 25 (1981): 1–40.

8 Z. Szajkowski, 'Sufferings of Jewish Emigrants to America in Transit through Germany', *Jewish Social Studies* 39 (1977): 105–16.

9 Geheimes Staatsarchiv Preussischer Kulturbesitz, Berlin-Dahlem Rep 76 VII B Nr 3005 die Einrichtung und Verwaltung des (staatlichen) Hygienischen Instituts in Posen 1901–4, 'Geschäftsbericht für das Rechnungsjahr 1903'.

10 W.U. Eckart, 'Von der Idee eines "Reichsinstituts" zur unabhängigen Forschungsinstitution: Vorgeschichte und Gründung des Hamburger Instituts für Schiffs- und Tropenkrankheiten, 1884–1901', in R. vom Bruch and R.A. Müller (eds), *Formen ausserstaatlicher Wissenschaftsförderung im 19. und 20. Jahrhundert*, Stuttgart, Franz Steiner, 1990, pp. 31–52; L. Wess, 'Tropenmedizin und Kolonialpolitik: Das Hamburger Institut für Schiffs- und Tropenkrankheiten, 1918–1945', *1999* 1992: 38–61; S. Wulf, *Das Hamburger Tropeninstitut 1919 bis 1945*, Berlin, Reimers, 1994.

11 Staatsarchiv Hamburg (STAH), Hafenarzt I Nr 135 Verwendung von Kohlenoxydhaltigen Gasen (Generatorgas) für Rattenvertilgung 1899–1905. BAP 15.01 1165 Desinfektion der Schiffe 1903–10. Reichsgesetzblatt (1907) 511.

12 Bayerisches Hauptstaatsarchiv Muenchen (BHSTA) M Inn 62407 *Vollzug des Gesetzes betr die Bekämpfung gemeingefährlicher Krankheiten, Anweisung zur Bekämpfung ansteckende Krankheiten im Eisenbahn Verkehr*, Berlin, 1905.

13 BHSTA MA 95773 Bekämpfung gemeingefährlicher Krankheiten Reichskanzler to Bayer Staatsministerium 30.iv.1913.

14 STAH II F6 Unterbringung der Auswanderer vor deren Einschiffung Bd III 1908–38, letter from Hafenarzt 26.v.1913.

15 Mary Antin, *A Promised Land*, Boston, 1912, pp. 174–7; repr. Princeton, Princeton University Press, 1969. A description of two weeks' experience of quarantine in Hamburg in 1894 is cited in

Markel, *Quarantine*, chap. 1. U. Weisser (ed.), *100 Jahre 1889–1989 Universitätskrankenhaus Eppendorf*, Tübingen, Attempto, 1989, p. 43.

16 STAH II F6 Unterbringung der Auswanderer vor deren Einschiffung Bd I 1886–1906, Bd II 1906–8, Bd III 1908–38; Sthamer, *Die Auswanderer-Hallen in Hamburg*, Hamburg, n.d. (*c*.1900–4); B. Nocht, *Die Auswandererobdach und die gesundheitspolizeiliche Überwachung der Auswanderer in Hamburg*, Hamburg, 1901. The quotation is from Sophia Kreitzberg, cited in B.C. Hamblin, *Ellis Island: The Official Souvenir Guide*, Santa Barbara, 1994, p. 12.

17 Staatsarchiv Bremen (STAB) A 4 No 290 betr Besichtigung der Auswanderer-Kontrollstationen an der russischen österreichischen Grenze und in Ruhleben und Leipzig, report by Nocht and Tjaden 20.VII.06. Prussian MdI report 19.IV.07. STAB 4, 21 – 502 Auswanderungswesen, Bd 1 1904–13, report by Tjaden, 'Auswandererungswesen in Bremen', 10.VI.07, pp. 6–7.

18 M. Just, *Ost- und südosteuropäische Amerika-Wanderung 1881–1914*, Stuttgart, Franz Steiner 1988, pp. 30–1, 77–85, 106–14.

19 STAH F6 Bd II. Szajkowski, 'Sufferings of Jewish Emigrants'.

20 STAB 4,21–470 Fleckfieber (Flecktyphus) und Läusebekämpfung, report by Tjaden, 21.XI.08.

21 J. Wertheimer, *Unwelcome Strangers: East European Jews in Imperial Germany*, New York and Oxford, Oxford University Press, 1987, pp. 50–1.

22 Just, *Ost- und südosteuropäische Amerika-wanderung*, p. 114. Howard Markel has examined these perceptions in the Yiddish-American press, see Markel, *Quarantine*.

23 STAB Nr A.4.No 300a, report by Tjaden and Nocht, 20.VII.06.

24 D. Dwork, 'Health Conditions of Immigrant Jews on the Lower East Side of New York, 1880–1914', *Medical History* 25 (1981): 1–40; A.M. Kraut, 'Silent Travellers: Germs, Genes and American Efficiency', *Social Science History* 12 (1988): 377–94; Kraut, *Silent Travellers: Germs, Genes and the 'Immigrant Menace'*, New York, Knopf, 1994; V.A. Harden, *Inventing the NIH: Federal Biomedical Research Policy, 1887–1937*, Baltimore, Johns Hopkins University Press, 1986, pp. 11–16; H. Markel, ' "Knocking Out the Cholera": Cholera, Class and Quarantines in New York City, 1892', *Bulletin of the History of Medicine* 69 (1995): 420–57, see p. 454 for the mortality of migrants.

25 See Evans, *Death in Hamburg*, pp. 280–4, 299–300, for the suggestion that cholera was transmitted to Hamburg by Russian Jewish transmigrants.

26 M. Hart, 'Moses the Microbiologist: Judaism and Social Hygiene in the Work of Alfred Nossig', *Jewish Social Studies*, n.s., 2 (1995): 72–96.

27 *Reichstag*, 47 sitting (27.II.95), Antrag Frh. v Hammerstein, Fr v Manteuffel auf Vorlegung eines Gesetzentwurfs nach welchem Israeliten, die nicht Reichsangehörige sind, die Einwanderung über die Grenzen des Reichs untersagt wird.

28 *Völkischer Beobachter* (22 December 1941).

29 Hart, 'Moses the Microbiologist', *passim*.

30 G. Frey, 'Zu den Juden in Polen', in Frey, 'Das Gesundheitswesen im Deutschen Verwaltungsgebiet von Polen in den Jahren, 1914–1918', *Arbeiten aus dem Reichsgesundheitsamt* 51 (1919): 632–5, also see pp. 724–5 on the lack of impact; Frey, *Bilder aus dem Gesundheitswesen in Polen (Kongress-Polen) aus der Zeit der Deutschen Verwaltung*, Berlin, 1919 (*Beiträge zur Polnischen Landeskunde*, n.s., 7: 70–1); I.B. Singer, *Mayn Tatns Bays-Din-Shtub*, Tel Aviv, 1979, p. 300.

31 Frey, 'Gesundheitswesen', pp. 647, 710–11; Frey, *Bilder*, pp. 69–91.

32 W. His, *Die Front der Ärzte*, Bielefeld and Leipzig, Velhagen & Klasing, 1931, pp. 39, 91–4; Weindling, 'The First World War and the Campaign Against Lice: Comparing British and German Sanitary Measures', in W.U. Eckart and C. Gradmann (eds), *Die Medizin und der Erste Weltkrieg*, Pfaffenweiler, Centaurus, 1996, pp. 241–72; Frey, 'Gesundheitswesen', pp. 615, 623–4, 631, 637–9, 722–3; Frey, *Bilder*, pp. 117–24.

33 His, *Front*, pp. 39, 91–4; Frey, 'Gesundheitswesen', pp. 584, 591, 731–3; Frey, 'Bilder', p. viii; Halbjahresbericht des Verwaltungschefs bei dem Generalgouvernement Warschau für die Zeit vom 1. April 1917 bis zum 30. September 1917, p. 28.

34 'Sanitärer Wideraufbau Serbiens: Festschrift anlässlich einjährigen Bestehens des k und k Militär-General-Gouvernements in Serbien', *Der Militärarzt* 51 (1917): 2–3 (3 February), 4–5 (10 March), 6 (14 April).

35 Frey, 'Gesundheitswesen', pp. 642–3; GSTA Rep 76 VIII B Nr 3774 Drews of Prussian Ministry of the Interior (MdI) to Reichskanzler, 18.II.18; Prussian MdI, 20.IV.18, BAK R 86/1040 Bd 6 Besprechung, 9.III.18. Rep 76 VIII B Nr 3775 Prussian MdI meeting of medical officers 26.X.18. For comparison of the epidemics of 1916–21 with those of 1940–1, see W. Hagen, 'Das Gesundheitswesen der Stadt Warschau September 1939 bis März 1941', Archives of National Institute of Hygiene Warsaw. Hagen considered there was a 'Jewish epidemic' of 1916–18, and a 'Polish epidemic' of 1918–21.

Chapter 11

'Savage civilisation'

Race, culture and mind in Britain, 1898–1939

Mathew Thomson

Within the history of science the nineteenth century has been regarded as a pivotal period in the development of racial thought, with 'scientific racism' reifying race as biologically fundamental and immutable. Even though the polygenist theory that races were different species had been largely discredited by the second half of the century, it was superseded by a model which fixed races on a hierarchical scale of physical and mental evolution and thus naturalised the cultural gulf between 'primitive' and 'civilised' societies. The psychological theories of British writers such as Francis Galton and Herbert Spencer, and techniques to measure the power and qualities of mind, such as anthropometry and craniology, contributed to the development of this evolutionary model in the final decades of the century.[1] However, the extent to which 'scientific racism' was predominant beyond its own ideologues is more open to question. Even within the still largely amateur field of British anthropology, published papers on craniology and anthropometry were a small minority compared to those taking a more cultural and historical approach.[2] Moreover, looking at the question from the broader perspective of a historian of British society and culture, José Harris has suggested that although ideas about race were 'omnipresent' in mid-Victorian Britain, they had 'only the sketchiest of roots in biological thought' and were more likely to be expressed in terms of constitutional tradition and political culture. And even as biologistic connotations of 'race' came to the fore at the turn of the century, it 'did not invariably have the specifically ethnic and exclusionary connotations that a later generation might suppose'. It could refer to nations, groups within the nation, public health, sex, or the condition of the whole human species. Harris may overstate her case, but she does cast into doubt the hegemony of 'scientific racism' in turn-of-the-century Britain, suggesting instead that we need to think in terms of a series of parallel and overlapping 'race' discourses.[3]

The emergence of psychology as an experimental science in the early twentieth century provided the opportunity to demonstrate that racial difference and inequality rested on innate mental ability. Moreover, for the first time psychologists moved beyond theoretical speculation to test such questions in the field. The most famous of such investigations, the Torres Straits expedition of 1898, is considered in the first section of this chapter. It is argued that a closer examination of the 'savage' in fact had the opposite effect: rather than confirming biologically based otherness and inequality, it helped reveal the 'savage' and 'primitive' basis of the 'civilised' mind, and enforced the idea that cultural heritage was fundamental in shaping individual psychology. Such theoretical positions were suited to a translation back to the British domestic environment. First, they resonated with the cultural model of race which already circulated at a popular level. Second, they could address issues of national and individual identity which seemed particularly pressing in the era of World War I and its aftermath. Third, although a current of scientific racism persisted (particularly within anthropology), it was being modified to emphasise culture and its authority was being seriously eroded, with science itself undermining assumptions about innate difference and inequality, with the ontology of 'race' cast into confusion and with racism ideologically discredited, particularly in the shadow of Nazism.[4] And finally, local circumstances meant that there was simply less opportunity for a race-difference discourse to thrive than, for instance, in the United States or in Britain's own colonies: concern over immigration had subsided since a brief flurry of xenophobia at the turn of the century, as had the scale of immigration, and there was no major or particularly visible problem of race relations, or at least none that could not be conceptualised more readily in terms of culture than biology. Struggling to demonstrate the importance of their discipline as an applied science in schools, factories, the army and the clinic, British psychologists had little incentive or opportunity to focus on race as a category of difference. They were closely involved in the eugenics movement; however, even here discussion was surprisingly rare, apart from the obsession with the decline of 'the race' (that is, of the British population) itself. The greatest 'racial' threat was deemed to be that of Britain's own 'mental defectives' and, although the terminology of 'mongol' was still a commonplace for one section of this class, this no longer connoted a distinct racial identity.[5] When psychologists did undertake studies of ethnic minorities within Britain (as in the examination of the intelligence of Jewish schoolchildren), their findings were as likely to point to the mental parity or even superiority of these groups and to highlight the role of cultural difference in mediating outcomes.[6] Indeed if one concentrates on British psychologists working in Britain alone, as opposed to those working or with experience in the colonies, it is the relative absence and moderation, rather than the occasional and often casual presence, of scientific racism which is the more noteworthy.[7]

What this chapter attempts to demonstrate, however, is that if one goes beyond the paradigm of scientific racism and appreciates the broader contemporary resonances of 'race', then a racial dimension can still be distinguished alike within academic and popular psychological thought. Thus although the Torres Straits psychologists would move away from a racism which emphasised innate, biological inequality and clear-cut racial divisions, they would refashion the dichotomy between the 'primitive' and the 'civilised' in terms of mind and culture and embed this at the very heart of their new psychology. The second section of the chapter concentrates on the subsequent writing of William McDougall, the member of the expedition who made the most concerted attempt to construct a new racism in response to the anthropological experience, bringing culture to the fore alongside biology in a manner which resonated with the longer tradition of ideas about national character. His openly racist views were hardly typical of his profession, it must be noted, and they attracted growing criticism, but he was one of the most widely read psychologists of the era (his *Introduction to Social Psychology* of 1908 entering its twenty-third edition in 1936 and his *Psychology: The Study of Behaviour* selling over 100,000 copies during his lifetime) and as such he provides a valuable window on the nexus between academic and popular thought.[8] The final sections of the essay move further into the popular arena, highlighting the continued articulation of racial dimensions to mind that lie well outside the paradigm of 'scientific racism'.

Translations between psychology and anthropology

The Torres Straits expedition of 1898 is recognised as a key moment in the history of anthropology, but its significance for the development of British psychology has attracted less attention.[9] Expedition members W.H.R. Rivers, William McDougall and C.S. Myers were among the first generation of British psychologists to be engaged in laboratory-based research: Rivers was one of Britain's leading authorities on the psychology of visual perception; Myers, a talented musician, was engaged in research on the psychology of music and hearing, and McDougall conducted research into colour perception. Through the Torres Straits and subsequent expeditions their psychological perspective was translated into the discipline of anthropology and, in turn, a comparative and anthropological dimension would be translated into their research and writing on the mind.

Although polygenist theories had generally been rejected by this time and replaced by a notion that there was a basic 'psychic unity' between all races of humankind, this had left great scope for differentiating between levels of evolutionary development. The Torres Straits investigators were deeply influenced by such a perspective. Rivers, for instance, in collaboration with neurologist Henry Head, had already conducted a series of experiments on the return of sensation to the arm after severing of nerves, finding two distinct levels of sensory nerves – the 'protocritic' and 'epicritic' – which, following the ideas of neurologist Hughlings Jackson, were taken as representing primitive and higher stages in the racial evolution of the nervous system.[10] The introduction of the 'primitive' subject into the field of research provided the opportunity to test and demonstrate such models.

In practice, as the Western researcher approached closer to the 'primitive' mind, assumptions about psychological difference were questioned as much as confirmed. For instance, there was waning support for the idea that the size and shape of the cranium were directly related to differences in intelligence or revealed essential mental differences between races. It was difficult to prove that the islanders had the more acute senses expected in a more 'primitive' stage of human evolution. And it was recognised that there were fundamental problems in making cross-cultural comparisons based on the new technology of the (culturally specific) psychological test. Besides, research was suggesting that any difference in mental ability between races was usually no more significant than differences within the races themselves.

Early-twentieth-century psychology was a science of individual difference.[11] The anthropological experience would help to reposition the individual within the group. Though Rivers and his co-workers did undertake tests on individuals, as they had in their Cambridge laboratory, their attention was inevitably drawn to the strange culture they encountered, and to the way this affected individual behaviour. Tests revealed differences in perception, but these were differences of degree and differences which reflected the cultural environment more than innate ability. The anthropological experience forced Rivers to retreat from his evolutionist position.[12] Recognising that social environment was more important than innate ability he adopted a 'diffusionist' position in which the transfer of culture – 'the contact of peoples' – interacted with individual psychology.[13]

Following their anthropological experience, interwar British psychologists such as Myers, McDougall and F.C. Bartlett, another leading Cambridge psychologist, resisted the mechanistic behaviourism which dominated American interwar psychology. The Britons would argue that there could be no such thing as an 'individual psychology': all psychology was necessarily social.[14] McDougall went so far as to launch a campaign for a new discipline of 'social psychology'.[15] Though critical of McDougall's vision of basing social explanation on individual psychology when anthropology had revealed the fallacy of assuming that a single psychological theory could be applied across cultures, Rivers likewise recognised that psychology could no longer stand apart from a study of culture.[16] Significantly he called his major anthropological study a 'history' of Melanesian society and made the transfer of ideas, beliefs and traditions between societies just as crucial as innate evolutionary development.[17] This interest in culture was imported into his study of World War I shell-shock victims, where he attributed the high rate of mental breakdown among British officers to their public-school, stiff-upper-lip culture which repressed release of tension through instinctive flight.[18] Historians have regarded the wartime shell-shock experience as a crucial moment in forcing psychologists to study their subjects within a social situation. Undoubtedly it was, but it should be borne in mind that the anthropological experience had set a precedent for the study of the individual within the field: Rivers, McDougall,

Myers and Elliot Smith had all gained experience in the anthropological field before their innovative wartime work.[19]

In living in the field, the anthropologists lost many of their prejudices about 'savages'. It rapidly became apparent that these populations were not, in any straightforward way, 'native' or 'primitive': they each had their own long histories of culture-contact and racial mixing. The evident fragility of these cultures in the face of the most rapid and powerful culture-contact yet – with Europeans – inevitably attracted concern and focused anthropological attention on recording the last traces of tradition before they disappeared. In doing so, the anthropologists' preconceptions about 'otherness' were worn away: not only was their opinion of the savage raised, but they were also forced to consider the persistence of the 'savage within' of civilised humanity. As McDougall put it in his *Pagan Tribes of Borneo*:

> the more intimately one becomes acquainted with these pagan tribes, the more fully one realises the close similarity of their mental processes to one's own. Their primary impulses and emotions seem to be in all respects like our own. It is true that they are very unlike the typical civilised man of some of the older philosophers, whose every action proceeded from a nice and logical calculation of the algebraic sum of pleasures and pains to be derived from alternative lines of conduct; but we ourselves are equally unlike that purely mythical personage.[20]

This experience encouraged McDougall to place instinct at the very centre of individual psychology when he came to write his highly influential *Introduction to Social Psychology* in 1908. Europeans possessed all of the instincts and irrational tendencies of the 'savage', the only difference being that these impulses were modified, trained and repressed in the 'civilising process'. The same thing was being revealed in the work of contemporary psychopathologists.[21] Clearly the individual psychology of the future had to embrace this irrational and instinctive side of people.

Finally, anthropological study of the 'diffusion' of culture encouraged psychologists to think about the layering of ideas in the development of civilised humanity. It was recognised that the powerful ideas which existed at a subconscious level in dreams and myths had great continuity over time and linked civilised humanity directly to its primitive ancestors. In a similar way folklorists were becoming interested in the continuation of myths and folk practices in civilised society, recognising that they were not mere legacies of the evolutionary past but continued to have an active function in the present.[22] The anthropological experience was crucial, for instance, in opening Rivers' eyes to the importance of ritual, myth and the irrational in human society, and he realised that such forces remained powerful in even the most civilised of societies, despite attempts at conscious rationalisation.[23]

In sum, the anthropological experience had four important influences on early twentieth-century British psychology: it redirected psychology into the field; it pushed psychology beyond the individual to the social; it demonstrated the importance of culture and thereby shifted attention away from a purely biological approach to race, and it focused attention on the power of instinct, the unconscious and the irrational within 'civilised' society.

Though this shift did undermine a crude biological determinism, it did so invariably by reconfiguring scientific racism rather than ending it altogether. This was most apparent in the psychology of the colonial subject. The idea that cultural differences could be explained in terms of innate biological difference alone was rejected. Instead it was suggested that minor racial, environmental and cultural differences became cumulatively more significant over many generations, with culture and mind constantly interacting and mutually reinforcing each other to construct unique and organic racial cultures. The mind of the 'savage' was therefore not wholly different to that of the 'civilised'; indeed 'primitive' mental types would be found in the most developed of societies, the difference being that they would be adjusted individuals in the culture of the former of these worlds and unable to cope successfully in the latter.

The work of C.G. Seligman, another member of the 1898 expedition and a man whose subsequent illustrious career in anthropology would centre on the 'points of contact' with psychology, demonstrates how scientific racism could be reconfigured through the emphasis on mind and culture. He rejected the diffusionist theory that differences and similarities between cultures could be explained by the historical transfer of knowledge – culture-contact – alone. Instead he related development and independent innovation to the level of mental evolution. He drew support from comparative research which claimed that the brains of Britain's 'mental defectives' and those of 'primitive' races tended to show a common inferior development of the outer 'supragranular' layer (that which developed latest in the evolutionary process and was devoted to the 'higher inhibitory, adaptive and intellectual side of life') alongside an overdeveloped 'infragranular' layer (that which was 'phylogenetically the older, concerned with deep-seated needs and instincts, the automatic "protopathic" side of life, unaffected by environment').[24] Social problems, it was suggested, emerged when people with poor supragranular development were expected to cope with the demands of a highly civilised society: hence both the growing problem of mental deficiency in Britain, and the apparent inability of colonial subjects to cope with the impact of white civilisation.[25] His increasing interest in psychodynamic theories did not end his belief in a mental basis to cultural differences between races. The supragranular/infragranular model was now used to defend the idea that 'the communication between the unconscious and conscious is freer in savages than Europeans'.[26] Likewise he adopted Jung's idea that there were two distinct temperaments – the introvert and extrovert – to position the savage as the unrepressed but unreflective primitive.[27] Over time, however, Seligman would come to minimise differences and to stress the essential likeness between the minds of different races: for instance, he would trace common features in the dreams of civilised and savage cultures and he would regard common cultural traits in isolated peoples as evidence of a basic unity within the species. He would also emerge as an active opponent of Nazi racism in the 1930s.[28] Nevertheless, it is clear that such psycho-cultural theories could perpetuate a racist scientific justification for colonialism.[29] And, although such models would be of little direct concern to domestic practitioners of the 'psy' disciplines and were rejected by the increasingly dominant functionalist school of anthropology in interwar Britain, they were important for the increasing number of experts who became tools of Empire.[30] Here, psychology would continue to diagnose the colonial subject as both child-like and mentally unstable, and therefore in need of responsible rule, moral guidance and a culture to gradually elevate the 'primitive' mind to civilisation. Even then, such minds were liable to breakdown under the stress of a too-rapidly encroaching civilisation, with revolt against colonialism simply one more sign of mental pathology.[31]

William McDougall: the racialisation of national culture

Domestically the reconfiguration of psychological racism, from an emphasis on biology to an emphasis on culture, can be traced through a more detailed analysis of William McDougall and his racialisation of national identity.[32] In McDougall's view racial differences had emerged hundreds of thousands of years ago, and had remained virtually static ever since (the course of evolution being incredibly slow and human culture holding back natural selection by protecting the weak).[33] Moreover, his anthropological experience had shown that there was a considerable overlap between the mental abilities of all races; the main differences lay within, rather than between, races.[34] However, over thousands of years these differences of degree, in intelligence, instinctive character and temperament, did have an immense influence in organically shaping culture and environment, and this in turn magnified the effect of mental differences between nations. In sum, with the significance of biological difference undermined, culture came to the rescue of racism.

McDougall was attracted to the idea that the inheritance of memory might also contribute to distinct national identities. If a cell could inherit a genetic code inscribing future development of the organism, and carrying the genetic 'memory' of thousands of generations of ancestors, it seemed feasible that mental memory might similarly store the experiences of racial ancestors. Attracted by Jung's idea of a collective unconscious of myths and archetypes, he entered analysis under the Swiss doctor after World War I. He was disappointed by the limited results, but maintained an open mind, rationalising that he himself was 'too mongrel-bred to have clear-cut archetypes'.[35] In the behaviour of young children and 'primitive' peoples, he found plenty of circumstantial evidence to suggest that ideas were indeed inherited.[36] He even conducted his own Lamarckian experiment into the inheritance of learnt behaviour in rats and claimed to have achieved an 80 per cent improvement over 18 years.[37]

McDougall rejected the idea that there was an Aryan race or that nations constituted individual races, but he did accept that European peoples were a mix of three earlier races: the Mediterranean, the Alpine and the Nordic. Thus, although there was no British or German 'race' as such, historical and sociological analysis suggested that the racial mix did have a long-term effect on culture.

For instance, the contrast between the 'subservience' of the French people and the 'independent spirit' of the English could be traced far back through history and mapped onto the different racial mix of the two populations. Thus English character was not simply a product of a history of resistance, rather this resistance was the product of an innate predisposition to resist which was magnified by the tradition. Innate racial differences may have been minor, but manifested in culture over a long period of history they led to distinctive national cultures, organically in harmony with distinctive national character. As such, anthropology and psychology offered the key to a new scientific understanding of history.[38] In an era of heightened national consciousness and growing criticism of racism it is perhaps unsurprising to see racial difference being translated into this organic, cultural mode.[39] In McDougall's terms, the 'culture species' replaced the race.[40]

Although he accepted that the intelligence of 'primitive' peoples was not greatly inferior to civilised humanity, McDougall's views on cultural evolution still naturalised a racial hierarchy and justified a conservative stance on issues of race. He was pessimistic about the civilising of primitive peoples, for although they might make very rapid intellectual progress, the evolution of a matching organic culture was a much slower process. Left without a system of customs and social sanctions, and unable to adapt to the rapid social and cultural changes of civilisation, such peoples would be wiped out.[41] Where racial and cultural differences were small, racial mixing could be healthy and in fact beneficial, as in the emergence of a British people (following the diffusionist anthropological position, progress emerged from the contact of cultures, whereas isolation could lead to cultural degeneration, as in the case of the Chinese).[42] However, where the gap between races was large, as with negroes and whites in the United States, the result was a biologically inferior stock and one with serious moral problems because of the racial 'culture clash'. The dire consequences of such interbreeding had been demonstrated in the unfortunate and unstable history of India.[43] Even within Britain itself, McDougall feared that the pressures of rapid development were disrupting an organic culture. Like other eugenists he was particularly worried about a dysgenic decline in fertility among the professional and middle classes, and he attributed this to the development of intellect (culture) at the expense of instinct (biology). The same 'parabola of peoples' had characterised other great civilisations. If the natural history of culture was allowed to play its course, Britain was faced with inevitable decline; if her leaders and citizens could be made conscious of this destiny they might actively change it.[44] A new era of cultural evolution beckoned, in which the 'race' had the opportunity to take control of the evolutionary process, both by moulding its own social environment and culture in line with its innate character and by eugenic control of the quality of stock (vital once evolution became predominantly cultural and therefore dependent on brain power).

McDougall's advocacy of a 'social psychology' rested on his view that individuals were innately social creatures. Again he had detected the 'gregarious instinct' in his study of primitive society.[45] However, it did not disappear in civilised humanity. In fact, alongside the maternal instinct and an imitative tendency, it was vital for social development. He did not share the predominantly negative view of many continental thinkers that such instincts necessarily led to a dangerous loss of conscious control and descent into pathological mass behaviour. In his view these social instincts were the key to social evolution, providing an unconscious source of attraction towards the common culture, traditions and history which unified society and gave direction to the nation.

In his *Group Mind* of 1920, McDougall argued that the psychological ties between the individuals of an organic and culturally bonded group, such as a nation, gave the whole a mind-like property; the mind of the individual after all (like that of the group) was simply a collection of disparate ideas and instincts organised into a whole, and the larger part of each individual's mind (again like that of the group) lay outside conscious control. Attracted by the contemporary interest in vitalism and dissatisfied with sensationalist psychology when it came to explaining instincts or psychic experiences, he was drawn to the idea that there was a psychic force which ran alongside the physical – a 'psycho-physical dualism'. As such, the persistent character of a people – the 'soul of the race' – might stem from more than a continuity of germplasm: it might reflect 'an enduring psychic existent of which the lives of individual organisms are but successive manifestations'.[46] And, with modern psychopathology suggesting that personality could be literally dissociated, he suggested that there was a physiological 'collective unconscious' of groups of purposive cells within mind which mirrored the collective unconscious of individual minds within society.[47] Thus the individual mind became a repository for a racialised national history which was both biological and cultural.

The culture of racial memory

The translation of racial thought into ideas about individual minds and their relationship to culture reached well beyond academic debate.[48] The intellectuals and novelists of this era tended to be acutely alert to developments within science and often played a vital role in conveying such ideas to a broader educated audience.[49] However, this was not a one-way process. As has already been pointed out, there was already a well-established intellectual tradition of thinking about race in terms of cultural tradition. Moreover, just as the culture of Melanesia or Borneo had opened the eyes of the psycho-anthropologists, the rapid and sometimes painful transition to modernity provided subject material and stimulus for the domestic reconceptualisation of mind and its relationship to culture.

Nowhere within popular culture was the diffusion of ideas about race as culture more evident or significant than in thinking about national identity.[50] Though critical of McDougall's idea of a 'group mind', political theorist Ernest Barker's influential writing on English national character clearly demonstrates the existence of a shared pool of organicist ideas. Writing in 1927, he described race as:

> something more than a passive stuff or substratum. The racial blend of a nation may serve as a selective agency which chooses for survival this or that mental structure – a form of law, or a variety of religious belief – because it is most congenial to its own hidden character.

Immigration was a problem, not because of the racial inferiority of the migrants, but because 'a nation may lose the integrity of the solid core which is the basis of its tradition. And the nation which loses its tradition has lost its very self.'[51] This model of the organic nation persisted in his edited collection of 1950, *The Character of England*, in which the national character was seen as pervading virtually every aspect of the culture: for instance, its 'outdoor life' (with an essay from Vita Sackville-West on the organic design of the English country house and the rejection of the Palladian style), its 'homes and habits', and the 'English and the sea'.[52] Language was a particularly rich storehouse for generations of national consciousness, for:

> if race counts for the anthropologist, the language-group must count for the historian, who may find in its original language – so far as it can be recovered or reconstructed – a treasury of the thoughts which once were common to a group of peoples now speaking different tongues, and still may unite them loosely by the memories they have bequeathed and the sympathies they have engendered.[53]

As anthropology had shown, words had a power of their own beyond mere meaning – a totemic as well as an analytical value. By returning to the Anglo-Saxon roots of English one could reach back to a language which still functioned at an unconscious and instinctive level, in contrast to the Latin and French aspect of the language which was implanted on top at a more analytical, conscious and therefore less vigorous level.[54]

A search for the racial origins of the English nation was also pursued through folklore study and archaeology.[55] The popular enthusiasm for such activities reflected the fact that this was a search for a cultural lineage which was seen as still actively shaping the national character. As such it was, in Barker's view, a kind of civic duty 'to know the pit from which we are dug and the rock from which we are hewn'.[56] The discovery of such a past also had a regenerative function, as captured in H.G. Wells' *The Secret Places of the Heart* of 1922. Here psychologist Dr Martineau, fictional author of *The Psychology of the New Age*, attempts to restore the depressed entrepreneur Sir Richmond Hardy through a tour of the ancient sites of south-western England. Hardy draws on the remnants of the primitive culture to retrieve that side of himself stifled through the strain of civilisation. As he puts it:

> Today, among those ancient memories, has taken me out of myself wonderfully. I can't tell you how good Avebury has been for me. This afternoon half my consciousness has seemed to be a tattooed creature wearing a knife of stone. ... When we stood on the wall here in the sunset I seemed to be standing outside myself in an immense still sphere of past and future. I stood

> with my feet upon the Stone Age and saw myself four thousand years away.[57]

Wells returned to this theme in his autobiography of 1934, where he sees himself as being tied to the primitive through the ancient structure of the brain and sees individual evolution in terms of a struggle to reach beyond the confines of self to an understanding of this broader racial consciousness.[58]

The idea that racial memory was embedded in the individual even entered analysis of such an unlikely area as the national obsession with golf:

> The little white ball represents nothing less than the skull of your enemy. When you smite it with brassy or cleek, your nerves thrill to the very stimulus which maddened generations of your ancestors through ages of paleolithic savagery in tribal warfare … it carries back the soul of the twentieth century Briton to a very remote and barbaric stage in human evolution. This psychic return to neolithic barbarism and to paleolithic savagery is the secret of golf. It is the reason of the rapid spread of golf-mania among nations of city-dwellers who suffer more and more from the strain of the ever-increasing rapidity of social evolution.[59]

The themes echo Wells' *Secret Places of the Heart*: civilised man is still fuelled by ancient, instinctive drives, but is under strain because of higher inhibitions and the lack of avenues for release in modern society; though repressed, the primitive becomes an essential part of the civilised; the solution, and the path to continued harmony and evolution, is the development of a self which is at one with its cultural (and thereby racial) past, as well as its present.

Such a use of racial history as something which was integral to the self (rather than simply a marker of the biological 'other') can also be found in the work of Edward Carpenter, an eccentric, prophet-like, but nevertheless influential and widely read figure, whose views on racial memory were in fact integral to his better known activity as a socialist and sex reformer.[60] As Carpenter argued:

> All the instincts, all the devices, all the mental and physical adjustments by which during the centuries the Ego obtained expression for its own nature and qualities amid the outer conditions in which the race existed, are (together with that nature and those qualities) summed up and represented in his corporal organism; and within it the immense heritage of race-memory is stored. The 'I', the Ego, of his race is not only present, manifesting itself in Time and History – but an aspect, an affiliation, of it is now, today, present in that man, in his body. ... At the back of our eyes, so to speak, and in the profound depths of the race-life (of which each individual is but a momentary point) is stored the remote past of the world; and through our eyes look the eyes of our dead ancestors.[61]

In the next stage of evolution human beings would learn how to reach into their racial consciousness and thus gain a full understanding of self and its integration within the whole. At present, ancestral memories, in the form of myths, symbols and instinctive patterns of behaviour, influenced individual action only at an unconscious level. For Carpenter and others (such as his admirer Marie Stopes) the sexual act was so important because it involved a loss of self-consciousness and the release of powerful race memories: 'The mortal figure without penetrates the immortal figure within; and there rises into consciousness a shining form, glorious, not belonging to this world, but vibrating with the agelong life of humanity, and the memory of a thousand love-dramas.'[62] Through the physiological imprint of myth-making over generations of racial development the character of races had become markedly different.[63] However, a heightened racial consciousness would reveal the universal patterns which underlay racial myths, and in so doing would in fact disrupt the very stability of racial categories:

> When the consciousness deepens to that of the universal life, and to the point whence as it were the different races have radiated, then the figures of the gods grow dim and lose their outline, the rivalries and mutual recriminations of the various human ideals cease to have the old poignancy and interest; and their place is taken by a profound sense and intense realisation of the unity and common life of all races and creatures; by a strange and novel capacity of understanding and entering into the habits of distant beings or peoples; and by a mysterious

> sense of power to 'flow down' into these forms and embody therein a portion of the life universal. And with all this come naturally great changes in the institutions and political forms of peoples, and the spreading of genuine Democracy and Socialism over the Earth.[64]

As such, Carpenter's vision of accessing race memory looked to the ultimate subversion of race as a category of difference.

Anthropologising national culture

By the late 1930s, with race de-emphasised as a category of fundamental biological difference, the study of cultural difference emphasised (particularly within the increasingly dominant school of functionalist anthropology) and the primitive recognised within the civilised, the emergent Mass Observation movement attempted to reverse the anthropological gaze by making the everyday life of the British population the object of study. Having completed an account of his own anthropological experience in the New Hebrides, Tom Harrisson had set up Mass Observation with sociologist Charles Madge in 1937. Harrisson's experience had taught him that the study of a truly 'primitive' society was becoming impossible under the impact of Western colonialism, and suggested that it was time instead for the study of 'normal man' and the '[b]lack shirt and red'.[65] The title of his account – *Savage Civilisation* – scorned the very notion of a clear dichotomy between the savage and the civilised: 'one only needs to watch a "savage" becoming "civilised", to see how ephemeral many of our superficial criteria are. … What oceans of error we should have been spared if those who wrote about the "savage", primitive mentality, had done more primitive living'. Therefore he now consciously projected the character of primitive people and their culture into an analysis of twentieth-century Britain. Indeed the whole project was premised on the idea that irrational superstition was still a powerful unconscious force in modern society and that, if anything, such ideas were becoming stronger because of the stresses and complexity of modernisation and the exploitation of the condition by advertising, the press and political propaganda.[66] Mass Observation hoped to open the eyes of the public to this phenomenon, through active involvement in studying their own society and through the publication of results. As such it was a project of civic self-education, and one which aimed to counter the loss of social consciousness within an atomising mass society (a devastation which echoed that encountered by anthropologists in their studies of primitive cultures on contact with civilisation).[67] Finally, emphasising the racial and cultural relativity of the enterprise, Madge and Harrisson called for investigators from other racial groups and societies who would 'see ourselves as others see us', and perhaps even more significantly (as well as realistically) they called for lay investigators from within Britain's own general public. In sum, the project pointed towards a collapse of the boundary between and hierarchy of academic and popular knowledge: anthropology, like contemporary dynamic psychology, was now recognised as a way of understanding that was embedded in and constrained by its own culture, and the very possibility of fully knowing the 'other' was called into question.

Conclusion

This chapter has presented two main arguments. The first has been that for a complex of reasons British psychological thought in the period 1898–1939 was noteworthy less for the persistence of scientific racism than for the relative lack of interest (particularly domestically) in this issue, and for the withdrawal from hard-line positions on innate biological inequality to an emphasis instead on the cumulative influence of culture on mind. Even when considering McDougall, who was clearly exceptional in the degree and extremism of his interest in this area, what stands out are the unorthodoxy of his theoretical models of race and his contortions to elevate the significance of culture once he was forced to recognise the lack of a fundamental difference in mental potential between 'primitive' and 'civilised' humans. The second argument, however, has been that we need to look beyond this rather limited paradigm of a science of racial difference and inequality to recognise the existence of multiple discourses of race. And in this respect it has been argued that the influence of racial thought in fact remained fundamental in both academic and popular psychology. For instance, national character was essentially racialised as the natural outcome of an organic fit between culture and the mind of the people. Psychological theory internalised a racial history of cultural difference within the individual psyche through the models of primitive and civilised layers of the mind, the 'protocritic' and 'epicritic', the extrovert and the introvert, the unconscious and the conscious, and the instinctive and the intellectual. And the path from savagery to civilised individual and social development was recast as no longer a simple transition from one side of the divide to the other, but a question of harnessing both sides and matching both to the social environment through an understanding of culture, history and psychology. The psychological exchange with anthropology contributed to this reorientation, but the search for an individual identity which went beyond the civilised, rational self to link up with primitive instincts, an organic nation and its past, or a universal racial consciousness, should also be seen as the reaction to a more general modernist crisis of identity caused by the instability of a rapidly changing society. In highlighting this, the chapter has attempted to show how the history of the diffusion of racial knowledge can move beyond a restrictive paradigm of control or construction against the 'other' towards an understanding of the ways in which race could inform the self-construction of identity, connecting individuals with their pasts, their communities and nations, and even liberating their behaviour.[68]

Notes

1 D. Lorimer, 'Theoretical Racism in Late Victorian Anthropology, 1870–1900', *Victorian Studies* 31 (1987–8): 405–30.

2 Lorimer, 'Theoretical Racism', p. 411.

3 José Harris, *Private Lives, Public Spirit: A Social History of Britain, 1870–1914*, Oxford, Oxford University Press, 1993, pp. 233–7. Despite his intention to highlight the significance of scientific racism in the last decades of the century, Lorimer is also forced to acknowledge that the willingness to generalise about racial difference owed less to science than to 'habits of mind shaped by the larger social and cultural environment. Much of the Victorian discussion of race took place in a haphazard fashion, mixing the observations of travellers with commonplace prejudice' ('Theoretical Racism', p. 428).

4 For the argument that within British anthropology the functionalist approach of Malinowski (which emphasised culture and imported a Freudian perspective) continued to be paralleled by a physical anthropological tradition, see Paul Rich, 'The Long Victorian Sunset: Anthropology, Eugenics and Race in Britain, *c.*1900–1948', in Rich, *Prospero's Return? Historical Essays on Race, Culture and British Society*, London, Hansib, 1994, pp. 53–66. However, Rich also recognises the emerging critique: 'The Baptism of a New Era: The 1911 Universal Race Congress and the Liberal Ideology of Race', *Prospero's Return*, pp. 67–84. This is convincingly pushed further in Elazar Barkan's authoritative work, *The Retreat of Scientific Racism: Changing Conceptions of Race in Britain and the United States between the Wars*, Cambridge, Cambridge

University Press, 1992; Nancy Stepan, *The Idea of Race in Science: Great Britain, 1860–1960*, London, Macmillan, 1982, pp. 140–69. For contemporary examples of the new scientific critique of racism, see G. Spiller, 'Science and Race Prejudice', *Sociological Review* 5 (1912): 331–48; Julian Huxley and A.C. Haddon, *We Europeans: A Survey of 'Racial' Problems*, London, Jonathan Cape, 1935.

5 It is also worth bearing in mind that when John Langdon Down coined this term in reference to a supposed physical likeness, he was attacking the polygenist theory of race which was used to defend slavery in the era of the American Civil War. By labelling sections of Britain's own population as 'mongoloids' (he also marked out other racial types within the population, such as 'malays' and 'negroids'), he was suggesting that there was no species gulf between whites and blacks, and that examples of all stages of human evolution, and degeneration – as in the case of the 'mongol' – could be found within the 'Caucasian' race; see Lilian Zihni, 'The History of the Relationship between the Concept and Treatment of People with Down's Syndrome in Britain and America from 1886 to 1967', unpublished University of London Ph.D. thesis, 1989, pp. 43–54. On the subsequent history of the concept, see Mark Jackson's chapter in this volume (Chapter 8).

6 Graham Richards, *'Race', Racism and Psychology: Towards a Reflexive History*, London and New York, Routledge, 1997, pp. 187–223.

7 It should be noted that even critics of racism were willing to accept the existence of innate biological differences. See, for instance, J.B.S. Haldane, *Heredity and Politics*, London, Jonathan Cape, 1938, pp. 128–53. Equally the use of terms such as 'savage' and 'primitive' remained commonplace; see Barkan, *Retreat of Scientific Racism*, p. 23; George Stocking Jr, *Race, Culture and Evolution: Essays in the History of Anthropology*, New York, Free Press, 1969, p. 132. The fact that individuals who attacked scientific racism could adopt such language indicates once again the need to develop a model of parallel 'race' discourses.

8 In his survey of racism within British psychology during this period, Graham Richards (*'Race', Racism and Psychology*, pp. 199–200) finds only one other leading British psychologist, R.B. Cattell, to have been similarly forthright on the subject; for example, see Cattell's *Psychology and Social Progress*, London, C.W. Daniel, 1933. Interestingly both moved to the United States. And it should be noted that it was in this more politicised environment that McDougall made his most overt racist statement and attracted the most criticism after he had emigrated, with the publication of *Is America Safe for Democracy?* (1921), which was republished in modified form in Britain as *National Welfare and National Decay*, London, Methuen, 1921. It is however difficult to disentangle criticism over his racism from the probably more central attacks on his theoretical positions. For McDougall's own views and for bibliographic details of his work, see A.L. Robinson, *William McDougall: A Bibliography, Together with a Brief Outline of His Work*, Durham, NC, Duke University Press, 1943.

9 There is an excellent account of the influence of the psychological perspective for anthropology: Henrika Kuklick, *The Savage Within: The*

Social History of British Anthropology, 1885–1945, Cambridge, Cambridge University Press, 1991. Historians of psychology have paid far less attention to this important dialogue, though this has recently been remedied in Richards, *'Race'*, pp. 41–64.

10 Ian Langham, *The Building of British Social Anthropology: W.H.R. Rivers and His Cambridge Disciples in the Development of Kinship Studies, 1898–1931*, Dordrecht and London, Reidel, 1981, pp. 55–64; Richard Slobodin, *W.H.R. Rivers*, New York, Columbia University Press, 1978.

11 Nikolas Rose, *The Psychological Complex: Psychology, Politics and Society in England, 1869–1939*, London, Routledge, 1985.

12 W.H.R. Rivers, 'The Ethnological Analysis of Culture', Presidential Address to Section H of the British Association in 1911; repr. in Rivers (ed.), *Psychology and Ethnology*, London, Kegan Paul, 1926, pp. 133–7.

13 W.H.R. Rivers, *The History of Melanesian Society*, Cambridge, Cambridge University Press, 1914, vol. 2, p. 595; Kuklick, *The Savage Within*, pp. 125, 164.

14 For instance, see F.C. Bartlett, *Psychology and Primitive Culture*, Cambridge, Cambridge University Press, 1923.

15 W. McDougall, *An Introduction to Social Psychology*, London, Methuen, 1908.

16 W.H.R. Rivers, 'Sociology and Psychology', *Sociological Review* 16 (Autumn 1916); repr. in Rivers, *Psychology and Ethnology*. Similarly, despite being attracted by Freudian theory (like Rivers), Malinowski was critical of the universalism of ideas such as the Oedipus complex; see his Letter to the Editor, *Nature* 3 November 1923: 650–1.

17 Rivers, *The History of Melanesian Society*, vol. 2, p. 596; L. Gome, 'Sociology and the Basis of Inquiry into Primitive Culture', *Sociological Review* 11 (1909): 317–37.

18 For a perceptive and historically informed interpretation of the links between Rivers' anthropological and psychological thinking, see the Booker Prize-winning novel by Pat Barker, *The Ghost Road*, London, Viking, 1995. On shell-shock, see M. Stone, 'Shell-Shock and the Psychiatrists', in W. Bynum, R. Porter and M. Shepherd (eds), *The Anatomy of Madness*, London, Routledge, 1985, vol. 2, pp. 242–71.

19 Kuklick, *The Savage Within*, pp. 165–74.

20 William McDougall and Charles Hose, *The Pagan Tribes of Borneo*, London, Macmillan, 1912, vol. 2, p. 211.

21 For instance, Freud's views on repression influenced Wilfred Trotter, *The Instinct of the Herd in Peace and War*, London, Ernest Benn, 1916, p. 48.

22 For instance, see R. Marett, 'A Sociological View of Comparative Religion', *Sociological Review* 1 (1908): 48–60; J.W. Slaughter, 'Psychological Factors in Social Transmission', *Sociological Review* 1 (1908): 149. Marett drew directly on Rivers' work. Though part of the generation of 'armchair' anthropologists, his call for active involvement in folk practice as a route to understanding pointed towards an anthropology of the field (see R. Marett, *Psychology and Folk-Lore*, London, Methuen, 1920, pp. 1–26).

23 W.H.R. Rivers, 'Dreams and Primitive Culture', *Bulletin of the John Rylands Library* 1918: 25; Rivers, 'Sociology and Psychology', p. 17. Because of the power of rationalisation in civilised society, Rivers suggested that it was easier to interpret the minds of Melanesians through behaviour than it would be the inhabitants of an English or Scottish village.
24 R.J.A. Berry (ed.), *Stoke Park Monographs on Mental Deficiency and Other Problems of the Human Brain and Mind: No. 1. The Burden Memorial Volume*, London, Macmillan, 1933.
25 C.G. Seligman, 'Psychology and Racial Difference', in J.A. Hadfield (ed.), *Psychology and Modern Problems*, London, University of London Press, 1935, p. 64; Berry, *Stoke Park Monographs*, p. 237. For the colonial context of this work, see Jock McCulloch, *Colonial Psychiatry and 'the African Mind'*, Cambridge, Cambridge University Press, 1995, pp. 46–63.
26 Seligman, 'Psychology and Racial Difference', p. 68; C.G. Seligman, 'The Unconscious in Relation to Anthropology', *British Journal of Psychology* 1928: 18.
27 Seligman, 'Psychology and Racial Difference', pp. 86–98.
28 Barkan, *The Retreat of Scientific Racism*, pp. 30–4.
29 Megan Vaughan, *Curing Their Ills: Colonial Power and African Illness*, Oxford, Polity Press, 1991, pp. 100–28.
30 Headed by Polish-born Bronislaw Malinowski, Professor of Anthropology at the London School of Economics from 1927 to 1939, functionalists pushed further the shift of focus from the evolutionary or historical roots of cultures and peoples towards a sociology-style study of cultures in their own right. As such they de-emphasised innate racial differences and relativised cultural differences as functional rather than a sign of evolutionary development; see Kuklick, *The Savage Within*, pp. 264–8.
31 Kuklick, *The Savage Within*, pp. 182–241; B.J.F. Laubscher, *Sex, Custom and Psychopathology: A Study of the South African Pagan Natives*, London, G. Routledge & Sons, 1937; McCulloch, *Colonial Psychiatry and 'the African Mind'*.
32 W. McDougall (1871–1938) became Wilde Reader in Mental Philosophy at Oxford in 1904. After the war he moved to Harvard and then Duke University in the United States. He wrote extensively and was widely read; however, among his academic peers his ideas were regarded as increasingly eccentric. See Robinson, *William McDougall*.
33 McDougall, *The Group Mind: A Sketch of the Principles of Collective Psychology With Some Attempt to Apply Them to the Interpretation of National Life and Character*, Cambridge, Cambridge University Press, 1920, p. 212.
34 McDougall, *Group Mind*, p. 203.
35 William McDougall, *National Welfare and National Decay*, London, Methuen, 1921, pp. 133–4.
36 McDougall, *National Welfare and National Decay*, pp. 136–41.
37 McDougall, *The Riddle of Life*, London, Methuen, 1938.

38 McDougall, *Anthropology and History*, Oxford, Oxford University Press, 1920, p. 10.
39 P. Rich, 'Imperial Decline and the Resurgence of English National Identity, 1918–1979', in T. Kushner and K. Lunn (eds), *Traditions of Intolerance*, Manchester, Manchester University Press, 1989, pp. 33–52.
40 McDougall, *Anthropology and History*, p. 11.
41 McDougall, *Anthropology and History*, p. 12; McDougall, *Introduction to Social Psychology*, p. 232.
42 McDougall, *Anthropology and History*, p. 10.
43 McDougall, *Group Mind*, pp. 242–4.
44 McDougall, *Anthropology and History*, p. 74. On the authoritarian dimension to McDougall's calls for government led by psychological experts, see Reba Soffer, 'New Elitism: Social Psychology in Pre-War Britain', *Journal of British Studies* 8 (1969): 111–40.
45 McDougall, *Introduction to Social Psychology*, pp. 72–3.
46 W. McDougall, *Body and Mind: A History and Defence of Animism*, London, Methuen, 1911, p. 377. See also W. McDougall, *Modern Materialism and Emergent Evolution*, London, Methuen, 1934; McDougall, *The Riddle of Life*.
47 McDougall, *The Riddle of Life*, p. 221, also pp. 202–17. On dissociation of personality, see Ian Hacking, 'Multiple Personality Disorder and Its Hosts', *History of the Human Sciences* 5 (1992): 3–31.
48 Laura Otis, *Organic Memory: History and the Body in the Late Nineteenth and Early Twentieth Century*, Lincoln and London, University of Nebraska Press, 1994.
49 This is clearly the case with the three main figures discussed here: H.G. Wells, Edward Carpenter and Ernest Barker. For a general account which describes how intellectuals were influenced by contemporary science, see J. Carey, *The Intellectuals and the Masses: Pride and Prejudice among the Literary Intelligentsia, 1880–1939*, London, Faber & Faber, 1992.
50 It is seen as an important factor in the appeal of interwar, Baldwinite, Conservatism: see S. Nicholas, 'The Construction of a National Identity: Stanley Baldwin, "Englishness" and the Mass Media in Interwar Britain', in M. Francis and I. Zweiniger-Bargielowska (eds), *The Conservatives and British Society, 1860–1990*, Cardiff, University of Wales Press, 1996, pp. 127–70. For more general coverage, see R. Colls and P. Dodd (eds), *Englishness: Politics and Culture, 1880–1920*, London, Croom Helm, 1986. For examples of the various ways in which national character was conceptualised in the writing of this period, see D. Trotter, *The English Novel in History, 1895–1920*, London, Routledge, 1993, and J. Giles and T. Middleton (eds), *Writing Englishness, 1900–1950*, London, Routledge, 1995, which suggests that education was an important avenue for the propagation of organicist notions of national identity (see, for instance, the extracts from Arthur Mee's *Children's Encyclopaedia*, pp. 63–6). Interwar Englishness has recently been presented as a feminised category, moving away from aggressive (masculine) imperialism towards a more inward-looking, domestic and private vision; see A. Light, *Forever England:*

Femininity, Literature and Conservatism between the Wars, London, Routledge, 1991. The models of identity presented in this chapter suggest that the domestic and imperial visions were in fact tied together by a particular form of racial thought; moreover, the primitive, instinctive dimension to identity reveals the continuity of a non-domesticated, non-'feminised' set of images associated with national identity.

51 Both quotations are from E. Barker, *National Character and the Factors in Its Formation*, London, Methuen, 1927, p. 47. See J. Stapleton, *Englishness and the Study of Politics: The Social and Political Thought of Ernest Barker*, Cambridge, Cambridge University Press, 1994.

52 E. Barker, *English National Character*, London, Oxford University Press, 1950. The wartime threat to the nation probably revived such a naturalisation of the national character; see, for instance, Arthur Bryant's best-selling history, *English Saga, 1840–1940*, London, Collins, 1940. On the way in which this affected post-war immigration debates and thinking about the difficulties of integration, see C. Waters, ' "Dark Strangers" in Our Midst: Discourses of Race and Nation in Britain, 1947–1963', *Journal of British Studies* 36 (1997): 207–38. Waters, however, may underestimate the significance of a cultural racism – and the contribution of science to this racism – that already existed in interwar thinking.

53 Barker, *English Character*, p. 25.

54 Trotter, *The English Novel in History*, p. 157; Ernest Jones, 'A Linguistic Factor in English Characterology', in E. Jones, *Essays in Applied Psycho-Analysis*, London, Hogarth Press, 1951, pp. 88–94.

55 On folk study, see Georgina Boyes, *The Imagined Village: Culture, Ideology and the English Folk Revival*, Manchester, Manchester University Press, 1993. The English Folk Song Society was founded in 1898, followed by the English Folk Dance Society in 1911.

56 Barker, *National Character*, p. 45.

57 H.G. Wells, *The Secret Places of the Heart*, London, Cassell, 1922. This reference is from a later collected edition, see H.G. Wells, *The Invisible Man, The Secret Places of the Heart, and God the Invisible King*, London, The Literary Press, n.d., pp. 194–5. As early as 1896 Wells had explored the plasticity of racial difference through his depiction of the mental and physical construction of men from beasts in *The Island of Dr Moreau* (London, Heinemann), in which the idea of the island laboratory also drew on the anthropological expeditions of the era.

58 H.G. Wells, *Experiment in Autobiography: Discoveries and Conclusions of a Very Ordinary Brain (Since 1866)*, London, Victor Gollancz, vol. 2, 1934, pp. 825–7. It should be noted that this use of racial identity by Wells is of a different nature to the biological racism and anti-Semitism which, controversially, was detected in his work by M. Coren (see Coren, *The Invisible Man: The Life and Liberties of H.G. Wells*, London, Bloomsbury, 1993, pp. 65–7).

59 Gilbert Slater, 'Concerning Golf (and Other) Balls', *Sociological Review* 4 (1911): 319–20. Slater was a writer and Principal of Ruskin College, Oxford. His article was not an exception. See, for instance, advice on reaching into the deeper levels of mind to improve one's golf and life

in L. Schon, *The Psychology of Golf*, London, Methuen, 1922; C.W. Bailey, *The Brain and Golf: Some Hints for Golfers from Modern Mental Science*, London, Mills & Boon, 1923.

60 Typically his often mystical ideas about mind are dismissed as a 'jumble of pseudo-scientific claims and assertions', despite the fact that Beatrice Webb, for instance, regarded it as the 'Metaphysics of the Socialist Creed'; see C. Tsuzuki, *Edward Carpenter, 1844–1929: Prophet of Human Fellowship*, Cambridge, Cambridge University Press, 1980, p. 164. For more serious consideration of his ideas on sex reform, though still not of his ideas on mind, see Sheila Rowbotham, 'Edward Carpenter: Prophet of the New Life', in S. Rowbotham and J. Weeks, *Socialism and the New Life*, London, Pluto Press, 1977.

61 Carpenter, *The Art of Creation: Essays on the Self and Its Powers*, London, George Allen, 1904, pp. 96, 133.

62 Carpenter, *The Art of Creation*, p. 137. This mystical and racial dimension to sex was more widespread, present in the work of novelist D.H. Lawrence (such as *The Rainbow* of 1915) and even in the best-selling sex-advice manual of the era (Marie Stopes, *Married Love*, London, Putnam, 1918, pp. 23–30). It should also be noted the Wells' Hardy character was to find release and a return to health through sex.

63 Carpenter, *The Art of Creation*, p. 152.

64 Carpenter, *The Art of Creation*, p. 216.

65 Tom Harrisson, *Savage Civilisation*, London, Victor Gollancz, 1937, pp. 343, 366–7.

66 Charles Madge and Tom Harrisson, *Mass Observation*, London, Frederick Muller, 1937, pp. 13–19.

67 Madge and Harrisson, *Mass Observation*, p. 31.

68 For the 'other' as central in fashioning national identity, see L. Colley, 'Britishness and Otherness: An Argument', *Journal of British Studies* 31 (1992): 311; for the classic account of the colonial experience as providing the 'other', see E. Said, *Orientalism*, London, Routledge, 1978. Carolyn Steedman has highlighted the limitations of this rather restrictive model in much recent work on identity in 'Inside, Outside, Other: Accounts of National Identity in the Nineteenth Century', *History of the Human Sciences* 8 (1995): 59–76.

Chapter 12

'New men, strange faces, other minds'

Arthur Keith, race and the Piltdown affair (1912–53)

Jonathan Sawday[*]

The mystery of the beginning of all things is insoluble by us … I for one must be content to remain an agnostic.

(Charles Darwin, *Autobiography*, 1876–81)[1]

I remember the bat-winged lizard birds,
The Age of Ice and the mammoth herds,
And the giant tigers that stalked them down
Through Regent's Park into Camden Town.
And I remember like yesterday
The earliest Cockney who came my way,
When he pushed through the Forest that lined the Strand,
With paint on his face and a club in his hand.

(Rudyard Kipling, 'The River's Tale', 1911)[2]

The Piltdown 'fraud' or 'hoax' is a subject of abiding public fascination.[3] It is not difficult to understand this interest. In the early 1950s, when the fraud was unmasked, the terms 'science' and 'scientist' had become as much metaphors for human hope, discovery and optimism, as simple words with which to describe a particular human activity and those who pursued that activity. Scientists were perceived in the popular imagination as figures of authority who had about them something of the nature of a priestly caste. In their reserved and austere communion with 'Nature', in the deployment of an increasingly specialised language for communication with one another, and in the immense (and

* I should like to acknowledge the advice of Dr Bernard Harris and Professor Clive Gamble (both of the University of Southampton) in the preparation of this essay.

growing) financial investment which was needed to support scientific research, an immeasurable divide seemed to have opened up between the world of the scientist and the layperson.[4]

By exposing Piltdown as a fraud, the divide, if it did not vanish, seemed somehow measurable. Science was no longer a suprahuman activity. Rather, like all other human activities, it was seen to be subject to the everyday world of imperfect human morality. Hence, as well as being the occasion for a good deal of *schadenfreude* on the part of the public at the expense of the scientist, the fraud suggested that the usual human emotions were in play even within the scientific community: ambition, vanity, envy, greed, maliciousness and sheer delight in mischief-making. Ironically, of course, it was the application of rigorous scientific methodology which finally revealed the fraud for what it was: a clumsy attempt at fabricating the fossilised remains of a human-like creature which had never existed in nature. But, following the exposure of the fraud in 1953, the hunt was on for the perpetrator or perpetrators. Various candidates have been (and are still being) proposed as the chief 'fraudster'.[5] However, in searching for the culprit(s) a much more important series of questions remained unasked, let alone unanswered. Why, particularly within British scientific and medical circles, was Piltdown accepted for so long? What are its claims to be taken seriously – if not as part of the history of human origins, then as part of a larger cultural history of science and its intersection with other forms of knowledge? Above all, what does the fabrication of 'Piltdown Man' – a creature organised on the basis of supposedly Darwinian principles – have to tell us about the fascination with 'race' and theories of so-called 'racial decline' in the first half of the twentieth century? Concentrating on the career of one of the first and most distinguished of the Piltdown 'interpreters', Sir Arthur Keith, this chapter sets out to explore these questions within the context of the forty-year-long 'career' of 'Piltdown Man': one of the most notorious scientific frauds of the age.

Writing the Book of Nature

For Charles Darwin, Nature spoke volumes. True the record was imperfect, but Nature nevertheless presented herself in an intelligible language. In reading Nature's Book, however, the problem was one of discontinuity. 'I look at the history of the world imperfectly kept', Darwin wrote in *The Origin of Species* (1859),

> and written in a changing dialect; of this history we possess the last volume alone, relating only to two or three countries. Of this volume, only here and there a short chapter has been preserved; and of each page, only here and there a few lines.[6]

Darwin's task, then, was to reconstruct the Book of Nature; to produce a coherent narrative which would account for the diversity of life as it was to be observed both in the living world of the present, and in the vanished world of the past, of which the only memorials were fossil remnants. But to reconstruct the Book of Nature is not to rewrite it. For others who came after Darwin, the incomplete nature of the record offered both a challenge and an opportunity. The challenge was to piece together the scattered fragments of the natural record on the principles established by Darwin. The opportunity (or the temptation) was to supplement the incomplete volume: to provide an entirely new page, but written in a hand indecipherable from the authentic original.

Such a page – for a time held to be authentic, but eventually proved to be a forgery – is represented by the Piltdown 'discoveries' of 1912–15. The Piltdown 'discoveries' were once constituted as key moments in the sciences of anthropology and prehistoric archaeology. The discovery of 'Piltdown Man' (or *Eoanthropus Dawsoni* as the creature was once known) in a Sussex gravel-bed – a being who appeared to possess the skull of a modern human and an ape-like jaw – was once held to be the triumphal vindication of Darwin's evolutionary theories. Here at last, and in England, was the so-called 'missing link': the final and irrefutable evidence of the shared origins of modern humanity and modern apes. But Piltdown also appeared to refute one of Darwin's more uncomfortable speculations. In *The Descent of Man* (1871) Darwin had tentatively posited a likely point of origin for the human species:

> In each great region of the world the living mammals are closely related to the extinct species of the same region. It is therefore probable that Africa was formerly inhabited by extinct apes closely allied to the gorilla and chimpanzee; and as these two species are now man's nearest allies, it is somewhat more probable that our earliest progenitors lived on the African continent than elsewhere.[7]

Unwilling to press this speculation too far, Darwin drew back from a firm conclusion:

> But it is useless to speculate on this subject; for two or three anthropomorphous apes … nearly as large as man … existed in Europe during the Miocene age; and since so remote a period the Earth has certainly undergone many great revolutions, and there has been ample time for migration on the largest scale.[8]

This hasty qualification to the 'out of Africa' hypothesis left ample room (or so it seemed) for Piltdown to flourish. As Richard Leakey has observed, when Darwin advanced the idea that human beings had emerged from Africa, 'no early human fossils had been found anywhere; his conclusion was based entirely on theory'.[9] An African origin for humanity, moreover, flew in the face of that colonial disdain which held that Africa, the home of 'primitive' peoples, could hardly have rivalled Europe or Asia, with their ancient and flourishing civilisations, as an appropriate birthplace for modern humanity.[10]

So Piltdown insinuated itself into what might be termed a pair of Darwinian 'gaps'. First, there was the chronological 'gap' in the fossil record, where evolutionary theory suggested that there ought to be evidence of some kind of 'transitional' species between human and ape. Second, there was the 'gap' in the geographical location of human origins; Piltdown – the English 'discovery' – handily supplied that missing fragment of the jigsaw puzzle as well. Yet, as further evidence on human origins accumulated in the interwar and immediate post-war years, Piltdown gradually began to appear as an anomaly. It was as if the English find was a fragment from an entirely different puzzle, which had been forced into the larger picture of human origins. Hence, following the exposure of the fraud in 1953, the almost audible sigh of relief with which W.E. Le Gros Clark, Emeritus Professor of Anatomy at the University of Oxford, was able to record that the Piltdown anomaly need trouble the world of science no longer: 'The elimination of "Piltdown Man" from further consideration greatly clarified discussions of the origin of man … it was entirely out of conformity with all the fossil evidence of hominid evolution available from other parts of the world'.[11] But Piltdown also served as a warning to the scientific community: 'this astonishing fraud … does serve to emphasise even more strongly the extreme caution which needs to be exercised in the interpretation of alleged fossils of quite unusual or unexpected type', concluded Le Gros Clark.[12]

The painting

What the event *should* have been (indeed what the event was between 1912 and 1953) is graphically displayed in the painting entitled 'A Discussion of the Piltdown Skull' by John Cooke, RA (Figure 12.1). This group portrait was completed in time for the May Exhibition of the Royal Academy in 1915, and met with considerable public acclaim. Cooke's portrait displays the chief (but not quite all of) the Piltdown protagonists. They are (standing in the back row, from left to right) Frank Barlow, technical assistant in the Department of Geology at the British Museum (Natural History), who was responsible for preparing plaster replicas of the Piltdown skull; Grafton Elliot Smith, Professor of Anatomy at Manchester University, responsible for describing the Piltdown cast; Charles Dawson, a solicitor from Uckfield in Sussex, the principal discoverer of the Piltdown material; Arthur Smith Woodward, Keeper of Geology at the British Museum (Natural History), who provided the first interpretation of the Piltdown skull and offered a reconstruction of the material; and (seated in the front row, from left to right) Arthur Swayne Underwood, Professor of Dental Surgery at King's College London, Smith Woodward's consultant on dental matters relating to the reconstruction of the Piltdown skull; Arthur Keith, Conservator of the Royal College of Surgeons, responsible for much of the anatomic work on the Piltdown skull; William Plane Pycraft, an osteologist and another whom Smith Woodward consulted; and, finally, Edwin Ray Lankester, a former Professor of Zoology at University College London, Professor of Comparative Anatomy at Oxford, and Director of the British Museum (Natural History), who supported Smith Woodward's interpretation of Piltdown. Of these eight individuals, four (Elliot Smith, Smith Woodward, Keith and Lankester) were either to receive knighthoods or were already knighted for their services to science.

The painting represents a meeting which took place at the Royal College of Surgeons on 11 August 1913. What does the painting tell us of the organisation of scientific method at the time of Piltdown? We stand beyond the picture-plane looking into a room full of characters who are oblivious to our gaze, intent upon the object of their study.

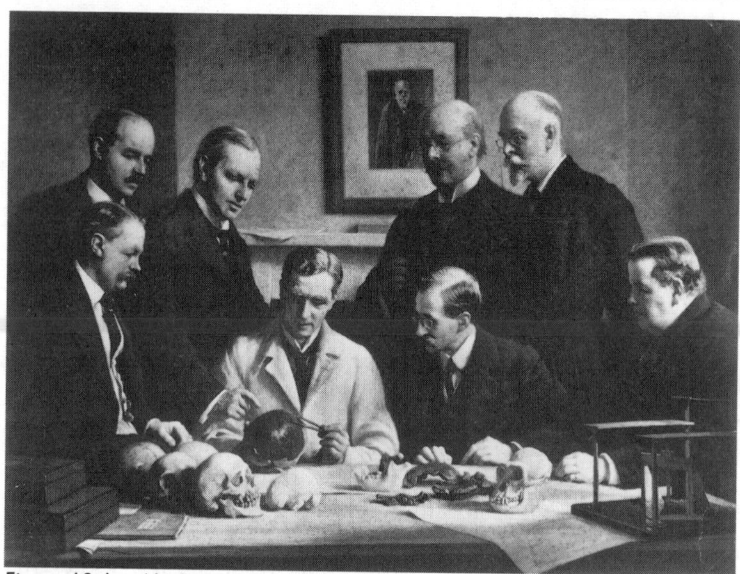

Figure 12.1 'A discussion of the Piltdown Skull'
Source: With permission, Natural History Museum, London.

The painting commemorates who was there, who was involved; the groupings of figures, their disposition in relation to one another, may also tell us something of (say) the relative intellectual or social status of the individuals depicted. We see the figures dispersed into a series of interlocked equilateral triangles – a device of group portraiture which is very much in the style of Rembrandt.[13] Two of these triangles meet (or share a common angle) in the left hand of Keith, which holds a pair of dividers. In Renaissance images, mathematical instruments (the square, the ruler, dividers and compasses) symbolised the rational plan according to which God had created the Universe. More specifically they came to be emblems of God as the divine 'architect' of the human frame.[14] Whether or not the artist is consciously evoking this iconological tradition, the dividers as instruments of accurate measurement had an immediate significance to the interpretation of Piltdown and to the genesis of Cooke's painting. One of the chief areas of contention among the experts who attempted to reconstruct the complete Piltdown skull from the fragments which had been 'discovered', was the precise cubic capacity of the creature's brain-case. Arthur Keith, the man in the white coat who is shown holding and measuring a cast of the 'reconstructed' Piltdown skull, believed that Smith Woodward's analysis of the cranial fragments (upon which the 'reconstruction' was based) had deprived the creature of some 250–300 cm^3 of brain-space. Keith's firm conviction, which he pursued in an exhaustive series of comparative anatomical studies, was that the 'Piltdown race' (as he termed those of whom the fragments were the only memorial) possessed 'a head above average dimensions, and a brain very little, if any, below the amount allotted to the average European of today'.[15] Smith Woodward and Keith found themselves locked in dispute over their differing hypotheses, and it was in an attempt to resolve this disagreement that the August meeting depicted in Cooke's painting took place.

But there was to be no resolution. Indeed, if anything matters became more heated. In his autobiography (published in 1950) Keith recorded the details of the dispute. Keith may well have felt some professional jealousy that he had not been consulted from the very outset about the discovery. Instead he was allowed to see the Piltdown material (and for a very short period of time) by Smith Woodward only after the discovery had been publicly announced.[16] At a subsequent discussion at the Royal Society in 1913, at which Elliot Smith read a paper on the brain of Piltdown Man, there was a furious argument. Keith objected to Elliot Smith's use of the flawed reconstruction of the Piltdown brain-case:

> in the discussion which followed I did not mince my words in pointing out the glaring errors in the reconstructed brain-cast he exhibited to the meeting. It was a crowded meeting, and it so happened that he and I filed out side by side. I shall never forget the angry look he gave me. Such was the end of a long friendship.[17]

So, although Cooke's painting is concerned with measurement, interpretation and the unfolding of scientific 'truth' through the processes of rational observation, it also conceals enormous professional and institutional rivalry.[18] The sombre-suited Edwardian experts appear to be caught in a moment of dispassionate enquiry, yet the reality of many of the Piltdown discussions was quite different.

There is, of course, one more figure in the painting who, from a compositional point of view, occupies the most important position of all. At the very mid-point of the image, on the wall behind the group, hangs a representation of John Collier's portrait of Charles Darwin, now in the National Portrait Gallery. This image forms the apex of a third triangle, uniting the complete composition, with the two other angles of this triangle indicated by the skull on the left (in Keith's hand) and the skull on the right (just between the left hand of Pycraft and the left hand of Lankester). The two skulls face one another, in grinning opposition. The skull on the left is that of a modern human being, that on the right the skull of an anthropoid primate – a gorilla. With his left hand, Arthur Keith measures the cast of the skull, the cranial capacity of the human part of Piltdown, leaving the animal part – the jaw fragment – on the table. Science is thus measuring that which defines the human in respect of the ape. The sight-lines of the surrounding group converge on this moment of revelation, while one pair of eyes stares challengingly back out of the picture-plane towards us. Darwin watches us, as before our eyes, his theory of the primate origin of humanity is triumphantly vindicated.

Looking at the picture, in which the animal and the human are shown gazing at one another beneath the supposedly dispassionate eye of science, it is difficult to resist the suspicion that Cooke had in mind the famous closing passage of Darwin's *The Descent of Man* (1871):

> Man may be excused some pride at having risen, though not through his own exertions, to the very summit of the organic scale; and the fact of his having thus risen, instead of having been aboriginally placed there, may give him hope for some higher destiny in the distant future. … We must, however, acknowledge, as it seems to me, that man with all his noble qualities, with sympathy which feels for the most debased, with benevolence which extends not only to other men but to the humblest living creature, with his god-like intellect which has penetrated into the movements and constitution of the solar system – with all these exalted powers – Man still bears in his bodily frame the indelible stamp of his lowly origin.[19]

Certainly, Cooke's portrait registers the pride of the moment. But the image somehow resists the brooding, Hamlet-like quality of

Darwin's closing sentence, where the 'indelible stamp' of 'lowly origin' acts as a counterpoise to the exalted claims of the 'risen ape' of humanity.

But, of course, the picture is a fake. It never happened like this. Or rather it shows two forgeries in operation. The first forgery we are happy to accept, since this is the forgery implicit in any such act of commemoration and representation. Cooke, the artist, was not there at the meeting which the painting purports to represent, and instead painted each figure separately at a series of individual sittings, a device common in such portraits.[20] The second forgery is more difficult to stomach.

Piltdown in context

Between 1912 and 1915 a series of 'discoveries' at Piltdown in Sussex were announced whose cumulative effect was to suggest that, some 500,000 years ago, the human lineage (in the words of Arthur Smith Woodward) had 'already differentiated into two widely divergent groups'.[21] Of those two groups, one – the Neanderthal type – could now be considered (in the words of a contemporary report) to be no more than

> a degenerate offshoot of early man while surviving modern man may have arisen directly from the primitive source of which the Piltdown skull provides the first discovered evidence.[22]

'Piltdown Man' – the 'primitive source' of modern humanity – had displaced the cumbersome Neanderthals from the human line and at the same time 'purged' that lineage of a supposedly unprepossessing ancestor.[23] But, above all, Piltdown was a British discovery, made on native English soil. Before 1912 all significant ancient hominid fossil remains had been found in places other than the British Isles. Chief among these discoveries were those of an army officer and former lecturer in anatomy at the University of Amsterdam, Eugene Dubois, who in 1894 announced the discovery of *Pithecanthropus erectus* (Java Man, now known as *Homo erectus*) – a find which divided European scientific authorities, some arguing that *Pithecanthropus* was a species of extinct anthropoid ape, while others argued that it was a human precursor, and still others argued that the remains were 'intermediate between the great apes and humans'.[24] Prior to the work of Dubois, the chief contender for the title of earliest human type had been Neanderthal man, whose remains, after the 1860s, were found at various continental European locations, but particularly in France and Belgium. In 1907 German scientists announced the finding of 'Heidelberg Man', a discovery that further seemed to underline the insularity, both literal and metaphorical, of British anthropology. All that could be offered as evidence of human-type activity in the British Isles were the disputed claims of Galley Hill Man and Ipswich Man, claims which were pressed by some of those represented in Cooke's portrait of the Piltdown group.

The picture that emerges, then, is one which is familiar to students of late imperial history. In the final years of the nineteenth century and the opening years of the twentieth, anthropology as a science could be understood as just one of many cultural manifestations of the competing claims of rival European powers in the colonial sphere. At issue was not just the priority of the discovery – who was to be the first to find the 'missing link' – but what may be termed the 'territoriality' of evolution. This scramble was to result in bizarre accusations and counter-accusations between, in particular, the French, the British and the Germans. For example, in 1909 French palaeontologists were outraged by the decision of the Berlin Museum für Völkerkunde to pay 125,000 francs for a pair of skeletons discovered on French territory.[25] At the same time, British anthropologists (referred to dismissively by the French as *chasseurs de cailloux* – pebble hunters) had complained as early as the 1860s that French peasants were manufacturing 'prehistoric' flints for sale.[26] National prestige was considered to be at stake, a prestige that in 1907 led the Berlin Academy of Science to mount a lavish expedition to Java in the hope of replicating and, if possible, trumping the work of Dubois. We can understand the foundation of the *Institut de palaeontologie humaine* in Paris prior to 1912, as well as the displacement of English by French as the language of anthropology and prehistoric archaeology in the same year, as part of this European-wide rivalry.[27]

This, then, is the macro-political context of Piltdown. Cooke's painting is celebrating not simply a scientific discovery, but just as significantly, in the year (1912) that a British expedition arrived second at the South Pole, the priority of British intellectual if not physical endeavour. But in 1953 the whole edifice – which was questioned from the start by numerous authorities, not all of them non-British – collapsed. The scientific tests to which the Piltdown fragments had been subjected by Joseph Weiner and Kenneth Oakley made it indisputable that the Piltdown material – the fossilised skull fragments, the canine tooth, the jaw bone, the associated 'tools' (which included the famous cricket bat) – were all forgeries.[28]

At this point, of course, Cooke's painting takes on an entirely new resonance. Rather than being celebratory, it appears to be almost hilariously ironic. The figure of Darwin looms from the shadows accusingly, an eminent Victorian aghast at the mistake (or rather the crime) which his Edwardian progeny are about to commit. The skull of the primate on the right lends the image to an alternative tradition of seventeenth-century portraiture. It grins over at its modern counterpart – a Rochesterian presence – in a mocking echo of the ape who appears so frequently in seventeenth-century images undercutting the vaunting claims of human reason. Similarly the skull on the left begins to appear as a *vanitas* image, an ironic commentary on the ephemerality of mortal fame. The prominence of the hands resting on the table or wielding the tools of scientific enquiry, a prominence which in 1915 had signified an alternative sign of humanity beyond that of the mental capacity which Arthur Keith is busy measuring – the capacity, that is, to make tools – now begs the question as to which hand had perpetrated the crime.[29] Whatever the answer to that question might be, we have to admit that after 1953 the portrait is incomparably richer than it appeared prior to Oakley's and Weiner's battery of tests. From being an interesting Edwardian genre painting, it has been transformed into a minor classic in the psychology of both art and science. Not to say criminology.

Arthur Keith and 'race'

In Cooke's painting it is Arthur Keith – the man in the white coat – who actually holds the Piltdown cast in his hand. A key figure in the Piltdown affair, Keith for many years was represented as the innocent dupe of the fraudster or fraudsters. Recently, however, Keith's presumed innocence in the affair has been challenged.[30] Certainly Piltdown coincided with a turning point in his professional and social life: in 1913 he was elected a Fellow of the Royal Society, having been rejected the previous year, and in 1914 he was elected to the Athenaeum.[31] Of greater interest, however, is the way in which Keith's interest in 'racial science' is subtly entwined within the Piltdown story and its aftermath. For Piltdown is a story about 'race', or rather the 'decline' of a 'race', which was echoed in other areas of British intellectual life in the period prior to the revelation of the fraud.[32]

The facts of Keith's life are these: born in Scotland in 1866, he graduated from the University of Aberdeen in 1888 and went as a physician to the goldfields of Thailand (or Siam as it then was). It was in Siam that he first began to work on primate evolution, under the direction of C.P. Gibbons. Returning to London in 1892, he studied anatomy at University College London and became Senior Demonstrator of Anatomy at the London Hospital in 1895. Between 1895 and 1908 Keith concentrated mainly on human anatomy, doing work on the sinoatrial node – the 'pacemaker' – of the heart. In 1908 Keith became Conservator of the Royal College of Surgeons and was thus in charge of one of the greatest collections of comparative anatomy and pathology in Europe. This was the position Keith held at the time of Piltdown. Up to this point Keith's career was one of steady if unremarkable progress. But it was his prominence in the Piltdown interpretations which brought him to the attention of a wider public. His anthropological interests began to predominate over anatomy, to the extent that he became one of the principal international authorities on human fossils. He was President of the Royal Anthropological Institute (1914–17), President of the Anatomical Society (1918), Honorary Secretary of the Royal Institution (1922–6) and President of the British Association for the Advancement of Science (1927). He was knighted in 1921 and awarded honorary degrees from the universities of Aberdeen (twice), Birmingham, Oxford, Durham and Manchester. He died in 1955 (just two years after Piltdown was announced as a forgery), a venerated and respected scientist, who was to be described in Robert Ardrey's *African Genesis* – a best-selling popular account of human origins – as 'the grand old man of British anthropology'.[33]

But this tells us nothing of the *unconscious* of Piltdown and its cultural importance. Nor do the bare bones of Arthur Keith's distinguished scientific career (he was the author of over 500 papers, articles, books and reviews) open the door to that climate of feeling which both created Piltdown and allowed it to flourish for nearly forty years within British scientific circles. Rather we have to read between the lines of Keith's own story to reveal his continuing (but evolving) fascination with the 'problem' of race, racial origin and racial variation. In tracing that story we can begin to see both how Piltdown was a vehicle for that fascination and how assumptions about race coloured the ways in which the Piltdown fragments were interpreted and evaluated in the light of developments in the application of evolutionary theory to fossil remains.

Keith's scientific career began in Siam. It was during these years (1889–92) that Keith determined on two interests which were to dominate his life: his interest in evolutionary theory and his interest in racial theory. It was in Siam that he began, as he later claimed, to describe what was there to be observed in the diversity of races. The observation of diversity, rather than hierarchy or superiority, was his goal. But Keith also believed that races could be classified according to their degree of 'aggression'. Comparing himself to his native servant – Nuan – Keith observed that as a member of a 'superior race' (as he then believed he was):

> I was aggressive, proud, assertive, and competitive, whereas Nuan was none of these things. I did not then know that the difference between Nuan and myself was due to his being a member of a non-aggressive race, while I came of the most aggressive of evolutionary stocks.[34]

In Keith's view the relationship between 'races' (not individuals) was one of struggle, with each 'race' competing against each other 'race'. These Social Darwinist views were to inform Keith's thinking for the rest of his life. In effect Keith was paraphrasing the views of the 'archetypical' Social Darwinist, Herbert Spencer, who in his *Principles of Psychology* (1855) observed that:

> It needs only to contrast national characters to see that mental peculiarities caused by habit become hereditary. We know that there are warlike, peaceful, nomadic, maritime, hunting, commercial, races – races that are independent or slavish, active or slothful … [35]

The difficulty was how to define a 'race'. For Keith this was a lifelong problem. As early as 1895, for example, Keith had embarked on a massive project in which he attempted to correlate features of the external human ear with a putative notion of racial 'origin'. Drawing on the example of John Beddoe, whose *The Races of Britain* had appeared in 1885, Keith set about creating a means of testing the interrelationship and origin of different populations, using the ear as a clue to the 'relation of one race of mankind to another, and of one species of animal to another'.[36] In all, Keith observed the ears of over 15,000 individuals between 1895 and 1897, compiling records drawn from observations made in central and western Germany, Scotland, England, Wales and Ireland. This work was undertaken, for the most part, covertly, although 'observations on the insane and criminals were made more leisurely'.[37] What were the conclusions of this exhaustive attempt at classification?

> For the main purpose of my inquiry – the relationship of one group of people to another – this labour of mine has been a complete failure … it brought me face to face … with the method of statistical inquiry and showed me how far that manner of inquiry is likely to help us in settling racial affinities. It brought home to me the fact that the statistical method is one which raises rather than answers questions; it produces data but it cannot explain them.[38]

Mere measurement, then, was no guide to the definition of 'race'; a more integrated approach was required, as Keith chided himself: 'one cannot determine the relationship by taking into consideration one point only … to settle the affinities of a people one must take into consideration every one of the characters of body and mind'.[39]

For all that the statistical method had produced inconclusive results, Keith's interest in racial classification never waned. Between 1910 and 1911, on the eve of Piltdown, Keith once more revisited the problem of race in a series of articles in *Nature*, the *Lancet* and the *Journal of the Royal Anthropological Institution*.[40] Much of this work was occasioned by a new set of observations and anatomical dissections. In 1906 he undertook the task of dissecting a 'pygmy child' who had 'arrived in England for exhibition purposes', and measuring the ears of other equatorial Africans. His dissections and measurements led him to 'regard pygmy people as sports which have arisen in diverse places at diverse times'.[41] During this period Keith was testing the hypothesis that so-called 'racial' variation was pathological in origin. In pursuing this line of research, Keith was willing to bend the ethical rules of the medical profession. In 1911 he recorded his 'purchase' of the body of an East End clerk who had died exhibiting the symptoms of a hormonal disorder – acromegaly – which contorts the features so that they come to resemble those attributed to the Neanderthal type. The clerk's family, who were poor, received £25 and their funeral expenses were paid by Keith. The chairman of the Museum Committee was alarmed at Keith's activity, since the 'purchasing' of bodies in this way was illegal. Keith's main concern, however, was not so much the moral scruples of the Museum Committee, but the difficulty of getting the expenses of the transaction reimbursed.[42]

In 1915 Keith presented his views on the Piltdown material in his *The Antiquity of Man*, where he offered the following conclusion to the complete work:

> It is only when we come to draft a genealogical tree ... that we realise the true significance of those extinct human types. When we look at the world of men as it exists now, we see that certain races are becoming dominant; others are disappearing. The competition is world wide and lies between varieties of the same species of man. In the world of fossil man the competition was different; it was local, not universal; it lay between human beings belonging to different species or genera, not varieties of the same species.[43]

The extinct Piltdown 'race', in other words, posed a warning for the future. Universal racial competition, as it appeared in the world of the present, was a variation on a much older theme: the local competition of 'species or genera'. But, no matter how far up the evolutionary tree the large-brained (in Keith's view) Piltdown creature appeared to have climbed, his fate was to be displaced by other human 'species'. Such a struggle, Keith believed, was still to be observed among modern humankind. By 1915, when these words were published, the issue of 'dominant races' in Europe had become, of course, hugely significant. The war concentrated the minds of Keith and his contemporaries, to the extent that the conflict began to be described in evolutionary terms. Thus in the revised second edition of *The Antiquity of Man*, published in 1925, Keith wrote an 'Additional Note to Preface' (dated July 1915) in which he observed:

> we have burst into a critical phase in the evolutionary progress of mankind; we have had to lay aside the problems of our distant past and concentrate our thoughts and energies on the immediate present. Liège and Namur, which figure in this book as the sites of peaceful antiquarian discovery, have become the scenes of bloody war.[44]

Although the present seemed to have displaced the past as a matter of immediate concern, yet, as Keith explained, 'there may be some who will wish to survey the issues of the present fateful period from the distant standpoint of man's early evolution'. An understanding of evolution, in other words, would help to explain the present baffling conflict which itself represented a 'critical phase in the evolutionary progress of mankind'.[45]

By the time that the second edition of *The Antiquity of Man* was published, Keith had begun to turn more determinedly from the past to the present, and from thence to the future. In the early 1920s he had become interested in Galton and eugenics. Keith regarded Galton as 'one of the most originally minded of all British anthropologists'.[46] Of eugenics Keith later observed that he drew back from joining the society not only because of other demands on his time, but because 'I could not make up my mind as to the kind of people my country might be in need of fifty years hence'. But this liberal sentiment was to be undercut by the authentic voice of the proto-eugenicist, since Keith continues: 'the kind that would not be needed – the undesirables – presented an easier problem'.[47] One perhaps ought to note here that this throwaway comment concerning the 'undesirables' was written in 1947. Despite (or perhaps because of) his views, Keith served on a commission which surveyed the state of the nation's health. Not surprisingly Keith found plenty of evidence of 'Grade C men', particularly in the northern industrial towns.[48] It was in the 1920s, too, that Keith began to argue against the League of Nations, an organisation which would, he believed, result in 'emasculating mankind and bringing it to the kind of peace which is to be found in a cabbage patch'.[49] In 1926, the year before his election to the Presidency of the British Association, Sir Arthur (as he now was) began to study the cartoons in *Punch*, observing that 'many of its drawings were faithful representations of British types of men and women'.[50] In 1930 he was in Egypt and the Middle East, practising once more what he termed 'racial diagnosis' and observing the 'inbred, pallid,

Samaritans'.[51] In September 1930, the year in which he was given honorary degrees by Aberdeen and Oxford, after meeting Captain George Pitt-Rivers, President of the International Organisation of Eugenists, Keith was writing enthusiastically of the eugenic programme. He drew back from advocating 'compulsory methods' of selection, observing that 'our methods should be educational'. But he goes on to compare the lives of city dwellers with those of 'our tribal ancestors', noting the disastrous effects of 'modern civilisation on the minds and bodies of those who are subjected to it for many generations'.[52]

This theme of 'racial preservation' was to be developed in many of Keith's subsequent writings, but most notably in his Rectorial Address to the students of Aberdeen University in 1931, which was entitled 'The Place of Prejudice in Modern Civilisation'. Keith's Rectorial Address (also published in 1931) was written, he later acknowledged, under the influence of Adolf Hitler, whom he termed a 'student of evolution' whose chief mistake was to 'force the pace of evolutionary change'.[53] Keith's address presented a heady mixture of Scottish nationalism and patriotism, aimed at those who believed that 'there can never be health in our modern world until all mankind sleeps under the same tribal blanket'. The metaphor is revealing in that it hints at Keith's continuing fear of miscegenation and hybridity.[54] Against such sentiments Keith deployed 'race prejudice' which, he argued, 'works for the ultimate good of mankind, and must be given a recognised place in all our efforts to obtain natural justice for the world'. His address concluded:

> Nature keeps her human orchard healthy by pruning; war is her pruning hook. … As a gardener Nature has two sides, a good and a bad. She plants and she also prunes. If we accept her, we have to accept her altogether. Sooner or later she brings the false prophet to book.[55]

That last allusion is obscure, although Keith believed he knew who would be counted as a true 'prophet', though unrecognised in his own land. Of the subsequent career of Captain Pitt-Rivers, for example, he wrote:

> He joined the party of Sir Oswald Mosley and shared the fate of leading members of that party when the second world war

> came. In my opinion his liberty should never have been suspended; he had, and has, an abiding love of his country.[56]

In 1934 Keith was studying the history of the Jews, and becoming involved in a controversy in the letters page of *The Times*. The statesman Sir John Simon, annoyed at having Jewish parentage ascribed to him, had written to *The Times* claiming that he was 'Aryan'. Leading anthropologists had responded, protesting against the use of a term which was in vogue among the Nazis. Keith argued that the Nazi use of the term did not invalidate it since, though neither Germans nor Jews could anatomically term themselves a 'race', nevertheless they both 'felt' that they were different. Race, Keith concluded, was therefore a distinction of the spirit (perhaps an imagined community) as much as it might be understood as a physical manifestation.[57] Such a transcendent view of racial distinction returns us to the abortive ear measurements of 1895–7, when Keith concluded that 'to settle the affinities of a people one must take into consideration every one of the characters of body and mind' (see above, p. 272).

The example of Nazi Germany in the 1930s came to haunt Keith's later works. In particular his *Essays on Human Evolution* (1946) and *A New Theory of Human Evolution* (1948) – the former described by Ardrey as 'a marvellous volume' – were indebted to the Nazi 'evolutionary' experiment.[58] In these two late works, composed when Keith was nearing the end of his scientific career, the theory of 'group evolution' is offered. Group evolution is rooted, Keith argues, in the study of both living cultures (particularly Germany in the 1930s) and the extinction record of fossilised human remains. Group evolution differs from the common (mis)understanding of Darwinian evolution as a struggle between individuals, since it identifies two forms of essentially tribal activity as the dynamo of evolution. One form may be termed 'intratribal' and constitutes cooperative human behaviour between members of the same tribe. The other form is 'extratribal' or 'intertribal' activity, whose methods are 'cruel, merciless and completely immoral'. What each tribe is struggling to preserve is its emotional bond to the 'soil' and its 'common kinship, real or assumed, sometimes spoken of as the blood bond'.[59] In a subsequent essay ('The Behaviour of Germany Considered from an Evolutionary Point of View in 1942') Keith drew on his reading in *Mein Kampf*, *The Times* and the July 1937 issue of the *Journal of Racio-Political*

Correspondence (published by the German Bureau for Human Betterment and Eugenics). His aim was to analyse Hitler's response to Eden's January 1937 statement that German race theory stood in the way of a common discussion of European problems. Hitler's reply, that it was the 'duty' of each race 'to preserve the purity of the blood which God has given it', was discussed by Keith in the following terms:

> Here we have expounded the perfectly sound doctrine of evolutionary isolation; even as an ethical doctrine it should not be condemned. No German must be guilty of 'the greatest racial sin' – that of bringing the fruits of hybridity into the world. The respective 'genes' of Germany must be kept uncontaminated, so that they may work out the racial destiny of the German people without impediment.[60]

Writing of the methods of the Nazis after 1933, Keith argued that isolation, the condemnation of 'cosmopolitanism', the doctrine of 'soil and blood', the use of force, compulsion and the concentration camp, all of these methods 'yet may be justified by their evolutionary result', even if (he acknowledges) they can form no part of a system of ethics. For ethics must always succumb to the evolutionary imperative. Or, to put it in Keith's own words, 'good men … do not desire to discriminate between races, but the distinctions implanted by nature are too conspicuous'.[61]

'A steady man-ward movement': The reforging of Piltdown

But what does this have to do with Piltdown, and the events in Sussex and London of 1912 to 1915? Is it not the most grotesque distortion of archaeological method to retrieve artifacts (here the writings of Sir Arthur Keith over a period of some fifty years) and then proceed to construct a picture of the culture which produced those artifacts, or texts, which has no regard to the geological strata in which they are to be found? Isn't this, after all, precisely what the Piltdown forger or forgers attempted? The answer, of course, is that Piltdown did not end in 1915, but continued throughout the 1920s, 1930s and 1940s. Its significance, within the overall political and intellectual context of the years leading up to the outbreak of World War II, may be traced in two remarkable diagrams published in 1915 and 1931 respectively. The first diagram, to be found in Keith's *The Antiquity of Man* (1915), shows a genealogical tree of human evolution (Figure 12.2). In the full flush of Piltdown, we see an ascending 'tree' from whose 'trunk' branch the various hominid stocks. Thus *Pithecanthropus* branches away to extinction, as does Neanderthal and *Eoanthropus* or Piltdown Man. But we can also see here how the human 'races' diverge at roughly the same chronological moment. In Keith's thinking, the separation of the modern 'races' takes place at the beginning of the Pleistocene, some 400,000 years ago.

In 1931, the year in which Keith delivered his Rectorial Address in Aberdeen, he published a revised edition of his 1915 work under the title *New Discoveries Relating to the Antiquity of Man*. The revisions, in fact, were so comprehensive as to make *New Discoveries* an entirely new book. In *New Discoveries* Keith's diagram of human evolution has become more complex (Figure 12.3). The complexity is a function of having to accommodate new information, in particular the discovery by Raymond Dart in 1924 of *Australopithecus* in the Northern Cape Province of South Africa, together with the discovery in the late 1920s of *Sinanthropus Pekinensis* or 'Peking Man'. *Australopithecus* challenged the primacy of Piltdown and suggested Africa as the true location of human origin. Again we see the wavering lines of hominid species branching from the main human stem to totter towards extinction. But note what has happened at the top of the stem. 'Mongaloids' [*sic*] and 'Europeans' diverge from one another in the Pleistocene, some 200,000 years before the present, while 'Negroes', 'Negroids' and 'Australoids' are shown to have left the ascending stem much earlier (in the Pliocene epoch). Thus a schematic hierarchy, based on chronology, has been established. But note, too, what has happened to Piltdown. It has been moved from the left-hand side of the stem where it was placed in 1915, to the right-hand side. At the same time a helpful note below the diagram interprets the revised scheme for us: 'The divergence of the human stem towards the right is intended to indicate a steady man-ward movement'. Thus Piltdown – the native British discovery of 'The First Englishman' (the title, incidentally, of Arthur Smith Woodward's 1944 account of the Piltdown affair) – is, oddly, the most human of all. On the other hand, all races to the left of Europeans have just lost their status as full members of the modern stem of humanity: they exist on borrowed time.

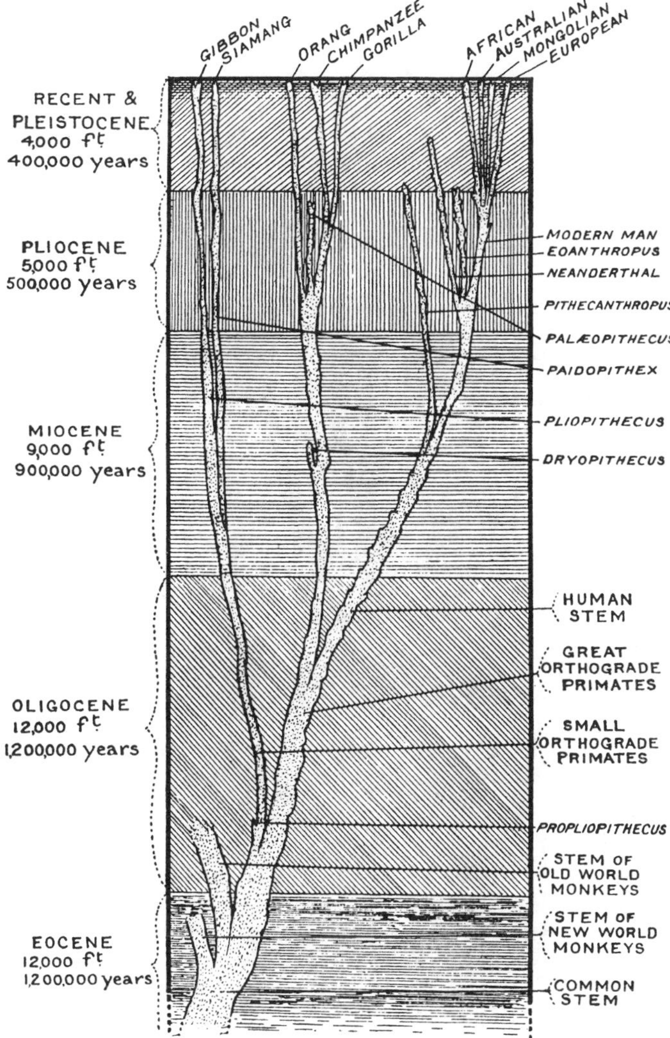

Figure 12.2 Genealogical tree, showing the ancestral stems and probable lines of descent of the higher primates

Source: Arthur Keith, *The Antiquity of Man*, 1st edn, London, Williams & Norgate, 1915.

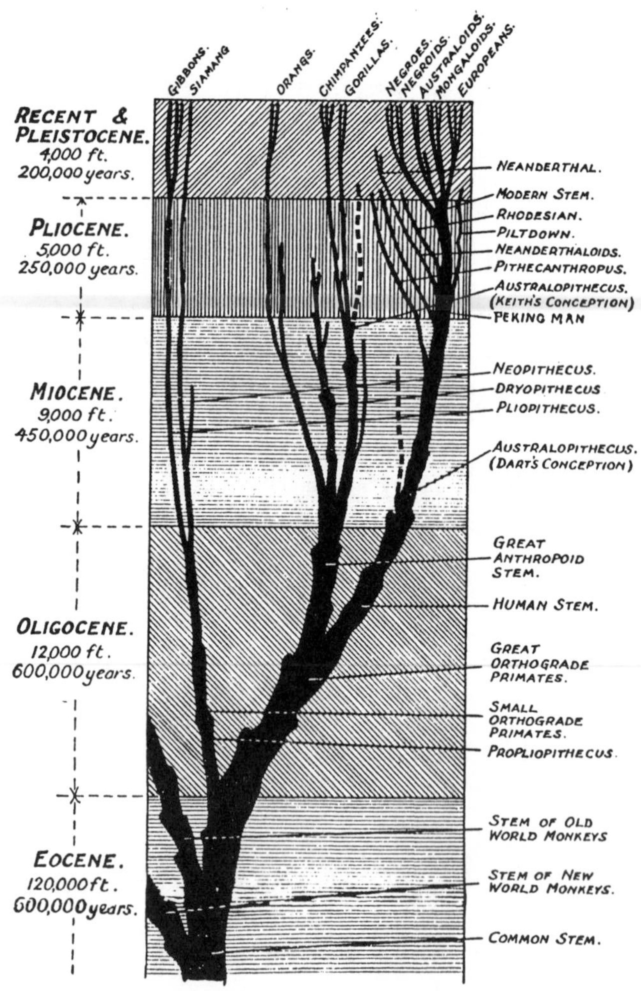

Figure 12.3 Diagrammatic synopsis of human evolution

Source: Arthur Keith, *New Discoveries Relating to the Antiquity of Man*, London, Williams & Norgate, 1931.

Note: An evolutionary tree of Man and Ape is represented against a background of geological time. The separation of human and anthropoid stems is represented as having taken place in the oligocene period, while the breaking up of the human stem to form species and races – known to us by fossil remains – is depicted as having occurred in the pliocene and early pleistocene periods. The divergence of the human stem towards the right is intended to indicate a steady man-ward movement.

In these diagrams Piltdown was being given a new identity by Keith. In effect the forgery was being reforged or at least remoulded. With Dart's discoveries in Southern Africa, Keith could no longer claim an unchallenged position for the ancient man of Sussex. Thus *Australopithecus* appears twice in the 1931 diagram. Keith assigns Dart's African discovery (the dotted stem) to the non-human family of chimpanzees and gorillas, though acknowledging that other authorities would place him firmly in the human stem nearly 200,000 years earlier. But Piltdown now exists as a terrible warning. This 'essentially modern type' (Keith explained in 1931) who lived 'at the western end of the Old World' rejoiced in a brain which 'in point of size, reached almost the modern standard' when compared, for example, to those inhabitants of the eastern end of the Old World who were 'low and small-brained types'.[62] Yet his large brain, his essential modernity, did not save him from extinction, even if he was considered to be 'the ancestor we have been in search of during all these past years'.[63] Piltdown thus represented an evolutionary paradox. If the mark of human modernity was understood as a function of brain size (or, to be more precise, cranial capacity), then how was it that this large-brained creature nevertheless appeared to have succumbed to the evolutionary imperative?

From the paradox of Piltdown, Keith was able to draw a moral. Sometimes evolution had to be helped if the fate of the Piltdown 'race' was to be avoided. In 1931, the year in which Keith presented his revised version of Piltdown, he also published a small volume in the 'Today and Tomorrow' series entitled *Ethnos or the Problem of Race*. In *Ethnos*, Keith wrote:

> If Eugenists have their way, and ultimately I have no doubt they will obtain the ear of statesmen, then a new phase – a conscious phase – in the evolution of mankind will be initiated. If we find that the way we are living is leading us straight to physical and mental bankruptcy then we can no longer afford to be mere pawns on the chessboard of evolution; we must somehow take a hand in the game.[64]

Conclusion: 'Taking a hand in the game'

Whoever planted the Piltdown fragments was indeed, in Keith's phrase, prepared to 'take a hand in the game'. But what exactly was the game which was being played out? In his 1927 Presidential Address to the British Association in Leeds, Keith explained the rules of the game which he believed the Piltdown creature had played so unsuccessfully. 'The guide to the world of the past', Keith wrote,

> is the world of the present. In our time man is represented not by a single type but by many and diverse races – black, brown, yellow, and white; some of these are rapidly expanding, others are as rapidly disappearing. Our searches have shown that in remote times the world was peopled, sparsely it is true, with races showing even a greater diversity than those of today, and that already the same process of replacement was at work.[65]

In 1915, in his first interpretation of Piltdown, Keith had written that local competition 'lay between human beings belonging to different species or genera, not varieties of the same species' (see above, p. 273). Understanding this chronologically distant struggle of different species might help the understanding of contemporary competition between otherwise similar 'races', he believed. But in 1927, in this account from the Presidential Chair of the British Association, Keith has elided the distinction between 'species' and 'race', 'local' and 'universal', and even past and present. Further, instead of learning from the past, he now believed that the past must be interpreted in the light of present understanding. Finally, the distinction between a 'race' and 'species' has been collapsed altogether into a single term: 'greater racial diversity'. By collapsing these categories, Keith had cleared the ground, intellectually, for his writings of the 1930s and 1940s, so that the racial programme of Nazi Germany, for example, could be understood as 'the perfectly sound doctrine of evolutionary isolation'. The alternatives had become clear: either a never-ending war between 'races' (or what Keith had once described as 'human beings belonging to different species or genera' in the context of the distant past) or racial separation.

A page or so later, in the same Presidential Address, Keith turned to the subject of Piltdown. 'We may confidently presume', he wrote, 'that this individual was representative of the people who inhabited England at this remote date.'[66] Yet how easy it might have been to have misinterpreted this representative individual:

> If merely a lower jaw had been found at Piltdown, an ancient Englishman would have been wrongly labelled 'Higher Anthropoid Ape'; if only the thigh-bone of Pithecanthropus had come to light in Java, then an ancient Javanese, almost deserving the title of anthropoid, would have passed muster as a man.[67]

It was as if, for Keith, unwary anthropologists might themselves commit the sin of miscegenation – of causing all humankind to sleep 'under the same tribal blanket' as he was to express the matter to the students of Aberdeen in 1931. At stake was the creation of artificial or hybrid evolutionary forms by the anthropologist as much as by 'Nature' – an irony when the hybridised nature of the Piltdown creature is recalled. The large brain of Piltdown, Keith believed, was the stamp in the passport which admitted these Sussex fragments to the style of 'ancient Englishmen', just as securely as the ape-like skullcap of the 'ancient Javanese' would ensure that he would never 'have passed muster as a man'.

If we turn now, for the last time, to the image of the man in the white coat measuring a possibly human skull, we have a third level of irony with which to read the image – but it is not, I think, productive of laughter. A group of scientists are debating which features should be accounted human and which simian. The fact that the individual upon whom they are concentrating their attention was an artificial hybrid, of a kind which never existed in nature, is no longer of any consequence to this exercise in taxonomy. If we end Piltdown in 1915, then we might conclude that the forgery is an unfortunate incident in the history of science. But, as the subsequent career of Arthur Keith indicates, Piltdown did not end in 1915. Rather, a distinguished scientist who was at the very centre of the establishment, who was being honoured by the scientific intelligentsia of interwar Britain, who was one of the foremost popularisers of a form of Darwinian theory, and whose articles on evolution and race were appearing in *The Times*, the *Daily Express*, the *New York Times*, the *Illustrated London News*, the *Evening Standard* and *Evening News*, and the *Daily Mail* throughout the 1930s, had not only found room to 'explain' Piltdown, but had turned the fragments deposited in, and then retrieved from, a Sussex gravel-bed into a memorial to the first example of European racial extinction.

Notes

1 Charles Darwin, 'Autobiography' (composed *c.*1876–81), in Gavin de Beer (ed.), *Charles Darwin, Thomas Henry Huxley: Autobiographies*, London, Oxford University Press, 1974, p. 54.
2 Rudyard Kipling, 'The River's Tale (Prehistoric)', in *Rudyard Kipling's Verse: Definitive Edition*, London, Hodder & Stoughton, 1946, p. 709.
3 The Piltdown affair has been variously described as both 'fraud' and 'hoax'. The word 'fraud' – with its connotations of criminal deception – suggests a deliberate attempt to mislead, or to pass off as authentic that which is, in fact, inauthentic, in order to gain 'an unjust advantage' or to 'injure the rights or interests of another' (*OED*). 'Hoax' on the other hand suggests a more general attempt to discomfort, embarrass or hold up to ridicule those who lay claim to a specialised knowledge of the discipline in which the 'hoax' has been perpetrated. Perhaps the chief distinction between the two is that the 'fraudster' would not wish their activities to be uncovered, while it is of the essence of the activities of the 'hoaxer' that their activities (if not their identity) *should* be exposed, since it is only in exposure that the experts' credulity is demonstrated. To put this another way, for as long as a 'fraud' is not discovered, it must remain a 'fraud'; once the 'fraud' is announced, then it may exhibit all the characteristics of a 'hoax'. In this account, I have throughout preferred the term 'fraud' when describing the Piltdown affair.
4 Much of the esteem in which scientists were held in Britain in the post-war period was derived from the perception that science and technology had enjoyed a particularly 'good war'. On scientific and technological change in the war years and after, see Eric Hobsbawm, *Age of Extremes: The Short Twentieth Century, 1914–1991*, London, Michael Joseph, 1994, pp. 264–5, 522–57. The divide between scientists and non-scientists is perfectly expressed in the ferocious public interchange which took place between F.R. Leavis and C.P. Snow, following Snow's Rede Lecture of 1959.
5 The vast weight of literature and commentary on Piltdown as a fraud has probably supplanted the (earlier) literature on Piltdown as a genuine discovery. A full bibliography of that literature up to 1990 may be found in Frank Spencer, *The Piltdown Papers, 1908–1955*, London, Natural History Museum Publications, Oxford University Press, 1990. Candidates continue to emerge for the title of chief fraudster: see, for example, Henry Gee, 'Box of Bones "Clinches" Identity of Piltdown Palaeontology Hoaxer', *Nature* 381 (23 May 1996): 261–2.
6 Darwin, *The Origin of Species by Means of Natural Selection* (first published 1859), 6th edn, London, John Murray, 1910, p. 271.
7 Darwin, *The Descent of Man and Selection in Relation to Sex* (first published 1871), 2nd edn, London, John Murray, 1882, p. 155.
8 Darwin, *The Descent of Man*, pp. 155–6.
9 Richard Leakey, *The Origin of Humankind*, London, Phoenix, 1995, p. 2.
10 Leakey describes the 'disdain' of British anthropologists for the 'out of Africa' hypothesis, a disdain which was amplified in the early twenti-

eth century when human fossils began to be uncovered in Europe and Asia. The Piltdown 'fossils', of course, substantiated the claims of a European origin for humanity. See Leakey, *The Origin of Humankind*, p. 2.

11 W.E. Le Gros Clark, *The Fossil Evidence for Human Evolution*, Chicago, University of Chicago Press, 1955, p. 87. Le Gros Clark was co-author of the original paper which unmasked Piltdown as a fraud, see J.S. Weiner, K.P. Oakley and W.E. Le Gros Clark, 'The Solution of the Piltdown Problem', *Bulletin of the British Museum (Natural History) Geology Series* 2 (1953): 139–46.

12 Le Gros Clark, *Fossil Evidence for Human Evolution*, p. 87.

13 One of the earliest examples of the scientific 'commemorative' portrait is Rembrandt's 'Anatomy of Dr Tulp' of 1631 – a painting which virtually established the genre of which Cooke's image is a much later example.

14 See S.K. Heninger Jr, *The Cosmographical Glass: Renaissance Diagrams of the Universe*, San Marino, Huntington Library, 1977, p. 151; Jonathan Sawday, *The Body Emblazoned: Dissection and the Human Body in Renaissance Culture*, London and New York, Routledge, 1995, p. 74.

15 Arthur Keith, *The Antiquity of Man*, 1st edn, London, Williams & Norgate, 1915, p. 355.

16 See Arthur Keith, *An Autobiography*, London, Watts, 1950, p. 325.

17 Keith, *An Autobiography*, p. 327.

18 In a revealing phrase, Keith wrote of Smith Woodward that 'he had no special knowledge of the human body' and that 'no doubt he was just as jealous for the interests of his institution as I was for mine'. The implication is that Keith believed the Piltdown fragments should have been placed in his keeping at the Royal College of Surgeons, rather than with Smith Woodward at the Natural History Museum in South Kensington (see Keith, *An Autobiography*, p. 324). It has also been suggested to me, in discussions of Cooke's painting in seminars at Keele University, Sussex University and the University of Southampton (1995–7), that there is a hint that Keith, the only figure to be shown wearing a laboratory coat, is being depicted as a somewhat subservient 'technician' working under the 'instruction' of his rival, Elliot Smith, who is gesturing towards the cast which Keith is holding.

19 Darwin, *The Descent of Man*, p. 619.

20 Frank Spencer, *The Piltdown Papers, 1908–1955*, London, Natural History Museum Publications, Oxford University Press, 1990, p. 113. Spencer notes (p. 113) that Cooke's picture excited great interest when it was first exhibited in 1915. Photogravure reproductions, signed by the artist, were available for purchase at three guineas.

21 Cited in Spencer, *Piltdown: A Scientific Forgery*, London, Natural History Museum and Oxford University Press, p. 46.

22 *Nature*, 12 December 1912.

23 The story of the expulsion from the human lineage of Neanderthals by Piltdown is told in Erik Trinkaus and Pat Shipman, *The Neanderthals: Changing the Image of Mankind*, London, Pimlico, 1994, pp. 199–207.

24 Trinkaus and Shipman, *The Neanderthals*, p. 144.
25 Trinkaus and Shipman, *The Neanderthals*, p. 179.
26 Trinkaus and Shipman, *The Neanderthals*, pp. 91–7.
27 For further accounts of this 'scramble', see John Reader, *Missing Links: The Hunt for Earliest Man*, 2nd edn, London, Penguin Books, 1988, chaps 1–5; Roger Lewin, *Bones of Contention: Controversies in the Search for Human Origins*, London, Penguin Books, 1989, chaps 1–2.
28 One of the best accounts of the unmasking of Piltdown as a fraud is still to be found in J.S. Weiner, *The Piltdown Forgery*, London, Oxford University Press, 1955. See also Francis Vere, *The Piltdown Fantasy*, London, Cassell, 1955; Ronald Miller, *The Piltdown Men*, London, Scientific Book Club, 1974.
29 The idea that the identity of the fraudster(s) was known outside the scientific community seems first to have been posited by Le Gros Clark, in a letter (dated 9 August 1954) to J.S. Weiner. Le Gros Clark had noticed similarities between the Piltdown story and Rudyard Kipling's short story 'Dayspring Mishandled', first published in 1928 and republished in *Limits and Renewals* (1932). 'Dayspring Mishandled' revolves around a forged manuscript but, as Weiner noted in a letter to Le Gros Clark (dated 17 August 1954), 'Dayspring is poetical for the break of day or the dawn' and the scientific name of Piltdown Man was *Eoanthropus Dawsoni*: the 'dawn man of Dawson' (Charles Dawson being one of the principals concerned in the affair, while Kipling himself was an active member of the Sussex Archaeological Society). See Spencer, *Piltdown Papers*, pp. 249–50.
30 See Pat Shipman, 'On the Trail of the Piltdown Fraudsters', *New Scientist* 6 October 1990: 52–4. Dr Caroline Grigson, on the other hand, believes Keith to be innocent and that the chief culprit remains Charles Dawson; see Grigson, 'Missing Links in the Piltdown Fraud', *New Scientist* 13 January 1990: 55–8. For a further discussion of the identity of the forger(s), see William T. Stearn, *The Natural History Museum at South Kensington: A History of the British Museum (Natural History), 1753–1980*, London, Heinemann, 1981, pp. 245–6.
31 In 1913 Keith felt that his election to the Royal Society was a goal he 'expected to reach ten years ago'. He was particularly pleased to be able to record in his diary that his election to the Athenaeum in 1914 was under 'the special rule', which meant that he did not have to endure the usual waiting period of fifteen years following his entry into the Candidate's Book by Sir Clifford Allbutt in February 1913. See Keith, *An Autobiography*, pp. 363–4.
32 On late nineteenth-century beliefs in 'racial decline' or 'degradation', particularly in relation to the influence of Count Gobineau, the first volume of whose *Essay on the Inequality of Races* (1853–5) was translated into English in 1915, see Robert J.C. Young, *Colonial Desire: Hybridity in Theory, Culture and Race*, London and New York, Routledge, 1995, pp. 99–117. See also Dorothy Porter, 'Enemies of the Race: Biologism, Environmentalism and Public Health in Edwardian London', *Victorian Studies* 34 (1990–1): 147–78.

33 Robert Ardrey, *African Genesis: A Personal Investigation into the Animal Origins and Nature of Man*, London, Collins, 1961, p. 17. Ardrey's thesis is, as he acknowledges (p. 273), indebted to Keith's *Essays on Human Evolution* (1946). For Keith's biography, see Charles Coulston Gillispie (ed.), *Dictionary of Scientific Biography*, New York, Charles Scribner & Sons, 1973, vol. 7, pp. 278–9; Trevor I. Williams (ed.), *A Biographical Dictionary of Scientists*, 3rd edn, London, Adam & Charles Black, 1982, pp. 285–6.

34 Keith, *An Autobiography*, p. 119.

35 Herbert Spencer, *Principles of Psychology*, quoted in George W. Stocking Jr, *Race, Culture and Evolution: Essays in the History of Anthropology*, Chicago and London, University of Chicago Press, 1982, p. 240. On Social Darwinism, see Greta Jones, *Social Darwinism and English Thought: The Interaction between Biological and Social Theory*, Brighton, Harvester Press, 1980; Douglas Lorimer, 'Theoretical Racism in Late-Victorian Anthropology, 1870–1900', *Victorian Studies* 31 (1987–8): 405–30.

36 Keith, 'The Results of an Anthropological Investigation of the External Ear' (presented 16 June 1906), in *Proceedings of the Anatomical and Anthropological Society of the University of Aberdeen, 1904–1906*, Aberdeen, Aberdeen University, 1906, p. 218. On Beddoe and other nineteenth-century attempts at racial classification, see Young, *Colonial Desire*, pp. 55–89.

37 Keith's method was to jot down 'on slips of stiffish paper' carried in the palm of his hand the 'colour of hair, sex, type of ear, degree of infolding [of the ear], condition of the auricular tip' of those he passed in the street. In this way, samples of the populations of Leipzig, Hamburg, Aberdeen, Whitechapel (in London), Liverpool, Belfast, Cork, and many other British, Irish and German cities were taken. See Keith, 'Results of an Anthropological Investigation', pp. 227–8.

38 Keith, 'Results of an Anthropological Investigation', p. 239.

39 Keith, 'Results of an Anthropological Investigation', p. 233.

40 See Keith, 'The Position of the Negro and the Pygmy amongst Human Races', *Nature* 84 (14 July 1910): 54–5; Keith, 'The Anthropology of the Ancient British Races', *Lancet* i (1911): 722–4; Keith, 'On Certain Physical Characters of the Negroes of the Congo Free State and Nigeria ... ', *Journal of the Royal Anthropological Institution* 41 (1911): 40–71.

41 Keith, *An Autobiography*, p. 339.

42 Keith, *An Autobiography*, p. 335.

43 Keith, *The Antiquity of Man*, 1st edn, p. 506.

44 Keith, *The Antiquity of Man*, 2nd edn, London, Williams & Norgate, 1925, vol. 1, p. xxiii.

45 Op. cit.

46 Keith, *An Autobiography*, p. 399.

47 Keith, *An Autobiography*, p. 400.

48 On fears over 'physical deterioration' in the period, see Bernard Harris' essay 'Pro-Alienism, Anti-Alienism and the Medical Profession in Late-Victorian and Edwardian Britain' (chapter 9 in this volume).

49 Keith, *An Autobiography*, p. 436.

50 Keith, *An Autobiography*, p. 499.
51 Keith, *An Autobiography*, p. 540.
52 Keith, *An Autobiography*, p. 553.
53 Keith, *An Autobiography*, p. 563.
54 This fear may be traced back to Keith's years in Siam. In a revealing passage in his autobiography, Keith describes the erasure of the word 'cohabitation' in his diary entries for October 1889. Reconstructing his own diary, Keith observed: 'The details have vanished from my memory; I do not think it was attended by any consciousness of sin. Siamese women from the European point of view were of easy virtue; the finest maiden in the province, if she was free, was willing to surrender herself to the embrace of a temporary husband for the payment of 80 ticals (£8); most of my fellow-officers were "temporary husbands" ' (*An Autobiography*, p. 118).
55 'Sir Arthur Keith's Rectorial Address', *Aberdeen University Review* 28 (1930–1): 258–60.
56 Keith, *An Autobiography*, p. 553.
57 Keith, 'The Aryans', *The Times* 8 and 13 August 1934.
58 Ardrey, *African Genesis*, p. 189.
59 Keith, 'Evolution and Ethics', in *Essays in Human Evolution*, London, Watts, 1946, p. 6. Many of the essays to be found in the collection first appeared in the *Literary Guide* between January 1943 and July 1944. Keith notes (*Essays in Human Evolution*, p. vii) that on first publication these essays 'met with a mixed reception'.
60 Keith, 'The Behaviour of Germany Considered from an Evolutionary Point of View in 1942', in *Essays in Human Evolution*, p. 9.
61 Keith, 'Christianity versus Evolution', in *Essays in Human Evolution*, p. 66.
62 Keith, *New Discoveries Relating to the Antiquity of Man*, London, Williams & Norgate, 1931, p. 292.
63 Keith, *New Discoveries*, p. 467.
64 Keith, *Ethnos or the Problem of Race Considered from a New Point of View*, London, Kegan Paul, 1931, p. 16.
65 Keith, *Concerning Man's Origin*, London, Watts, 1927, p. 8.
66 Keith's confidence in the 'representative' nature of the Piltdown individual was surely misplaced. In 1925, in the enlarged edition of 1915's *The Antiquity of Man*, he was unsure even as to the possible sex of the creature under examination, an uncertainty which persisted in the 1931 account. See Keith, *The Antiquity of Man*, 2nd edn, 1925, vol. 2, pp. 592, 594; Keith, *New Discoveries*, p. 458.
67 Keith, *Concerning Man's Origin*, p. 11.

Index